MW01259030

"*Mapping Apologetics* provides the most complete and best analysis to date of my overall apologetic approach."

John Warwick Montgomery, distinguished research professor of philosophy, Concordia University, Wisconsin; director of the International Academy of Apologetics, Evangelism and Human Rights, Strasbourg, France

"Brian Morley shows mastery of the details of my approach, including the qualifications and nuances."

John Frame, professor of systematic theology and philosophy, Reformed Theological Seminary

"In the volume *Mapping Apologetics*, Brian Morley treats the reader to an overview and examination of several very useful apologetic methods for defending the Christian faith. At several points, what impressed me were the careful nuances that Brian made time and again when he could have settled simply for repeating other commonly-stated reports, but which would have been quite inaccurate. His careful avoidance of such common pitfalls helped to produce some of my appreciation for his treatment."

Gary R. Habermas, distinguished research professor and chair, department of philosophy, Liberty University and Baptist Theological Seminary

"Dr. Brian Morley has provided us with an excellent survey of the major approaches to Christian apologetics. *Mapping Apologetics* is well-informed, even-handed, charitable and insightful. It will be a very helpful resource for anyone seeking to think through the important question of how Christians should contend for the faith 'once for all delivered to the saints' (Jude 3)."

James N. Anderson, associate professor of theology and philosophy, Reformed Theological Seminary, founder, www.vantil.info

"Many works on Christian apologetics make the mistake of disconnecting arguments for the Christian faith from the specific assumptions, perspectives and theology of the person advancing those arguments. As an antidote to this disconnection, Brian Morley discusses a helpful range of Christian apologetic perspectives and uncovers how and why each perspective shapes their arguments as they do. Not only do we learn about various important Christian apologists—a worthwhile task in its own right!—we see powerful and tangible examples of how the roots of our theology connect to and feed the various branches of our apologetic arguments. Anyone who considers themselves a Christian apologist should read and benefit from Morley's important volume."

Jim Beilby, professor of systematic and philosophical theology, Bethel University, author, *Thinking About Christian Apologetics*

"Dr. Morley is a careful scholar who does assiduous research and painstaking analysis. His long teaching experience of apologetics shines through in this much-needed volume in a day when the diverse approaches to defending the Christian faith are often misunderstood and misrepresented. Morley has conscientiously checked the primary sources and, when possible, he has directly confirmed the accuracy of his accounts by consulting with the apologists whose views he describes. This volume will prove to be an invaluable resource for teachers, students and all Christians who want to enhance their understanding of recent developments in the field of apologetics."

Mark M. Hanna, professor of philosophy, Veritas Seminary, and author of *Biblical Christianity: Truth or Delusion?*

"In his book *Mapping Apologetics*, Brian Morley aims to give us a remarkably readable survey of the most influential apologetic approaches current and has remarkably achieved that aim. His analysis lays bare the main lines of each representative apologist's thought. Methods are both described and critiqued. But Brian bends over backwards in his attempt to be fair and accurate with each one. His evaluations are both to the point and irenic. The book strives to keep the technical jargon to a minimum and largely succeeds. When technical language is necessary, the terms are carefully explained both in the text and at the end of each chapter. The book will serve well undergraduate and graduate students seeking to understand diverse apologetic approaches extant today."

Paul R. Thorsell, professor of theological studies, Cedarville University

MAPPING
APOLOGETICS

COMPARING CONTEMPORARY APPROACHES

BRIAN K. MORLEY

IVP Academic

An imprint of InterVarsity Press
Downers Grove, Illinois

InterVarsity Press
P.O. Box 1400, Downers Grove, IL 60515-1426
ivpress.com
email@ivpress.com

©2015 by Brian K. Morley

All rights reserved. No part of this book may be reproduced in any form without written permission from InterVarsity Press.

InterVarsity Press® is the book-publishing division of InterVarsity Christian Fellowship/USA®, a movement of students and faculty active on campus at hundreds of universities, colleges and schools of nursing in the United States of America, and a member movement of the International Fellowship of Evangelical Students. For information about local and regional activities, visit intervarsity.org.

All Scripture quotations, unless otherwise indicated, are taken from the New American Standard Bible®, copyright 1960, 1962, 1963, 1968, 1971, 1972, 1973, 1975, 1977, 1995 by The Lockman Foundation. Used by permission.

Cover design: David Fassett

Interior design: Beth McGill

Images: red pushpin: © vicm/iStockphoto
  red ribbon: © t_kimura/iStockphoto
  topographical map: © drlogan/iStockphoto

ISBN 978-0-8308-4067-0 (print)
ISBN 978-0-8308-9704-9 (digital)

Printed in the United States of America ∞

 As a member of the Green Press Initiative, InterVarsity Press is committed to protecting the environment and to the responsible use of natural resources. To learn more, visit greenpressinitiative.org.

Library of Congress Cataloging-in-Publication Data
Morley, Brian.
 Mapping apologetics : comparing contemporary approaches / Brian K. Morley.
 pages cm
 Includes index.
 ISBN 978-0-8308-4067-0 (pbk. : alk. paper)
1. Apologetics--History--20th century. I. Title.
BT1117.M67 2015
239--dc23

                               2014044449

P	23	22	21	20	19	18	17	16	15	14	13	12	11	10	9	8	7	6	5	4	3	2	1
Y	34	33	32	31	30	29	28	27	26	25	24	23	22	21	20	19	18	17	16	15			

To my wife Donna:

after God himself,

his greatest gift.

CONTENTS

INTRODUCTION

On March 9, 1974, Japanese lieutenant Hiroo Onoda walked out of the jungle on a remote island in the Philippines, finally convinced that World War II was over—twenty-nine years after it had ended. Trained as an intelligence officer in guerilla warfare, he was told to survive at all costs. No matter what happened, his superiors would come for him.

Just a few months after his arrival in 1944, the allies overwhelmed Japanese defenses, and Hiroo's band of five hid deep in the jungle, surviving on what they could find. When the war ended many attempts were made to find and convince the remaining soldiers to come out. Newspapers and even letters from relatives were left, which they found, along with leaflets. But how could the war have ended so quickly? And why were there spelling errors in the leaflets? Hiroo's own brother even came and attempted to speak to him over a loudspeaker. The band considered each piece of evidence, and always concluded that the enemy was trying to deceive them. One by one they died, the last one after twenty-seven years in hiding, leaving Hiroo alone.

Finally, a Japanese student tracked Hiroo down and befriended him. He could not surrender, Hiroo explained, until his commanding officer ordered him to do so. The student returned to Japan, and the government found his commander, now a bookseller, who returned in his tattered uniform and personally gave the order. Hiroo, still in his uniform, with sword on his side and his working rifle in his hand, was relieved of duty, and wept. Philippine president Ferdinand Marcos pardoned him for the approximately thirty people he had killed over the years, because the soldier had believed he was still at war. Hiroo returned to a world vastly changed, realizing that his beliefs had been completely wrong for nearly thirty years.

Hiroo illustrates the problem of belief, what to accept as evidence and as valid explanation, how to weigh assumptions, and much more. We make such complex decisions in our own lives, over both minor beliefs and major ones. And we all come to and hold the most crucial beliefs of our existence—our worldview—entailing whether to believe in a God, how to live, and what to do about an afterlife, if there is one.

There could not be a more important question than how we are to decide what to believe. That is the subject of this book.

SCOPE

There are a number of conflicting approaches, as we shall see. Some approaches have been used to support a wide variety of worldviews, and some have been developed and used in a uniquely Christian context. I have chosen those most discussed today, the live options, as represented by those who have had a major part in shaping them. In a few cases the choice was difficult, and different ones could have been made. I would like to have written much more, covering the work of more apologists in each of the major categories, but the book's total length would have been daunting.

I have tried to represent each thinker fairly, as they would describe their views. I have had the privilege of meeting and talking to most of the those I have written about (including the late Greg Bahnsen), and whether by personal contact or only via their writings, I am glad to have been exposed to such brilliant minds who have worked hard on these complex issues over a lifetime. I am grateful to those who, despite very busy schedules, were able to review what I had written about them and to offer some input: John Frame, Alvin Plantinga, Mark Hanna, Gordon Lewis (on his views and E. J. Carnell's), Norman Geisler, Richard Swinburne, John Warwick Montgomery (who also gave helpful input on my concluding chapter) and Gary Habermas. James N. Anderson[1] kindly went over my chapter on Cornelius Van Til and gave some helpful input. Their input was not only valuable but also reassuring and encouraging. I'm also grateful to InterVarsity Press's anonymous reviewer for detailed, thoughtful input.

I have tried to be not only fair but also clear, so as to be accessible to readers who have no special background in apologetic methodology. To that end I have explained terms and kept specialized words to a minimum. I have traded the tech-

---

[1]James N. Anderson is associate professor of theology and philosophy at Reformed Theological Seminary in Charlotte, North Carolina, and supervises www.vantil.info/.

nical rigor that characterizes purely academic writing for readability for a wider audience (and in some cases have refrained from referencing more technical sources). Incidentally, I have occasionally used a male pronoun to refer to both men and women where my intention is obvious, and I sometimes use both a male and a female pronoun ("he or she") to make that clear. Where it is not awkward I use "their." Biblical quotations are from the New American Standard Bible.

Along the way I repeat a few things briefly, by way of reminder, so the reader does not have to search back through the book, and so that the chapters stand alone better, in order to aid the reader who does not go through the book quickly. The structure of every chapter is not identical. Some stop to compare apologetic approaches, and in others more time is spent exploring the criticisms.

To benefit the reader with some background in the topic of the book, and to serve the advanced reader, I have also sought where possible to bring out the deeper, underlying issues separating the views, most of which are philosophical, having to do with issues such as the following: how we know, how we have certainty (and how certain we can be); the relation between faith and evidence; the possibilities of reasoning by way of deduction, induction and abduction; the role of assumptions and presuppositions; the relation between evidence and worldview; the validity of intuition as a way of knowing and its possible divine origin; and whether we can know some things without inferring them from other things we know (i.e., foundationalism). Through all this I hope to bring the issues into sharper focus so as to facilitate more constructive dialogue on the subject of apologetic methods.

The focus of the book is on understanding the theories and how they see each other, so I have kept my own views to a minimum, adding my conclusions and constructive insights in a final chapter. (Perhaps I'll have the opportunity to expand those into a book.) Where I have made my own brief addition that could be mistaken for the view of the featured apologist, I usually precede it with something like, "We could add that. . . ." In a few places, I have added the thoughts of others to the material about the featured apologist, in order to broaden the reader's knowledge a bit (the longest addition being a section on miracles in the chapter on evidentialism). In a few sections in which I develop the thinking of the featured apologist, I include a brief criticism from another thinker in order to save the reader from having to go back from the criticism section and search to connect the criticism with the apologist's view.

My twenty-five years of experience as a professor led me to add a list of terms, discussion questions and suggestions for further reading. That teaching experience has shown me too that complex issues are best understood if they can be viewed from different angles, and more than once.

In order to increase understanding of where the approaches lead, I have included something of how they would actually be used, focusing on some of the best insights that each has to offer. Some approaches require a bit more detail to show what the apologist is doing and how it all fits with their method. For example, I summarize Norman Geisler's rationale for selecting the right test for truth, review his criteria for selecting a worldview and finally show how he applies this method to arrive at theism. It requires some detail to see the systematic nature and rigor of his approach. So at the end of the book the reader will come away with not only the theories but also their application.

As I mentioned at the beginning of this introduction, I have focused on those who are currently influential, which is why I have chosen, for example, Van Til over Abraham Kuyper. I have also focused on those whose work in the field has been sustained, original and extensive. That entails choosing, for example, Gary Habermas over Josh McDowell, even though as a popular writer, the latter has had enormous influence. My only regret is that the purpose of this book and the constraints on its length do not permit more attention to those who have made very worthy contributions in the past, such as Gordon Clark and C. S. Lewis, and more recently, John Feinberg, the late Paul Feinberg, Douglas Groothuis, Ravi Zacharias and K. Scott Oliphint, to name just a few. It is regrettable that only a few pages can be given to Francis Schaeffer, who had an enormous influence in his day, but is not as well-known to younger people, and shied away from discussions on apologetic theory, most notably with Van Til, who was eager to engage him.

Each apologist can be unique, but can also in some ways resemble the characteristics of someone representing a different approach. William Lane Craig, for example, is not far from Alvin Plantinga in his emphasis on the personal, inward awareness of God, yet he is thoroughly classical in how he makes his case to others. John Warwick Montgomery, a staunch evidentialist, regards C. S. Lewis as something of a mentor. They are similar in the breadth of their interests, pioneering the use of literature to communicate the gospel, and it seems, similar in their personalities.[2] But in overall approach, C. S. Lewis is in the classical camp.

One of my hopes for this book is that more people will gain a good grasp of

---

[2]To me they both seem expressive, creative and interested in all of life's possibilities.

this crucial field of apologetic methods. When the subject is taught often only one approach is presented, and students are left with little or no grasp of anything else—and don't really even understand the approach they are supposed to accept and use. Those who are introduced to the issues outside of a classroom tend to read only apologists from their own camp.

If progress is to made on a subject so vital, we will need a new generation of people who are interested in doing serious work. Most of those who have labored in this field in modern times are at or past retirement, or have already passed on. My real hope is that this book will help motivate some people to take up this work and carry it forward.

I can't thank InterVarsity Press enough (especially Andy Le Peau and Al Hsu) for their great patience and encouragement as I struggled with a hellacious onslaught of challenges that greatly slowed progress on the book. I can't imagine a better publisher, and I am honored they are doing this book. I am also grateful for Mark Hanna, who first introduced me to this topic when I was a seminary student. Not only was he kind and encouraging, but his grasp of all things apologetic has also always been inspiring. I owe thanks to the sabbatical committee, which granted me time to work on this book and on *God in the Shadows: Evil in God's World*.[3] I also want to thank my wonderful wife, Donna, for her continual support, as well as her example of discipline and passion in the research and writing of her own books.

OVERVIEW

This book is organized according to a schema, represented in the chart below, that I have used through much of my twenty-five years of teaching this subject. It is not perfect, but I have found that it aids understanding the relationships among the views.

On the far left is fideism (from the Latin for "faith"), according to which belief cannot or should not be supported by evidence of any kind. On this view, faith and reason are in separate, nonoverlapping circles. If we have faith, we have no reasons to believe; if we have reasons to believe, we do not need faith. Some people are fideists because of such convictions about the nature of faith; others believe that the fallen mind is incapable of processing reasons, or that the subject is simply beyond the mind's grasp. The resulting view is that faith must

---

[3]Brian Morley, *God in the Shadows: Evil in God's World* (Geanies House, Fearn, Ross-shire, Scotland: Christian Focus, 2006).

Approach	Fideism	Presuppositionalism	Reformed epistemology	Experien- tialism	Pragmatism
→ Increasing emphasis on objective, independently existing evidence →					
Defining characteristics	•Faith unsupported •Faith and reason don't overlap •Or reason is beyond the mind's grasp •Or the mind is too fallen	•Starting points are necessary presuppositions unprovable by independent evidence •No independently known facts •"Borrowed capital" •Autonomy is the problem •No common "notions" •Reasoning must be circular, deductive, indirect, *from* Christianity •Transcendental argument •Range of presuppositionalists, from Van Til to Frame	• Awareness of God (*sensus divinitatus*) is grounded in how we are made, and triggered •Christian faith a gift •Classical foundationalism too narrow •God is properly basic •Faith can exceed reasons	•Experience alone •Experience is only proof we can have or only proof we need	•Accept what works •Has a wide variety of forms
Adherents	•(Pascal) •Kierkegaard •Barth	•Van Til •Bahnsen •Frame (modified key points)	•Alvin Plantinga	—	•C. S. Peirce •William James •John Dewey •Richard Rorty
Criticisms	•Subjective •Unbiblical	•Amounts to fideism •Transcendental argument cannot prove the Christian God	•Cannot rule out other beliefs, like the Great Pumpkin	•Experiences must be interpreted	•What works ≠ truth •What works is vague
Epistemo- logical starting point	Faith	Presupposition	Immediate awareness	Experience	Workability
Summary	No reasons or certainty; entirely subjective and volitional	No independent facts as reasons	Intuitions plus ancillary reasons	One type of evidence, but subjective	One type of evidence that links internal and external

Figure 1. Chart of Apologetic Approaches.

Veridicalism	Combinationalism	Classical apologetics	Evidentialism	Rationalism
→ Increasing emphasis on objective, independently existing evidence → Cumulative case, common ground				
•Givens + corroboration •Givens are known intuitively and certainly, can be corroborated •Universal givens can be known by all and constitute cognitive neutral ground •God is a universal given •Special givens are known by Christians •Common ground = human needs, common experiences •No *spiritually* neutral ground •Eight kinds of "seeing"	•Christianity a hypothesis to be tested •Three-aspect test: rational (self-consistent); empirical (fits relevant facts); existential (can be lived)	•Prove theism, then Christianity •Prove theism using theistic proofs: cosmological argument, teleological argument, moral argument •Prove Christianity (same as evidentialists)	•Evidence points to Christianity •Theistic arguments useful but not necessary •Facts point to best interpretation •Prophecy and resurrection prove the Bible •Use universally accepted facts (Habermas)	•Absolute certainty •Start from indubitable point •Reason using deduction •Build up to worldview
•Mark Hannah	•E. J. Carnell •Gordon Lewis •Francis Schaeffer	•Norman Geisler •William Lane Craig •J. P. Moreland •R. C. Sproul •Richard Swinburne	•John Warwick Montgomery •Josh McDowell •Gary Habermas	•Descartes
•Givens cannot rationally ground belief	•Three tests are unworkable	•Main critics are presuppositionalists •There is no common ground •Must reason *from* Christianity	•Facts must be interpreted •Facts cannot point to their interpretation	•Indubitable starting points cannot lead to a worldview without adding along the way
Givens and corroboration	Three-aspect test	Two-step argument	Facts pointing to interpretation	Deduction from certain starting point
Internal givens and objective corroboration	Hypothesis tested internal to theory, externally with facts and existentially	Uses cosmos and order to prove interpretive framework (theism), then uses facts of history	Proves Christianity using many objective, independently existing facts	Certainty is absolute; nothing is subjective or volitional

Figure 1 (continued).

be purely a gift from God. Fideists who tilt toward a Calvinistic view of salvation (according to which God predestines individuals for salvation) may see the action of the mind as irrelevant. Because the ultimate cause of belief is divine choice, God bypasses the intellect.

Fideism is thus a denial of apologetics, which makes it different from other views. All the views to the right hold that there is at least some overlap between faith and reason, that there are reasons of some kind for belief.

On the far right of the chart is rationalism, which claims complete proof for belief. The classic example is René Descartes (1596–1650), who lived in the tumultuous aftermath of the Reformation, when the Continent was divided over religious belief. He sought certainty by starting from something he could not doubt, then building up from there he used deduction, a form of reasoning that guarantees the truth of the conclusion if we accept the premises. In spite of his original approach and rigorous effort, virtually everyone today sees Descartes as coming short of providing the level of certainty he offered.

So the far left and the far right are opposites: faith can have no support, and faith has complete support.

Just to the right of fideism is presuppositionalism, which says we can have no direct proof for either God or Christianity. That means we cannot make either one the conclusion of a noncircular argument. In a traditional argument, premises are known independently of the conclusion and are offered as grounds for the conclusion. The problem with this, says the founder of presuppositionalism, Cornelius Van Til, is that nothing can be known independently of God because ultimately truth is whatever God says it is. God does not "know" an independently existing reality, rather, he determines that reality. He knows the lights are on in the room because he determined that they would be on. Adam fell when he tried to become independent of God, determining for himself what is true and morally right. Fallen humanity's problem is not primarily ignorance, but rebellion. The unbeliever does not need to merely add a few facts to his worldview but to completely tear it down and rebuild one that makes God the source and guarantor of every fact. So to encourage the nonbeliever to think he can know premises and determine truth independently of God is to inflame the problem. Furthermore, even if such a process results in a person affirming the Bible as the Word of God, he has in effect passed judgment on God, when God should be passing judgment on him. As well, things can be tested only using something higher and more ultimate, yet nothing can be more ultimate than the Word of God. Despite all this, the presuppositionalist says we can have absolute proof for the Christian God, because only if he exists can we know anything. Only if the Christian God exists and knows everything—as well as determines everything—is knowledge of any kind about anything possible. All other viewpoints fail because they claim to be true yet cannot properly account for how we have knowledge. So while there is no direct proof, there is absolutely certain indirect proof for Christianity. Christianity is a presupposition we cannot do without. It is claimed that even attempts to disprove Christianity must assume it is true; thus we can know Christianity transcendentally, as a necessary assumption. Also, the Bible is self-attesting: God's sheep hear his voice (Jn 10:27).

This view is next to fideism because it bases knowledge on a presupposition (roughly, a commitment to a foundational assumption) rather than anything known independently. Proponents see their view as akin to rationalism, which offers absolute certainty for knowledge, whereas many critics see it as closer to fideism, because it works by presupposing rather than directly proving.

Note that there is a wide range among presuppositionalists, from those who follow Van Til with little or no modification, such as Greg Bahnsen, to those who have modified the view considerably, such as John Frame. Some of Frame's modifications, such as acceptance of some use of induction, of the transcendental argument as a direct as well as an indirect proof, and acceptance of the cumulative force of arguments, would put him on the right side of the chart. There are also those who take the label of presuppositionalist who emphasize Van Til's rejection of traditional, direct proof but want little or nothing to do with his indirect proof. I knew one professor who called himself both a presuppositionalist and a "biblical fideist." So on the chart we can have a left side of presuppositionalism, which is closer to fideism, and a right side, which sees a robust role for proofs of different kinds. In the middle would be Van Til and Bahnsen. Frame would be on the far right, ideally on a line that extends to the right side of the chart (which would best be indicated by an arrow, since an actual line might be visually confusing).

Gordon Clark and Carl F. H. Henry represent a more deductive form of presuppositionalism, in which the Bible is posited as true, and what can be deduced from it is also true. Unlike Van Til and Bahnsen, they do not try to justify Christian presuppositions transcendentally, that is, as the only basis for reason. Herman Dooyeweerd (DOE-yuh-vaird; 1894–1977) took some of the foundations laid by Abraham Kuyper (1837–1920) in a different direction than Van Til.

John Frame has sought to remain true to Van Til's central insights while modifying significant aspects of his approach. He maintains his former teacher's convictions that since facts are not independently existing realities, we cannot simply see which interpretation fits best and use them independently to decide on an interpretation (the view of evidentialism), and there can be no neutral ground. He emphasizes the important nuance that it is really statements of facts that are not separate from interpretation.

Frame says that in an argument, because the premises commit us to the conclusion, they therefore commit us to what the premises presuppose, making presuppositions a kind of conclusion. Presuppositions are commitments that govern our other beliefs, and as such they are not defeasible (cannot be defeated by evidence and argument) unless a contrary presupposition is adopted. Since all thought is dependent on God, who makes all argument possible, we should not encourage the nonbeliever to think otherwise.

Contrary to Van Til, Frame believes that there can be real agreement between the believer and nonbeliever, induction can be acceptable in apologetics and the transcendental approach is an overall goal and not a single argument—there being no way the Christian God of love, justice, patience, wisdom and more must be presupposed in order for anyone to understand and talk about anything. He also believes that there is no essential difference between direct and indirect reasoning; therefore, the major difference between presuppositional and traditional apologetics may be the intent of the apologist to acknowledge God as sovereign and the source of all meaning, intelligibility and rationality, that is, the ultimate authority for human thought.

Frame adds the extremely important stipulation that interpretations can be verified on the basis of facts. In other words, we can compare the data of the mind with the data of the external world. Interpretations can be verified by comparing them with facts, and facts can be verified by comparing them with interpretations. Neither one is a brute, incorrigible standard.[4]

These and other modifications make presuppositionalism much closer to traditional apologetics, and give it access to a large array of more traditional arguments. Frame adds his own highly constructive innovations, holding that as nonomniscient beings we can see things in different perspectives that are simultaneous and overlapping, where each can contain the other. Knowledge, for example, is a matter of sense experience, reason and feeling.

To the right of presuppositionalism is the Reformed epistemology of Alvin

---

[4]Personal email correspondence with Frame, Aug. 24, 2013.

Plantinga. He challenges the notion that belief must be proportional to evidence such that we are entitled to believe only as much as we can prove. In answer, he points out that people commonly and rightly believe many things they would have trouble proving, such as that the world was not created with apparent age only a few minutes ago, or that people have minds like us and are not merely cleverly designed robots. So it is rational to believe in God to a degree greater than we can prove. The level of proof that would be required to justify a belief as crucial as Christianity would be very high, and we have that level for virtually no philosophical beliefs of that magnitude. Knowledge of God is the result of an inner knowing, what Calvin called the *sensus divinitatis*, which arises in us because of how we are made. The catalyst for that knowing can be different for different people, perhaps the grandeur of mountains, or the starry sky. Knowledge of Christianity comes by an inner knowing that is a special gift of the Holy Spirit. The inner knowing of both God and Christianity is not evidence for a conclusion, but an immediate knowing (like knowing we have pain, or that we exist). Plantinga affirms the value of arguments, but alone they hold little promise of being sufficient to truly justify belief in God or Christianity.

Reformed epistemology is to the right of presuppositionalism because it affirms a role for independent proofs, but it is on the left side of the chart because it is a type of intuition that grounds faith.

Next is experientialism, especially of the sort where an experience is taken as grounds for the conclusion that God exists or that Christianity is true. In this type, experience is evidence for the conclusion. This would include such things as experiences of answered prayers, or providential care, or an awareness of God that is the basis for the conclusion that God is there. What is unique about this method is that such experiences are the only basis for belief. Other methods to the right of it accept experience as one proof among many. To the left of the view, fideism accepts no proof, presuppositionalism does not regard experience as proper proof for God or Christianity and Reformed epistemology regards experience as a direct knowing, but not evidence for a conclusion. So coming from the left side of the chart, experientialism is the first view that accepts something as independent grounds to justify belief.

Although I have met people who take an experientialist approach to justifying belief in God or Christianity, it is difficult to find whole books supporting the view. People who take the view generally regard their experiences as adequate to justify only their own beliefs, and do not expect mere reports of their experiences to be sufficient for someone else; thus others would need to have their own experiences. So it is not hard to see why few would see the value in writing about their experiences as a way to convince others. This book does not have a chapter on the approach, but it includes a brief critique by Norman Geisler. The problem with experientialism is that experiences must be interpreted. A person can have an experience, but that does not mean we must—or even can—take it at face value. Someone's experience of their dead ancestor appearing to them could be interpreted in a number of ways, as could a person's experience of the Hindu god Shiva. Whether such things are regarded as real, imaginary, demonic apparitions or whatever depends on what other beliefs we hold as true. Furthermore, how do we resolve conflicts between experiences? Therefore, experience is widely regarded as insufficient as the sole means of proof, though it typically appears as one type of evidence in the apologetic methods to the right of it on the chart.

Next we add pragmatism, which essentially offers one source of justification, that of workability. There are both simple and sophisticated forms of this view, but the idea is, if it works we can accept a belief as verified to some degree. There is a difference between the (more radical) claim that workability equals truth, or is what we mean by truth, versus workability as an indicator of truth. The latter view is often added into the mix of possible methods of justification among views to the right of pragmatism on the chart. I have chosen not to use the available space in the book to detail pragmatism because, so far, its best-known philosophical forms have not been as popular as other approaches among those seeking to know or justify theism or Christianity. The view has been developed by C. S. Peirce (pronounced "Purse"; 1839–1914), William James (1842–1910) and recently by neopragmatist Richard Rorty (1931–2007). I have included brief criticisms of pragmatism made by Norman Geisler.

Moving again to the right on our chart, veridicalism, developed by Mark Hanna, sees knowledge as grounded in givens,[5] which are known intuitively and with certainty, and are not inferred from other things we know. All humans can benefit from universal givens, some of which cannot be coherently denied (because denying them would require assuming them), such as our own existence,

---

[5]"Literally anything that can be veridically, nonpostulationally, and nondiscursively grasped by consciousness is a given. And if it is susceptible of apprehension by all human beings in principle, it is a universal given." Mark M. Hanna, *Crucial Questions in Apologetics* (Grand Rapids: Baker Book House, 1981), p. 117.

and the principle of noncontradiction. Awareness of the existence of the God of theism is a universal given. Christians benefit additionally from special givens, including awareness that God cares for them, that the Bible is God's Word (which is self-attesting only to believers[6]) and that he or she is saved. Because universal givens are knowable independently of a worldview and within any worldview, they form cognitive neutral ground. There is, however, no spiritually neutral ground, since everyone either accepts or rejects what can be universally known about God.[7] There is common ground consisting of human needs, such as guilt and loneliness, as well as cultural patterns of thinking and acting.[8] Though known immediately, givens can be corroborated in different ways, for example, by reflection, and by their connection to other givens.[9] Some are known because they are undeniable, and others can be supported by evidence and inference. Some arguments for theism are inductively strong, such as the kalam cosmological argument, and the teleological argument from fine tuning of the universe for life.[10] In all it can be shown that God is the best explanation. A case can also be made for Christianity. The essential beliefs of Christianity are givens that can be corroborated. They are not arrived at from nontheological data or premises.[11] Citing Christ's statement that some see without "seeing" (Mt 13:13), Hanna identifies eight kinds of "seeing," only one of which is physical. Each has two poles, relating to its reality (metaphysical) and its knowability (epistemological). They are physical, intellectual, introspective, intersubjective (awareness of other persons and one's relationship to them), moral, aesthetic (which can grasp objective beauty) and spiritual (one mode that is common to all humans, another that is unique to Christians). Some forms of seeing overlap and interact; for example, spiritual seeing requires some use of intellectual seeing. He argues (in a forthcoming book) that biblical theism is the only adequate explanation of the eight modes of seeing and their objective correlates.

Next is the view called combinationalism. According to the combinationalism[12] of E. J. Carnell and Gordon Lewis, traditional proofs for the existence of God are inadequate for the same reason that the empiricism they are implicitly based on

---

[6]Ibid., p. 103.

[7]Ibid., p. 105.

[8]Ibid.

[9]Ibid., p. 101.

[10]Phone conversation with Mark Hanna, Oct. 16, 2013.

[11]Hanna, *Crucial Questions*, p. 121.

[12]The name was not chosen by Carnell, but it is used in Norman Geisler's widely read *Christian Apologetics*, 2nd ed. (Grand Rapids: Baker Books, 2013).

is inadequate: you can never arrive at what is immutable, universal and necessary from what is finite. If you cannot arrive at God from experience, you must bring God to experience, in the form of a hypothesis to be tested. This does not mean our faith is weak or tentative, only that to be intellectually honest, as God would have us be, we must at least in principle be rational in our faith. In this sense we treat Christianity as a hypothesis, and like any hypothesis, it must not contradict itself. Anything self-contradictory cannot be true, but what is noncontradictory could be true. To see if it is true, we check it with all relevant facts, looking for contradictions between the hypothesis and the facts. The hypothesis should be applicable to life in the sense that it can be lived out without contradiction. There is common ground between believer and nonbeliever, consisting, for example, in the principle of noncontradiction, values, ethics and the need for love. Furthermore, worldviews typically overlap in areas that are impersonal and nonmetaphysical. Even science, properly practiced, can be carried on between believer and nonbeliever. But worldviews diverge as soon as questions of ultimate meaning and purpose arise. We can prove that Christianity is true to the extent that we can prove any real-world belief is true, that is, with high probability. Yet we can have complete inner assurance, "certitude," that it is true. Combinationalism is to the right of pragmatism on the chart because it tests belief using an objective standard, that of consistency. A hypothesis must be consistent within itself, consistent with the facts and capable of being lived out consistently.

In the next column is classical apologetics, which is practiced by people as diverse as C. S. Lewis, William Lane Craig, J. P. Moreland, R. C. Sproul, John Gerstner and Norman Geisler. This approach aims first to prove theism, the general belief that God is, for example, omnipotent, omniscient, omnipresent, holy, creator and sustainer of the universe. If theism is not proved first, proof for the resurrection, for example, would not necessarily be interpreted theistically by the unbeliever. Of course if the unbeliever already accepts theism, proving it is unnecessary.

Classical apologists use theistic arguments (though they are also used by some apologists who use other methods). They are types or families of arguments in that there are a number of variations to each. The cosmological argument essentially reasons from the existence of the universe to a creator. One form argues that God is a necessary being, that he must exist in every possible world. Another argues that everything needs an adequate cause; thus the universe needs an adequate cause, and that cause is God (he is not a thing, and is uncaused). The teleological argument reasons from design in the universe to a designer. Modern science has uncovered intricate design in DNA, for example. We are also discovering the amazing extent to which the universe has been finely tuned to allow for life. The moral argument, which is not used as widely as the cosmological and teleological arguments, argues from the existence of objective moral obligations to a higher moral being as the grounds of such obligations.

Norman Geisler believes we must use a different approach to prove the truth of a worldview versus truth within a worldview. He uses six first principles of reality, which cannot be denied, because any attempt to deny them would use them (similar to Hanna's view). We do not need to prove them; we simply "see" that they are true once we understand them. One first principle (stated informally) is that "something exists." Anyone who attempts to deny that is admitting they exist. Another is the principle of noncontradiction, which would also be assumed by anyone attempting to deny it. Once alternatives are eliminated and theism is proved, Geisler shows that Christianity explains all the known facts in the most consistent way.

To the right of classical apologetics, and just left of rationalism (on the far right), evidentialism has been popularized in recent decades by Josh McDowell, who was influenced by John Warwick Montgomery. Gary Habermas has also been influential and widely known. The view does not require that theism be proved first. While most evidentialists accept theistic arguments and would use them, they do not believe it is necessary to first prove theism. Unlike classical apologists, evidentialists believe that, at least to some extent, facts point to their proper interpretation. So evidentialists typically work to prove the resurrection after supporting the veracity of the Bible (e.g., John Warwick Montgomery), or at least the believability of very widely accepted crucial facts (e.g., Gary Habermas). Many of the same facts and approaches used by evidentialists are used by classical apologists in their second step, which seeks to prove Christianity.

Let's review the chart again, this time more briefly. For fideism there can be no proof, but there is certitude from faith in revelation. For presuppositionalism there can be no direct proof of Christianity, but we must presuppose it: roughly, assume it by conviction and necessity. The case must ultimately be circular. Revelation is known of its own authority, but we can have proof because it must be presupposed. For Reformed epistemology noncircular arguments are acceptable in principle, and should be developed, but they are not adequate to ground something as crucial as religious faith. Belief in God is an

awareness that can arise in us because of the way we were created, and belief
in Christianity is a divine gift. Moving right, experientialism is the first view
that accepts something as decisive, standalone evidence for the conclusion that
Christianity is true. The evidence is internal and subjective. Pragmatism deals
with workability, which is a more objective form of experience and is therefore
to the right of experientialism. (Note that what "works" can be defined differently by different people.)

Moving further right (but not including rationalism on the extreme right nor
combinationalism) we have views that accept induction as an important and effective method of proof for religious belief. They (including combinationalism)
also accept a cumulative case, that is, layers of proof adding up to form a stronger
case overall. Religious experience and workability in life (including giving life
meaning) also typically play a supporting role in an overall case (whereas with
experientialism experience is the only proof). Veridicalism accepts both givens
that are known intuitively and that are undeniable, and effective corroboration,
through evidence and reason. Everyone can have an immediate awareness of God,
and the Christian can have an additional awareness of some essentials of Christianity. In its emphasis on direct awareness it is like Reformed epistemology, but in
veridicalism corroborating evidence can be strong and decisive. So like Reformed
epistemology on its left, it has a place for intuition, but like views on its right, it
has a place for a convincing case based on evidence.

As we continue to move right, intuition (similar to "self-attesting" for presuppositionalism) plays less of a role, and there is more emphasis on independently
existing objective evidence as grounds for belief.[13] There are also more such
objective criteria, until we get to evidentialism, which appeals to a multiplicity
of individual facts.

Combinationalism accepts livability as a test of a hypothesis, but only as one
of three aspects of consistency, whereas to the left pragmatism viewed livability
as the main criteria, and to the right of combinationalism, livability is viewed
as only one of a number of factors in an overall case.

Classical apologetics accepts arguments for theism and for Christianity, typically insisting (like presuppositionalism) that a worldview determines the interpretation of facts. But like the views on the right side of the chart, that
worldview is established by something other than a necessary assumption (for

---

[13]Presuppositionalists would say that the transcendental argument provides objective evidence, but
they would not say that it is "independently existing," since no facts exist independent of God.

Geisler, it is by undeniable first principles, but unlike presuppositionalism, they are necessary in every worldview; cf. Hanna).

Evidentialism is the near polar opposite of presuppositionalism, affirming that facts can be known independently of the views that interpret them, and that facts can even point to the correct interpretation.

I once showed this chart to Greg Bahnsen, who not surprisingly said that presuppositionalism should be on the right, next to rationalism, as offering absolutely certain proof for belief. In response I pointed out that certainty was secondary; the primary order of the chart was appeal to independent evidence for the conclusion: So fideism appeals to no independent evidence. Presuppositionalism appeals to a presupposition but not to independent evidence as grounds for belief (i.e., no direct proof). Reformed epistemology appeals to intuition. Experientialism appeals to one subjective criterion as evidence for a conclusion; pragmatism, to one external criterion. Next is veridicalism, which appeals to givens plus external and independent evidence. Then comes combinationalism, with its appeals to consistency of hypothesis and fittingness with the facts plus livability. Then classical apologetics appeals to independent evidence for theism and Christianity. And finally evidentialism appeals to a multiplicity of independent facts—the opposite of presuppositionalism's view that there are no independent facts. Bahnsen thought for a few seconds and said, "That could work . . . that could work."[14] I then mentioned that I always tell my students that presuppositionalists see their view as close to rationalism as far as both offer certainty. I add that they would see their presuppositionalism as different from rationalism's method of using independent evidence (Descartes, for example, famously beginning from his own thought—again, the opposite of presuppositionalism, which begins with God as the standard of truth). If it were not visually too complicated, on the chart I might put fideism, presuppositionalism and rationalism each at different points of a triangle so that presuppositionalism could be equidistant from the faith of fideism and the absolute proof of rationalism, yet unique. But over the years students have generally confirmed that it would be too complicated, and thus unhelpful.

Before we begin, it is worth briefly recounting why fideism, which challenges the legitimacy of apologetics, is biblically inadequate. Here are just a few examples of biblical reasons for belief. Moses asks God for signs to show his people that he has divine authority (Ex 4:1), which God grants, and later he grants

---

[14]Personal conversation after Bahnsen was a guest speaker in my apologetics class, Master's College, Newhall, California, in the fall of 1993.

abundant signs in the confrontation with Pharaoh (Ex 7–11). In the wilderness, God supernaturally demonstrates his presence, his provision for his people and his backing of Moses' leadership. In the conquest of the Promised Land, God divides the Jordan (Josh 3:17), gives victories over superior forces (Josh 1:4-9; 3:10-17) and extends daylight (Josh 10:12-14). He grants miracles for Gideon (Judg 7:16-22), Samson (Judg 14:6, 19; 15:15; 16:3) and others. Prophets such as Elijah predict events and perform miracles. Jesus' life fulfills a number of prophecies and is attested by miracles. He points to them as grounds for belief (Lk 24:27; Jn 10:37-38). When John the Baptist doubts, Jesus points to evidence that matches prophecy (Mt 11:4-5; cf. Is 29:18). Jesus meets Thomas's doubts with evidence (Jn 20:27). After the resurrection, he gives "many convincing proofs" (Acts 1:3; cf. Lk 24:39). John recounts some of Jesus' supernatural deeds as a way of inspiring saving faith (Jn 20:30). The supernatural authority of the Seventy (Lk 10:17) and the apostles (2 Cor 12:12) is attested by miracles. Paul argues from Scripture that Christ had to suffer and rise again (Acts 17:2-3), and he regards the resurrection as "proof to all men" (Acts 17:31; cf. Rom 1:4). Some do believe because of miracles (Jn 12:11; Acts 9:42; 13:12).

As mentioned above, this does not show that an unproblematic appeal to miracles and prophecy can be made today, but that Scripture uses reasons in support of faith. Just how that should be done is the subject of this book.

PART ONE

Foundational
Issues

1

APOLOGETICS IN THE BIBLE

Some have claimed that the Bible contains no apologetics, and that we look in vain for any attempt to prove the existence of God. It simply assumes the existence of God, and we should do the same. But this view overlooks the fact that the Bible was written mostly for the benefit of believers, not for unbelievers. And looking for answers to atheists—of which there were very few in Israel and not that many in the classical world—overlooks the way believers dealt with the challenges of the day. The main question in ancient times, reflected in the Old Testament, was not whether God exists but which God should be obeyed and served. A major issue in the New Testament was, who is the person of Christ?

OLD TESTAMENT

Much more work needs to be done on the subject of apologetics in the Bible, especially in the Old Testament. We can, however, identify some general themes.

God's power to act is given throughout the Old Testament as a reason to believe and trust in him. He supports those who obey, honor and trust him, confidently expecting him to act (e.g., Is 49:23). He also provides for them, guides and protects them and even cares for their descendants (Deut 28:1-14). Those who oppose him he will oppose in a myriad of ways (e.g., 1 Sam 2:30; Ps 18:26). There are anomalies, such as Job, but in general there is a sharp contrast between the well-being of those who love and serve him versus those who oppose him. Though the people might not have thought of it primarily as a source of confirmation, there is some explanatory power, and thus confirmation, in the correlation between personal and national faithfulness to Yahweh and well-being in the past and present and as a predictor of the future; and conversely for correlation between lack of faithfulness with trouble in the past, present and future.

God's actions had, understandably, more apologetic impact on the ancient peoples who witnessed them and, in the case of Israel, passed down the memories of them. For example, many of those who saw Israel defeat powerful enemies became convinced of Yahweh's reality (Josh 2:9-11). The persuasiveness of an argument from events to the God behind them is felt less today since it depends on accepting the Bible as an accurate historical record. Today, owing to several centuries of attacks on the historical credibility of the Bible, many unbelievers doubt its historical accuracy (what the Christian should do about that doubt is partly the subject of this book).

Isaiah exemplifies an important type of Old Testament apologetic reasoning. To make it vivid he offers a courtroom proceeding, with evidence and witnesses, challenging opponents,

"Present your case," the LORD says.
"Bring forward your strong arguments." (Is 41:21; cf. Is 43:26; 45:21)

The proceedings contrast Yahweh, the true God, with idols, which are made by very human craftsmen from ordinary materials (Is 40:18-20; 41:6-7; 44:9-20). Whereas idols cannot save, Yahweh can vanquish enemies (Is 41:11-12), sustain life (Is 41:17-18) and fructify the land (41:19). He does it in order

that they may see and recognize,
And consider and gain insight as well,
That the hand of the LORD has done this,
And the Holy One of Israel has created it. (Is 41:20)

Idols are mere "wind and emptiness" (Is 41:29) that can neither answer nor deliver (Is 46:7; 45:20)—in fact the idols themselves have gone into captivity (Is 46:2).

In similar reasoning, the psalmist says that idols are merely "the work of man's hands." They cannot speak, see, hear, smell, feel or move. Those who make and trust them "will become like them" (Ps 115:4-8; cf. Ps 135:15-18). Habakkuk also contrasts trusting in something one has made rather than God (Hab 2:18). Jeremiah emphasizes that only the true God, not idols, can give rain (essential to life in a desert; Jer 14:22)—a point that Elijah dramatically demonstrates in his showdown with the false prophets and their idols (1 Kings 17–18).

This type of reasoning was well understood by other ancient peoples. When the Assyrians go against Israel, the spokesperson says to Hezekiah that it is futile to trust that Yahweh will deliver them. No other gods have delivered their people from Assyria, and Yahweh will be no different. Hezekiah prays that God will show he is superior to the idols, and God responds by giving them victory (Is 37). When the Syrians invade Israel in the hill country and suffer defeat, they suppose it is because Yahweh is a God of the hills. If they fight on the plains, they reason, their own gods will be stronger and will defeat Israel. Yahweh makes sure the Syrians are defeated on the plain as well, to show he is Lord over all (1 Kings 20:23, 28).

Ancient societies had many supposed gods and prophets speaking for them. Even Israel, at times, had prophets representing other gods, as well as prophets who spoke falsely in the name of the Lord. The genuine prophets of the true God were at times validated by performing miracles. The woman of Zarephath understands this when Elijah raises her son. She says, "Now I know that you are a man of God and that the word of the LORD in your mouth is truth" (1 Kings 17:24). One of the most dramatic miracles in the Old Testament is Elijah's showdown with the false prophets on Mt. Carmel, when their god cannot cause their sacrifice to spontaneously burn up, whereas Elijah's God can. "When all the people saw it, they fell on their faces; and they said, 'The LORD, He is God; the LORD, He is God'" (1 Kings 18:39). Additionally, one of the most memorable events in Israel's history, one that defines them as a nation, is the miracle of the exodus. The clear implication, reiterated throughout the Old Testament, is that they could have come forth only if their God was real.

In the Old Testament, the ability to foretell the future is also a clear mark of the true God himself. Isaiah proclaims that Yahweh alone can predict the future (Is 41:23), "declaring the end from the beginning" (Is 46:10). God explicitly identifies this ability as a way to discern between one who speaks for him and one who does not: "'How will we know the word which the LORD has not spoken?' When a prophet speaks in the name of the LORD, if the thing does not come about or come true, that is the thing which the LORD has not spoken. The prophet has spoken it presumptuously; you shall not be afraid of him" (Deut 18:21-22).

The prophetic tradition that was validated formed a cohesive whole in that each contribution constructed a harmonious message. In many cases they knew their contemporaries, and even validated their message (e.g., Elijah's mantle passed to Elisha, 2 Kings 2:13).

NEW TESTAMENT

The New Testament reflects important apologetic themes found in the Old. For example, Christ clearly and repeatedly appeals to prophecy to show that he represents the true God. He came as the fulfillment of the predictions.

Christ also uses miracles as an additional way to demonstrate that he speaks for the living God. He goes so far as to say, "If I do not do the works of My Father, do not believe Me; but if I do them, though you do not believe Me, believe the works, so that you may know and understand that the Father is in Me, and I in the Father" (Jn 10:37-38). Nicodemus is one who clearly grasps the significance of Christ's miracles, saying, "Rabbi, we know that You have come from God as a teacher; for no one can do these signs that You do unless God is with him" (Jn 3:2). John closes his Gospel by saying that he has recorded some of Jesus' miracles in order that people might come to believe in him and thereby have salvation (Jn 20:30-31).

Acts also records numerous miraculous events performed by or on behalf of the apostles (e.g., Acts 3:7; 14:10). Miracles as divine credentials will be used again by the two witnesses in Revelation 11:5-6.

It is common to hear—even from pulpits—that miracles never change the mind of anyone; they merely confirm the faith of believers and harden the disbelief of nonbelievers. But the idea is simply not biblical. When Jesus raises Lazarus, "many of the Jews who came to Mary, and saw what He had done, believed in Him" (Jn 11:45). The Pharisees become concerned that if Jesus goes on performing such miracles, "all men will believe in Him" (Jn 11:48). When Peter raises Aeneas, "all who lived at Lydda and Sharon saw him, and they turned to the Lord" (Acts 9:35). When Peter raises Tabitha, "it became known all over Joppa, and many believed in the Lord" (Acts 9:42). When Paul blinds Elymas the magician, "the proconsul believed when he saw what had happened" (Acts 13:12). Jesus expects that miracles will convince people, and condemns Chorazin, Bethsaida and Capernaum (Mt 11:21, 23) for failing to respond to them. (This is not to say that citing the miracles of the Bible will have the same apologetic effect today that it had in biblical times, for reasons we will mention briefly when we discuss David Hume.) There is a sense in which, for some people, their response to a miracle may have merely manifested the underlying condition of their heart such that those who were open responded, whereas those who were already hardened rejected the miracle and the message. But that is different from the miracle itself always and only either confirming people in belief or hardening them in unbelief, but never convincing.

Jesus also defends his message with scriptural arguments. For example, he confronts his opponents with the fact that the Messiah will be the son of David, and yet David can also call him "Lord" (Mk 12:35-37). And he defends his message logically. When his opponents claim that he casts out demons by the power of Satan, Jesus points out the absurdity of the idea that Satan would fight his own forces. It is a move in logic called a reductio ad absurdum, in which you show that your opponent's position leads to an absurdity (Mt 12:25-26; Mk 12:26; Lk 11:17-18).

Like Jesus, the apostles seek to convince people of the truth. In his Pentecost sermon, Peter reasons with his Jewish audience from Scripture, appealing also to Jesus' miracles (Acts 2:22) and the resurrection (Acts 2:24). Paul customarily goes to synagogues and "reason[s] with them from the Scriptures, explaining and giving evidence" (Acts 17:2-3; cf. Acts 18:4, 19; 19:8). Acts notes with approval those who were powerful at defending the truth of the gospel and refuting objections (Stephen, Acts 6:10; Paul, Acts 9:22; Apollos, Acts 18:28). Paul includes the ability to refute those nonbelievers who contradict sound doctrine as a qualification of an elder (Tit 1:9; nonbelievers, cf. Tit 1:10-16).

In Galatians Paul answers what was no doubt an objection from some Jews: How could Jesus be the Messiah, or even be sent from God, if he was hanged on a cross and died? Paul acknowledges that anyone hanged on a tree is cursed, but explains that Christ died a substitutionary death for sin, taking the curse for our sin on himself (Gal 3:13; see Deut 21:23). He also defends salvation by grace through faith in the face of Jewish and Judaizing tendencies to depend on works (Gal 3:6-12).

Paul changes his approach when talking to non-Jewish audiences. After healing a man at Lystra, he confronts the peoples' devotion to the Greek deities. He says that God "did not leave Himself without witness, in that He did good and gave you rains from heaven and fruitful seasons, satisfying your hearts with food and gladness" (Acts 14:17). All the while God had been showing people his true nature through his providential care and the beneficent regularities of nature. This echoes the words of Psalm 19, "The heavens are telling of the glory of God" (Ps 19:1). The regularities of the universe (Ps 19:2, "day to day," "night to night") give clear nonverbal testimony (Ps 19:3, "no speech, nor are there words") that reaches "through all the earth" (Ps 19:4).

Paul's most extensive recorded presentation to Gentiles is his remarkable sermon in Acts 17 to some of the intelligentsia of the day. Discussion of the sermon could fill a chapter of its own, but we could say briefly that he first gets their attention (Acts 17:22-23), then says things that agree with their views (Acts 17:24-29), and goes on to raise issues that conflict with their views (Acts 17:30-31). To those unfamiliar with the relevant Greek philosophical views, it appears that Paul is confronting them from start to finish. But actually he is showing some agreement. He no doubt was well acquainted with the views of the Stoics, in part because his hometown, Tarsus, was a major Stoic center. Stoics held that God is not confined to temples and idols (Acts 17:24), nor is he like the mythic gods who have needs (Acts 17:25). He is much bigger than that (Acts 17:29). He is immanent in the world (Acts 17:27). Furthermore (in contrast to much Greek cultural chauvinism), Stoics held that humanity is a unity[1] (Acts 17:27-28). But just when his audience would have felt like standing and cheering, Paul confronts both the Stoics and Epicureans with those parts of the gospel that would have been foreign to any Greek. He mentions judgment through Christ and the resurrection (Acts 17:31). The Greeks held that the body imprisons the soul, so the idea of rejoining one's body in the afterlife would have made no sense. And that's when the meeting breaks up (Acts 17:32).

Some Christians regard Paul as having erred in his Acts 17 presentation. Some also regard 1 Corinthians 2:1-5 as a statement of confession and resolve not to dabble in philosophical talk again, but instead to give a straightforward presentation of the gospel. However, those who hold the sermon to be no less exemplary than Paul's other evangelistic speeches point out that Paul gives no indication to the Corinthians that he is thinking about his speech in Athens. Nor do the passages necessarily conflict. He says to the believing Corinthians that he wants their faith to rest on the power of God rather than human wisdom, and he focuses on Christ. To the unbelieving Athenians he compares and contrasts their views with Christianity, and talks about Christ.

There is no indication in either context that Paul does anything wrong. It would be hard to imagine Luke leaving out any such indication since the speech is so important. It is the most detailed of the apostle's encounters with Gentiles, and it is in no less than Athens, the center of thought in the ancient world. Furthermore, the supposedly errant features of the speech are also in his brief address at Lystra (Acts 14:15-17): he quotes no Scripture, and does not focus on Jesus as Messiah (incidentally, he also mentions God's patience, Acts 14:16; cf. Acts 17:30). It is here that he appeals to natural revelation (beneficent order, Acts 14:17). So if Paul is wrong in Acts 17 he is also wrong in Acts 14, yet neither context indicates he is.

Luke ends his account of the speech with its results. Some reject the message, some want to hear more and "some men joined him and believed"

---

[1]Michelle V. Lee, *Paul, the Stoics, and the Body of Christ* (Cambridge: Cambridge University Press, 2008), pp. 88–95.

(Acts 17:34). One convert is no less than Dionysius the Areopagite, who tradition says became important in the early church. So if the speech was a failure, it had a remarkable effect.

Though Paul appeals to natural revelation and quotes no Scripture, he does present scriptural ideas. It seems he expects certain things to be clear to people even apart from Scripture—which fits what he says in Romans 1. There he explains that all people are accountable and without excuse because they can have some basic knowledge of God and his moral law (Rom 1:19, 32; cf. Rom 2:14-15): "*For since the creation of the world* His invisible attributes, His eternal power and divine nature, have been clearly seen, *being understood through what has been made*, so that they are without excuse" (Rom 1:20 [emphasis added]). He does not go into detail, but it seems that everyone can make a simple inference to the existence of God. Creation allows people to clearly see "His invisible attributes, His eternal power and divine nature" (Rom 1:20). Those who worship some demeaning and idolatrous distortion of God are denying that basic awareness available to every human (Rom 1:21, 23). There is an alternate view that in Romans Paul is referring to a noninferential, or nondiscursive, awareness of God, that we simply become aware of God without it being a conclusion (which as we shall see, is held by Alvin Plantinga, and is considered possible by William Lane Craig).

Whatever is available about God through inference or immediate awareness is, however, not specific enough to include the gospel. Paul says that the contents of the gospel come only through a human messenger: "How will they hear without a preacher?" (Rom 10:14).

Luke weaves into his writings his own defense of Christianity, though it is rarely recognized as such by modern readers because he was responding to the first-century situation. Christianity looked like a troublemaker's religion because it was often associated with conflict, riots and imprisonment. Even its founder was executed as a common criminal. The Roman writer Tacitus says that after Christ's execution, "a most mischievous superstition, thus checked for the moment, again broke out not only in Judaea, the first source of the evil, but even in Rome, where all things hideous and shameful from every part of the world find their centre and become popular."[2]

---

[2]Tacitus, *Annals* 15.44. *Complete Works of Tacitus*, trans. Alfred John Church, William Jackson Brodribb and Sara Bryant (New York: Random House, 1942), edited for Perseus Digital Library, http://www.perseus.tufts.edu/hopper/text?doc=Perseus%3Atext%3A1999.02.0078%3Abook%3 D15%3Achapter%3D44.

In response, Luke documents how the proceedings against Jesus were illegal.[3] He was not convicted in a bona fide court. Pilate declares his innocence three times (Lk 23:4, 14, 22), and so does the Roman centurion attending his crucifixion (Lk 23:47; Matthew even includes a statement by Pilate's wife about Jesus's innocence; Mt 27:19). Luke includes that the hostility toward this innocent and once popular man came from jealous and hypocritical religious leaders. As to how the Son of Man could be the victim of scheming people, the answer is that he was no mere victim, but everything was following a divine plan. John even includes a prophetic explanation as to how Jesus could have chosen a traitor for a disciple (Jn 3:18; see Ps 41:9).[4] The Gospels show Jesus in confident submission during the trials and crucifixion.

As for trouble encountered later by Christ's followers, Luke shows in Acts how much of it came from jealous leaders (e.g., Acts 13:45; 14:2, 19; 17:5, 13; 21:27). To counteract them he records how many officials were favorable toward the disciples. One proconsul was favorable, and even believed (Acts 13:7, 12). At Philippi the chief magistrate apologized to Paul and Silas for the illegal beatings (Acts 16:37-38). The proconsul of Achaia ruled that accusations against Paul were merely internal to Judaism; they were guiltless as far as the government (Acts 8:12-13). In Ephesus civic leaders were friendly to Paul and publicly absolved him of wrongdoing (Acts 19:13-14). The Roman commander at Jerusalem, Claudius Lysias, reported to Governor Felix that Paul had done nothing deserving death or imprisonment (Acts 23:29). After hearing Paul's case, Felix kept him in prison an inordinate amount of time in hopes of receiving a bribe and wishing to curry favor with the Jews (Acts 24:25-27). Festus and Agrippa heard his case and declared that he had done nothing deserving death or imprisonment (Festus: Acts 25:25-27; Agrippa: Acts 26:31-32).

Luke also records illegal proceedings against Paul that end with Paul graciously overlooking the offenses (Acts 16:23-40; 22:24-29). Acts closes with Paul carrying on his full missionary activity from prison, right under the watchful eye of the guard. Had anything illegal been going on, he would certainly have been stopped.

As to the argument that Jesus could not be the Messiah because the Jews rejected him, Luke records Stephen's speech in detail, according to which Israel had a long history of rejecting the prophets, so this was nothing different (Acts 7:51-52). Mark

---

[3]F. F. Bruce, *The Defense of the Gospel in the New Testament*, rev. ed. (Grand Rapids: Eerdmans, 1977). I am indebted to Bruce for pointing out the various elements included by Luke.
[4]Avery Dulles, *A History of Apologetics* (1971; repr., Eugene, OR: Wipf & Stock, 1999), p. 5.

also makes a point of Israel's rejection of God and his messengers (Is 6:9 in Mk 4:12; Is 29:13 in Mk 7:6-7; Ps 118:22-23 in Mk 12:10-11). In fact, the theme of divinely super-intended hardening appears in all four Gospels (Mt 13:14-15; Lk 8:10; Jn 12:40) and Acts (Acts 28:26-27). Paul develops the theme in relation to God using that hardening in order to bring Gentiles into his plan of salvation (Rom 11:8-10, 25).

The theme of Israel's rejection of truth is given prophetic implications when Mark and Luke record the astounding prediction that the temple would be destroyed (Mk 13:2; Lk 19:44), which was fulfilled in A.D. 70.

The early church also began defending the resurrection. Matthew answers the charge, which was apparently circulating, that the disciples stole Jesus' body. He explains that the story was concocted by the chief priests with the cooperation of the soldiers (Mt 28:11-15). Paul offers the eyewitness accounts of Peter, the Twelve, James, "all the apostles," five hundred people and himself (1 Cor 15:5-8). Luke records Paul's defense before authorities, in which he offers his encounter with the resurrected Christ (Acts 9:3-6) as the reason for his own remarkable conversion (Acts 22:3-14; 26:9-18).

Matthew includes a full exposure of the deficiencies Jesus opposed in the Judaism of his time and that gave him and the disciples so much trouble. Acts 23 charges the leaders with obsessive outward conformity and the desire for attention while being inwardly ungodly, missing the entire essence of a righteous life and persecuting those who are truly serving God. Far from pleasing God, they incur his wrath and lead followers disastrously astray. They will in no way enter heaven, it is said (Acts 23:13; cf. Acts 5:20).

A more philosophical challenge seems to have arisen late in the first century, as what appears to be early forms of Gnosticism began to emerge. (Paul seemed to be opposing an early form of Gnosticism in Colossians.) In keeping with a major theme in Asian thought, Gnosticism held that the physical realm is bad and the spiritual realm is good. This entailed that Christ could not have been fully physical and that his incarnation must have been only apparent. In answer to this, John begins his epistle with an affirmation that Christ was physical: "What we have *heard*, what we have *seen* with our eyes, what we have *looked at* and *touched* with our hands, concerning the Word of Life" (1 Jn 1:1 [emphasis added]).

So, understood in context, the Bible is rich in apologetic content. There are also verses that moderate the importance of evidence. After giving Thomas the proof he requests, Christ says, "Blessed are they who did not see, and yet believed" (Jn 20:29). And Paul tells the Corinthians he does not want to speak with "persuasive words" lest people's faith rest on "the wisdom of men" (1 Cor 2:4-5; cf. 1 Cor 1:17; 2:1).

The various approaches to apologetics seek to give a coherent account of these and other biblical passages.

2

APOLOGETICS IN HISTORY

A survey

Apologetics has followed a long, winding path as it has interacted with the many intellectual and cultural changes and upheavals of the past two millennia. While the history of apologetics could constitute a detailed study in itself, surveying some of the highlights and flow will give us background for understanding the apologetic approaches that have been proposed in modern times.[1] And as always, grasping the past can help prepare us for the future.

THE EARLY CHURCH

Christianity was born as a movement within Judaism, so its early focus was on Jewish objections, while Paul also dealt with Gentile issues. In A.D. 70, Rome smashed Judaism as a national and cultural force, after which Christianity interacted mostly with the classical world. Almost from the beginning followers of Christ were not accepted by Judaism, so they lost the acceptance Rome gave to recognized religions—exposing Christians to persecution for two centuries. Christians raised suspicion by giving ultimate allegiance to Christ rather than Caesar, refraining from bawdy public feasts, the bloodlust of the gladiatorial games and military service, which entailed immorality and pagan worship. For this they were regarded as haters of humankind,[2] and mistaken for atheists because their God was

---

[1] What follows is a series of brief, suggestive highlights, not a complete survey, so a number of significant individuals have been left out.

[2] Tacitus says that Nero blamed the great fire in Rome on Christians because he needed a scapegoat to quell the rumor that he himself had started it. The Christians, "who are hated for their abominations," were arrested and condemned, "although not so much for the fire itself as for their hatred of humankind." *Annals*, trans. Cynthia Damon (New York: Penguin Classics, 2013), 15.44.

not visible in idols. Ignorant rumors arose over Christian practices of "love feasts," the use of "brother" and "sister" even for one's spouse (which sounded like incest) and talk of "eating" the body and blood of Christ in Communion. Christians were blamed for the many troubles of the empire on the grounds that they had offended the gods by neglecting their worship, a view encouraged by the idol makers, temple builders, priests and soothsayers (Acts 19:24-29).[3] One holding facility became so jammed with Christians that some suffocated before they could be executed.[4] Meanwhile the lower classes flocked to a religion that eschewed class consciousness and regarded all people as equal before a God of love.

By the second century, apologists arose to win civil justice for the church as well as new converts. They gave less attention than some to miracles, probably because they did not want their accounts to be confused with pagan stories. One exception was Quadratus, who wrote in A.D. 125 that some who were cured by Jesus survived to his day.[5] It was common for apologists to point out that pagan idols, which were often made with precious stones and gold, had to be guarded so they wouldn't be stolen, so how could they provide protection when the needed it? How could they be above humans when they were made by them?[6]

Many argued for the moral and intellectual superiority of Christianity. Aristides of Athens argued (*Apology*, ca. A.D. 125) for the superiority of Christianity, saying barbarians worship objects that must be moved by higher powers, Egyptians worship lowly things like plants and reptiles and Greek deities are immoral. Such gods had been invented, he said, so people could indulge in unrestrained vice. Jews, he said, worship the one God, but mix it with superstition and the notion that God needs our sacrifices. Christians worship the one God and strive for a moral life, to the point of loving their enemies.[7] Justin Martyr (ca. 100-ca. 167) came out of Greek philosophy to Christianity, believing the latter to be "the only sure and useful philosophy." He said that philosophers had been enlightened by the *Logos* (Jn 1:9), a term used by the apostle John that appears in Greek philosophy as far back as Heraclitus (500 B.C.). He addressed the emperor, but also

---

[3]Pliny, governor of Bithynia, complained to Emperor Trajan in A.D. 112 that the pagan temples were nearly deserted and those who sold sacrificial animals were impoverished.

[4]Justo L. González, *The Story of Christianity* (1984; repr., two vols. in one, Peabody, MA: Prince Press, 1999), 1:46-47. Known from a letter sent from churches in Lyons and Vienne (in Gaul) to fellow believers in Phrygia and Asia Minor.

[5]Eusebius, *History of the Church* 4.3.1-2, cited in Avery Dulles, *A History of Apologetics* (1971; repr., Eugene, OR: Wipf and Stock, 1999), p. 25. His work survives as only a line in Eusebius.

[6]González, *Story of Christianity*, 1:56.

[7]Dulles, *History of Apologetics*, p. 25.

got a wide audience, saying Christians are moral and follow a moral founder whose life fulfilled prophecy. In his *Dialogue with Trypho*, who was a Jewish man, he compares law and gospel, and uses prophecy to argue for Christ as Messiah. Breaking with the irenic apologetics of the time, Justin's pupil Tatian (*Address to the Greeks*) scorned pagan deities for their immoral deeds, said that positive aspects of Greek culture were borrowed from other cultures and even pointed out that their beloved Greek language, which supposedly separated them from barbarians, was spoken differently in the various regions of Greece. He hoped to show that Christianity is superior, and thus win tolerance for it. Athenagoras (*Plea for the Christians*, ca. 177) argued for toleration on the grounds that the empire already accepted a wide variety of religious views and that Christians had high morals, condemning abortion, infanticide and gladiatorial games. In all, they were no threat to the empire; on the contrary, they prayed for government.

As Christians were answering cultural charges, Gnosticism had grown to a full worldview by the mid-second century, teaching that the highest being is pure God, from whom emanates successively lesser beings, each having a greater amount of matter. According to one view, the God of the Old Testament is responsible for evil and should not be trusted, whereas little can be known of the high God. He would never become incarnate as lowly matter; thus either Christ was ghostlike, or "Christ" came on Jesus at baptism and left at the cross. He supposedly taught secret knowledge only to his inner circle, which was not written but passed orally. Possession of it brings salvation. In answer, Irenaeus (ca. 130–ca. 200; *Against Heresies*, ca. 185) said that Gnosticism was a contradiction in that it offered knowledge of an "unknown" God. He had been under Polycarp's ministry, whose life had overlapped the apostolic age, so Irenaeus could state with authority that there was no such secret teaching passed down from the apostles. He emphasized the unity of the church and the succession of its teaching, from the apostles to current times. To answer Gnosticism, he developed relatively sophisticated ideas of the Trinity and nature of Christ.

Christianity was growing its own worldview, notably in Alexandria, Egypt, where Clement (150–ca. 215) ran a school that continued until the Muslim conquest. He taught that the Greeks had borrowed from the Old Testament, and since all truth comes from God, Christians can use it.

Tertullian (ca. 160–225), an attorney, questioned the policy that Christians were to be persecuted but the government was not to initiate investigations to find them. If they were criminals, said Tertullian, they should be sought out as such; if they were not, they should be acquitted. As far as undermining the empire by not honoring the gods, Rome was great before being devoted to them, and besides, they took them from vanquished peoples. No one can prove they exist, whereas the God of the Bible can be proved by prophecy, including prophecy that the Jews would be afflicted if they were unfaithful to God, and they have been sent wandering. Christians do not worship the emperor but pray for him and obey the laws—who would want forced worship anyway? Persecution would never stop belief, he said, since "the blood of Christians is seed" (*Apology* 50). To the Jewish community, he offered that Christ fulfilled prophecy, as well as fulfilled the law and superseded it (*Against the Jews*). In contrast to the use early apologists made of classical philosophy, Tertullian rejected it as a source of truth equal to revelation.

Origen (ca. 185–ca. 254; *Contra Celsum*) was Clement's pupil and succeeded him as head of the school. He answered the anti-Christian Celsus in a five-hundred-page response, the first full Christian counteroffensive. He argued that because of his high moral character, Christ would not have made up a story about his virgin birth, neither would he or his followers have died for a fraud. He charged Celsus with arbitrarily relying on some biblical passages while regarding others as myths, and holding biblical history to an impossible standard that would also eliminate events everyone accepts as historical, such as the Trojan War. As to Christ not being able to predict his betrayal and death, he could foresee events that he chose not to prevent—not so unlike Socrates. Origen makes a positive case for Christ from prophecy, miracles and the power of God still evident in the Christian community. Christianity is morally superior to paganism in its view of God and ethics, and those who convert to it are morally transformed.

Christians also appealed to recent events. Galerius, the Roman ruler responsible for the worst persecution, fell ill with an excruciating, repulsive disease. It prompted him to pardon Christians in 311, asking in return that they pray for the empire. He died a few days later. Constantine soon conquered the empire in the name of Christ, and Christianity eventually became the religion of the empire. Lactantius (240–ca. 320) interpreted these events apologetically, saying that Galerius's repentance had come too late to avoid God's judgment. Contrary to the view of the Stoics, God is involved in human events. While paganism is full of contradictions, Christianity can be demonstrated by prophecy, and its revelation gives ultimate truth. Eusebius (ca. 260–339) argued for Christianity not only from prophecy, miracles and the integrity of the apostles, but also from history. God had superintended the unity of the empire for the sake of the spread of the gospel, and he had worked through Constantine. Athanasius (ca. 293–373), whose tireless efforts helped defeat the Arian doctrine that Christ is created, also argued from historical events. Christian truth is winning everywhere, he said, and proof of Christ can be found in his workings in the world. Chrysostom (347–407) too regarded the rise of Christianity, and its morality, as a type of evidence. He was, however, harsh in arguing against Jews, which set an unfortunate precedent.

In the face of persecution that had been horrific at times, Christianity had survived and grown. Partly in response to what it determined were heresies, it had defined the essentials of its theology. The apologetic response went far beyond theology, to include issues that were legal, social, ethical, historical and philosophical. The young church's broad thinking and flexibility is a good reminder that the apologetic task goes beyond the theological and philosophical—and must ultimately be determined by the challenge (an ethos echoed in the broad engagement with culture found in the apologetics of C. S. Lewis and John Warwick Montgomery). Whatever the effect of the response, which is hard to assess, it was backed up by the moral testimony of a church that had met distortions, hatred and violence with love and forgiveness—making credible its message of a God who cares and forgives. Though hated and suppressed in its beginnings, Christianity eventually grew in respect and popularity until it became the dominant religious force in the empire, a fact that would itself be used as evidence that God was behind it, growing it from a mustard seed to a bountiful tree (Mt 13:31-32).

AUGUSTINE

In an age when Christianity still had some competition from paganism, Augustine (354–430) emerged as a pastor whose writings were to be the most influential since Paul, and are still in bookstores after sixteen hundred years. As a young man he wandered from the Christian faith of his devout mother, wrestling in part with the problem of evil. After a sudden conversion, he developed the idea that evil is not inherent in things, but is a matter of the use that moral beings make of them.[8] Evil is not a thing brought about by God, so he is not to blame. It is in a sense an absence, as blindness is a lack of sight. As divine grace is God's free gift, no one can blame God for not giving it—since grace is by definition undeserved. Sin is a lack of virtue, as cowardice is a lack of bravery, but the fault lies in the will of the

---

[8]Augustine, *On the Morals of the Manichaeans* 8; the chapter is titled "Evil Is Not a Substance, but a Disagreement Hostile to Substance," www.newadvent.org/fathers/1402.htm. Augustine uses the analogy that a scorpion's poison is not bad for it but is bad for humans.

person who failed to do good. God did good by creating beings with free will, and the blame falls solely on us for misusing it.

Against skeptics, Augustine pointed out that we have certainty about many things, such as the principle of noncontradiction (put simply, a proposition and its denial cannot both be true). We also know we exist, and we can even be certain that we have doubt, a theme later expanded by René Descartes. So, ironically, skepticism is actually a kind of covert knowledge claim. (Mark Hanna's veridicalism and Norman Geisler's classical apologetics, as we shall see, make use of an immediate knowing that is certain.)

In general, according to Augustine, our knowledge is of material and nonmaterial things. Knowledge of the material is less certain because things change and our senses change.[9] Knowledge of the nonmaterial comes from the mind, to which God gives the ability (illumination) to know eternal truths. The fact that our finite minds can grasp eternal truths points to the existence of a God who makes this possible, since both he and what we know are eternal and true. (We will see how Alvin Plantinga argues that divine creation explains the mind's ability to grasp truth better than atheistic evolution.) Sense objects, too, such as living things, point to God in that they could not have created themselves. Moreover, finite things require the existence of something permanent to explain how they came into being.

When Rome was sacked by the Goths in 410, Christians were blamed because they had defected from the gods that had given protection. Augustine answered extensively with the first philosophy of history, *The City of God*. Misfortunes happen to everyone,[10] and Rome's defeat could be explained by the dynamics of war, not failure to honor the pagan gods. The empire had been defeated when the pagan gods were widely worshiped,[11] and its current weakened state was due to its vices. In ancient times, Rome was virtuous, and God had spared it despite its pagan worship.[12] It was the Christian influence that had spared Rome from complete destruction, and in a display of divine providence, the invaders had spared the churches. The world, he said, divides spiritually into the heavenly city, consisting of those who love God and seek his glory, and the earthly city, dominated by the love of self and exaltation of all things worldly.[13] They have contended since the fall of humanity, and only the heavenly is eternal.

---

[9]Many find in views like this an echo of the Platonism Augustine had held as a young man.
[10]Augustine, *The City of God* 1.
[11]Ibid., 2.
[12]Ibid., 5.
[13]Ibid., 14.28, "Of The Nature of the Two Cities, The Earthly and the Heavenly."

Augustine focused on spirituality and morals, not general knowledge and science. It is better to be ignorant yet humble than to pry into secrets and become proud.[14] As to the relation between faith and reason, reason is needed to understand what we believe.

In Augustine the divergence between Christian and classical thought was set. The Greeks focused on understanding nature, humanity and how to form a good society; evil is mere ignorance of the good; focus was on the good life. Christians focused on God and his moral requirements and believed that evil is a matter of the will, not the intellect.

THE MIDDLE AGES

Little by way of apologetics developed in the so-called Dark Ages. However, at the end of this period, the archbishop of Canterbury Anselm (1033–1109) devised the controversial ontological argument for the existence of God.[15] God is the greatest possible being. If God exists only in the mind then he would not be the greatest possible being (because something that exists outside the mind is greater than a mere notion that exists only in the mind). Therefore, God must exist not only in our minds but also in reality. (Alvin Plantinga recently strengthened the ontological argument by casting it in modal logic, a modern innovation.)

By the mid-twelfth century, Aristotle was reintroduced via new translations and took the intellectual world by storm. His views that the world is eternal, that God is aware only of himself and that sin is ignorance were of particular concern to his medieval interpreters. Thomas Aquinas (1225–1274) sought to harmonize Aristotle with Christianity where possible, rejecting the elements of his thought that contradicted doctrine. We can know something of a cause from its effects, Aquinas said, so we can know something of God's existence from the world, a line of reasoning he developed in five arguments. But this knowledge is vague and must be filled out with revelation. Some things can be known only from reason (e.g., specific facts about the world), some things can be known only from revelation (e.g., the Trinity), but some things can be known by both, as when we know some general things about God through the world.

Augustine had contrasted the earthly and the heavenly. Plato had contrasted the realms of the seen and the unseen, the place of God and the forms. Aquinas joined

---

[14]W. T. Jones, *A History of Western Philosophy* (New York: Harcourt, Brace, & World, 1952), p. 386.
[15]It is an a priori argument as opposed to an a posteriori one. The latter is an argument that in some way depends on reflecting on our knowledge of the world; an a priori argument does not.

realms, as Aristotle (who, for example, joined forms and objects) had. For Aquinas, since God was both Creator and author of the Bible, the two are in harmony. Any conflict between science and Scripture is only apparent, caused by errors in science or exegesis. So ignorance is the problem—not the desire for more knowledge than God wants us to have. Augustine had made knowledge a product of divine enablement (illumination), and separated divine and human wisdom. Aquinas held that the mind can grasp things directly, following Aristotle's view that the mind can grasp essences. All content in the mind comes through the senses, a claim typically made by empiricists. Aquinas held that philosophy reasons from information given by the senses, whereas theology works from revelation and is held on faith. Reason can neither prove nor disprove doctrine. Like all fields, philosophy and theology are based on first principles that cannot be proven but must be assumed. (We will see that a major issue dividing certain apologetic methods is the relationship between assumption and proof.) Rationalists like Plato, by contrast, claim that significant knowledge comes from the mind's grasp of truth (usually eternal truths), and that the senses can tell us only what is probably true. Empiricists regard rationalists as in danger of having ideas that are out of touch with reality.

Not everyone was enthused about bringing faith and reason so close together. Meister Eckhart (1260–1328) held that God is above our rationality, including our concepts and categories, and insisted that we must make a mystical and suprarational connection to the divine.

John Duns Scotus (1265–1308) mounted a very different challenge. The medieval synthesis of knowledge that reached a high point in Aquinas relied on the conviction that we can know truth by thinking rationally, since a rational God made the world. That he made our minds with rational capabilities closed the loop, ensuring our knowledge. The preferred method of reasoning was deductive, by which the conclusion is certain if the premises are true and the argument is valid. That is because the conclusion does not go beyond the premises. For example, all the chairs in this room hold five hundred pounds; this chair is one of those; therefore it holds five hundred pounds. The conclusion only brings out an implication of what was already accepted in the premises.

But for Scotus, saying that God acts rationally wrongly puts his will under his intellect. Instead, God can do absolutely anything he wants, not only what is rational. Consequently, if God does not have to do what is rational, then we cannot necessarily know truth through reason. There is no guarantee that the conclusion we reach in our mind is true in reality. Instead of thinking our way to truth, we have to go out and observe what God chose to do. This argument shifted the primary way of knowing from reason to observation, and helped start the scientific age. Aquinas had harmonized faith and reason by means of a rational God who both created the world and inspired the Bible. Scotus separated theology and philosophy. We can know little of God's existence from his effects, as Aquinas had claimed; rather, we have to take spiritual things more on faith. Reason, which now had little place in spiritual knowledge, became a purely secular tool. Besides, just as the will is primary in God, so it is in humans. Therefore, God is not much interested in illuminating our minds; he is focused on modifying our conduct. And because God's will is primary in ethics too, what is good is simply a matter of God's choice. He does not will something because it is good; it is good because he wills it. So even right and wrong cannot be discovered; it has to be revealed. God could have chosen almost anything to be right and wrong.

Where Aquinas and many medieval thinkers had put theology over philosophy and all other fields, theology was now separated from philosophy, and thus in effect isolated from it (contrary to what Scotus had intended). Knowledge would develop independently of theology, and joining with unrestrained reason, it would eventually come back to challenge every aspect of religious belief. This is one factor that set the stage for the modern challenge to religious knowledge. (Some contemporary apologists attempt to argue that theism is the best explanation for things like the efficacy of logic, whereas presuppositionalists attempt to argue that the God of Reformed Christianity is the only grounds for reason.)

William of Ockham (ca. 1280–1349) further limited the importance of reason by saying that categories exist only in the mind. We see a person, John, and that is all that exists in the real world. The categories of "man," "human," "student" that we might apply to him are only in our mind. We should not create more than what is absolutely necessary to explain something, a principle that came to be known as "Ockham's razor." This tended to reduce things to what is observable, making it more difficult to prove God. When science began to develop physical explanations, it was used to discourage supernatural ones. Ockham also attacked the prevailing Aristotelian emphasis on goals ("final causes") as God-given and thereby objective. As science and the modern mind developed, the idea came about that only *what* happened is objective; *why* something happened is purely subjective.

The need for God—and the ability to prove his existence—was beginning to fade from the Western mind.

At this point we can identify some broad trends. Augustine emphasized the difference between heavenly and earthly wisdom, trusting the deliverances of the mind and revelation rather than knowledge from the senses. Heavenly and earthly mindsets ("cities") have little in common. Aquinas connected our knowledge of the world and revelation, emphasizing that we can know something of God through empirical investigation. Everyone can see effects, and can reason from them to causes. We shall see something of these broad themes continued in contemporary apologetics.

THE REFORMATION

The Reformation did more than challenge theology, it shook epistemology (the study of the possibility and limits of knowledge) by seeking to replace the authority of the church with the individual and his conscience, as grounded in the Bible. John Calvin (1509–1564) accepted that creation bears witness to the Creator, but sin renders that witness ineffective unless it is "illumined by the inner revelation of God through faith."[16] Evidences are not strong enough to establish faith, but for those who have faith, evidences are "very useful aids" and offer "wonderful confirmation."[17] Evidences for the Old Testament include the heavenly character of its doctrine, agreement of all its parts, its effect on us, its sheer antiquity, miracles performed by God's messengers, fulfilled prophecy and preservation of the Bible through persecution. Evidences for the New Testament include its preservation through persecution, the transformation of the apostles, the agreement of diverse people who believe it and their godly character, and the witness of the martyrs.[18] There are "other reasons, neither few nor weak," but those who try to use them to establish faith (rather than confirm it) are "acting foolishly, for only by faith can this be known."[19]

Humanism had been growing since the late Middle ages, becoming recognizable as a new movement. At first it represented simply a renewed interest in learning and the possibilities of this life. Later it would take God out of the center of its worldview and replace it with humanity. Christianity as it had developed under the Reformers' emphasis on the inability of good works to contribute to salvation seemed unnecessarily disparaging of humanity and the pos-

---

[16]John Calvin, *Institutes of the Christian Religion*, ed. John T. McNeill, trans. Ford Lewis Battles, Library of Christian Classics 20 (Philadelphia: Westminster, 1960), 1.6.14 (p. 68).

[17]Ibid., 1.8.1 (p. 82).

[18]Ibid., 1.8–9 (pp. 81–92).

[19]Ibid., 1.8.13 (p. 92).

sibilities of this life.[20] Those possibilities seemed brighter with the dawning of science—if only religious fervor could be held back by tolerance. (Baruch Spinoza [1632–1677] even celebrated doubt as a way to chill religious fervor.)

Blaise Pascal's (1623–1662) apologetics are too complex and fragmented to summarize easily, but he is best known for his wager, which is unique as an argument from utility (i.e., that it is useful to believe). As popularly summarized: If the believer turns out to be right, he gains everything, but if it turns out he is wrong, he loses little (assuming a moral life is a good life). If the atheist is right he gains nothing, and if it turns out he is wrong he loses everything. No rational person would bet against Christianity. Pascal's wager has been criticized for not arguing that the object of belief is true, but considering all his other writings, Pascal did not intend it as the only reason to believe.[21]

Greek skepticism, which had been rediscovered in the fifteenth century,[22] exposed the vulnerability of knowledge and evoked a strong, lasting response from philosophers and apologists throughout this general period. Various strategies were attempted to defeat it. It is perhaps unfortunate, however, that so much attention was diverted to it, since the number of people who have held it has always been relatively small. That has remained true even up through the modern period (though lately the numbers have been going up).[23]

Though some, like Aquinas and Raymond Lull (ca. 1232–ca. 1315), interacted with Islamic thought, apologetics has done relatively little with other religions and has made an effective response to sects only in the latter part of the twentieth century. This is due in part to the West's being largely isolated from other religions until the nineteenth century.

---

[20]The Platonic leanings of society, reflected in the church, encouraged a focus on unseen perfections, which for Christians were found in heaven. This life seemed little more than preparation for the next, a view reinforced by various troubles of the age, and by the periodic ravages of the bubonic plague.

[21]Pascal is often regarded as a fideist, one who offers no reasons to believe. Despite the fact that the wager reasons from decision theory rather than epistemology, and he spoke of irrational motivations of the heart, he also offered other supports for faith in his varied writings.

[22]Greek skepticism was rediscovered through the writings of Sextus Empiricus, the skeptical works of Cicero and an account by Laertius of ancient skepticism in his *Lives of Eminent Philosophers*. The first known reference to Sextus Empiricus in Renaissance Europe is a letter from humanist Francesco Filelfo to Giovanni Aurisa in 1441. Richard Popkin, *The History of Scepticism from Savonarola to Bayle*, rev. ed. (New York: Oxford University Press, 2003), pp. 17, 19.

[23]Rieke Havertz, "Atheism on the Rise Around the World," *The Christian Science Monitor*, August 15, 2012, www.csmonitor.com/World/Global-News/2012/0815/Atheism-on-the-rise-around-the-globe. The number of atheists has been relatively small in the West, being only 5 percent in the United States. This does not mean that atheism is insignificant or should not be vigorously addressed. In China 47 percent are atheists, the most of any nation, and it is on the rise globally.

The Enlightenment and Modernity

The fighting that followed the Reformation, which had secular as well as religious motives, brought much bloodshed and destruction, with perhaps as many as one-quarter to one-third of Germans dying in the Thirty Years' War. Religious intolerance replaced heresy as the perceived danger to society, and conversely, tolerance grew to become the chief virtue. Furthermore, people began look to science for hope instead of religion, further reducing the status of the latter.

Responding to the intellectual ferment and uncertainties of his day, René Descartes (1596–1650) sought to make his Christian worldview as certain as possible by founding it on what he could not doubt, namely, that he was thinking (doubting is a form of thinking, and one cannot doubt that he is doubting). After thus establishing his own existence as a thinking being, he sought to establish God's. Everything needs a sufficient cause, he said, and since our idea of God is of an infinite being, we finite beings could not have caused it. The cause must be God himself. And since that idea is of a perfect being, he cannot be a deceiver because deception is an imperfection. Our "clear and distinct" ideas must be true, otherwise God would be a deceiver; but being perfect, he would not deceive us. He also constructed an ontological argument: we have a clear and distinct idea of a perfect being, who must exist, since perfection requires existence. Pierre Gassendi (1592–1665) replied that if something lacks existence it does not lack perfection, it lacks reality. Later Immanuel Kant and Bertrand Russell would make similar objections.

So Descartes thought he had proved the existence of himself, God and the world, in that order. His rational approach differed from the empirical approach of Aquinas and others, who start from the world and argue to a creator (cosmological argument) or an orderer (teleological argument).

Descartes's new approach had begun not from what we know (ontology), but from how we know (epistemology). He tried to go from a single point of knowledge to all his essentials beliefs. He was a foundationalist in that he sought to ground knowledge on beliefs that do not need to be supported by other beliefs—we simply know them (more about this in the chapter on Alvin Plantinga, who seeks to expand what we can know without proof to include God). Descartes's version was radical in holding that those unsupported beliefs must be true, since they are clear and distinct.

Up until Descartes's time and for another two and a half centuries, hardly anyone doubted that it was possible to obtain objective, universal truth. Many regarded it as something of a cognitive duty to get truth that transcends our personal situation and culture. Philosophers, theologians and scientists sought—and typically thought they had found—the truth. Nor was there any doubt that gaining the truth was possible, that the more control humans had over things the better and that we were making steady progress toward truth and a better future. Suspending as much as possible one's assumptions and viewing something from a neutral perspective seemed ideal. These bold claims would fade by the mid-nineteenth century, leaving a fragmentation that is sometimes loosely referred to as postmodernism (though it is difficult to make this a strict, chronological development, since similar themes can be found earlier). Whether it is possible to view anything from neutral ground, apart from our perspective, or whether our perspective determines what we see and how we see it, is part of the contemporary debate over apologetic methods. On the left side of the chart in the introduction, presuppositionalism tends to see presuppositions as highly determinative, whereas on the right side, evidentialists believe facts can point us to the right interpretation. A major difference between evidentialists and classical apologists is that the latter hold that a worldview (a perspective with the broadest impact on our other beliefs) has a great effect on how we interpret evidence.

In the formative era of science, it was thought that people with different perspectives could agree on a method by which to resolve differences in beliefs, requiring only minimal assumptions. That method formed common ground, agreed on by those holding different perspectives, theories or even worldviews. It was thought that each side could then argue for the truth of their position using what was common, in effect pointing out the fit between the facts and their theory. It was thought to be possible for the individual to find truth that is fully, finally and independently true, if incomplete. In the twentieth century the role of assumptions and prior cognitive commitments seemed more pervasive, and doubts arose that there could be such a thing as neutrality or even objectivity (a view developed in Van Til's presuppositionalism).

Scientific discoveries of mathematical regularities in nature gave rise to deism, which held that God caused the universe, then caused nothing after that. Like the perfect watchmaker, his watch never needed resetting with supernatural interaction. This ruled out miracles and divine revelation. Everything essential was made known through reason. Robert Boyle (1627–1691) argued for revelation on grounds that Christian doctrine is sublime, that miracles can be known and that Christianity has been beneficial to society.

John Locke (1632–1704) used reasoning from sense knowledge to get objective truth, an approach that continued to gain popularity with the scientific movement. Science soon settled on a harmony between theory and experimental data as the indicator of truth. If the experiment does not turn out as the theory led us to expect, we adjust the theory, or perhaps redo the experiment. Medieval modes of reasoning gave way to reasoning from observation, which favored induction: many cases of *x* could be observed, from which we draw a conclusion about all cases of *x*.

Against deism, Joseph Butler (1692–1752) argued that miracles cannot be dismissed merely because they are singular events, since there are unique events in nature itself. If revealed religion is more self-consistent and conducive to morality than natural religion, it should be preferred.[24] Some things in revelation are obscure because our minds are limited, but that does not count against their divine authorship any more than unknown aspects of nature count against its being created. That some do not have access to the Christian religion is not so different from God bestowing natural benefits unevenly.[25] In all, the case for faith is about as strong as can be made for other practical decisions in life, even those with the gravest consequences.[26]

David Hume (1711–1776) rejected theistic arguments and miracles, pitting our extensive experience that nature is inviolate against any report of a case where it was not, and casting doubt that any report could be sufficiently reliable (more about this in the chapter on evidentialism). William Paley (1743–1805) mounted arguments against Hume, in part using arguments that had already been made, such as the analogy of a watch obviously pointing to a watchmaker. In a broader sense, Hume undermined confidence in sense perception alone, which motivated Immanuel Kant (1724–1804) to join sense perception with mental categories. The senses give us data, and the mind organizes it. But that means that we cannot know reality for what it is, because we cannot get past our mind's interpretation. Nevertheless, we have to assume some things transcendentally; that is, unless we assume their existence we cannot make sense of experience. (Van Til used a similar approach, which he claimed conclusively demonstrates Reformed Christianity, in that we must presuppose it to know anything.)

In an era when some doubted our access to reality, Friedrich Schleiermacher (1768–1834) made religion essentially a matter of feeling rather than knowledge

---

[24]Dulles, *History of Apologetics*, p. 141.
[25]Ibid.
[26]Ibid., p. 142.

(a subjectivism with echoes in contemporary relativism). Christianity is superior, he claimed, not because it is "true" but because it represents a higher
form of God consciousness.[27]

Søren Kierkegaard (1813–1855) eschewed proof and made faith essentially a commitment. Others emphasized ethics (e.g., Walter Rauschenbusch, 1861–1918, the
social gospel). Pragmatists like John Dewey (1859–1952) focused on what "works."
G. F. W. Hegel (1770–1831) built an entirely different worldview around a God who
envelops the world like a mind, and whose development is clearly known through
its expression in history. On his view, even God is changing, and contradictions do
not point to eternal truths but are the dynamic of progress, the "dialectic." Forms of
his idealist philosophy dominated the nineteenth and early twentieth centuries, until
it was overturned in part by the efforts of atheist Bertrand Russell (1872–1970) and
G. E. Moore (1873–1958). Cornelius Van Til interacted with idealism, adopting some
of its terms to do so, which created a controversy within Reformed circles.

CONTEMPORARY

In the continuing doubts about our grasp of reality, some narrowed the scope of
what we consider knowledge, with science usually providing the paradigm.
However, some discoveries have challenged even the belief that we have direct
access to the world via science; for example, in non-Euclidian geometry the
shortest distance between two points is not necessarily a straight line.[28] In a
celebrated experiment, Werner Heisenberg (1901–1976) discovered that we
cannot know the exact location and speed of a subatomic particle, which seems
to undermine the determinism of Newton's worldview and reinstate uncertainty.
Albert Einstein's (1879–1955) theory of relativity was taken to imply there are no
absolute truths or ethical norms (which dismayed Einstein). Even knowledge of
the self, which had been a fundamental certainty since Descartes, was undermined by Sigmund Freud (1856–1939) in his assertion that we are subject to
subconscious forces we don't fully grasp. Rather than respond to hostile views
with traditional arguments, he tended to interpret them in terms of his theory,
alleging the opponent had various psychological motives to reject his ideas. This
"hermeneutic of suspicion" had been used by Karl Marx (1818–1883) and Friedrich
Nietzsche (1844–1900), and finds parallels in some contemporary thought.

---

[27]Paul Thorsell suggested this insight.
[28]On mathematics and postmodernism, see Vladimir Tasic, *Mathematics and the Roots of Postmodern Thought* (New York: Oxford University Press, 2001).

Karl Popper (1902–1994) challenged science as a way of knowing, arguing that a theory is not proven in any final sense, but we hold it only until it is proven wrong. According to Thomas Kuhn (1922–1996), science does not make steady progress but holds to a paradigm until problems overwhelm it, and there is a shift to another one, with no guarantee that it is closer to the truth.

Parallel developments loosened the connection between language and the world. They are illustrated in Ludwig Wittgenstein (1889–1951), who initially held that propositions picture reality and are connected to it, and are either true or false. He shifted to the view that the meaning of a proposition is its use, so for example the meaning of "God exists" depends on how people use it and how they live. Earlier, Ferdinand de Saussure (1857–1913) had said, roughly put, that words connect concepts to sounds—not directly to reality.

These and many other developments contributed to what is loosely called postmodernism, the very existence and identify of which is controversial. In the broadest terms we can say that it emphasizes the difficulties of grasping absolute truth in a way that transcends a particular perspective. It is not strictly a chronological development, since there have been extreme doubts about the possibility of knowledge since ancient times (e.g., Heraclitus, ca. 535–ca. 475 B.C.; Gorgias, ca. 483–ca. 376 B.C.), and conversely, it does not dominate the contemporary scene. In the opinion of some, it is nothing more than modernity pushed one step farther.

Apologetic responses have varied widely. Myron Penner emphasizes the subjective aspect of truth: "We won't, in other words, get to the bottom of reality to perceived reality as it really is apart from how it is for us."[29] He suggests changing discussions of truth from "correspondence" to "edification," avoiding "the modern split between objective and subjective (as if they were separate spheres of reality), which privileges objectivity in truth and denigrates an emphasis on subjectivity as a relativistic denial of truth."[30]

Rick Richardson, summarizing the work of George Hunter, points favorably to Celtic Christianity, contrasting it with Roman Christianity. The Celts emphasized humanity's connection to nature; the achievements of humanity and not just its sinfulness; God's immanent presence rather than transcendence; divine dynamic activity rather than maintenance of stability and order; the advancement of a Christian movement through community rather than maintenance of insti-

---

[29]Myron Bradley Penner, *The End of Apologetics: Christian Witness in a Postmodern Context* (Grand Rapids: Baker Academic, 2013), p. 110.
[30]Ibid.

tutions and traditions; indigenous and contextual work within culture rather than the regarding of one's own culture as superior; areas of spiritual interest in other religions that can be used in communication rather than written off as irrelevant or as manifestations of the demonic; creative use of art, drama, music, story, analogy and poetry to encourage experience of the truth rather than only explanations of the truth; the welcoming of nonbelievers to be involved in the Christian community. All these Richardson and Hunter see as having contemporary relevance, especially to a society influenced by postmodern themes.[31]

Don Everts and Doug Schaupp find five common thresholds that postmoderns cross in coming to Christ, and they advocate fostering those experiences, moving from distrust to trust, from complacency to curiosity, from being closed to change to being open to change, from meandering to seeking to making a personal decision.[32]

A response that has considerable support among academic apologists is to carefully confront the epistemological inadequacies of postmodernism, especially with regard to theories of truth, knowledge and justification, and views of logic and the like.[33]

Legal apologetics deals less with metaphysical realities and the fine points of epistemology and more with the evaluation of specific claims, using a method that is already agreed on by society. Evidentialists regarded these as special advantages, especially in the current epistemological climate. The method began with Hugo Grotius (1583–1645) and was developed by Thomas Sherlock (1678–1761) and Simon Greenleaf (1783–1853). It has been advanced today by John Warwick Montgomery (1931–).

The apologetic methods explored in this book are connected to the developments of the past and address the challenges of the present. They represent the lifelong efforts by some of the best minds in Christendom to answer what could be viewed as life's most important question: How do we know religious truth?

---

[31]Rick Richardson, *Evangelism Outside the Box* (Downers Grove, IL: InterVarsity Press, 2000), pp. 56–60.

[32]Don Everts and Doug Schaupp, *I Once Was Lost* (Downers Grove, IL: InterVarsity Press, 2008), pp. 23–24. Their wording of the fifth is, "To cross the threshold of the kingdom itself."

[33]See, e.g., John S. Feinberg, *Can You Believe It's True? Christian Apologetics in a Modern and Postmodern Era* (Wheaton, IL: Crossway, 2013). For such a complex subject, the book is remarkably clear.

PART TWO

Apologetic
Methodologies

– 3 –

CORNELIUS VAN TIL

Christianity is an intellectual commitment we cannot do without

Presuppositionalism claims to be something of a Copernican revolution in apologetics, so it is not surprising that it has caused a great deal of controversy. It takes a fairly wide variety of forms, a fact not sufficiently acknowledged by all who count themselves presuppositionalists.

It began with Cornelius Van Til (1895–1987), whose family moved from Holland to Indiana when he was ten years old. His love of farming, which he got from his family, stayed with him all his life, and often showed up in his illustrations. He attended Calvin College, then Calvin Theological Seminary, which were both run by the Christian Reformed Church, of which his family was a part. After one year at Calvin, he left for Princeton Theological Seminary, which at the time was conservative Presbyterian. He earned a ThM from the seminary and a PhD from the university. He taught briefly at Princeton, then in 1929 helped start Westminster Theological Seminary in Pennsylvania, where he taught until his retirement in 1972.

Several who knew him have described him to me as personal and caring. He was generous with this time, spending hours with students, speaking in churches and even in nursing homes.[1] Not everyone could follow his teaching, however. John Frame, who was in his classes, described his pace as at times "dizzying."

---

[1]John Frame, *Cornelius Van Til: An Analysis of His Thought* (Phillipsburg, NJ: P & R, 1995), pp. 28–29.

He rarely defined his concepts precisely. When students asked for definitions or tried to reduce his arguments to a logical sequence, Van Til usually resisted. What he did in such cases was to back up and start over, using essentially the same language he had used before. He seemed to think that regular repetition of certain ideas would result in their entering the students' minds by a kind of osmosis.[2]

Frame recalls that brighter students had trouble engaging him because he would answer in roundabout monologues that resembled preaching. To answer one simple question that Frame asked, Van Til insisted on going clear back to Genesis, ending with Revelation; then he went through the whole history of philosophy. Eventually Frame forgot his question entirely. He says that Van Til regarded even small deviations from his views as concessions to non-Christian thought, and dissenters were made to "feel guilty."[3] Students who asked too many hard questions were "dismissed as Arminian or worse."[4] Adding to the problem, former students have often remarked that the content was the same for every course Van Til taught.[5] Despite his style of communication, he had a good sense of humor,[6] was generous with his time and generally endeared himself to his students. He inspired a loyal following and influenced a wide variety of people, and his many years of devoted teaching contributed to a shift in Reformed thinking on apologetics.

Nevertheless, his academic legacy has been somewhat clouded by conflicting claims about his views. Frame observes that "even today there are many—both allies and opponents of Van Til's ideas—who have extremely confused notions of what he actually taught."[7] The charge that a given critic or even proponent does not understand Van Til is unusually common. Frame attributes this not only to Van Til's way of communicating ("inadequate definition, analysis, and argument"[8]) but also his academic isolation, due in part to his harsh criticism of other theological traditions and his preference for confrontation over dialogue.[9] And because his books and journal articles were put into print with little of the critical input that normally precedes academic publishing, he was not forced to clarify and strengthen his writing. Christian philosopher and theologian Colin

---

[2]Ibid., p. 30.
[3]Ibid.
[4]Ibid., p. 17.
[5]Timothy I. McConnel, "The Historical Origins of the Presuppositional Apologetics of Cornelius Van Til" (PhD diss., Marquette University, Milwaukee, WI, 1999), p. 47 n. 71.
[6]Frame, *Cornelius Van Til*, pp. 27-28.
[7]Ibid., p. 161 (Frame comments on specific people in a footnote).
[8]Ibid.
[9]Ibid.

Brown observes that Van Til "spends a good deal of time reiterating points without really explaining them."[10] Gary North appreciates his insights, but says, "His books all wind up talking about the same dozen themes," and if his books had no covers you could not tell what they were about or who it was intended to refute.[11] A student once introduced Van Til as the world's most intelligent man because "no one, but no one" could understand him.[12]

He never tired of fighting beliefs that he felt threatened the purity of Reformed thought. A friend who watched him debate at Boston University said, "He graciously, respectfully, but incisively told them that they were going to hell."[13] He was often at the center of controversy. "Perhaps I was brought into the world to be a nuisance to others," he wrote to a friend.[14] He also doubted the value of his writings, characterizing them privately as "a lot of noise and no results."[15] Nevertheless, those writings have been some of the most influential in modern apologetics.

Whatever the problems, his friend R. J. Rushdoony had no trouble understanding and appreciating him. In a letter to Van Til he said, "I believe that the problem your readers have can be summed up under two heads, first sin, and second, laziness."[16]

Another reason people have a hard time with Van Til's views is that he grew up academically in another era, when idealism held sway. Also, he developed his views against the background of Dutch thinkers like Abraham Kuyper, rather than the Scottish realism that was embraced by so many traditional apologists.

INFLUENCES

Most of us are realists of one sort or another. Realism, simply put, is the view that truth and the reality it connects with are independent of minds. For the realist, a

---

[10]Colin Brown, *Philosophy and the Christian Faith* (Downers Grove, IL: InterVarsity Press, 1969), p. 249. Frame reminded me of this comment, *Cornelius Van Til*, p. 32.

[11]Gary North, *Dominion and Common Grace* (Tyler, TX: Institute for Christian Economics [Dominion Press], 1987), pp. 10–12; quoted in Frame, *Cornelius Van Til*, p. 33.

[12]William White, *Van Til, Defender of the Faith* (Nashville: Thomas Nelson, 1979), p. 182.

[13]T. Grady Spires, "A Tribute to Cornelius Van Til," *Christianity Today*, December 30, 1977, p. 20. Quoted in John R. Muether, *Cornelius Van Til: Reformed Apologist and Churchman* (Phillipsburg, NJ: P & R, 2008), p. 202.

[14]Van Til to Theodore J. Jansma, April 30, 1948; Cornelius Van Til Archive, Westminster Theological Seminary. Quoted in Muether, *Cornelius Van Til*, p. 139.

[15]Van Til to Henry Van Til, undated, ca. 1945, Family Letters from Reinder Van Til. Quoted in Muether, *Cornelius Van Til*, p. 142.

[16]R. J. Rushdoony to Cornelius Van Til, Feb. 27, 1967; Cornelius Van Til Archive, Westminster Theological Seminary. Quoted in Muether, *Cornelius Van Til*, p. 216. Rushdoony wrote *By What Standard* (Phillipsburg, NJ: P & R, 1959). Van Til regarded it as a simple and clear treatment of his views.

proposition is true or false regardless of what we think. Thus it is either true or false that there are undiscovered subatomic particles. Realism, like most views, comes in degrees. Most realists do not go so far as to say, for example, that pain would exist even if there were no minds to feel it. There are also various types of realism. Moral realism, for example, is the view that some things are right or wrong whether we think so or not.

So for the realist, things have real existence, and our minds have the capacity to know those independently existing things. For the typical theist who is a realist, God too knows what exists. If the chair is at the table, God knows it is there, and we can know it is there because he has given us the capacity to know reality (though partially and imperfectly).

By contrast, idealism holds that reality is ultimately mind dependent. If "the rose is red and smells sweet," it is because someone can perceive it—or at least we cannot make such a statement about the rose without referring to mental processes.

To again simplify, for realists, minds know a reality that is independent of them. For idealists, reality, truth and the mind that knows them are inextricably linked. According to less extreme forms, one cannot explain a thing without reference to a mind. In more thoroughgoing forms of idealism, a mind determines reality. For German philosopher George W. F. Hegel (1770–1831) reality is the expression of the mind of God (*Geist*). So when we look at reality and the unfolding of history, we are seeing the mind of God. British philosopher George Berkeley (1685–1753; pronounced BARK-lee) went so far as to claim that things have no existence apart from a mind to perceive them. Things exist because God perceives them. His mind makes them "real."

Idealism, in a highly developed form, was the dominant view from the nineteenth to the early twentieth centuries. Then it was overthrown by realism, which was the dominant view until it was challenged by various types of postmodernism in the past couple of decades. The point is that when Van Til was educated and developed his thought, idealism was dominant. His style of thinking, the questions he sought to answer and even his vocabulary were molded by idealism.

Van Til was well acquainted with the idealism of his day. At Calvin College, the only philosophy professor was W. Harry Jellema, who wrote his dissertation on idealist Josiah Royce. The text for his philosophy class, which Van Til was in, was idealist F. H. Bradley's *Appearances and Reality*. And when Van Til was at Princeton, the philosophy department was directed by British idealist Archibald

A. Bowman. Nevertheless, while Van Til admired aspects of idealism[17] he clearly rejected major tenets of it. His dissertation, "God and the Absolute," argued that the God of absolute idealism could not be the Christian God.

It was a matter of fractious debate during the 1940s and 1950s whether Van Til was too influenced by idealism. Some criticisms came from Christian philosophy professors[18] who were concerned partly because Van Til adopted idealist terms such as *brute facts, concrete universal, limiting concept, apparent contradiction, one and many, absolute system, eternal novelty* and *logic* when designating general methodology. The very term *presupposition* was used by idealism.[19]

To his critics, Van Til's use of such concepts was a corruption of Christianity. But Van Til answered that if we are to win people we must "speak to them in their language." The apostles did this, he said, when they used the Greek term *logos* for Christ.[20]

Though Van Til rightly convinced most people he was no idealist, some could find in his thought a very faint echo of a mild idealism. For example, in his theory of truth, which is distinct from his theory of knowledge, he insists that viewpoints (which no doubt include theology, philosophy and apologetics) are interconnected wholes such that they must be accepted or rejected entirely. This was a factor that led him both to reject most of traditional apologetics and to insist that the Christian viewpoint must be presented, as much as possible, in its entirety. Such emphasis on the "whole" was characteristic of idealism, though defenders could say that he was in no way influenced by idealism. He also regards knowing as ultimately a matter of agreeing with God. To know something about a thing is to agree with what God believes about it. (Of course they would need to have rational grounds for what they believe, since accidentally having a true belief would not be knowledge.) This sounds more like idealism than realism in that realists usually talk more in terms of our knowing reality directly: we humans have the ability to know reality as it is—the same reality that God

---

[17]"It is marvelous that out of such a soil the lofty ethics of idealism in all its forms has sprung. It can only be the common grace of God that accounts for it." Cornelius Van Til, *The Defense of the Faith*, 3rd ed. (Phillipsburg, NJ: P & R, 1979), p. 64. McConnel ("Historical Origins," p. 586) brought this quote to my attention.

[18]Jesse DeBoer taught philosophy at the University of Kentucky. Clifton Orlebeke taught at the University of Rhode Island. Most of the criticism of Van Til appeared in the journal *The Calvin Forum*. See Timothy I. McConnel, "The Influence of Idealism on the Apologetics of Cornelius Van Til," *Journal of the Evangelical Theological Society* 48, no. 3 (September 2005): 558-62.

[19]Frame, *Van Til*, p. 21.

[20]Van Til, *Defense of the Faith*, p. 23 n. 1. McConnel pointed me to this ("Historical Origins," pp. 586-87).

knows directly (and, some would add, determines). Thus it is usually said that our view is true when it matches reality, not when it matches God's mind. It is more common among theists to refer to God's knowledge as matching, or "corresponding to," reality (albeit a reality that he created, sustains and controls), and our knowledge as true because it matches reality as well. Our knowledge reflects God's knowledge because both of us grasp the same reality (although of course our knowledge is imperfect and incomplete while his is infinite, and he created and controls the reality we know). The view that truth is, in this way, a matter of corresponding to reality is called the correspondence theory of truth.

Van Til's view that truth is a matter of agreeing with God could be one reason some have thought that he rejected the correspondence theory of truth in favor of the coherence theory of truth,[21] according to which something is true if it fits with everything else we believe[22] (more about the correspondence versus the coherence theories of truth in the chapter on E. J. Carnell). But to be more precise, in emphasizing revelation as foundational to all types of knowing, Van Til held to parts of, as well as criticized, all the dominant theories of truth: correspondence, coherence and pragmatic.[23] None of this, of course, makes him an idealist.

Divine Sovereignty and Apologetics

The point that truth is whatever God determines it to be is central to Van Til's epistemology, which is built on his deep conviction that God is central to all knowing. For him, the hallmark of human fallenness is denying God's authority over us, which crucially includes God's authority to determine truth. Thus intel-

---

[21]Carl F. H. Henry, *God, Revelation, and Authority*, vol. 1, *God Who Speaks and Shows: Preliminary Considerations* (Wheaton, IL: Crossway, 1976), p. 237.

[22]There are, of course, variations of the coherence theory. On one version, for example, the body of knowledge with which a view must fit with (cohere with) is the total of all human knowledge. For different versions of coherentism, see James O. Young, "The Coherence Theory of Truth," in *The Stanford Encyclopedia of Philosophy*, ed. Edward N. Zalta, Summer 2013 ed., http://plato .stanford.edu/archives/sum2013/entries/truth-coherence/.

[23]Greg L. Bahnsen, *Van Til's Apologetic: Readings and Analysis* (Phillipsburg, NJ: P & R, 1998), p. 164. Van Til said, "From this presentation of the matter, it is clear that what we mean by correspondence is not what is often meant by it in epistemological literature. In the literature on the subject, correspondence usually means a correspondence between the idea I have in my mind and the 'object out there.' In the struggle between the 'realists' and the 'subjective idealists' this was the only question in dispute. They were not concerned about the question uppermost in our minds, i.e., whether or not God has to be taken into the correspondence. We may call our position in epistemology a Correspondence Theory of Truth, if only we keep in mind that it is opposed to what has historically been known under that name." *In Defense of Biblical Christianity*, vol. 2, *A Survey of Christian Epistemology*, Works of Cornelius Van Til (Phillipsburg, NJ: P & R, 1969), chap. one, sec. two, "Analysis and Synthesis."

lectually, fallenness is characterized by trying to know truth apart from God rather than acknowledging him as the author of truth.

It follows that failing to believe in the truth of God's Word (which for Van Til must be interpreted from a Reformed perspective) is more a matter of rebellion than ignorance. Thus submitting to God is not merely a matter of doing what he wants but is also in large part a matter of accepting what he says in his Word as truth.

Van Til goes even further from the typical language of realism in his effort to be true to the concept of divine sovereignty, which is so central to Calvinism: God does not know reality as something external to himself, he knows the world through his will. God does not know that the sun is shining today because it is shining, he knows it because from all eternity he willed it to shine today. Thus God knows himself—not external reality—first and foremost. Van Til holds this view not from any influence of even a mild idealism, but because of his commitment to Calvinism. He was expressly against all but a distinctly Reformed apologetic, and his approach to apologetics can function under no other interpretation of divine sovereignty and control.

That God is the Creator[24] and sole ultimate determiner of all there is forms the core of Van Til's apologetic and is the basis for its most innovative, controversial and misunderstood concept. Put simply, reality is a unity, and facts are related to each other only because the Christian God created and determines everything. Greg Bahnsen, who focused much of his academic ministry on expounding and propagating his former teacher's views, explained it by saying that the Christian God is the only basis for our experience of order, which is characterized by unity (which includes "causal connections between events, conceptual continuity, logical necessity, moral absolutes, etc."[25]), as well as by "connections, sameness, generalization, universality, lack of change, or continuity."[26] God is also behind our experience of disorder, which includes "diversity, particularity, individuality, novelty, uniqueness, change, or discontinuity."[27] To the nonbeliever, the diversity looks like chaos, but for the believer, it is all in the plan of God. The nonbeliever looks to chance to bring forth something new, but the believer knows all is foreordained so there is no such thing as chance. Because everything fits into the plan of God, there is no such thing as a "brute" fact, one

---

[24]Van Til, *Defense of the Faith*, p. 43.
[25]Bahnsen, *Van Til's Apologetic*, p. 140 n. 134.
[26]Ibid., p. 141 n. 137.
[27]Ibid.

that is uninterpreted (by God or a human), that could be used to interpret other things. There is an apparent tug of war between chance and necessity, necessity being demanded by natural laws and the principle of noncontradiction. But that is only an appearance resulting from a failure to see God as the author of everything. Such failure makes "nonsense" out of experience. Only (Reformed) Christianity can make sense out of both order (unity) and change (diversity).

According to Van Til, if God did not create and control everything, we could not know anything because on a non-Christian worldview, "all things in this universe are unrelated and cannot be in fruitful contact with one another."[28] Van Til claimed that for anything in the universe to be understandable it must fit into a larger interconnected whole, like a web, or as he called it, a "system." Not only must there be those connections between individual things and the whole, but also at least one mind must know all the connections as well as know everything there is to know. That being is God, whose mind knows those connections because he determined them. And though no human will ever know all that God knows, it is only God's knowledge of everything that makes even our partial knowledge possible. As Van Til put it, "It is true that there must be comprehensive knowledge somewhere if there is to be any true knowledge anywhere but this comprehensive knowledge need not and cannot be in us; it must be in God."[29] Furthermore, since each fact or individual thing gets its "meaning" from its relation to the whole, each thing expresses the whole. That is why, in his view, each fact reveals, at least to some extent, the God who created the whole. And that is also why explanations need to be made, where possible, in wholes.

INTELLECTUAL COMMITMENTS

To reiterate: Van Til believes that the truth is in the whole, and that all things are connected. So to understand a cow eating grass one must understand the grass, photosynthesis, dirt and its chemistry, biochemistry and the physics it is based on, gravity—literally everything in the universe.[30] And because to under-

---

[28]Van Til, *Defense of the Faith*, p. 43.

[29]Ibid., p. 41.

[30]Cornelius Van Til, "A Christian Theistic Theory of Knowledge," *The Banner* 66, no. 1809 (1931): 984, 995. In "The Works of Cornelius Van Til, 1895-1987," CD-ROM (Oak Harbor, WA: Logos Library System, 1987): "I see a cow. I say it is an animal. But what is an animal? To answer that question fully I should be able to say what life is for a cow is living [sic]. I watch the cow eat grass. Does the grass live too? Yes it does. The grass grows out of the ground. Does the ground live also? No it does not. But some say that it does. At any rate I see that the lifeless is indispensable for the living. Hence I cannot say what life is unless I can also say what the ground is. I

stand any fact one must understand its place in God's plan, there is no useful common ground in principle between the believer and nonbeliever with respect to the nonbeliever's ultimate commitments. Each sees everything differently. For example, when the Christian and the atheist look at the same tree, one sees a creation of God, something with divine purpose. The other sees only the product of blind evolution. So there is nothing in common that could be used for apologetics. It does no good to point to the created thing or its divine purpose because the atheist's view already rules out created things and divine purposes. Similarly, it will do no good to point to a miracle, since the atheist could at most see it as a freak of nature, like a two-headed calf, rather than an act of God—because he has already decided there is no God.

There is no neutral ground, and nothing is untouched by one's intellectual commitments. In this way epistemology is entwined with theology and no one is truly neutral. They are either submitted to God or they are in rebellion. They do not need to merely add to their worldview some additional knowledge about God, they need a "head-on collision" that will confront their entire way of knowing and attitudes. They have to be confronted about leaving God out of the very foundations of knowledge, that every fact can be known only for what it is in the plan of God, and without God no fact has any connection to any other fact. Therefore the nonbeliever cannot be confronted merely about one area of thought (e.g., the "spiritual" part) or about the conclusions of his or her thought (e.g., that it is better to interpret the world as created by God). For Van Til, the nature of such a total confrontation makes apologetics closer to evangelism than has traditionally been supposed.

For Van Til, only the Christian has a basis for science, logic and ethics. That is because only the Christian God, by virtue of his creation and plan for everything, provides for order, predictability and necessity.[31] Furthermore, if God did not create everything then nothing would be connected to anything else, and words would not even connect to other words and communication itself would be impossible. For that matter, one part of a human would not connect to another. The world itself would be a "vacuum."[32]

---

cannot really say what a cow is until I can tell what the whole of physical reality is." Accessible at *Presuppositionalism 101*, http://presupp101.files.wordpress.com/2011/08/van-til-collection-of-articles-from-1920-1939.pdf.
[31]Bahnsen, *Van Til's Apologetic*, p. 112.
[32]Cornelius Van Til, *In Defense of Biblical Christianity*, vol. 1, *The Protestant Doctrine of Scripture*, chap. seven, part one (Phillipsburg, NJ: P & R, 1967), Logos Bible Software Library, The Works of Cornelius Van Til.

All of this contrasts with the more conventional thinking that things can be connected whether or not God determines all aspects of their existence. Leaves are still on trees whether God put them there or not. One part of DNA is connected to another part whether God determined it to be so or not. And we can detect those connections. Traditional apologetics takes, for example, observations of order and concludes that a divine orderer is the best explanation (not, as Van Til claims, the only explanation), because competing worldviews can explain order, just not as well. Traditional apologetics, on the one hand, thus moves from evidence to a conclusion based on that evidence. Van Til, on the other hand, proceeds from the assumption that our experience and knowledge of order is valid, to the preconditions of that knowledge, which he says can be found only in the God of Reformed Christianity. Where traditional apologetics uses induction, deduction and the principle of noncontradiction to point to the truth, Van Til emphasizes that each of these tools, while valid, is valid only because of the God of Reformed Christianity.

INDIRECT PROOF

He sees his argument as a reductio ad absurdum, that is, an argument that reduces the opposing argument to an absurdity. A person who claims an alibi, for example, is in a sense using a reductio argument by showing that the accusation that he committed a crime entails the absurd idea that he could have committed it when he wasn't there. In the Gospel of Luke, Christ uses this type of argument to counter the accusation that he casts out demons by the power of Satan in that the accusation entails the absurd idea that Satan would be fighting himself (Lk 11:18). It is a type of deductive reasoning, which means that if we assume the premises are true then conclusion has to be true (as long as the argument is constructed properly, of course). This is the basis for Van Til's claim that his argument for Christianity is not just highly probable but absolutely certain. He strongly opposed apologetic reasoning that concludes Christianity is only highly probable. Since inductive arguments show that their conclusions are only highly probable and not that they are absolutely certain, he opposed apologetics based on induction. Induction itself he saw as a valid form of reasoning that can give us and even the non-Christian knowledge about things, but an inductive argument for Christianity does not do justice to the power of the case. Besides, as a number of Reformed thinkers view it, a probabilistic case—even with a highly probable conclusion—is not enough to hold people accountable before God.

Nothing less than absolute certainty will do. So the Christian should not claim merely that God probably exists.

Van Til added an appeal to the Trinity to his central argument. His basic argument was that individual things ("particulars") must connect to a greater whole ("universals") if they are to have any "meaning," thus making knowledge impossible without the God of Reformed Christianity. Even the details of history are particulars that must relate to larger patterns if they are to have meaning.[33]

> The many must be brought into contact with one another. But how do we know that they can be brought into contact with one another? How do we know that the many do not simply exist as unrelated particulars? The answer given is that in such a case we should know nothing of them; they would be abstracted from the body of knowledge that we have; they would be abstract particulars. On the other hand, how is it possible that we should obtain a unity that does not destroy the particulars?[34]

This problem of the "one and the many" has its solution in the Trinity, Van Til claimed. In God, "the one and the many are equally ultimate. Unity in God is no more fundamental than diversity, and diversity in God is no more fundamental than unity. The persons of the Trinity are mutually exhaustive of one another. The Son and the Spirit are ontologically on par with the Father."[35] Thus only the Trinity can provide an adequate grounds for knowledge.

Van Til considered his overall approach a transcendental case for Christianity, or an "indirect" proof. The idea of a transcendental argument was brought into Western thought by German philosopher Immanuel Kant (1724-1804), who argued that even if we cannot know or prove some things directly we can still show that we must assume their existence to make sense of experience. Thus we can posit the existence of God, the soul and the world. Presumably even a skeptic would have to assume the existence of those things to make sense of experience. As philosopher Barry Stroud puts it, "Transcendental arguments are supposed to prove that certain particular concepts are necessary for experience or thought;

---

[33]Cornelius Van Til, *Common Grace* (Phillipsburg, NJ: P & R, 1947), p. 2. I am indebted to Mc-Connel, "Historical Origins," p. 141, for pointing me to this passage.

[34]Van Til, *Defense of the Faith*, pp. 25-26. See R. J. Rushdoony, "The One and the Many Problem—The Contribution of Van Til," in *Jerusalem and Athens: Critical Discussions on the Philosophy and Apologetics of Cornelius Van Til*, ed. E. R. Geehan (Phillipsburg, NJ: P & R, 1971), pp. 339-48; Van Til responds approvingly on p. 348. Rushdoony also wrote *The One and the Many: Studies in the Philosophy and Order of Ultimacy* (repr., Vallecito, CA: Chalcedon/Ross House Books, 2006).

[35]Van Til, *Defense of the Faith*, p. 25.

they establish the necessity or indispensability of certain concepts."[36] But that does not mean that rationally demonstrating the existence of God, for example, was without problems. Kant found the traditional proofs for God to be flawed, which left him without rational or logical proof. Yet he went on to suggest that it seems God exists because without him and the afterlife there is no assurance that moral actions will be rewarded. According to W. H. Walsh, his moral argument gave him "not objective knowledge, but a species of personal conviction."[37] So in general, we can be rationally certain of no more than how we experience the world, not the way it is in itself.

Van Til embraced the basic transcendental strategy while rejecting what he saw as Kant's failure to include God as a precondition of knowledge. He regarded Kant as an example of autonomous, non-Christian thinking.

While Kant left the knower agnostic about reality, Hegel wrote that reality can be known because, as an expression of God, it is visible for everyone to see, even through events of history. As a German idealist, he emphasized the whole of reality. Since reality is a whole, we cannot prove our worldview with traditional premises and a conclusion, because the very premises, the reasoning process—virtually everything—is included in the worldview. Arguments on this scale are inevitably circular, but not viciously so. The whole worldview stands or falls by how well it interprets the world.[38] It is a clear break with traditional proofs, in which the conclusion must not be included in the premises. Traditionally, premises provide independent grounds for accepting a conclusion; one accepts the conclusion based on the strength of the premises. Descartes famously sought to prove his Christian worldview by building up from a single point, popularized as "I think therefore I am." By contrast, Hegel sought to prove the whole. Van Til, incidentally, knew Hegel's thought and logic well, having had two doctoral courses on him, including one on his logic, under professor A. A. Bowman.[39] For

---

[36]Barry Stroud, "Transcendental Arguments," *The Journal of Philosophy* 65, no. 9 (May 2, 1968): 243.

[37]W. H. Walsh, "Immanuel Kant," in *The Encyclopedia of Philosophy*, ed. Paul Edwards (New York: Macmillan, 1967), 4:317.

[38]Tom Rockmore says of Hegel, "In his alternative analysis, the initial point of the theory is demonstrable only a posteriori in terms of the explanatory capacity of the framework to which it gives rise, in fact the relation of thought to its object, or being. Clearly this kind of epistemological strategy is circular, although not in a vicious sense, since the appropriateness of the beginning of the explanatory framework, and accordingly the claim to know, is demonstrated in terms of the result upon which it then depends, instead of making the result depend on its relation to the starting point of the theory." Tom Rockmore, *Hegel's Circular Epistemology* (Bloomington: Indiana University Press, 1986), pp. 10–11.

[39]Eric D. Bristley, *Guide to the Writings of Cornelius Van Til, 1895–1987* (Chicago: Olive Tree Com-

Van Til, the whole of Christianity constitutes a transcendental proof because only its worldview can interpret the world; specifically, only it can provide the foundation of thought and experience.

Van Til would disagree with views of knowledge that were popular for several centuries after Descartes, in the rise of the modern era, which held that we have to start with how we know, epistemology. That approach emphasizes the knower and the process of knowledge. It was typically thought that we could, to a great extent, put aside our intellectual commitments, presuppositions and biases, and get to the truth as it exists. Rationalists (who hold that at least some knowledge can come through the mind without coming through the senses or from experience[40]) like Descartes thought we could come up with true concepts. Empiricists, like John Locke (1632–1704), held that we could get to the truth through our senses. The growing enterprise of science was arriving at the view that when our theories, or concepts, harmonize with the observations in our experiments, we have the truth.

Van Til, by contrast, holds that we have to start with what we know, that is, what we think is true (ontology), which for him is contained in our theology, including ideas about such things as God, the Bible and fallenness. He developed his view at the beginning of a trend in Western thought that sees objectivity as difficult or even impossible to obtain, where there is no neutral ground because everything is interpreted by one's perspective (roughly, one's intellectual commitments, viewpoint or presuppositions). Also, such things as the mathematics of curved surfaces and the inaccessibility of subatomic particles seemed to make it impossible to get to the world as it is, apart from interpretation, and therefore apart from perspective. Philosopher of science Thomas Kuhn (1922–1996) said in his groundbreaking book, *The Structure or Scientific Revolutions* (1969), that science does not make steady progress from one unified perspective held by everyone, but moves in a series of shifts, from one entire conceptual viewpoint ("paradigm") to another. Even if two viewpoints use the same key words, they mean something different by them because the viewpoint defines those very key words. A word like *atom* could mean something different in each of two competing theories. In a book published seven years later, Van Til said something similar with regard to the different meanings given to terms like

---

munications, 1995). The two doctoral courses are listed under 1923b.

[40]*Rationalism* is a broad term, and there are many types. The brief characterization here is not intended to cover all of them in any precise way.

induction and *deduction* when used by Christians versus non-Christians. (I know of no reason to think Van Til got his views from Kuhn.)[41]

For Van Til the transcendental nature of his proof is more than an intellectual strategy. It harmonizes with his view of humanity and of the nature of sin versus righteousness, which points to a theme of his, that apologetics and theology are entwined more than is normally recognized. By confronting the nonbeliever with the need to acknowledge God from the start, it challenges what Van Til believes to be the very essence of sin: to think and act autonomously, or independently of God. Traditional apologetics inflames human fallenness, he thought, by allowing person to think they can decide truth. By presenting evidences and inviting the person to draw the conclusion that Christianity is true, the traditional apologist reinforces the idea that we can think autonomously, without putting God at the center of the knowing process. Such an approach makes humanity the judge of God rather than God and his Word the judge of humanity. It is not a man's place to decide whether the Bible is in fact the Word of God. His responsibility is to submit to the Bible as part of personal submission to God. The nonbeliever does not have a knowledge problem, he has a sin problem. The answer is to submit to God and his Word, not to assert that he is qualified to judge what is truth. Only God can do that.

Fallen humanity wants to think "univocally," as if humanity and God face the same reality, as if we can know that the sun is shining as a fact that exists in and of itself apart from what God has determined. According to correct thinking (i.e., unfallen thinking and redeemed thinking) the sun is shining because God determined it would be so in his plan from all eternity; it is so because God makes it so. We do not know it as an independent fact, but by "thinking God's thoughts after him." In this sense we must be content to have "derivative" or "analogical" knowledge, that is, knowledge derived from God. Our thoughts must be "receptively reconstructive" in that they must follow what God says (or more precisely, determines) is true. But instead fallen humanity wants to be

---

[41]Van Til, *A Survey of Christian Epistemology*, p. v. The wording appears in the 1969 version, in the table of contents. The material had been reworked and expanded over the years. As an earlier syllabus it was titled "Metaphysics of Apologetics" and was only forty-six pages. A search of *The Works of Cornelius Van Til* (CD-ROM) turns up neither "Thomas Kuhn," "Thomas S. Kuhn," nor "The Structure of Scientific Revolutions." Though it's not clear if or how much Van Til thought about Kuhn's ideas, it is likely anyone interested in philosophy of science, or even developments in philosophy in general, would be familiar with his work. The idea that terms are interpreted differently within competing theories is often referred to as "incommensurability." It is a matter of some debate how far Kuhn took it, and to what extent commitment to different paradigms hinder communication between theories.

"creatively constructive," that is, we want to determine the standard of truth and thereby think apart from God.

Van Til's use of the term *analogical* has caused some confusion because of its use in certain medieval discussions. Thomas Aquinas said that our knowledge is analogical rather than univocal, but an example of what he meant is that the word *strong* in "God is strong" does not have exactly the same meaning as *strong* in "weightlifters are strong." God never tires, does not use energy and so on. The exact meaning of *strong* depends somewhat on the thing we are talking about. For Aquinas analogy has to do with the way meanings relate to natures. For Van Til it has to do with God and his will as the foundation for knowledge. Besides what he said about analogy, Aquinas said that we can know things by their effects, so we can know something of God by his effects—what he causes. (He did not believe we can know much about God that way; for detailed knowledge of God we need the Bible.) Thus we can start from knowledge of things around us and conclude there is a God. For Van Til, this more traditional view is backwards. We must presuppose the (Reformed) Christian God if we are to know anything.

Van Til was clear that people do know things despite the fact that they refuse to acknowledge God as the foundation of all knowledge. They have knowledge only because they covertly function on the assumption that the God of (Reformed) Christianity exists. As Van Til put it, they use "borrowed capital." That is the only way they can have unity between particular things and categories, continuity between the future and the past, a basis for reason and morality and so on. They know things, but only because they do not actually live by the worldview they profess. Instead they borrow from (Reformed) Christianity, a theme later developed by Francis Schaeffer, though he applied it more to morals than to thought. The apologist should confront this hypocrisy.

For Van Til this is related to the possibility of showing the non-Christian the dissonance within his own belief system. Such "internal critique" is made "from within the context of his assumptions and aims—rather than an external criticism of the unbeliever's position simply for disagreeing with the Christian position."[42] Van Til sought to show, for example, that the non-Christian "makes nonsense" of his experience, and cannot even account for knowledge of any kind. The Christian invites the non-Christian to examine the Christian's own view from within, viewing the world through Christian glasses, and to discover

---

[42]Bahnsen, *Van Til's Apologetic*, p. 140 n. 135.

how it can account for knowledge, make sense of experience and more. What is discouraged, however, is the non-Christian's attempt to critique the Christian's worldview using non-Christian presuppositions, since according to Van Til such presuppositions destroy the possibility of all knowledge and argument. As Bahnsen puts it, "The ultimate truth—that which is more pervasive, fundamental, and necessary—is such that it cannot be argued independently of the preconditions inherent in it. One must presuppose the truth of God's revelation in order to reason at all—even when reasoning about God's revelation."[43] In his view this does not nullify the Christian's argument, it illustrates it.

The relationship between God's knowledge and human knowledge was a point of friction between Van Til and Gordon Clark, and Van Til joined those who tried to block Clark's ordination to the Orthodox Presbyterian Church in 1944. Clark eventually left the denomination, calling it an "isolationist porcupine,"[44] yet the two men were careful to be cordial and respectful.[45]

For Clark, human knowledge must at some point coincide exactly with God's knowledge or it is not knowledge, and "man can have no truth at all."[46] For us to "know" that $2 + 2 = 4$ God must know that same thing, even if he knows infinitely more about it. But for Van Til this challenged the incomprehensibility of God. He maintained that at no point is our knowledge exactly the same as God's— which left the critic wondering how we could know anything at all. Reformed theologian Robert Reymond, though mainly sympathetic with Van Til, believes that Van Til ends up in the same place as Karl Barth, though for Barth truth is existential whereas for Van Til it is objective and biblically propositional.[47]

Clark emphasized that logic is an expression of God's mind, and Van Til emphasized that it is indeed grounded in God, neither higher than him nor independent of him. As Bahnsen characterizes his view, "an allegedly 'autonomous' use of logic destroys its foundations or intelligibility, while the true foundation for the intelligibility of logic (God's mind revealed to men) cannot

---

[43]Greg L. Bahnsen, *Always Ready: Directions for Defending the Faith*, ed. Robert R. Booth (Atlanta: American Vision; Texarkana, AR: Covenant Media Foundation, 1996), p. 75.

[44]Gordon H. Clark, "Blest River of Salvation," *Presbyterian Guardian*, January 10, 1945. Quoted in Muether, *Cornelius Van Til*, p. 108.

[45]Ibid., pp. 101, 210.

[46]Gordon H. Clark, "Apologetics," in *Contemporary Evangelical Thought*, ed. Carl F. Henry (Great Neck, NY: Channel Press, 1957), p. 159.

[47]Robert Reymond, *The Justification of Knowledge: An Introductory Study in Christian Apologetic Methodology* (Phillipsburg, NJ: P & R, 1976), p. 105.

as such be subordinate to man's use of logic for its own acceptability."[48]

For Van Til truth is a unit such that if we know anything exactly we know literally everything (recall that to know the cow eating we must know photosynthesis, molecular biology and on to all of knowledge). He separated "truth," which is stated in propositions, from "knowledge," which is much broader. Knowledge includes truth, which is stated in propositions, but differs from person to person because knowledge is related to the whole of what a person knows, the integration and coherence of their knowledge, the way they know it (e.g., intuitive vs. discursive), the ethical relation of the knower to God, the knower's knowledge of the terms in the proposition and their relationship to all other reality, and their knowledge of the implications of the proposition.[49]

Van Til emphasized that the Christian's view of things is entirely different, in principle at least, from the non-Christian's view. The nuances are important to the difference between his view and more traditional views of apologetics. In traditional apologetics "common ground" usually refers to beliefs the believer and nonbeliever hold in common. Those common areas are used to formulate premises that will help convince the other person of a conclusion. This is ideal for reasoning in general, regardless of the subject matter. You try to pick premises the other person agrees with as much as possible. Where there is disagreement about the truth of a premise, you will have to use additional arguments to support your premise.

But for Van Til, the "common ground" between believer and nonbeliever consists of what is actually common between them: they live in the same universe run by the same God. That is the metaphysical situation.[50] But of course what most apologists are interested in are the concepts about those things, what Van Til calls "common notions" ("self-conscious interpretations," as Bahnsen describes them).[51] Since the unbeliever's worldview is completely opposed to the believer's (the nonbeliever being in rebellion against God) there is in principle—in their worldview—nothing in common between them. And since every fact and experience is interpreted by, and connected to, a worldview, there is no neutral ground between the believer and nonbeliever. That is, there is nothing

---

[48]Bahnsen, *Van Til's Apologetic*, p. 236 n. 174. Bahnsen notes a misunderstanding by Ronald Nash and others.

[49]Gilbert B. Weaver, "The Concept of Truth in the Apologetic Systems of Gordon Haddon Clark and Cornelius Van Til" (PhD diss., Grace Theological Seminary, Winona Lake, IN, 1967), p. 156.

[50]Van Til, *Defense of the Faith*, p. 153.

[51]Bahnsen, *Van Til's Apologetic*, p. 424.

they know and interpret the same way (though in actual thinking the non-believer may borrow covertly from the Christian worldview).

But this describes only what Van Til considers to be the epistemological situation. If that were all there was to it, the nonbeliever would have no knowledge because there would be in principle no way to know the world. Does that mean the nonbeliever in fact has no knowledge or can gain no knowledge? Van Til assured critics that he believed nothing "so absurd as that."[52] He said, "Many non-Christians have been great scientists. Often non-Christians have a better knowledge of things of this world than Christians have."[53] That is because no nonbeliever is entirely consistent with their worldview. So there is no overlap between believer and nonbeliever strictly speaking, in principle, conceptually ("epistemologically"); but there is overlap in what they actually believe ("psychologically"). This is partly because pressing in on the nonbeliever is the fact that he is made in the image of God, and there is clear revelation in nature and in Scripture.[54] So the nonbeliever ends up believing what the believer's worldview alone actually authorizes. But on the basis of his own worldview, the nonbeliever has no right to hold what he actually believes.

It is precisely this difference on which Van Til builds his apologetic efforts. He wants to show the nonbeliever the difference between what he believes and what his worldview authorizes him to believe. But again, Van Til does not want to use the difference to formulate a traditional argument, which uses premises that lead the nonbeliever to a conclusion based on the premises. Such traditional reasoning would only reinforce the nonbeliever's sense that he can autonomously determine what is and is not true. Van Til wants instead to force the nonbeliever to reevaluate his presuppositions and adopt (Reformed) Christian ones.

As he sees it, the error of traditional apologetics is to take the areas of actual agreement and use them to argue for Christianity, as if the nonbeliever's thinking need only be made more complete. Van Til wants to take a wrecking ball to the nonbeliever's entire foundation with the claim that all knowledge depends on presupposing (Reformed) Christianity. As he put it, we should not appeal "to 'common notions' which Christian and non-Christian agree on, but to the 'common ground' which they actually have because man and his world are what

---

[52]Van Til, *Defense*, p. 103.

[53]Cornelius Van Til, *An Introduction to Systematic Theology* (Phillipsburg, NJ: P & R, 1974), p. 83, in chap. seven, sec. B, "Revelation About Nature from Man, Psycho-Physics," Logos Bible Software Library, The Works of Cornelius Van Til. See also quote in Bahnsen, *Van Til's Apologetic*, p. 415.

[54]Bahnsen, *Van Til's Apologetic*, p. 425 n. 94.

Scripture says they are."[55] Again, we have to be careful to understand what Van Til means by "common ground": when most traditional apologists seek to use "common ground" they mean roughly what Van Til rejects as "common notions."

For Van Til, believer and nonbeliever indeed have a "point of contact," something in common that the believer can use to argue for his worldview, but as noted, it is in no way the common ground of traditional apologetics. The point of contact as Bahnsen describes it is "what they have in common as rational creatures of God who know their Creator."[56] It is not that their worldviews overlap at some point as if they had any ideas in common, or that there is neutral ground between them; rather, the non-Christian has contact with the reality that the (Reformed) Christian knows correctly. The non-Christian denies and suppresses the point of contact, something the Christian should point out and confront. Van Til seemed to suggest that one reason believers do not do so is that they fear nonbelievers and want to please them.[57] But he was quite willing to confront. "If I have not offended you," Van Til said in a simulated gospel presentation, "I have not spoken of my God. For what you have really done in your handling of the evidence for belief in God is to set yourself up as God. You have made the reach of your intellect the standard of what is possible or not possible."[58]

Important parts of the discussion about apologetic theory among Reformed thinkers take place with reference to the nature of common grace, a topic that deals with the issue of how God works with fallen humanity. For Van Til, common grace is negative, consisting of how God restrains fallen humans. For him, problems arise when common grace is taken to be constructive, supposing that fallen people can gain positive knowledge of spiritual truth in the form of natural theology. He held that knowledge the nonbeliever has of truth and God comes from his being made in God's image, the clarity of revelation in nature and the like. Since it cannot be obliterated in the nonbeliever, it need not be built by reasoning, especially not reasoning from supposed neutral ground. He

---

[55]Cornelius Van Til, "My Credo," in Geehan, *Jerusalem and Athens*, p. 21. "My Credo" was his most succinct statement of his views. Bahnsen, *Van Til's Apologetic*, p. 727 n. 11, documents earlier versions.

[56]Bahnsen, *Van Til's Apologetic*, p. 105 n. 49.

[57]In a mock dialogue, the more traditional apologist, Mr. Grey, thinks to himself regarding the nonbeliever (Mr. Black), "And he is pretty strong. So it is best to make a compromise peace with him. That seems to be the way of the wise and practical politician." Later Mr. Grey will "try to please" the nonbeliever. Van Til, *Defense of the Faith*, pp. 233, 246.

[58]Van Til, "Why I Believe In God" (Updated Edition, 1976), "The Works of Cornelius Van Til, 1895-1987," Guide number 1976.e.

thought Benjamin Warfield on the one hand was right that we can gain knowledge from the world around us, but wrong that fallen humanity could interpret it correctly. Fallen humanity misrepresents and suppresses it. Kuyper on the other hand was right about fallen humanity's estrangement from God, but wrong that consequently intellectual arguments would do no good.[59]

Van Til also sees problems with traditional uses of theistic arguments. As we've seen, he does not advocate using evidence as independent grounds for the conclusion that God exists, as if a nonbeliever could leave his thinking intact and merely add views about God, and as if the nonbeliever could decide what is and is not true—something only God can do. Humans must agree with God rather than try to usurp his place by determining what is true. So people must simply submit to the Bible as the Word of God, not evaluate whether it is true. While this sounds fideistic (i.e., that there can be no evidence for faith), recall that Van Til also holds that if we do not presuppose the Christian faith we cannot make sense of anything. As he sees it, this amounts not merely to inductive probabilities for the faith but also to absolute proof.[60]

In Van Til's view, if we use anything to prove that the Bible is the Word of God we in effect put it above the Bible, making it a higher authority. But since nothing can be higher than God, nothing can be used to verify that the Bible is true. And if the Bible needed anything to verify it, it would not be God's Word. On this much he and E. J. Carnell agreed.[61] Attempting to show that the Bible passes a test would be, to quote Van Til, "blasphemous."[62] Bahnsen adds that "God makes a radical demand on the believer's life which involves never demanding proof of God or trying Him. . . . No one can demand proof from God, and the servant of the Lord should never give in to any such demand."[63] The apostles were "not afraid of evidence" but never argued on the basis of it. They preached it without "feeling any

---

[59]Cornelius Van Til, *Christian Theory of Knowledge* (Philadelphia: Presbyterian & Reformed, 1969), pp. 245-46. I was led to this by McConnel, "Historical Origins," p. 43.

[60]As to Van Til's appeals to evidence, see Tom Notaro, *Van Til and the Use of Evidence* (Phillipsburg, NJ: P & R, 1985).

[61]Van Til, "Response by C. Van Til" [to Gordon Lewis], in Geehan, *Jerusalem and Athens*, p. 361.

[62]Ibid., p. 368. Van Til was referring specifically to Carnell's assertion that the Bible passes the test of "systematic consistency." Even attempting to show that it passes such a test "would be, already, to give the wrong answer. Such a question, as well as any man-made method devised to answer it, would be blasphemous. I remind you of Carnell's own words which I quoted earlier, 'If the Word required something more certain than itself to give it validity, it would no longer be *God's* Word'" (emphasis original).

[63]Greg Bahnsen, "The Impropriety of Evidentially Arguing for the Resurrection," *Synapse* 2 (1972): www.cmfnow.com/articles/PA003.htm.

need to prove it to skeptics; they unashamably [*sic*] appealed to it as fact."[64] The bottom line is that the sinner needs a "changed heart and Spiritually opened eyes, not more facts and reasons. . . . The only tool an apologete needs is the word of God, for the sinner will either presuppose its truth and find Christianity to be coherent and convincing (given his spiritual condition and past experience) or he will reject it and never be able to come to a knowledge of the truth."[65]

Van Til says the Bible is "self-authenticating." This self-authentication takes place apart from the inward testimony of the Holy Spirit, which as Bahnsen sees it is the cause of "the subjective personal response given by men to the Bible's own testimony."[66] Rather, self-authentication is "the objective and self-evidencing testimony of the Bible itself as a written message, regardless of the subjective response given to that testimony by men."[67] How does this work? "Men are so constituted as to recognize these words as the authoritative voice of their Maker speaking to them. Scripture's divine quality is perceived directly, just as the sweetness of candy or the wetness of water is immediately experienced without discursive argumentation."[68] (A discursive process is one that uses reasons rather than intuition.)

It would do no good to appeal to miracles to support the truth of the Bible, since an opponent can simply reply that we need to broaden our idea of what is possible. We cannot show that a miracle has taken place until we show that the event in question is indeed impossible, which cannot be demonstrated until all possible tests have been done.[69]

As far as evidences for the resurrection, Bahnsen says that their only proper use is to confirm the faith the believer already presupposes.[70] They are not for nonbelievers.

The critic would point out, however, that more traditional apologists claim not that God "probably exists" but that the case for God can be based on induction and thus the conclusion can be shown to be highly probable. The believer can have 100 percent faith even if the conclusion can be publicly demonstrated to be only 97 percent certain (more about that in the chapter on Alvin

[64]Ibid.
[65]Ibid.
[66]Bahnsen, *Van Til's Apologetic*, p. 198 n. 84.
[67]Ibid.
[68]Ibid., pp. 200–201.
[69]Cornelius Van Til, "Why I Believe in God," reprinted in Bahnsen, *Van Til's Apologetic*, p. 135. Van Til was illustrating his point by quoting William Adams Brown, *God at Work: A Study of the Supernatural* (New York: C. Scribner's Sons, 1933), p. 169.
[70]Bahnsen, "Impropriety."

Plantinga). An additional distinction can be made between what can be publicly demonstrated in an argument, the stuff of most apologetics, versus the sorts of inner assurances that are not normally offered publicly because they have force only for the individual who has them. These would include an inner sense of God's existence, prayers known to be answered only by the individual who prayed and so on. As far as people being accountable only for what is known with absolute certainty rather than high probability, the Bible indicates that people are accountable for things that are known only by high probabilities. For example, the people of Chorazin and Bethsaida should have known from Christ's miracles that he was sent from God (Mt 11:21; Lk 10:13) even though it is at least possible that apparent miracles can have a source other than God (Ex 7:22; Mt 24:24; Rev 13:14).

So Van Til holds both that it is wrong to offer to the non-Christian evidence as grounds for the conclusion that the Bible is the Word of God, or evidence as grounds for the conclusion that Christianity is true. The Bible is self-attesting, and we must presuppose it as such because not doing so would be absurd. Some misunderstandings surrounding Van Til are due in part to such seemingly antithetical positions: we have certainty about God and Christianity, not because we can offer evidence for them as conclusions, but because we must presuppose their truth.

Van Til did the same thing with theistic proofs that he did with evidences for Christianity. He did not reject them outright but radically recast them to fit his presuppositional approach. The most obvious difference is how he would use them, not as independent grounds for the nonbeliever to consider and add the conclusions to his existing worldview, nor as something that the nonbeliever can autonomously determine is true. Instead they have to be part of an overall comparison between the believer's and the nonbeliever's worldviews. And the proof for the Christian's worldview is that it is the only view that "does not annihilate intelligent human experience."[71] As he put his central insight, "The only 'proof' of the Christian position is that unless its truth is presupposed there is no possibility of 'proving' anything at all."[72]

The traditional ontological proof is based on the very concept of God. For Van Til this relates to the view that unless God exists, nothing is intelligible (a very different concept from the traditional ontological argument, however).[73]

---

[71]Van Til, *Defense of the Faith*, pp. 196–97; quoted in Bahnsen, *Van Til's Apologetic*, p. 616.
[72]Van Til, "My Credo," p. 21.
[73]Bahnsen, *Van Til's Apologetic*, pp. 620–21.

The traditional cosmological argument is based on the idea that, since every-thing has a cause, the universe must as well, and that cause is God. (There are actually a number of forms of the cosmological argument.) While Van Til holds that the argument is flawed, he still holds that causality makes sense only from within the Christian worldview. The nonbeliever (by which Van Til usually means the atheist, apparently) has no supernatural basis for regularities in the universe.[74] The teleological argument is based on order, and for Van Til God can be the only valid source of order.[75] As he says, "The true theistic proofs undertake to show that the idea of existence (ontological proof), of cause (cosmological proof), and purpose (teleological proof) are meaningless unless they pre-suppose the existence of God."[76]

Van Til argued against the mentality prevalent in the Enlightenment and the rise of science that we can put aside our biases and crucial assumptions and look at evidences objectively: that we can agree on a methodology (e.g., the scientific method) that could be adopted by those holding competing viewpoints, and in so doing could understand the world "out there," facts as they are in themselves. This "modern" viewpoint has come under suspicion in recent decades as the notion of objectivity has come under attack. One such attack is that there is no such thing as a neutral perspective because one's viewpoint determines how "facts" are interpreted. And since perspectives interpret everything, there is no neutral ground left on which people of different viewpoints can agree and argue for their respective positions.

Aspects of that attack remind us of Van Til's position. However, he would argue strongly against the view that the dominant role of perspectives and the lack of common ground entail that we cannot know truth objectively. As he would claim, we know with certainty what we are forced to presuppose, and in his view, we are forced to presuppose, (Reformed) Christianity. So unlike mod-ernists like Descartes, we cannot start with how we know (epistemology) and proceed to what we know (ontology). We have to begin with our convictions about what we know and believe.[77]

---

[74]Ibid., pp. 617–19.

[75]Ibid., p. 620.

[76]Cornelius Van Til, "A Letter on Common Grace," in *Common Grace and the Gospel* (Philadelphia: Presbyterian and Reformed, 1972), p. 190; Bahnsen pointed me to this quote, *Van Til*, p. 621.

[77]Other sections will feature a summary of the apologist, but since Van Til's views have been so important to modern apologetics, I will be summarizing and reviewing them in various places throughout the book in order to compare and contrast them with other thinkers. So I will dispense with a summary here.

CRITICISMS

Through intense give-and-take Van Til largely answered critics who said that he had capitulated to idealism. He is sometimes regarded as being an outright fideist, though as we have seen he opposed the view. More difficult to assess is the criticism that his views amount to fideism. Norman Geisler concludes that the way Van Til's approach actually functions make him a "revelational fideist": he uses presuppositions fideistically in that the only proof for Christianity is that it must be assumed; there are no common ideas (or to use Van Til's word, "notions") between believers and nonbelievers; to show what reality is or isn't, we cannot use facts as such or even logic, since they are not independent of God, and treat them as independent or as a way to discover reality, which would make people "autonomous." It is not enough for Geisler that Van Til would use logic and facts in a case for Christianity, because for Van Til they must be used presuppositionally. Geisler says, "It would appear that the Bible is assumed to be true by an act of faith in its self-vindicating authority in an admittedly circular reasoning process. If that is the case, the 'proofs' of God and historical 'facts' of Christianity would have absolutely no meaning or validity outside the fideistic acceptance of the presupposition that Christianity is true."[78]

What makes the evaluation of Van Til complex is that he has two contrasting approaches. On the one hand the Bible must be accepted as God's Word because to do otherwise would be to challenge God when we what we owe him is submission; we have no right to test him or his Word, or to put some criteria for truth higher than his Word. This sounds like straightforward fideism. On the other hand Van Til holds that unless we assume the existence of the God of (Reformed) Christianity, there is no way to account for human knowledge and experience. Whether we think this transcendental move works or not, Van Til at least thinks he is offering airtight proof in that the atheist must assume the existence of God to even state his view. So Van Til does not stop at a fideistic embrace of Christianity. He offers what he claims is the strongest possible proof, which he believes goes far beyond the level of proof offered by more traditional apologetics.

Does his transcendental approach do what he claims? He approves a common criticism of traditional proofs for the existence of God, which points to the fact that they do not prove the existence of the uniquely Christian God. At most the cosmological argument, for example, proves the existence of a being sufficient to cause the universe; the teleological argument proves a divine orderer. That

---

[78]Norman Geisler, *Christian Apologetics* (Grand Rapids: Baker, 1976), p. 58.

leaves us far from the Christian God. Yet Van Til's own approach demands only the existence of a God sufficient to account for human knowledge and experience. It is difficult to see how his approach demands all the details of the Christian God. He does hold that the Trinity alone can account for the relationship between individual things and categories, what is called the problem of the one and the many. However, for such a pivotal and innovative argument, his appeal to the Trinity has gone largely undeveloped. Even if the being who can account for human knowledge and experience must be triune, this is still a long way from all the details of the uniquely Christian God, which includes, for example, God's love, patience, mercy, wisdom, providence, justice, immanence, transcendence and more. And we should note that proving the existence of such a being is a long way from proving Christianity, which includes such things as the inspiration of Scripture, incarnation, the two natures of Christ, resurrection, the plan of salvation and more. We will see that John Frame makes the same criticism of Van Til's approach to the transcendental argument.

As we have seen, Van Til would use evidences for Christianity, but only in a presuppositional way, not as independent evidence for a conclusion. More than one critic has wished he had spelled out that process in more detail.

Van Til sets a very high bar for his arguments. Christianity is not merely the best explanation, as is held by many traditional apologists. It is the only explanation that can possibly work. But the critic could wonder, why must the Christian God create and direct everything for there to be any connections between things? Leaves cannot be on trees and we cannot use language and categories to talk about them unless the Christian God put the leaves there? Is every other explanation for relationships between things impossible (Van Til's view)—or just very unlikely (the view of more traditional apologetics)? Do all other explanations for such things as logic, causality and morality fail completely? Or are they merely inadequate? Over the decades Van Til often repeated the claim that (Reformed) Christianity alone can account for human reasoning, and while he developed support for this innovative and crucial claim, we could wish that he said even more about why we cannot know anything unless the Christian God is in absolute control over everything.

As some see it, part of the problem with his transcendental approach is that we do not know every possible explanation. We know only the ones we and others have thought up. So how can we be absolutely sure that no other explanation will work—or work better? As Brian Bosse points out, the presuppositionalist compares Christianity to other worldviews that are said to be unable to provide a basis for rationality, but "he never demonstrates that there are no other worldviews that meet the necessary preconditions for knowledge. . . . It is from this basis that the apologist inductively concludes that all worldviews outside Christianity fail!"[79] So while the presuppositionalist claims to have deductive, or absolute, certainty, says Bosse, he really has only inductive certainty; in other words, high probability. Inductive certainty is what most traditional apologists offer, and Van Til criticizes them for it. Evidentialist John Warwick Montgomery says that we cannot prove Christianity merely by disproving all the alternatives because there is an infinite number of alternatives. Even if there were not and we disproved a finite number of alternatives, we cannot be absolutely sure that one of them has to be true.[80] James N. Anderson counters that "the possible alternatives (even if infinite in number) can be divided into a finite number of classes, and those classes of alternatives defeated."[81] This leaves open the question of whether we can be absolutely sure that we have identified all the classes of alternatives and know that a more adequate alternative does not exist.

In a related objection, Van Til's former student David Hoover says that a presuppositional argument can show only that Christianity is a sufficient grounds for rationality, but not necessary grounds. In practical terms, it can show that Christianity is one view that works, but not the only view that could work.[82]

Greg Bahnsen answers that Christianity is properly compared to its negation, not to alternatives one by one. He says, "It has never been held (from Kant onward) that a transcendental argument establishes necessity only by the exhaustive elimination of all real and imaginary ways of expressing the alternative (of which there is logically only one: the conclusion's negation)."[83] As far as assuming that one of the alternatives being considered must be true, Bahnsen says

---

[79]Brian Bosse, "Van Tillian Presuppositional Apologetics—A Critique Concerning Certainty," p. 10, http://www.christianlogic.com/images/uploads/Critique-VanTil.pdf.

[80]John Warwick Montgomery, "Once Upon an A Priori," in Geehan, *Jerusalem and Athens*, pp. 387–88.

[81]James N. Anderson, personal email correspondence, Oct. 28, 2013. He made a number of helpful suggestions on this chapter.

[82]David P. Hoover, "For the Sake of Argument: A Critique of the Logical Structure of Van Til's Presuppositionalism," IBRI Research Report 11 (1982), Interdisciplinary Biblical Research Institute, http://www.ibri.org/RRs/RR011/11vanTil.htm. Citations are from the online version. Hoover studied under Van Til, embraced his views and enjoyed a personal relationship with him, even as he moved away from his views, eventually embracing evidentialism. See also Hoover, *The Defeasible Pumpkin: An Epiphany in a Pumpkin Patch*, Interdisciplinary Biblical Research Institute (Amazon Digital Services: September 7, 2012), preface.

[83]Bahnsen, *Van Til's Apologetic*, pp. 487–88 n. 41.

that both sides of a debate must be assuming that at least one alternative validates language and thought, or they would not be debating.[84]

Bosse says that Bahnsen's claim (which, we could add, echoes Van Til's claim) that every alternative to Christianity crucially presupposes human autonomy has not been proved and is a mere assertion.[85] He reminds us that presuppositionalists claim that every view but that of (Reformed) Christianity presuppose human autonomy. Can we so sharply divide everything into the one correct view on one side and all others on the other? Would Van Til's approach be sufficient to rule out an alternative to Christianity that is very close to it, for example, a triune God who creates and is in sovereign control of everything but does not become incarnate, does not offer salvation by grace and has nothing to do with Israel?

Hoover finds another problem with Van Til's claim that the transcendental argument gives us deductive certainty. Van Til says, "The best and only possible proof for the existence of such a God is that his existence is required for the uniformity of nature and the coherence of all things in the world."[86] However, Hoover goes on, the assumed acquaintance with "the uniformity of nature and coherence of all things in the world" can be known only by an omniscient being. At the very most Van Til is entitled to claim that "the Christian's God is a sufficient condition to account for the world so far as his knowledge goes."[87] But sufficient is far less than necessary. This leaves us without deductive certainty and again gives us only the inductive certainty of traditional apologetics. But Anderson turns the objection around and says that Van Til is claiming that only an omniscient being can know that nature is uniform, and therefore our knowledge must be derivative of his. So no one could know or be justified in assuming the uniformity of nature unless God exists.[88]

A critic might also point out that Van Til assumes human knowledge and experience to be valid, and his apologetic aims to show how that this is so; yet the connection between the mental constructs that humans call "knowledge" and reality outside our minds has needed a bit of shoring up in recent decades. For that matter, how can we be absolutely sure that there must be some ultimate, transcendent grounding for everything? Or, what if the Reformed Christian

---

[84]Ibid.

[85]Bosse, "Van Tillian Presuppositional Apologetics," p. 19, says that he is responding mostly to Bahnsen's rebuttal in an extended footnote on pp. 487–88 of *Van Til's Apologetic*, but if Bahnsen or any other presuppositional apologist has more adequately defended against the criticisms he is unaware of it.

[86]Van Til, *Defense of the Faith*, p. 103; quoted in Hoover, "For the Sake of Argument."

[87]Hoover, "For the Sake of Argument."

[88]Anderson, personal email correspondence with the author, Oct. 28, 2013.

grounding is accepted, but can really offer only a better explanation for things (i.e., traditional apologetics), but not the only possible explanation, as Van Til claims?

Van Til seems to focus mostly on atheism, contrasting it with Reformed Christianity. But even in the United States less than 10 percent are atheists, the rest are Catholics, Jews, Muslims, Mormons, Jehovah's Witnesses, Buddhists and more. While he is not as explicit about these other views, as Bahnsen sees it, all non-Christian worldviews are based on human autonomy, and thus they fail to provide what is needed for rationality.[89] So while Van Til's unbeliever sounds like an atheist, he is considered to be the archetype of every non-Christian.

KEY TERMS

Analogical reasoning. In Van Til, being subject to God in one's thinking, thus, thinking God's thoughts after him. But in Aquinas, analogical predication is neither exactly the same (univocal) nor entirely different (equivocal). It is in one way the same and in another way different. God's knowledge, for example, is neither exactly like nor entirely unlike human knowledge. The meaning of "*x* knows" depends on the nature of *x*, whether human or divine. The difference between Van Til's use of "analogical" and the traditional use influenced by Aquinas has caused some confusion.

Antithesis. The contrast between Christian and non-Christian thought.

Autonomy. The sinful attempt by fallen humans to live as an authority unto themselves rather than submit to the one true authority of a sovereign God.

Borrowed capital. The non-Christian typically affirms truth for which his or her presuppositions provide no foundation. In that sense they borrow from the Christian's worldview.

Brute fact. A supposedly uninterpreted fact.

Certainty. Complete assurance that Christian beliefs are true. According to Van Til, this is not the inductive certainty of high probability, but the deductive certainty of a reductio ad absurdum, where competing views are reduced to absurdity because they can offer no foundation for knowledge of any sort, lacking the determinacy of a sovereign, divine will and the omniscient unity of a divine mind.

Chance. A typical feature of a non-Christian worldview in which events might or might not happen. For Van Til, this effectively destroys the possibility of knowledge since one event or state of affairs is just as likely as another, there being no way to predict events or know what is true. The antidote is the deter-

---

[89]Greg Bahnsen, *Van Til's Apologetic*, pp. 487–88.

minacy of a sovereign will, a feature of (Reformed) Christianity.

Circular reasoning. Reasoning in which the conclusion appears in one or more premises. Normally thought to be a fatal flaw, circular reasoning for Van Til is unavoidable and necessary in the case for Christianity.

Common ground. In traditional apologetics, beliefs and knowledge that can be had by both Christian and non-Christian that could form the basis for reasoning to the truth. Van Til preferred to call overlap between worldviews "common notions," and denied that there can be such if each consistently held their presuppositions. Christian and non-Christian do live in the same world, however, and both have at least some knowledge of the true God, though the non-Christian suppresses it. For Van Til, these are legitimate "points of contact" between Christian and non-Christian even if there is no overlap between their worldviews, consistently held.

Internal critique. Critique of the nonbeliever's views from their own assumptions and aims, rather than from the Christian's. Van Til believed this would reveal the inadequacy of the nonbeliever's worldview, showing, for example, that they cannot make sense of knowledge or experience.

Presupposition. A belief that governs other beliefs. An ultimate presupposition controls all other beliefs. Van Til used "starting point" in this sense of a governing idea.

Self-authentication. The ultimate authority in a worldview that justifies itself. Van Til held that God as the ultimate authority is self-authenticating and is known through Scripture. Those who are called by God recognize that authority.

Transcendental argument. A unique and crucial aspect of Van Til's apologetic approach in which he argues that only (Reformed) Christianity can provide a basis for knowledge or discourse of any kind. Using this approach, he rejects traditional apologetics, which claims to be able to reason from premises that can be known apart from a commitment to (Reformed) Christian beliefs. Yet he can also claim that his apologetic offers absolute certainty, because it reduces all other beliefs to absurdity (a reductio ad absurdum) since they cannot provide sufficient grounds for knowing anything. (Reformed) Christianity is therefore proved as an assumption that is absolutely necessary if we are to know anything at all. All apologetics should take the approach of "reasoning indirectly."[90]

---

[90]For a more complete list, see John M. Frame, *A Van Til Glossary, IIIM Magazine Online*, August 28–September 3, 2000, http://www.thirdmill.org/files/english/practical_theology/33822~8_30 _00_6-57-45_PM~PT.Frame.VanTil.Glossary.pdf.

Thinking It Over

1. What is idealism, and why have some identified Van Til with that viewpoint? What is your view?

2. What is the correspondence theory of truth? The coherence theory? Why have some thought Van Til held to the coherence theory?

3. Explain how God's knowledge has a central place in Van Til's epistemology.

4. What part does God's will have in his knowledge?

5. What place does submission to God have in Van Til's epistemology?

6. What place does God's ordering of the universe have in the possibility of human knowledge? (See especially Bahnsen's explanation.) How does the non-Christian rely on chance and necessity where the Christian appeals to God to explain order (unity) and change (diversity)?

7. What is the significance of "wholes" for Van Til? What do wholes have to do with meaning, and why must one mind comprehend everything for human knowledge to be possible, according to Van Til?

8. How does Van Til's view of the interconnectedness of all things shape his view that there are no common ideas among different worldviews?

9. How does Van Til attempt to show that the Trinity is necessary for knowledge?

10. After Descartes, it was common to start with how we know. What does Van Til start with, and why?

11. Explain the transcendental argument.

12. What is Van Til's view of "common ground," and how does it differ from traditional apologetics? What is the "point of contact" with the non-Christian?

13. What is Van Til's view regarding common grace, and how does he compare with the views of Warfield and Kuyper?

14. Why can we not use anything to prove the Word of God?

15. What does it mean that the Bible is self-authenticating? Why can't miracles prove its truthfulness?

16. Why have some critics, like Geisler, concluded that Van Til's presuppositionalism amounts to fideism? What do you think?

17. A criticism of the transcendental argument is that, contrary to Van Til, the

details of the Christian God are not needed to make knowledge possible; only a few essentials are needed. If so, says the critic, then Van Til's indirect approach to apologetics fails, along with his claim that people have to presuppose Christianity to make sense of the world. What do you think?

18. A theme in traditional apologetics is that Christianity can be shown to be the best explanation (other views explain, but not nearly as well), whereas Van Til says it is the only possible explanation. Which do you think is correct?

19. Do you think every alternative to Christianity presupposes human autonomy? (See the criticism by Bosse.)

20. Do you think any of the other criticisms have merit? If so, which? If not, name one and tell why.

GOING FURTHER

Bahnsen, Greg L. *Van Til's Apologetic: Readings and Analysis*. Phillipsburg, NJ: P & R, 1998.

Frame, John M. *Cornelius Van Til: An Analysis of His Thought*. Phillipsburg, NJ: P & R, 2009.

Geehan, E. R. *Jerusalem and Athens: Critical Discussions on the Philosophy and Apologetics of Cornelius Van Til*. Phillipsburg, NJ: P & R, 1971.

Muether, John R. *Cornelius Van Til*. Phillipsburg, NJ: P & R, 2008.

Notaro, Thom. *Van Til and the Use of Evidence*. Phillipsburg, NJ: P & R, 1980.

Rushdoony, Rousas John. *By What Standard? An Analysis of the Philosophy of Cornelius Van Til*. Philadelphia: P & R, 1959.

Sigward, Eric, ed. *The Complete Works of Cornelius Van Til*. Phillipsburg, NJ: P & R, 1996. CD-ROM.

Van Til, Cornelius. *A Christian Theory of Knowledge*. Philadelphia: P & R, 1969.

———. *Christianity and Idealism*. Philadelphia: P & R, 1955.

———. *Common Grace*. Philadelphia: P & R, 1947.

———. *Defense of the Faith*. 3rd ed. Phillipsburg, NJ: P & R, 1979.

———. *Defense of the Faith*. Edited by K. Scott Oliphint. 4th ed. Phillipsburg, NJ: P & R, 2008. [Annotated edition that restores the complete text.]

———. *Introduction to Systematic Theology: Prolegomena and the Doctrines of Revelation, Scripture, and God*. Edited by William Edgar. Phillipsburg, NJ: P & R, 2007.

– 4 –

JOHN FRAME

We see ultimate truth from
more than one perspective

John Frame (1939–) is perhaps the best-known presuppositionalist today and has worked to maintain Van Til's core insights while significantly modifying many aspects of his views. His bold moves have been seen both as moving presuppositionalism forward, and as changing it beyond recognition.

Frame came to Christ at the age of thirteen, having been influenced by a local United Presbyterian Church and a Billy Graham meeting. He majored in philosophy at Princeton University, where a Catholic professor sympathetically taught the views of Aristotle, Spinoza and John Dewey, causing Frame to conclude that not all differences between thinkers are matters of truth and error. Rather, despite genuine differences, each had a different way of looking at the same reality. That was the beginning of his seeing reality "perspectively."[1]

At Westminster Theological Seminary he met Cornelius Van Til, who emphasized in his teaching that Christ must govern our thoughts. Frame came to believe Van Til was the most important thinker since John Calvin. Van Til showed, according to Frame, that we have to "reject non-Christian presupposi-

---

[1]John M. Frame, "Backgrounds to My Thought," in *Speaking the Truth in Love: The Theology of John M. Frame*, ed. John J. Hughes (Phillipsburg, NJ: P & R, 2009), p. 13. The chapter is also at the *Frame and Poythress* website, http://www.frame-poythress.org/about/john-frame-full-bio/.

tions and seek to think consistently according to Christian ones."[2] Frame says that you will not understand him if you do not understand Van Til.

Frame developed the idea that as nonomniscient beings, we cannot see everything at once, so we must see reality from different perspectives. We have essentially three perspectives, on nature, man, and God (explained below). The threefold nature of things is rooted in the Trinity.

Frame was also influenced by the thought, life and ministry of Francis Schaeffer. Schaeffer had been a student of both Van Til and one of his critics, J. Oliver Buswell, and Schaeffer sought to reconcile the opposing views. Van Til wrote a book he never published that was critical of Schaeffer; however, Frame concluded that Van Til's views were closer to both Schaeffer and traditional apologetics than Van Til himself thought.[3]

After graduate work in philosophical theology at Yale, Frame taught at Westminster Seminary, where Van Til asked him to also teach courses in apologetics. There he met Greg Bahnsen as a student, and the two remained friends until Bahnsen's death in 1995. Frame helped start the Westminster campus in San Diego and taught there for twenty years, leaving partly because of contention over whether his views were sufficiently Van Tillian. He currently teaches at Reformed Theological Seminary in Orlando, Florida.

During over forty years of teaching he has published extensively[4] and carried on such diverse activities as preaching, worship music, writing some eighteen thousand in-depth emails since 2000 and keeping up a website with former student and lifelong friend Professor Vern Poythress.

RELATIONSHIP TO VAN TIL'S THOUGHT

Frame's strong intellectual connection to Van Til's central ideas have guided him throughout his academic career. But he also recognizes that a "movement" has grown up around Van Til. Many in a movement of any sort want only to convert everyone to it, and they value faithfulness to the leader, not criticism. Frame considers himself a "committed member"[5] of the Van Til movement in the sense that he would like to see everyone adopt Van Til's basic principles.

[2]Ibid.
[3]Frame concludes this from reading Schaeffer's "A Review of a Review," *The Bible Today* (October 1948): 7–9, also at *PCA Historical Center*, www.pcahistory.org/documents/schaefferreview.html.
[4]Bibliography at the *Frame and Poythress* website: www.frame-poythress.org/bibliographies/john-frame-bibliography/.
[5]Frame, *Cornelius Van Til*, p. 10.

But he insists that no one should be above criticism, and partly to combat the view that Van Til should not be constructively criticized, he wrote *Cornelius Van Til: An Analysis of His Thought*.[6] In another work he says,

> I take the movement mentality to be the exact antithesis of Christian scholarship, the chief rule of which is that we may not idolize men. I love and admire Van Til. . . . But I do not think we do Van Til—or even Calvin—a service by treating them as deuterocanonical. Godly scholars assume the existence of finitude and sin in every thinker, including themselves, and they insist on testing everything by God's Word alone. The best honor we can do for Van Til is to treat him critically, for only thus can we be serious in determining how to build on his foundation.[7]

Frame holds that apologetics is the "application of Scripture to unbelief" and is thus "a part of theology, not a 'neutral basis' for it."[8] So when we move from apologetics to theology, we do not go from what is common between believer and unbeliever to what is unique to the believer (typically the view of more traditional apologetics).

The relationship between knowledge held by the nonbeliever, the believer and God can shape one's view of apologetics. Frame says we should think of "facts" as the world seen from God's point of view, "or perhaps, when truly seen from a human point of view, and 'interpretations' as our understanding of those facts, whether true or false."[9] What is distinctly presuppositional is the idea that a fact is not a reality in itself apart from interpretation, human or divine, by which we test interpretations. So facts are not independent enough from interpretations that we can point decisively to them. Rather, facts and interpretations cannot be separated. They are interpreted through one grid or another, there being no neutral space in between. For Frame (and Van Til), we can never get past interpretations to independently existing facts, and "we have no access to reality apart from our interpretative faculties."[10] This is a major reason why presuppositionalists contend that there is no neutral ground on which to judge anything as true or false (as is claimed by traditional apologetics).

---

[6]See John M. Frame, *The Doctrine of God* (Phillipsburg, NJ: P & R, 2002), p. 762.
[7]Frame, *Doctrine of God*, p. 762. On pp. 763–64 Frame responds to a critic with a partial list of his agreements with Van Til.
[8]John Frame, *The Doctrine of the Knowledge of God* (Phillipsburg, NJ: P & R, 2002), p. 87.
[9]Ibid., p. 71.
[10]Ibid.

Frame makes the very crucial stipulation that we can verify our interpretations on the basis of facts, in effect comparing the data of the mind with the data of the external world. "But neither form of data is understood as a brute, incorrigible standard," he says.[11] So he believes that either data field can be compared with the other, "in effect verifying each by the other."[12] Interpretations can be verified by comparing them with facts, and what we think are facts can be verified by comparing them with our interpretations. This is not the view of evidentialists, that facts are independent enough to alone reliably point to their proper interpretations, but neither is it the view that interpretations completely dominate facts and determine them such that they can do nothing to inform our interpretations. He says that his view is closer to an interactive holism, reminiscent of W. V. O. Quine.[13]

On the contrasting traditional view of apologetics held by evidentialists (and to a lesser extent by a few classical apologists), there is enough distance between interpretation and fact that we can look at a fact and decide the best interpretation. A rough analogy would be the legal process, where both sides argue their interpretation of the evidence, or facts, and the jurors decide which interpretation best fits the facts.[14] Another analogy comes from the scientific method, where experimental data (facts) are compared against various theories (interpretations) for the best fit. The more traditional apologist argues that God or Christianity constitutes the best fit with the facts (though there are different approaches, as we will see).

On Frame's view, the relationship between our knowledge and God's (the focus of the controversy between Van Til and Gordon Clark) is not one of all or nothing; therefore, it is not the case that we grasp nothing of God's knowledge simply because we cannot grasp all of it. Knowing any statement, such as 2 + 2 = 4, is not known "once-for-all in completed fashion, so that one either does or does not know the meaning."[15] We can come to know more and more of the

---

[11]Personal email correspondence with the author, Aug. 24, 2013.

[12]Ibid.

[13]Ibid.

[14]In a technical sense, we could further divide this type of reasoning into inference to the best explanation, which considers which view best *explains* the facts, and which view provides a *ground* for the facts. Evidentialists like John Warwick Montgomery and Gary Habermas suggest that our understanding of facts can point to which best interprets them. For example (as we will see in a later chapter), given the facts of Hitler's extermination of Jews, the interpretation that he hated them and wanted them all dead is to be preferred over the interpretation that he loved them and wanted them to be in heaven as soon as possible.

[15]Frame, *Doctrine of the Knowledge of God*, p. 34.

implications of a statement. Of course God knows to an infinite degree, "but God also surely knows the same limited levels of meaning that we know, and within that sphere He communicates with a clarity that leaves us without excuse" (for our spiritual ignorance).[16]

The unbeliever too can know some of the same things as the believer, Frame says. Of course in special cases they can mean different things when using the same words, as when a heterodox thinker uses a "revelation" but defines it differently from the orthodox thinker. Van Til occasionally claimed that any agreement between the believer and nonbeliever is merely "formal,"[17] being only apparent and superficial, not substantive or real. That is largely because they are using different presuppositions, one holding to the biblical God, the other not. But Frame says this is not possible, because the nonbeliever would have an excuse for ignorance, which Romans 1 says he does not have; Scripture regards statements made by Satan and unbelievers as a mixture of truth and error, not as always being merely "formally" true; if agreement were only "formal" believers and unbelievers could not communicate; and purely formal agreement seems impossible anyway if there is always some overlap in meanings.[18]

If agreement between the believer and nonbeliever is real and not merely formal, then perhaps they necessarily fail to connect because the unbeliever puts a true statement into a network of false beliefs. But for Frame that idea, that true statements become false when they are put into a false system of beliefs, "is a kind of idealistic theory of language that has no Christian basis and would be rejected by almost all linguists, including idealist ones!"[19]

We could add that a similar discussion arose in philosophy of science around the views of Thomas Kuhn (1922–1996), who claims that science uses paradigms (roughly, shared beliefs and approaches to problems) to interpret the "facts." Rather like Van Til's view that presuppositions so determine our thinking that people using the same words mean different things, resulting in mere formal agreement, some interpreted Kuhn to be saying that a paradigm does the same thing to words that occur within a theory. Words like *mass* and *cause* have different meanings according to the theory in which they occur. Theories are thus "incommensurable" in the sense that there is no neutral language into which they

---

[16]Ibid.; see also, p. 38 n. 33.
[17]Cornelius Van Til, *Defense of the Faith*, 3rd ed. (Philadelphia: P & R, 1967), p. 59; cited in Frame, *Doctrine of the Knowledge of God*, p. 52.
[18]Frame, *Doctrine of the Knowledge of God*, pp. 52–53.
[19]Ibid., p. 53.

can both be translated.[20] Communication between people holding different paradigms can therefore be difficult because the same terms mean different things to different scientists, according to their respective paradigm. Comparison and evaluation of theories becomes difficult. On more extreme interpretations, the lack of neutral ground between paradigms makes it difficult or impossible to make a rational choice between them, so the choice has to be made another way. Borrowing the language of religion, fideism could be one way, where a person simply chooses to hold a view. Borrowing from some themes in literary theory, psychological and social subterfuge could be a factor in how people choose their paradigm and propagate it.[21]

All this was taken by some to mean (or at least taken that Kuhn meant) that at root science is not a rational enterprise. It was associated with the shift away from the traditional view of science, wherein facts can be seen more or less neutrally, and theories can be judged by how they fit with them. On the traditional view, science makes linear progress toward the truth. But on the new view, paradigms dominate the interpretation of the facts, and paradigm choice is not always entirely a scientific matter; thus there is no guarantee that science progresses toward the truth. Paradigms shift, but there's no guarantee it will result in progress.

Kuhn said he was "surprised" at the extreme interpretations of his views, such as that scientists could decide to believe whatever they wanted based on nothing more than "accident and personal taste," then enforce it by all available means.[22] He clarified that he meant only "local incommensurability," that the problems of translatability arises only for a small subgroup of terms. There are enough terms that do not change meanings across theories that theories can genuinely be compared, and a rational choice can be made. But Kuhn added that even

---

[20]Thomas S. Kuhn, "Reflections on My Critics," in *Criticism and the Growth of Knowledge*, ed. Imre Lakatos and Alan Musgrave (Cambridge: Cambridge University Press, 1967), pp. 266–67; quoted in Paul Hoyningen-Huene, *Restructuring Scientific Revolutions: Thomas S. Kuhn's Philosophy of Science*, trans. Alexander T. Levine (Chicago: University of Chicago Press, 1993), p. 214. The passage also appears in Thomas S. Kuhn, "Reflections on My Critics," in *The Road Since Structure: Philosophical Essays, 1970–1993*, ed. James Conant and John Haugeland (Chicago: University of Chicago Press, 2000), p. 36. Further citations are to this edition.

[21]For insights on how another thinker, Stanley Fish, views topics related to the question of presuppositionalism, see Mark L. Ward Jr., "The Dwarfs Are for the Dwarfs: Stanley Fish, the Pragmatic Presuppositionalist," *Answers Research Journal* 6 (2013): 265–78 (https://cdn-assets.answersingenesis .org/doc/articles/pdf-versions/dwarfs_Stanley_Fish.pdf).

[22]Kuhn, "Reflections on My Critics," pp. 155–56. See the section in the essay "Irrationality and Theory Choice," pp. 155–62.

those terms that do not change "are *not theory-independent* but are simply used in the same way within the two theories at issue."[23]

So we can see that the relationship between theories and facts is enormously important to our choice of apologetic methodology. Although theories and presuppositions differ (more for some apologists than for others), it matters whether they so determine the interpretation of facts and even the terms used (such as *cause*) that there is no room for going from facts upward to the best-fitting theory. Van Tillian presuppositionalists tend to think they do determine facts, whereas evidentialists think there is enough distance between theories and facts that facts can point to the theory that best interprets them. Classical apologist Norman Geisler agrees with presuppositionalists that there can be no interpretation of facts apart from a worldview-level theory and that there is therefore no way to go from the facts of the resurrection, for example, to theism. But he disagrees, as we shall see, with presuppositionalists as to how we determine that theism is the right theory. Though he is also a classical apologist, William Lane Craig allows for some reasoning from facts to theories, though he believes that in practice such a move is vulnerable to criticism in a way that reasoning from theory to facts is not. Therefore, he argues, it is stronger to first establish theism and then prove the resurrection.

We can now see why it is significant that Frame insists that words do not prevent the believer and nonbeliever from real communication, nor prevent the nonbeliever from having real knowledge. A more radical view that prevents communication and knowledge would lessen the nonbeliever's access to rational discussion, persuasion and, ultimately, rational choice. Frame's view that human knowledge can be more or less accurate may have a small, underlying part in permitting his conclusion that presuppositional apologetics is not as distant from traditional apologetics as many fellow presuppositionalists think. Undergirding his view is the conviction that knowledge is not all or nothing, which allows our knowledge to overlap with God's in some small way. Also undergirding his view is the idea that presuppositions do not affect meaning enough to preclude communication and knowledge.

The term *presuppositional* is unfortunate, Frame believes, because it seems to contrast with evidence. Also, believing that presuppositions have a role in thought and apologetics is not distinct to the view, since every apologetic method sees a

[23]Kuhn, "Commensurability, Comparability, Communicability," in Conant and John Haugeland, *The Road Since Structure*, p. 36 (emphasis added).

role for them.[24] Incidentally, Scott Oliphant of Westminster Theological Seminary suggests the name "presuppositional" be updated to "covenantal apologetics."[25]

Frame agrees with Van Til that apologetic reasoning should be transcendental in the sense that it must always reason under God's authority and never assume— or encourage the nonbeliever to assume—that we can do otherwise, or that there is some neutral way to see the world that does not include God. To reason transcendentally is to "present the biblical God, not merely as the conclusion to an argument, but as the one who makes argument possible. We should present him as the source of all meaningful communication, since he is the author of all order, truth, beauty, goodness, logical validity, and empirical fact."[26]

He has come to believe that Van Til overstated the difference between presuppositionalism and traditional apologetics. Van Til tended to portray apologetics as it was done before him as the story of compromise, as trying to reason on a neutral basis, "but his analysis does not establish the crucial point of his critique: that the tradition assumes reality to be intelligible apart from God," and "he ignores ways of interpreting these traditional arguments as aspects of his own transcendental apologetic."[27] In his characteristically irenic and humble spirit, Frame urges us not to "overestimate the importance of our own insights at the expense of others. Nor should we interpret other writers in the worst sense possible, as Van Til has sometimes done. Rather, we should give them the benefit of the doubt, as we would wish others to give that benefit to us."[28]

Frame sees the transcendental approach as more of a goal than a single argument. It is not, as some Van Tillians have supposed, "a simplification of apologetics: in place of the many complicated arguments of traditional apologetics, we now have only one."[29] We do not have a "'magic bullet,' a simple, straightforward argument that would destroy all unbelief in one fell swoop."[30] Van Tillians expect to prove "that all the elements of biblical theism are presupposed in intelligible

---

[24]John Frame, "Presuppositional Apologetics," in *Five Views on Apologetics*, ed. Steven B. Cowan (Grand Rapids: Zondervan, 2000), p. 219 n. 16.

[25]Scott Oliphant, *Covenantal Apologetics: Principles and Practices in Defense of Our Faith* (Wheaton, IL: Crossway, 2013), p. 25.

[26]Frame, "Presuppositional Apologetics," p. 220.

[27]John M. Frame, "The Thought of Cornelius Van Til," lecture outline, *Reformed Perspectives*, http://reformedperspectives.org/articles/joh_frame/VT_The%20Thought%20of%20Cornelius%20Van%20Til.html.

[28]Ibid.

[29]Ibid.

[30]John Frame, *Cornelius Van Til: An Analysis of His Thought* (Phillipsburg, NJ: P & R, 1995), pp. 316–17.

communication,"[31] but most do not seem to grasp the enormity[32] of the task,
Frame observes. Van Til's argument from intelligibility and predication would
have to prove such doctrines as the Trinity, sovereignty, foreordination, creation,
providence, love, justice,[33] personhood, transcendence, immanence, infinity,
wisdom, omnipotence, omnipresence and more.[34] As a preconditions of rationality, must God be just? Must he also be loving? Wise? Van Til criticizes other
approaches to apologetics for merely proving a generic God, even though those
apologists go on to use other arguments to prove the Christian God. But how
many of the attributes of the Christian God are absolutely necessary to undergird
the process of human knowledge and communication? Frame sees no way to
conclude the existence of the distinctly Christian God in one simple argument. It
will take many subarguments and is actually a very complex task. He sees no
reason why a number of arguments used by traditional apologists cannot be used
in the endeavor, as long as they are tuned to the overall goal of showing that there
can be no intelligibility apart from him—the overarching transcendental goal.

Just how a Van Tillian apologetic approach would be executed in practical
terms is not as obvious as it could be. Frame says, "One weakness in Van Til's
own writings is the lack of specific arguments. Van Til always said that there was
an 'absolutely certain argument' for Christianity, but he rarely produced an example, except in the barest outline form."[35] To those in the presuppositional
movement, Frame says it is important

> for us to move beyond the traditional Van Tillian preoccupation with meth-
> odology. Van Tillian courses in apologetics, including mine, have focused far
> too much on methods, especially upon distinguishing our methods from those
> of other schools of thought. More time should be spent on developing actual
> arguments. We need to spend more time addressing unbelievers and less time
> arguing with one another over methods. Students of Van Tillian apologetics
> need to be far better informed about Christian evidences and about the current
> situations that the apologist must address.[36]

---

[31]Ibid., p. 316.
[32]"Enormity" in the sense of immensity, see *Merriam-Webster Collegiate Dictionary*, 11th ed., s.v.
"Enormity," http://www.merriam-webster.com/dictionary/enormity.
[33]Frame, *Cornelius Van Til*, pp. 315–16.
[34]Frame, *Apologetics to the Glory of God*, p. 73.
[35]Ibid., p. xii.
[36]Frame, *Cornelius Van Til*, p. 400. He thanks Greg Bahnsen for impressing on him the need to
move beyond a preoccupation with apologetic method (i.e., the theory of apologetics rather than
its application).

Frame says that his "account of Van Til allows us to take a somewhat less apoc-
alyptic view of methodological differences among apologists, so that we can
indeed concentrate on fulfilling the Great Commission."[37]

A major modification that allows Frame to consider a broad array of apologetic arguments is that, in stark contrast to Van Til, he does not rule out the use
of induction. Van Til thought that if we claim anything less than absolute certainty we are "virtually admitting that God's revelation to man is not clear."[38]
While Frame agrees that the evidence for Christian theism is "absolutely compelling" and not merely probable, he also believes that an argument may fall
short of certainty and be merely probable on a practical level due to sin, misunderstanding or incomplete knowledge. He does not believe that "Scripture
forbids us to explore areas that we don't entirely understand; quite the contrary
(Gen 1:28ff)."[39] So to legitimately say that an argument is probable is "to say that
one portion of the evidence, not well understood by a particular apologist,
yields for him an argument which is at best possible or probable." He relates this
to the three main approaches to probability. The frequentist view measures the
likelihood of something relative to a statistical sample, so is not relevant. The
logical view considers the likelihood of a hypothesis relative to a body of evidence, and Frame considers that to be absolutely certain (i.e., a probability of 1
on a scale of 0 to 1). The subjective view considers probability to be a matter of
an individual's belief, and it is here that Frame believes probability can be applied to apologetics: "Both the apologist and his hearers are often left with uncertainties because of inadequacies in the formulation of the argument and in
our reception of it. And where there is suspicion of at least some legitimacy to
uncertain reasoning, we may speak of some degree of probability."[40]

While human knowledge is fallible, and it is idolatrous to seek an infallible authority outside of Scripture, that does not mean we are left with uncertainty about
what God has said. Our certainty is based on our presupposition: "The very nature
of an ultimate presupposition is that it is held with certainty."[41] It is the ultimate
criterion of truth, the criterion against which all others are tested. There is no higher
criterion by which its certainty can be called into question; "thus by its very nature,

---

[37]Frame, *Cornelius Van Til*, p. 400.
[38]Cornelius Van Til, *Defense of the Faith*, 2nd ed. (Philadelphia: P & R, 1963), p. 104; quoted in
  Frame, *Apologetics to the Glory of God*, p. 81.
[39]Frame, *Apologetics to the Glory of God*, p. 81.
[40]Ibid., p. 81 n. 28.
[41]Frame, *Doctrine of the Knowledge of God*, p. 134.

such a presupposition is the most certain thing that we know."[42] All implications and applications are also certain; for example, if we are certain of "thou shalt not steal," we are also certain we should not embezzle. However, we may not always feel certain, due to sin, ignorance or limited knowledge of the Bible and theology.

In a sense, because "all knowledge can be seen as an application of our presuppositions, it is possible to say that all our knowledge is certain."[43] "God's revelation of himself in Scripture" is the Christian presupposition and is therefore the highest law of thought. In this way Scripture "justifies all human knowledge."[44] Some beliefs are justified explicitly by Scripture, such as God's love in Christ (Jn 3:16). Others are justified because they are deductions from Scripture, such as the Trinity. Beliefs that contradict Scripture are untrue, but many beliefs, like "Sacramento is the capital of California," are not in Scripture and do not contradict it. Yet there is a sense in which even they are "justified" by Scripture, in that we are commanded in Scripture "to use all diligence to discover the truth and live by it." As we do that, we discover that Sacramento is indeed the capital of California, so "in one sense, then, even beliefs of this sort are applications of Scripture. All knowing is theologizing!"[45] That of course does not mean that all knowledge can be derived from Scripture, but it does mean that Scripture warrants all knowledge.[46]

How do we justify belief in Scripture itself? We do it "by Scripture, of course! There is no more ultimate authority, no more reliable source of information, and nothing more that is more certain by which Scripture might be tested."[47] Yet that does not mean that "we may not use extrabiblical evidence in arguing for biblical authority."[48] We can and we should, "but as we select, interpret, and evaluate evidence, we must presuppose a biblical epistemology. Therefore, in a sense, our argument for Scripture will always be circular."[49]

Frame endorses a "biblical foundationalism" in which the "Bible contains knowledge about which we can be certain."[50] He does not accept foundationalism of the sort that seeks to trace all knowledge back to propositions that are known with certitude. He believes that rationalism (the view that we can have

---

[42]Ibid., p. 134.
[43]Ibid., p. 135.
[44]Ibid., p. 128.
[45]Ibid.
[46]Ibid., p. 129.
[47]Ibid.
[48]Ibid., p. 130.
[49]Ibid.
[50]Ibid., p. 129.

some knowledge that did not come through the senses, or from experience) and empiricism (knowledge comes from the senses) are both forms of foundationalism and wrongly attempt to find certainty outside of Scripture.[51]

Recall that according to foundationalism, beliefs are of two types: either known without being inferred from other beliefs (e.g., the lights are on, or my foot hurts), or they are known because they are inferred from other beliefs (I know electricity is coming into this house because I see the lights on). The competing view is that there is no such thing as a belief that is known by itself, and all our beliefs are inferred from other beliefs. We could add that only strong foundationalism, associated with Descartes, insisted that foundational (or "basic") beliefs are guaranteed to be true, and that all our knowledge must be linked with certainty to them (i.e., through deduction). Foundational beliefs were described as being not only certain and indubitable but also incorrigible in the sense that they could not be overturned by further knowledge. According to strong foundationalism, foundational beliefs can be known with certainty without being supported by other beliefs, and they can be used to prove other beliefs. Some call modest foundationalism the view that foundational beliefs can be known as well as used as premises to prove other beliefs even though they could turn out to be incorrect. On this view they can be not only fallible and dubitable but also revisable. According to weak foundationalism, foundational beliefs cannot be known in and of themselves without the support of other beliefs. Therefore we cannot simply stop at these beliefs when we are trying to prove something. We cannot say we believe *a* because of *b*, and *b* because of *c*; but we believe *c* by itself, without the support of any other beliefs, because it is a foundational belief. For weak foundationalists, then, a foundational belief must still be supported by other beliefs. Thus foundational beliefs are not known by themselves, but insofar as they are part of a web of beliefs that support each other. In this sense weak foundationalism is much like coherentism, the view that knowledge comes from the mutual support of beliefs, not the certainty of some beliefs we consider foundational. It is like knowing that we are right about a crossword puzzle because the answers all interlock (coherentism), not because we are absolutely sure of a few answers (strong foundationalism and modest foundationalism).[52]

---

[51]Ibid.

[52]Laurence BonJour, *The Structure of Empirical Knowledge* (Cambridge, MA: Harvard University Press, 1988), pp. 26–33; online at http://homepages.wmich.edu/~mcgrew/bonjour.htm. Ted Poston, "Foundationalism," *Internet Encyclopedia of Philosophy*, ed. James Fieser and Bradley Dowden, http://www.iep.utm.edu/found-ep/.

More modern forms of foundationalism accept that foundational beliefs can be mistaken, and many add that what is foundational to you, because it is obvious and does not need to be proved from other beliefs, might not be to me. Milder forms would say that a foundational belief is simply a stopping point of proof in our own personal thinking, that is, something we believe without having to prove it to ourselves from other beliefs. So for some more modern foundationalists, it is not about having infallible knowledge but about the structure of our thinking, that we can rationally hold some beliefs without having to prove them from other beliefs. It seems to me that presuppositionalists are saying something close to this, that we can hold to presuppositions without having to prove them from other beliefs, which must then be supported by other beliefs, which must in turn be supported by other beliefs, and so on. This is different from the Van Tillian claim that the Christian presupposition can be demonstrated transcendentally and by the impossibility of the contrary. It is true that presuppositionalists are claiming that knowledge is circular, but certainty does not come from the circle, however large, but from the certainty of the presupposition itself as the ultimate foundation for knowledge. Frame and Van Til insist that the Christian presupposition can be justified and that it is not a mere fideistic choice, but they also insist that we are not entitled to believe it simply because it can be justified; in fact, the Christian presupposition is supposed to be the source of justification, not merely one point in a circle. (More about foundationalism in the chapter on Alvin Plantinga.)

Both Frame and Van Til emphasize that the apologist must not be limited to argument, but should appeal to the knowledge of God that is innate in every human by virtue of their being created in the image of God, even if it is repressed. The apologist should appeal to this as a point of contact. Van Til holds that traditional apologetics mistakenly appeals to the nonbeliever's will and intellect. The problem is that the will is bound by sin, and the fallen intellect seeks to distort the truth and to think autonomously, that is, to think without acknowledging God's rightful place. Frame affirms Van Til's essential idea that since all thought must acknowledge God, the believer must never promote or accept "autonomous" thinking. However, the two apply that conviction differently. In Van Til's view, an apologist crosses the line when he uses any direct reasoning, such as, "There is causality, therefore God must exist." Only indirect reasoning is acceptable: "Without God, there can be no causality." As Van Til saw it, only the indirect form maintains Christian presuppositions throughout the argument. The direct form allows the nonbeliever to think autonomously by assuming that he knows what causality is and that he can form a conclusion without acknowledging God. Van Til thought that the premise "There is causality" allows nonbelievers to think they can know what causality is independent of God.[53]

Frame does not see it this way. Since he holds that there is no real difference between direct and indirect reasoning, there is no formal way to separate correct from incorrect reasoning. It is more a matter of the intent of the apologist. It is indeed a problem if the apologist allows or invites the nonbeliever to think autonomously, but whether he does cannot be determined by a single line of reasoning. Nor can it be determined simply by listening in to the apologist's interaction with the nonbeliever, since on Frame's view it is not necessary to bring the issue up in every apologetic encounter. Some apologists might not even be aware of differences in possible points of contact, so Frame says we cannot know if they are inviting people to sinfully suppose they can know what a "cause" is apart from God, or whether they are correctly appealing to their suppressed knowledge of God, by which they covertly know that God is the source and ground of all things, including causality. For Frame, the main consideration, then, is whether the argument is true. If it is, it will contact the unbeliever's repressed knowledge of God, even if the apologist did not intend to do so. Any truth will be a problem for the unbeliever's worldview, because it will not fit well.[54] So it comes down to whether we are wrongly accepting and addressing the nonbeliever's distorted worldview, or whether we are correctly accepting and addressing the undistorted revelation he covertly holds, despite the distorted worldview he professes.[55]

With important modifications in his view of negative argumentation, certainty and point of contact, Frame points out that "there is less distance between Van Til's apologetics and the traditional apologetics than most partisans on either side (including Van Til himself) have been willing to grant."[56] Presuppositionalists gain because "it opens to presuppositional apologists many, and perhaps all, of those

---

[53]But when the Christian is willing to accept the nonbeliever's viewpoint for the sake of argument, isn't he accepting the nonbeliever's autonomous thinking? No, says Frame (crediting Poythress for the insight). The Christian never really abandons his own presuppositions, even for a moment, "even when accepting the unbeliever's principles 'for the sake of argument,' he still is thinking as a Christian. What really happens in this second step, then, is that the Christian is telling the unbeliever how the unbeliever's principles look to him as a Christian." Frame, *Doctrine of the Knowledge of God*, pp. 359–60.

[54]Frame, *Apologetics to the Glory of God*, p. 84.

[55]Ibid., p. 85.

[56]Ibid.

arguments generally associated with the traditional apologetics in the past."[57]

Though Frame accepts direct arguments and allows for probability, he believes that the presupposition of Scripture and opposition to autonomy should be expressed even in our choice of words, tone of voice and personal piety when we interact with nonbelievers. We should communicate that we are committed to God and are not trying to search for abstract truth without him. So the attitude of heart becomes crucial to presuppositionalism: "It may no longer be possible to distinguish presuppositional apologetics from traditional apologetics merely by externals—by the form of argument, the explicit claim of certainty or probability, etc. Perhaps presuppositionalism is more an attitude of the heart, a spiritual condition, than an easily describable, empirical phenomenon."[58] Characteristics of "presuppositionalism of the heart" include a clear understanding of how our loyalties affect our epistemology, commitment to present the full teaching of Scripture without compromise, a determination to present God as "fully sovereign, as the source of all meaning, intelligibility, and rationality, as the ultimate authority for all human thought,"[59] and an awareness that the nonbeliever's thinking is affected by both a grasp of God and by rebellion against him. He then makes the notably irenic statement, "And if there are some apologists who maintain these understandings and attitudes without wanting to be called Van Tillians or presuppositionalists, I am happy to join hands with them."[60]

ARGUMENTS FOR GOD

With this in mind, we turn to Frame's outline of several arguments for God's existence. Although they resemble traditional theistic arguments, he notes that their ultimate conclusion is Van Tillian: "Nothing is intelligible unless God exists, and God must be nothing less than Trinitarian, sovereign, transcendent, and immanent absolute personality of the Scriptures."[61] No one argument can establish these truths, which is why he has several.

Frame's moral argument reasons that there must be objective moral values, which can be grounded only in a person who is absolute, since moral values are absolute. There must be one such being, because there is only one ultimate standard.

The epistemological argument starts with human rationality and concludes

---

[57]Ibid.
[58]Ibid., p. 87.
[59]Ibid., p. 88.
[60]Ibid.
[61]Ibid., p. 89.

that there must be a divine being who designed it. Only design can account for why the mind can interpret reality so well, and only a rational being can account for the normative element in logic by which we ought to believe what is logical. Only a divine being can ground truth and rationality as moral values, so ultimately the epistemological argument reduces to the moral argument.[62]

The amazing design in the world is the basis for the teleological argument, especially considering Aquinas's observation that unintelligent things (like matter and energy) work together for a purpose.

We can recognize human design and draw an analogy to design by a higher being. Frame proposes that evidence against a designer, such as the existence of evil, actually fits the Christian view as well. We would expect not only similarities between human and divine design but also differences—because humans and God are different, so the products of their design would be different. An opponent could reply that the evidence against design undermines the claim that it was designed at all, especially the claim that it was designed by a perfect designer. The difference between divine and human design is that God's designs should be even better, which makes evidence against design even more problematic. Frame likely has in mind, however, that a divine designer's knowledge and wisdom are so far above ours that perfections of design could appear to be flaws. Pain and evil would be prime examples.

The cosmological argument has many forms, and Frame highlights those that argue from causality, since he considers them the most intuitively cogent. His supportive remarks apply equally to the kalam argument (more on that in discussion of William Lane Craig's classical apologetics) and Thomistic-Aristotelian forms.[63] It is the nature of reason to search for causes, which roughly equate to reasons. The claim that some things in the world are uncaused is irrational (God is not "in the world" so can be uncaused[64]). And "if one event in the world lacks a cause, then the world as a whole lacks a cause. And if the world as a whole is without reason, then irrationalism triumphs."[65] We cannot claim there is no cause simply because we have difficulty finding one. If it is claimed that the world has no cause, then there is "no complete explanation, no complete reason why any event takes place."[66] The process of explanation goes infinitely back-

---

[62]Ibid., p. 109.
[63]Ibid., p. 110.
[64]Ibid., p. 111 n. 30.
[65]Ibid., p. 111.
[66]Ibid., p. 112.

wards with no endpoint. In the end "we are forced to choose between belief in a first cause and irrationalism," which is self-contradictory.[67]

Frame believes that the basic reasoning of Anselm's ontological argument is cogent, though the argument reduces to his argument from moral values. The problem is that "perfection" can mean different things. Existence can be or not be a perfection, depending on what we are presupposing. The argument proves the biblical God only on Christian presuppositions about existence and values. He notes that Anselm seeks not to understand that he may believe, but to believe that he may understand. To Frame, this captures something of a "presuppositionalism of the heart."[68] He concludes that the ontological argument is either a Christian presuppositional argument (and thus reducible to Frame's moral argument), or it is worthless.[69]

PROVING THE GOSPEL

Frame points out that while many divine attributes are clearly seen in creation (Rom 1:18-20) the message of the gospel is not (Rom 10:14-15). Scripture argues for its own credibility, and we ourselves needn't accept it on blind faith.

Frame takes as his starting point a Christian worldview, which he has established by his theistic arguments. These arguments demonstrate absolute-personality theism, found mainly in the biblical tradition or in traditions affected by it. If the absolute personality cares about humans, and the moral argument implies that he does, we would expect that he would make himself known. And "the Bible is the only major religious book which claims to fulfill that expectation, which claims to be the place where God presents his case to man."[70] In a claim that reminds us of Van Til, Frame says that there are really only two religions, so we do not need to study every world religion and philosophy. We are faced with either the wisdom of God or the wisdom of the world (1 Cor 1:18–2:16), so "in that sense, then, our theistic arguments have already settled the truth of the gospel, the total message of Scripture. Since there is no other logical candidate for a source of God's words, we must hear and obey that message."[71] But since he

---

[67]Ibid., p. 113.
[68]Ibid., p. 117.
[69]Ibid., p. 118.
[70]Ibid., p. 121. He maintains that a number of religions depend on the Bible yet distort its message, including Islam, modern Judaism, Roman Catholicism, Mormonism, Seventh-day Adventism, Christian Science and more (n. 2).
[71]Ibid., p. 121.

knows this particular argument will not convince many people, Frame pursues other evidence for the truth of the Bible.

Frame points out two ways to interpret Scripture, (1) in light of what it says about itself, which is the view of believers by the enablement of the Holy Spirit; or (2) as any other book. He claims that in traditional apologetics, "inquirers are told not to presuppose the full authority of Scripture as God's Word until after that authority has been proved by the apologist."[72] The impulse to examine Scripture without presupposing that it is supernatural got going about the year 1650, and has continued unabated. But Scripture's teaching about itself is credible, since "no other doctrine is compatible with absolute-personality theism." If God is revealing himself in the Bible, it has supreme authority, "and just as it cannot be disproved by something else of greater authority, so it cannot be proved in such a way. God's Word, like himself, must be supremely authoritative and therefore self-attesting."[73] This doctrine is taught by both the biblical writers and Jesus.

The Spirit does not work "magically," but through reasons, therefore, "the Spirit's work is not to persuade us of something for which there are no rational grounds, but rather to persuade us by illumining the rational grounds which obligate us to believe. Spirit-created faith is not 'blind.'"[74] God gives reasons and so should we.

A major line of evidence is prophecy, which involves the whole Old Testament, and there is the extensive witness to Christ in the New Testament. God also worked through miracles in biblical times, though we must be aware that today we have only the biblical testimony of miracles. Also, Scripture warns of the limits of miracles to persuade, which is brought up in the story of the man in hell who wants to warn his brothers but is told that if they did not believe Moses and the prophets they would not believe if someone rose from the dead (Lk 16:31). Yet Thomas believes in Jesus because of a miracle, and even John wrote about Jesus' miracles, expecting that people would believe because of them—even though like us today they would have only his written record of events (Jn 20:31). The greatest miracle is the resurrection, which Frame says is the "foundation stone of traditional Christian apologetics, and this is in general

---

[72]Ibid., p. 127.
[73]Ibid., p. 135.
[74]Ibid., p. 136.

an area where I do not differ from that tradition."[75] He recommends the works of classical apologist William Lane Craig and evidentialist Gary Habermas.[76]

Still, Frame emphasizes the biblical record as the main evidence. He revisits the interpretation of 1 Corinthians 15, in which Paul offers the eyewitness testimony of over five hundred people, most of whom were still living at the time (1 Cor 15:6). While Paul does appeal to the witnesses to establish the truth of the resurrection, "Paul's point is rather that the testimony to the resurrection was part of the apostolic preaching and is therefore to be accepted as part of that apostolic testimony."[77] The evidences come to us "with God's own authority," and "Paul asks the church to believe the evidence because it is part of the authoritative apostolic preaching."[78] An additional argument for the resurrection is that if the resurrection is denied, "the whole doctrinal content of Christianity must also be denied (vv. 12-19)."[79]

PERSPECTIVALISM

Frame has constructed his own extensive and innovative view of apologetics. It not only links apologetics with ethics but also develops the idea that as non-omniscient beings we see things from different perspectives that can be unified into a more holistic view of the world. Whereas Alvin Plantinga is convinced that we have no ethical duties to believe or disbelieve anything (partly on the grounds that what we believe is not under our direct control), Frame believes that epistemology is best regarded as a subdivision of ethics in that it describes our "obligations in the realm of knowledge,"[80] what we ought and ought not believe.[81] The connection between ethics and epistemology reinforces the centrality of presuppositions in that every belief presupposes an ethical value

---

[75]Ibid., p. 145.

[76]Specifically, William Lane Craig, *Apologetics: An Introduction* (Chicago: Moody Press, 1984), pp. 167–206; and Craig, *Knowing the Truth About the Resurrection* (Ann Arbor, MI: Servant Books, 1988). Also Gary Habermas and Antony G. N. Flew, *Did Jesus Rise from the Dead?*, ed. Terry L. Miethe (San Francisco: Harper & Row, 1987). Flew was an atheist at the time of the debate. In "Presuppositional Apologetics," p. 229 n. 42, he adds Josh McDowell, *Evidence That Demands a Verdict* (San Bernardino, CA: Here's Life, 1979), pp. 179–263.

[77]Frame, *Doctrine of the Knowledge of God*, p. 146. A similar point is made in Frame, *Apologetics to the Glory of God*, p. 58.

[78]W. C. Campbell-Jack and Gavin McGrath, eds., *New Dictionary of Christian Apologetics* (Leicester, England: Inter-Varsity Press, 2006), pp. 141–45.

[79]Frame, *Doctrine of the Knowledge of God*, p. 146.

[80]Ibid., pp. 73–74.

[81]Ibid., p. 109.

judgment, a claim to an ethical obligation or right to believe something. Thus there are no ethically neutral knowledge claims, only those that assume godly ethical standards and those that do not.[82]

That we can have different perspectives does not mean that all perspectives are somehow equal, nor that as we ourselves increasingly try to see things from different perspectives (such as when we walk all around a tree, or get input from someone) that they will begin to agree with everyone else's. People's perspectives will agree insofar as they embody the truth, and insofar as we can enrich each other by sharing the truth we have, knowledge can be a communal effort.

God's perspective encompasses all true perspectives, plus he sees things in ways we cannot. He sometimes gives us the benefit of various true perspectives, such as those of divinely inspired human perspectives of the four Gospels, and Kings and Chronicles.

There can be many of these simultaneously true, compatible and overlapping perspectives. You cannot have one perspective without the other, and with each you have the others. There can be a number of perspectives. Frame believes, for example, that the Ten Commandments are actually ten such perspectives on human life. But he and his longtime friend professor Vern Poythress see special significance in three perspectives. The Trinity constitutes three perspectives, though of course it is also much more in that it is three persons in one Godhead. Within the Trinity, "the Father is the supreme authority, the Son is the executive power, and the Spirit the divine presence who dwells in and with God's people."[83] Redemption reflects these in that there is "an authoritative plan, an effectual accomplishment, and a gracious application." In divine lordship, we have the same elements: divine authority, power and presence with his people. Revelation has a threefold perspective: general revelation, special revelation and revelation within the human heart (illumination, the testimony of the Spirit). Similarly, he finds triads in the offices of Christ and salvation.

In knowledge, there is sense experience, reason and feeling—three elements that secular philosophies have difficulty integrating. We sense the world God made and controls, the norm is God's revelation, and the subject is the knower in relation to God. Each contains the others: "Every item of true human knowledge is the application of God's authoritative norm to a fact of creation,

---

[82]Ibid., p. 109.
[83]John M. Frame, "A Primer on Perspectivalism," *Frame and Poythress* website, May 14, 2008, http://www.frame-poythress.org/a-primer-on-perspectivalism-revised-2008/.

by a person in God's image. Take away one of those, and there is no knowledge at all."[84] In the normative perspective, we ask, what do God's norms direct us to believe? In the situational, we ask, what are the facts? In the existential, we ask, what belief is most satisfying to a believing heart? Not only does each question help us answer the others, but they are also related in an overlapping way. The normative perspective contains all of reality because all reality is general revelation to us. The situational contains all reality because it is our whole environment. The existential contains everything because it is all of our experience. The normative includes the situational and existential in that

> to think according to God's norms is to take every fact (situational) and every experience (existential) into account. It is also true that the situational perspective includes the normative (for norms are facts) and the existential (for experiences are facts). And the existential includes the normative and the situational, for the norms and facts are aspects of our experience.[85]

The Bible is not merely one of the three perspectives (e.g., not the normative), but "it is a particular object within all three perspectives given to us by God to serve as the ultimate standard of human thought and life." It "governs all perspectives and determines how we should use them."[86]

When Frame refers to a "fact" he means a state of affairs, not merely a thing. He says, "States of affairs include things, together with their properties and relations to other things." Things can be designated by nouns, but states of affairs require sentences. Aristotle regarded reality as a collection of things, but Ludwig Wittgenstein (1889–1951) added that we must know their relationships. Alfred North Whitehead (1861–1947) further added that knowing reality requires knowing processes.[87] When Frame says that facts and interpretation are one, he really means that statements of facts and interpretations are one. A statement of fact is an assertion of some state of affairs, such as, "The chair is blue." Statements of facts are interpretations of reality. Therefore, a statement of fact may be true or false.

Frame integrates into apologetics both the principle of noncontradiction and

---

[84]Ibid.
[85]Ibid.
[86]Ibid.
[87]Frame, *Doctrine of the Knowledge of God*, pp. 99–100; see Ludwig Wittgenstein, *Tractatus Logico-Philosophicus*, trans. C. K. Ogden (New York: Routledge & K. Paul, 1992), sec. 1.1: "The World Is the Totality of Facts, Not of Things." Alfred North Whitehead, *Science and the Modern World* (New York: Macmillan, 1925; reprint, New York: Simon & Schuster; The Free Press, 1967), p. 72.

the internal knowledge of God. Together they solve the problem of how to handle a view that competes with Christianity. For example, the Muslim says the Qur'an is the Word of God, and the Christian says that the Bible is the Word of God. Like Van Til, Frame believes that all proof is ultimately circular (which, we saw above, he argues is not a problem if the circle is big enough). Frame says that, first, the Christian rejects Islam not arbitrarily but on the basis of God's revelation. Second, "our rejection of Islam is cogent for the same reasons that Christianity is cogent." Third, a broadly circular argument for Christianity will show that it is internally consistent, or holds together, in a way that will not be found in the competing view: "The non-Christian will be unable to maintain his system consistently, and he will rely on Christian concepts at crucial points."[88] Fourth, "because the Muslim is made in the image of God, at some level he is able to see the cogency of the Christian circle and the implausibility of his own."[89] It is similar to dealing with a paranoid person who reinterprets everything in a sinister way. In contrast with traditional apologetics, Frame says that you would not adopt a neutral position in order to convince him. Instead, "you simply proclaim the truth, together with the arguments for that truth (its rationale). You assume that no matter how ingenious the paranoid may be at assimilating your data into his system, he still 'knows' at some level, or at least is capable of knowing, that he is wrong and that you are right."[90]

Considering presuppositions versus conclusions to arguments, Frame finds there is no logical difference. In an argument, belief in the premises commits you to believe in the conclusion, and it also commits you to believe in what the premises presuppose. "Logically then, presuppositions are one kind of conclusion," Frame says. Psychologically, we believe the presuppositions of a premise more firmly than the actual premises.[91]

For Frame, insofar as belief in God is a presupposition, it is not merely basic, as Plantinga maintains (more on Plantinga's views later). The difference is that a presupposition governs our other beliefs, including what we accept as evidence and as valid arguments. As such it is not defeasible, that is, "not subject to rebuttal by evidence and argument unless another contrary presupposition is adopted."[92]

---

[88]Frame, *Doctrine of the Knowledge of God*, p. 132.
[89]Ibid.
[90]Ibid.
[91]Frame, *Apologetics to the Glory of God*, p. 105 n. 21.
[92]John M. Frame, "Reflections of a Lifetime Theologian: An Extended Interview with John M. Frame," in Hughes, *Speaking the Truth in Love*, p. 86.

CRITICISMS

While Frame believes that presuppositionalism is a more profound interpretation of Reformed convictions than Alvin Plantinga's Reformed epistemology, Plantinga himself thinks presuppositionalism is a "groping, implicit, inchoate" attempt at a view. Classical apologist William Lane Craig agrees.[93] Like many critics, he takes issue with the appeal to a circular argument, assuming Christian theism in some sense in order to prove it. Nevertheless, he believes presuppositionalism's central concept, the transcendental argument, can be very powerful. As we know, the term was coined by Immanuel Kant (1724–1804), who argued that the categories we use when we think are preconditions of rationality such that even an attempt to deny them would have to use them. He argued for a reality on grounds such that even a denial of it would have to assume it. Though Frame embraces this approach, Craig says that in his chapter in *Five Views on Apologetics*, Frame comes the closest to using a transcendental approach only when he says that we "should present the biblical God, not merely as the conclusion to an argument, but as the one who makes argument possible."[94] But then he fails to develop the argument. Instead, Craig says that Frame confuses a transcendental argument with what the medievals called *demonstratio quia*, "proof that proceeds from consequence to ground."[95] Richard G. Howe believes presuppositionalists frequently confuse the two, and arguments from consequence to ground are the turf of classical apologetics. For example, when the presuppositionalist argues that only Christian theism can ground morality, that is not a transcendental argument because morality is not necessary to deny morality. It is again arguing from consequence to ground.[96] Don Collett clarifies[97] that the transcendental approach is indeed unique in that it argues that *a*

---

[93]William Lane Craig, "Classical Apologetics," in Cowan, *Five Views on Apologetics*, p. 232.

[94]Frame, "Presuppositional Apologetics," p. 220; quoted by Craig in "A Classical Apologist's Response," in Cowan, *Five Views on Apologetics*, p. 233.

[95]Craig, "A Classical Apologist's Response" [to Frame], p. 233. He cites Thomas Aquinas, *Summa Theologiae* 1 a.2.2.

[96]Richard G. Howe, "Some Brief Critical Thoughts on Presuppositionalism," *The Virtual Office of Richard G. Howe, Ph.D.*, http://richardghowe.com/Presuppositionalism.pdf; adapted from chap. three of his doctoral dissertation, "A Defense of Thomas Aquinas' Second Way" (University of Arkansas, Fayetteville, n.d.), p. 11.

[97]Don Collett, "Van Til and Transcendental Argument Revisited," Trinity School for Ministry website, www.tsm.edu/sites/default/files/Faculty%20Writings/Collett%20-%20Van%20Til%20 and%20Transcendental%20Argument%20Revisited.pdf. This is an updated version of "Van Til and Transcendental Argument," *Westminster Theological Journal* 65, no. 2 (Fall 2003): 289–306. Page numbers are to the updated, online edition. Or see Donald Collett, "Van and Transcendental Argument Revisited," in Hughes, *Speaking the Truth in Love*, pp. 460–88.

presupposes *b* if *b* is a necessary precondition of the truth or falsity of *a*.[98] Put another way, *a* presupposes *b* if and only if *a* is neither true nor false unless *b* is true.[99] So a transcendental argument can work whether premises are true or false, because it focuses on the ground of the premises, not on whether they are true or false. Traditional arguments depend on premises being true. Van Til argues that he definitely uses the transcendental approach: "No human being can utter a single syllable, whether in negation or affirmation, unless it were for God's existence."[100] That approach is clearly different from the reasoning used by traditional apologetics.

Frame accepts the difference[101] but still insists—in sharp contrast to Van Til,[102] Bahnsen and others—that traditional apologetic reasoning can serve presuppositionalist goals. Using the concept that God's existence is a necessary ground for logic, Frame suggests one way to argue in a more traditional way with a presuppositional goal:

If predication is possible, then logic is reliable.

If logic is reliable, then God exists.

Therefore, if predication is possible, God exists.

Frame points out the usefulness of even the simple traditional argument known as *modus ponens*:

If predication is possible, then God exists.

Predication is possible.

Therefore God exists.

---

[98]Following Peter Strawson, *Introduction to Logical Theory* (London: Methuen, 1952), p. 175; Collett, "Van Til and Transcendental Argument Revisited," p. 24.

[99]Following Bas C. van Fraasen, "Presupposition, Implication, and Self-Reference," *Journal of Philosophy* (1968): 137; Collett, "Van Til and Transcendental Argument Revisited," p. 25.

[100]Cornelius Van Til, *A Survey of Christian Epistemology* (Phillipsburg, NJ: P & R, 1969), p. 11; quoted in Collett, "Van Til and Transcendental Argument Revisited," p. 12.

[101]John Frame, "Reply to Don Collett on Transcendental Argument," *Westminster Theological Journal*, 65 (2003): 307.

[102]Collett points out that Van Til knew some were saying his transcendental method is reducible to traditional reasoning, as Frame is today. Cornelius Van Til, *A Survey of Christian Epistemology* (Phillipsburg, NJ: P & R, 1969), p. 9; quoted in Collett, "Van Til and Transcendental Argument Revisited," p. 23.

Or, what looks more like Van Til's transcendental approach, the traditional argument form *modus tollens*:

If predication is possible, then God exists.

God does not exist.

Therefore, it is not the case that predication is possible.

Because we can reject the conclusion as absurd, it can function rather like a reductio ad absurdum, disproving what brought us to the absurdity. That is because what is absurd cannot be true, so whatever entails an absurdity cannot be true. That is the essence of a reductio argument. Recall that Van Til believed the approach to be the correct way to show non-Christian views to be false.

But this is where we see the possible implications of a fine point that could determine whether Frame can broaden presuppositionalism to include traditional apologetic arguments. Collett says that the *modus tollens* argument is not, strictly speaking, equivalent to a transcendental argument, because of course the argument depends on predication working in order to state the argument; simply put, statements have to have meaning in order to make an argument. But Collett points out that Van Til's transcendental argument is that there is no predication without God, so not even a *modus tollens* argument would work. Yet Frame claims we could construct a traditional argument that says, because we really do have *x*, then we must have God (e.g., we really do have predication, logic, morality and causality). Collett says Van Til's approach is more radical, and claims that if we don't have God then we can't form an argument of any kind since predication will not work at all—not even to form the argument.

Frame concedes that there are differences between a transcendental argument and traditional reasoning, but insists that a person could use traditional arguments and maintain presuppositionalism if they deny both that there is any valid thought apart from God (i.e., we cannot think autonomously) and that there is any neutral ground.[103] Frame says, "I think apologetics needs to have a transcendental direction or goal: we should be concerned to show that God is the condition of all meaning, and our epistemology should be consistent with that conclusion. But that conclusion cannot be reached in a single, simple syllogism. A

---

[103]Frame, "Reply to Don Collett," p. 309. He suspects that Collett would agree with him, based on email correspondence between them (p. 309 n. 4).

transcendental argument normally, perhaps always, requires many subarguments, and some of these may be traditional theistic proofs or Christian evidences."[104]

THINKING IT OVER

1. Who influenced John Frame?

2. What does Frame mean by a "movement," and how does he regard them? What is his attitude toward Van Til as a person? As a thinker?

3. What stipulation does Frame make regarding the verification of our interpretation of facts with the contents of the mind?

4. Explain what is meant by the distance between interpretation and fact. What does it have to do with apologetic methods?

5. How does Frame view the question of our knowledge versus God's knowledge (see Van Til vs. Clark), and why does the issue matter?

6. Can the believer and nonbeliever know the same thing?

7. What is meant by "incommensurable"?

8. In what ways does Frame think Van Til overstated the difference between presuppositional and nonpresuppositional apologetics? What constitutes a transcendental approach for Frame?

9. What does Frame think is the problem with the transcendental argument as Van Til stated it?

10. How does Frame regard induction?

11. Why does Frame regard a presupposition as "the most certain thing we know"?

12. How does Frame justify belief in Scripture? Can we use extrabiblical evidence?

13. What does Frame mean by "biblical foundationalism," and how does it differ from foundationalism?

14. Compare strong, modest and weak foundationalism.

15. For both Frame and Van Til, what can the apologist appeal to besides argument?

16. How does Frame differ from Van Til on the issue of indirect versus direct arguments?

17. If Frame does not limit presuppositional apologetics to deduction and indirect

---

[104]Frame, "Presuppositional Apologetics," p. 360.

arguments, what for him constitutes a presuppositional approach?

18. Summarize Frame's view of proofs for the existence of God.

19. What does Frame think of the Van Tillian idea that there are really only two religions?

20. What is Frame's view of prophecy and miracles?

21. How does Frame emphasize the biblical record?

22. Summarize Frame's view of perspectivalism.

23. What does Frame mean by a "fact"? How are they interpretations of reality?

24. How could the Christian approach the Muslim, for example?

25. What is the difference between a presupposition and a basic belief (cf. Plantinga)?

26. How does William Lane Craig clarify a transcendental argument? What does he say about Frame's use of the term?

KEY TERMS

Biblical foundationalism. The Bible contains knowledge for which we can have certainty. Frame believes that more traditional forms of foundationalism, which hold that some things outside the Bible can be known with certainty, represent an illegitimate attempt to find certainty outside of Scripture.

Perspectivalism. Nonomniscient beings can have many simultaneously true, compatible and overlapping perspectives. You cannot have one perspective without the other, and with each you have the others. God's perspective encompasses all true perspectives.

Transcendental argument. For Frame, such argument is an overall goal that must be reached through many subarguments. We cannot, with one argument, prove the Christian God because his unique attributes are not necessary for predication and knowledge.

GOING FURTHER

Frame, John M. *Apologetics to the Glory of God: An Introduction.* Phillipsburg, NJ: P & R, 1994.

———. *Cornelius Van Til: An Analysis of His Thought.* Phillipsburg, NJ: P & R, 1995.

———. *The Doctrine of God.* Phillipsburg, NJ: P & R, 2002.

———. *The Doctrine of the Knowledge of God.* Phillipsburg, NJ: P & R, 1987.

———. "Presuppositional Apologetics." In *Five Views on Apologetics,* edited by Steven B. Cowan, pp. 207–31. Grand Rapids: Zondervan, 2000.

Hughes, John J., ed. *Speaking the Truth in Love: The Theology of John M. Frame.* Phillipsburg, NJ: P & R, 2009.

– 5 –

ALVIN PLANTINGA

Belief in God is an immediate
awareness, and belief in
Christianity is a gift of God

Few contemporary apologists are as widely known as Alvin Plantinga, whom *Time* magazine called "America's leading orthodox Protestant philosopher of God."[1] The article notes that in a "quiet revolution," God is making a comeback, "in the crisp, intellectual circles of academic philosophers, where the consensus had long banished the Almighty from fruitful discourse."

Belief in God got little respect in philosophical circles as recently as the 1970s, when I majored in philosophy. When I asked one of my professors where I could go to study philosophy of religion on a graduate level, I was met with a blank look, then the suggestion that I consider going to a seminary. One person told me politely that (real) philosophers don't look into those kinds of questions.

But Plantinga was one force that changed all that. (William Lane Craig was another.) Rather than speak only to those who already hold his theological views, he has rigorously engaged the philosophical community through conferences, journals and academic presses. As he urges other believers to do in his "Advice to Christian Philosophers,"[2] he has both pursued philosophical topics

---

[1] "Modernizing the Case for God," *Time*, April 7, 1980, p. 66.
[2] Reprinted in James F. Sennett, ed., *The Analytic Theist: An Alvin Plantinga Reader* (Grand Rapids: Eerdmans, 1998), pp. 296–315.

that interest both him and other Christians, and he has built philosophically on his uniquely Christian assumptions and worldview. He did not confine himself to what the philosophical community regarded as interesting, nor did he proceed only from common ground with non-Christian thinkers.

A major thrust of his early apologetic work was to show that Christian belief can be rational even if unsupported by traditional evidence, there being in his view no adequate, noncircular arguments to be had for belief in God. Yet he has never regarded faith as a fideistic leap. Rather, it is a kind of knowledge that can be had immediately because of the way we are created and the action of the Holy Spirit, producing in us what Calvin called the *sensus divinitatus*—an intellectually grounded but noninferential awareness of the divine (which he admits is strongest for him when engaged in his beloved mountaineering).[3]

Born in 1932, he traces his roots on both sides of the family back to the *Afscheiding*, or Dutch religious succession of 1834, whose participants endured a great deal of persecution. Abraham Kuyper eventually emerged as a leading luminary of the movement. Plantinga's father was a professor of psychology at Calvin College, where Alvin became a student. Later, at Harvard, he encountered for the first time undeniably intelligent people who regarded his views with contempt, an experience that at first made him question his own beliefs. Two events helped him resolve his doubts. One gloomy night he was walking back to his room and he felt the overpowering presence of God.

> I suddenly saw or perhaps felt with great clarity and persuasion and conviction that the Lord was really there and was all I had thought. The effects of this experience lingered for a long time; I was still caught up in arguments about the existence of God, but they often seemed to me merely academic, of little existential concern, as if one were to argue about whether there has really been a past, for example, or whether there really were other people, as opposed to cleverly constructed robots.[4]

The second event occurred during a trip home, when he attended three class sessions taught by philosophy professor Harry Jellema at Calvin College. He was so impressed with his command of the subject and confidence in traditional Christianity that Plantinga decided to leave Harvard and return to Calvin, a

---

[3]Alvin Plantinga, "A Christian Life Partly Lived," in *Philosophers Who Believe: The Spiritual Journeys of Eleven Leading Thinkers*, ed. Kelly James Clark (Downers Grove, IL: InterVarsity Press, 1993), p. 61.
[4]Ibid., pp. 51-52.

decision he credits with shaping his entire academic direction and life. From his studies he took away the conviction that objections to Christianity are largely the outworking of non-Christian intellectual commitments. If that is the case, there is no such thing as neutral academics—a view he shares with Kuyper and Van Til. (Something Plantinga has said he regrets about Calvin College is a problem he finds in Christianity generally: a tendency to fight and sneer at each other instead of focusing on the real opponents outside.)[5]

When Plantinga finished his education he taught at Wayne State University in Detroit, then at Calvin for nineteen years and finally at Notre Dame (though a Catholic institution, the philosophy of religion program has many evangelicals), from which he recently retired. In all he has played an enormous part in shaping the next generation of theists and Christian thinkers.

In his first book, *God and Other Minds*,[6] Plantinga sought to answer the prevailing challenge to Christianity: that it is not believable because it lacks sufficient evidence. The challenge assumes an evidentialist approach to belief and proof, that to be rational our beliefs must have sufficient evidence, and, as a corollary, that our beliefs must be proportioned to the amount of evidence. This view, reflected in John Locke (1632–1704) and classically stated by W. K. Clifford (1845–1879),[7] casts belief and justification in terms of duty. Just as we have ethical duties, we have epistemic duties to form or not form beliefs under certain conditions.

In epistemology, evidentialism is the view that rational beliefs are those that can be supported by reasons or evidence of some kind. It is broader than what is referred to as evidentialism in apologetics, which is the view that Christianity can be supported in a one-step strategy, by appealing, for example, to a body of evidence for the resurrection and the believability of Scripture.[8] Apologetic evidentialists need not be epistemological evidentialists if for example they hold that it is rational to believe in Christianity with or without evidence. Evidence can be divided into propositional and nonpropositional types, the latter being things like intuition or Calvin's *sensus divinitatis*. Epistemological evidentialists

---

[5]Ibid., pp. 57–58.
[6]Alvin Plantinga, *God and Other Minds: A Study in the Rational Justification of Belief in God* (Ithaca, NY: Cornell University Press, 1967; 2nd ed., 1990). After developing his ideas for many years, Plantinga said with characteristic humility and a touch of humor, "From my present vantage point, *God and Other Minds* looks like a promising attempt by someone a little long on chutzpah but a little short on epistemology." Alvin Plantinga, "Afterword," in Sennett, *The Analytic Theist*, p. 353.
[7]"It is wrong, always, everywhere, and for anyone to believe anything upon insufficient evidence." W. K. Clifford, *Lectures and Essays* (London: Macmillan, 1901), p. 183.
[8]In this book, *evidentialism* refers to the apologetic view unless otherwise noted.

generally want to see propositional support, that is, roughly, statements about the way things are (more technically, "propositions") that can be taken to support the belief in question. In other words, they want to see an argument that supports the belief. Absent that, a belief is a matter of blind faith, or something like a hunch, but could not be called a rational conviction.

Rather than accept the evidentialists' requirements by attempting to construct a traditional argument for Christianity, Plantinga challenged the entire notion of traditional proof as the primary basis for belief. He pointed out that there are plenty of beliefs that we deem rationally acceptable even though we have little evidence for them. For one, we believe that other people have minds like ours and that they are not merely sophisticated robots. We also believe the world was not created a few minutes ago with apparent age, rings in trees, memories intact and so on. We would have a great deal of trouble proving either of these, yet we and others accept them—and clearly, we are rational for doing so. If it is rationally acceptable to believe those things without evidence, why can't it be rationally acceptable to believe in God or Christianity without evidence?[9] Arguments for the existence of God are not strong enough to be decisive, but neither are arguments against the existence of God. The attempt to set up requirements for rationality that rule out belief in God are very likely to also rule out beliefs even the objector wants to retain.

A few years later, in "Is Belief in God Rational?,"[10] he argued for his view more explicitly in terms of foundationalism. To review a bit and go further, according to foundationalism, we can rightly hold some beliefs without support from other beliefs, that is, without proof. Thus not every belief has to be supported. Not every belief has to be a conclusion, or an inference from other beliefs. We know our foot hurts not because we conclude it based on how big the rock was that fell on it. We just know it hurts. We know it without arguments or conclusions from other beliefs about rocks, inertia, feet and so on. We know that the lights are on in the room not because we reason that the switch on the wall is in the "on" position, or that we saw someone turn the lights on, or that we would not be able to see if the lights were not on. We just know the lights are on. We could come up with reasons why our foot hurts, or why we believe the lights are

---

[9]In an autobiographical chapter, Plantinga notes, amusingly, that when his wife heard his thesis that belief in God and belief in other minds are "in the same epistemological boat," she thought it "was one of the sillier things she had heard." Plantinga, "A Christian Life Partly Lived," p. 60. But in the field of religious epistemology, it was taken quite seriously.

[10]Alvin Plantinga, "Is Belief in God Rational?," in *Rationality and Religious Belief*, ed. C. Delaney (Notre Dame, IN: University of Notre Dame Press), pp. 7–27.

on, but we don't need to. We know those things without reasons. They are not inferences from other things we know.

So according to foundationalism, some things are known without support from other beliefs, while other things are known because we conclude them from other beliefs. For example we know the power is on in the building because we know the lights are on in the room. That the power is on is thus a conclusion based on knowing that the lights are on. But we do not know the lights are on because of another belief; we know it directly from our perceptions. Beliefs that are not conclusions from other beliefs are called basic beliefs.

A belief that is basic need not be a groundless assumption nor held out of sheer commitment. We may have good grounds for believing that our foot hurts, or that the lights are on, even if they are more like intuitions than conclusions. Basic beliefs are basic not because they are groundless but because they do not need to be supported by other propositions. For Plantinga the existence of God can be a legitimate basic belief, what he calls "properly" basic. That does not mean there are no arguments for the existence of God, nor that the theist should not try to show his or her beliefs are rational. Plantinga wants to show that theists are not irrational even if they are unable to demonstrate their beliefs conclusively from premises accepted by opponents.

Epistemological evidentialists generally also hold that to be intellectually responsible we should believe what is well supported, we should not be highly committed to beliefs that have no support and we should resist beliefs that are highly suspect in that there are many reasons not to believe them. So to believe that the Holocaust never happened would be rationally irresponsible if we recognize that there is considerable evidence that it took place and very little reason to conclude that it did not. In light of the evidence, the rational person would resist the conclusion that it never happened. To be highly committed to the belief that Hitler is alive and living in Brazil would also be irrational if there is little evidence for it. This leads to the idea that there are intellectual virtues, or doxastic virtues. This links beliefs and morals. Consequently, a problematic belief such as racial prejudice would not only be mistaken but also immoral. It also entails that there are epistemic duties, that is, things we should and should not believe.

Talk of epistemic virtues and duties assumes that we have some control over our beliefs, a view called doxastic voluntarism. Critics of the view object that we cannot will to have or not have beliefs. If we do not believe someone is knocking at the door, no amount of willing can change that. And if our will is not involved, it cannot be a moral issue. But while direct voluntarism claims that we can decide what we believe, indirect voluntarism says only that we can decide to expose ourselves to arguments and evidence for a viewpoint and hence that we have some indirect control over our beliefs.

Plantinga came to question the whole notion that rationality is a matter of believing what we ought. He argues that belief in God violates no intellectual duty or epistemic obligation even if it is not based on evidence in the form of propositions. Not only are we rational to believe in other minds, whatever our reasons may be, but we are also rational to hold some beliefs on the basis of, for example, our memories. When we remember something we do not take the content of that memory as propositional evidence; we simply recall, and believe, for example, that we had cereal for breakfast.

Plantinga called his view "Reformed epistemology" because he wanted to make an explicit connection to his Reformed tradition. Not everyone was happy with the name, and he later regretted it himself, since some mistook it for an affront to non-Reformed views like Catholicism.[11] As we will see, he came to hold that on apologetics the views of Calvin and Aquinas are not far apart.

Plantinga also began to take issue with classical foundationalism,[12] a view popular at least since the Enlightenment. On the classical view, not just any belief can be taken as basic—that is, can be believed by itself, without the support of another belief. René Descartes (1596–1650) held that beliefs that are clear and distinct can be basic. Such beliefs are self-evident and incorrigible, in that they cannot be doubted. If our clear and distinct ideas do not give us truth, Descartes reasoned, God would be a deceiver, and he is not. So it seems for Descartes that our basic beliefs cannot be wrong. Locke added sense perceptions to the list of potential basic beliefs.

Whereas Descartes seemed to think that our nonbasic beliefs should be connected ultimately to our basic beliefs through deduction (i.e., airtight reasoning, a very rigorous requirement) Locke allowed them to be connected through induction, that is, on the basis of likelihood. C. S. Peirce (1839–1914) added abduction, by which a conclusion is accepted because it is the best explanation for something. Classical foundationalism, then, requires that a belief be either basic, in which case it is either self-evident, incorrigible or

---

[11]Plantinga, "Afterword," in Sennett, *The Analytic Theist*, p. 354 n. 4.

[12]Alvin Plantinga, "Reason and Belief in God," *Faith and Rationality: Reason and Belief in God*, ed. Alvin Plantinga and Nicholas Wolterstorff (Notre Dame, IN: University of Notre Dame Press, 1983), pp. 16–93. For this theme in his later work, see Plantinga, *Warranted Christian Belief* (New York: Oxford University Press, 2000), pp. 82–85.

evident to the senses; or nonbasic, in which case it is ultimately connected to basic beliefs by deduction, induction or abduction.

One problem with this approach to knowledge is that it rules out many propositions that we legitimately take as basic, such as that I had lunch today, which is something I know from memory, not from other propositions. Another problem with classical foundationalism is that it cannot meet its own requirements. The view itself is not self-evident, incorrigible or evident to the senses; so it is not basic. But neither has any classical foundationalist been able to make an argument that has basic premises and proves classical foundationalism using deduction, induction or abduction. Plantinga concludes therefore that the view is "self-referentially inconsistent."[13]

Plantinga does not abandon foundationalism altogether, but insists that its criteria for what is basic are too narrow. Why accept as basic only those propositions that are self-evident, incorrigible or evident to the senses? Why can't belief in God be properly basic? If we can legitimately believe—without propositional evidence—in other minds, that the past goes back more than five minutes and that we had lunch, then why can't the theist believe in God on the same basis?

This is where Plantinga appeals to Calvin's *sensus divinitatis*, that awareness which all humans have of God through interaction with nature and their conscience. We are born with a capacity rather than actual content (like the ability to do arithmetic), and our experiences stimulate that awareness of God. Just what triggers it differs from one person to another. It may be the night sky, a sunset, the surf or an open field.[14] A sense of guilt might also give rise to a sense of God as the one who is displeased. The beliefs "just arise" within us; "they are occasioned by the circumstances, they are not conclusions from them."[15] It is not an inference in the sense that we see the starry sky and take it as evidence for the conclusion that God exists. We simply know God exists. It is similar to sense perception in that we do not take our seeing the starry sky as evidence for the conclusion that the starry sky itself exists; we see it and simply believe it is there, we do not conclude it is there. The *sensus divinitatis* is thus like "perception, memory, and a priori belief."[16]

To explain this crucial point in Plantinga a bit further, there are two ways to claim

---

[13]Plantinga, "Reason and Belief in God," p. 60. Plantinga is not arguing merely that classical foundationalism is wrong because it is not basic (as basic is described by classical foundationalism itself). The problem in his view is that, additionally, neither can it be shown from premises that are basic.

[14]Plantinga, *Warranted Christian Belief*, pp. 173-74.

[15]Ibid., p. 175.

[16]Ibid.

that our encounter with nature yields an awareness of God. One common view is that we see something in nature and we conclude there must be a God. We see, for example, that there is order in nature and we conclude there must be an orderer. That there is order in the universe is the premise, and the existence of an orderer is the conclusion, so we are making an inference. To use another example, we realize that everything around us could not come into being from nothing so we conclude there must be a creator. According to the competing view, held by Plantinga, our encounter with the world produces an immediate awareness in us that is not a conclusion. We see majestic mountains and we simply know God exists. It is an intuition, not a reasoning process by which we draw a conclusion. On this view the awareness of God is the result of the work of the Holy Spirit and the way we are made.

Plantinga's view that our awareness of God is an intuition rather than an inference is what allows him to say that it is basic. Recall that basic beliefs are not conclusions from other beliefs. They are simply there, like our awareness that the lights are on. Therefore if seeing order in nature gives rise to our idea that God exists without providing evidence for it—if the view that God exists is not a conclusion from the order but more like an intuition that arises when we see the order—then it can be part of the foundation for our thinking. It can be properly basic.

Plantinga points out a possible direction in which his model could be developed, which fits a nuance suggested by Aquinas. The role of the *sensus divinitatis* could enable us to see the truth of a crucial premise in a "quick" theistic argument, such as, "The heavens can be gloriously beautiful only if God has created them."[17] In Aquinas, knowledge of God can be "immediate" (an intuition) but also an inference. Thus the *sensus divinitatis* could be the means by which we see the truth of a premise. This would be significant because in an argument the conclusion is said to be true assuming the premises are true. But how do we prove the premises? We may need additional support for one or more of them, from additional arguments, which may include appeals to expert testimony, common sense, memory—or intuition, which can be provided by the *sensus divinitatis*. If so, it may remove the need for a backwards chain of arguments to support premises.

While foundationalism holds that some beliefs can be justified without being conclusions from other beliefs, the competing view is coherentism. Plantinga

---

[17]Ibid., p. 176. All of the quote was italicized in the original. For suggestions on how his model could be developed in the direction of the *sensus divinitatis* providing support for a premise, he recommends Michael Sudduth, "Prospects for 'Mediate' Natural Theology in John Calvin," *Religious Studies* 31, no. 1 (March 1995): 53.

says, "There is considerable confusion as to what coherentism is and no generally accepted account of the relevant coherence relations."[18] One suggestion has been that a proposition coheres with a set of beliefs if it is simply consistent with them. A problem is that two propositions could each be consistent with a set of beliefs but inconsistent with each other. Another suggestion has been that a proposition coheres with a set of beliefs if it is entailed in some way by members of the set. Still another is that the relationship is one of mutual explanation.

If I do not believe a proposition on the basis of evidence from other beliefs, then it is basic for me. Plantinga says that coherentism is not "the idea that in a coherent system each belief is evidentially supported by all the others, but rather that all the beliefs are properly basic, where the condition for being properly basic is being a member of a coherent set of beliefs."[19]

Since the network of all truths can be known only by an omniscient being, our knowledge is only partial, and "in a sense, we don't know anything, since all our beliefs are incomplete, but we can be said to know in part."[20] (Note how the view is reminiscent of Van Til, though he is not necessarily a coherentist.) While the strong view of coherentism was held by Hegel (1770–1831), F. H. Bradley (1846–1924) and Brand Blanshard (1892–1987), most modern coherentists claim it only as a theory of how beliefs are justified, that is, that beliefs are justified only by other beliefs that are in the web of what we know, and thus there is no such thing as a basic belief.[21]

Where foundationalism uses the metaphor of a foundation, coherentism uses the idea of a web. The strength of the web comes from the connections between ideas. We know it is raining even if we cannot see the drops perfectly, because we see wet streets, umbrellas and cars using their windshield wipers. No one belief is strong, or even validated by itself, but the whole of what we know stands or falls. Foundationalism, however, appeals to the strength of our basic beliefs, which can be known individually. We can know that $1 = 1$, or that the lights are on, or that we feel happy, without appealing to the whole of our knowledge.

Foundationalists object that if we do not accept some beliefs as basic and insist instead that all beliefs must be supported by other beliefs, then we can never

---

[18]Alvin Plantinga, *Warrant: The Current Debate* (New York: Oxford University Press, 1993), p. 66.
[19]Alvin Plantinga, personal email correspondence with the author, Sept. 9, 2013.
[20]Louis Pojman, *What Can We Know? An Introduction to the Theory of Knowledge*, 2nd ed. (Belmont, CA: Wadsworth, 2001), p. 116.
[21]For example, W. V. O. Quine, Wilfred Sellars, Gilbert Harman, Keith Lehrer and Laurence BonJour (see ibid.).

justify any belief. If we have to justify belief *a* by belief *b*, and belief *b* by belief *c*, and so on (which would be a linear approach, that is, going in a line), then we will have only an infinite string of unjustified beliefs. We have to stop somewhere, says the foundationalist, and that somewhere is at our basic beliefs, which serve to ground our knowledge. An alternative to a linear approach to justification is a circular one: *a* is justified by *b*, and *b* is justified by *c*, and *c* is justified by *a*. While most people find this unacceptable, coherentists generally think it is all right if the circle is large enough (the argument used by Van Tillians, though again, they are not necessarily coherentists). Besides, coherentists find beliefs mutually supportive. If you believe someone is innocent because they have an alibi, you can also believe their alibi because you think they are innocent.

Using coherence to justify beliefs has another problem: novels and dreams can be coherent, or noncontradictory, but they are not true. However, if a belief or theory contradicts itself it cannot be true. So most would say that for a belief or theory to be true it cannot contradict itself, yet that alone is not enough to show something is true. There has to be more than coherence, or noncontradiction. So a self-contradictory belief cannot be true, but a noncontradictory belief could be true. The problem is, it does not have to be true. Put more elegantly, coherence is necessary but not sufficient for justification.

It is not easy to see how young children and animals have knowledge if we require, as coherentists do, that the only grounds for a belief is another belief, and that all beliefs must fit together coherently. It seems children and animals have, at best, extremely simple belief systems. It is also more complicated for coherentists to justify beliefs about things that seem impossible to be wrong about, such as our feeling pain or depression. You can be wrong that you are injured, but can you be wrong that you feel pain? Can someone inform you that you are not depressed but are actually quite happy and don't know it? Foundationalists, however, say that some beliefs do not need to come from other beliefs. They need not be inferences but can have a different source, such as intuition. Knowing my foot hurts does not need to be a conclusion; I can just know it.

A weak coherence theory would see the coherence or fit of a belief with other beliefs (background beliefs) as only one test of its truth, other tests being such things as intuition, perception and memory. A strong coherence theory would see coherence as the only criterion of justification.

Some see coherence as only a negative test such that if a belief does not cohere or fit with other beliefs it is not justified. Others see coherence as a positive test such that if a belief fits with other beliefs it is justified. And some strong coherence views see coherence as both a positive and negative test.

Foundationalists and coherentists who hold that what makes a belief knowledge is that we have reasons for believing it adhere to a view called internalism. Historical internalists include Plato, Aquinas, Descartes, Locke and Bertrand Russell. Contemporaries include Roderick Chisholm, Keith Lehrer, John Pollack, Laurence BonJour, William Alston, Roberti Audi, Richard Foley, Earl Conee and Richard Feldman.[22] According to a strong version, in order to have knowledge, as opposed to a hunch or a guess, we must be aware of the reasons for believing something. We must have "reflective access to evidence that the belief is true."[23] On a weak version, we need only be able to call up, or produce, the reasons if needed; we need not have them in mind currently. Internalists contend that having reasons is necessary for knowledge. They emphasize the perspective of the subject, focusing on a person's reasons for holding a belief.

Externalists on the other hand argue that at least some of what makes for knowledge is outside our thought process. They emphasize objective grounds for belief, approaching knowledge from the perspective of an ideal observer, even if the individual with the belief in question does not have that knowledge. One argument for externalism is that if young children and animals can be said to know anything, it cannot be because they are able to marshal reasons in their mind, as the internalist claims. Another is that even the typical adult can have trouble articulating reasons for a belief, which internalists require for knowledge.

Plantinga has further engaged the field of epistemology, the division of philosophy that studies the nature of knowledge, as to how knowledge differs from mere belief, and how knowing differs from guessing. How does knowing that Barbara is in Barbados differ from merely believing it, or making a lucky guess that she is there? Traditionally the answer has been that knowledge is a true belief that is justified. A guess is not justified.

The time-honored consensus that was held since Plato, that knowledge is "justified true belief," was thrown into total disarray by a very brief paper by Edmund Gettier in 1963. Gettier, a colleague of Plantinga's at Wayne State University, over coffee one day expressed doubts that he would make tenure the following year because he had not published enough. He told Plantinga that he

[22]Ibid., p. 136.
[23]Earl Conlee and Richard Feldman, *Evidentialism: Essays in Epistemology* (Oxford: Oxford University Press, 2004), pp. 48–49.

had a short paper offering counterexamples to the traditional understanding of knowledge.[24] Gettier didn't think much of his paper, but its publication the following year caused a revolution in epistemology. Traditionally, someone knows something, if (and only if) (1) they believe it, (2) it is true and (3) their belief is "justified," that is, they have good reason to believe it. If one of those is missing they do not have knowledge. But Gettier proposed a counterexample in which Smith and Jones apply for the same job. Smith has strong evidence that Jones will get job (the company president has told him so), and he also knows that Jones has ten coins in his pocket (Smith has just counted them). So Smith is justified in believing that Jones will get the job and that Jones has ten coins in his pocket. Therefore, Smith is justified in believing that "the man who will get the job has ten coins in his pocket." But it turns out Smith, not Jones, gets the job. And Smith didn't realize it, but he himself has ten coins in his pocket. It is still true that the man who got the job had ten coins in his pocket—and though Smith was justified in believing it, he clearly did not "know" it. In a second example, Smith believes for very good reasons that his friend Jones owns a Ford. He also knows Brown, but has no idea where he is. So he believes that "either Jones owns a Ford or Brown is in Barcelona." But it turns out that Jones doesn't own a Ford, yet by sheer coincidence Brown is in fact in Barcelona. So Smith's belief was correct that "either Jones owns a Ford or Brown is in Barcelona," but we would not say he knew it.

In spite of years of work by epistemologists, there is still no agreement on how to solve the problem. Some still think that knowledge is a matter of justifying a true belief but that Gettier showed something more is needed to separate knowledge from luck. A fourth condition needs to be added to the three traditional conditions of knowledge (listed in the paragraph above). They generally still use the traditional term *justification*, which is a property of persons, and argue that a person can be justified in believing something. Others think Gettier showed that something is seriously wrong with the entire field of epistemology, which ought to quietly die. Plantinga is in a third camp, which holds that Gettier showed epistemology was on the wrong track with justification. Instead, he used

---

[24]Pojman, *What Can We Know?*, p. 82. For Gettier's paper see Edmund Gettier, "Is Justified True Belief Knowledge?" *Analysis* 23 (1963): 121–23. James Beilby notes that Roderick Chisholm found two earlier counterexamples by Alexius Meinong and Bertrand Russell that were similar to Gettier's, but they had gone relatively unnoticed. Roderick Chisholm, *Theory of Knowledge*, 3rd ed. (Englewood Cliffs, NJ: Prentice-Hall, 1989), cited in James Beilby, *Epistemology as Theology: An Evaluation of Alvin Plantinga's Religious Epistemology* (Aldershot: Ashgate, 2005), p. 75.

the word *warrant* to identify what must be added to a belief to make it knowledge. Warrant is a property of beliefs rather than persons. It not enough, it is said, for internalists to see if a person has the right reasons for holding a belief. It is too easy for a person to have sufficient reasons and still be wrong if their belief was formed in a way that is unreliable. So Plantinga focuses on the belief itself, specifically the way it is formed. Is it formed in a way that can be relied on to gives truth? This view, called reliabilism, is the dominant form of externalism. It says that knowledge is not a matter of the reasons in our mind, but the way a belief is formed, whether our belief-forming processes (memory, introspection, senses, testimony from others, reasoning) are functioning properly in the context. It is a matter of avoiding unreliable processes, such as confused or wishful thinking, hunches, guesses and hasty generalizations.[25]

Reliabilism has the advantage of validating that we know something even when we cannot give reasons for it. For example, we may have forgotten, or never have been able to articulate, the reasons why a particular belief is true. It therefore explains how children and animals can have knowledge. We can also be justified in holding a belief in spite of skeptics, because we need not have reasons that defeat them; we merely need to know we came to the belief in a reliable way.

Reliabilism has its own challenges. When can a belief-forming process be judged "reliable"? When it produces a true belief 90 percent of the time? For that matter, how many times must the process have been tried? Then there is the question of the particulars of any process. With regard to sight, for example, how close to us does something have to be? What speed can it be moving? How well lighted does it have to be? So to determine whether a car is a taxi, how close does it have to be, what speed can it be moving and how much light must be on it? Furthermore, every object is in a number of categories, so which do we use? The car may be in all the following categories: a car, a moving car, a car moving more than thirty miles per hour, a yellow car, an object viewed at dusk, a car viewed at dusk, an object viewed under yellowish street lights. If we make the category too narrow it will be in that category by itself (e.g., yellow car going thirty-seven miles per hour, under yellow light, moving away from us, on Hal-

---

[25]Alvin Goldman, "What Is Justified Belief?," in *Justification and Knowledge*, ed. George Pappas (Dordrecht, Netherlands: D. Reidel, 1979), reprinted in *Epistemology: An Anthology*, ed. Ernest Sosa and Jaegwon Kim (Malden, MA: Blackwell, 2000), pp. 340–52. In Goldman's view, it is not necessary that we know or believe that a belief is reliably produced. That is, we need not have metabeliefs (i.e., beliefs about our beliefs), otherwise children and animals could not know anything.

loween). If objects are in categories so narrow they are by themselves, then every true belief will be the result of a reliable process.[26] But if we draw the category too broadly, it will include too many false beliefs to be helpful. If, for example, viewing the car is considered simply a case of using our sight, we are too often wrong about what we think we see to call it a reliable process.

Plantinga is well aware of the problems of reliabilism. His own model, which resembles reliabilism, is based on (1) the idea of the proper function of belief-forming faculties. Faculties, such as our senses, are functioning properly when they are (2) functioning the way they were designed, ether by God, evolution or both.[27] To function the way they were designed, they must be (3) functioning in the right environment. That consists of not only the right general environment or the sort we find on earth (e.g., light, visible objects, regularities of nature—the "maxi-environment") but also the right particulars (the "mini-environment"). Our conclusions will go awry if there are problems with the mini-environment. A glance at a clock will normally give us accurate time, unless unbeknownst to us the clock has stopped. If the clock stopped at midnight we might check it exactly at noon and be accidently right about the time—therefore being lucky but not having knowledge (your belief is justified and true, but not knowledge).[28] The goal must be (4) to produce a true belief. Wishful thinking, for example, is not aimed at producing true belief.[29] And (5) the plan must be a good one; that is, "there must be a substantial objective probability that a belief of that sort produced under those conditions is true."[30] Furthermore, (6) there must be no defeaters (nothing can successfully contradict the belief, which is a theme found in coherentism).

Plantinga distinguishes between two types of objections to Christian belief. De facto objections claim that belief is factually in error, for example, because of pain and suffering, or because the doctrine of the Trinity is self-contradictory. He focuses on de jure objections, which claim that belief in Christianity is somehow flawed and unjustified, problematic and deficient. Freud offered such an objection

[26]Pojman, *What Can We Know?*, p. 149.

[27]The idea of design avoids the problem of calling any function "proper." A fish that is decomposing could be said to be functioning properly, but it clearly is not functioning the way it was designed. It was designed to swim and eat. Beilby, *Epistemology as Theology*, p. 83. Alvin Plantinga, *Warrant and Proper Function* (New York: Oxford University Press, 1993), pp. 22–24.

[28]Plantinga identifies this as Bertrand Russell's "pre-Gettier Gettier example." Alvin Plantinga, "Respondeo," in *Warrant in Contemporary Epistemology: Essays in Honor of Plantinga's Theory of Knowledge*, ed. Jonathan L. Kvanvig (Lanham, MD: Rowman & Littlefield, 1996), p. 309.

[29]Plantinga, *Warrant and Proper Function*, p. 42.

[30]Plantinga, *Warrant: The Current Debate*, p. 214.

when he claimed that belief in God is mere wishful thinking, a pathological coping strategy. Marx made a similar claim, grounding it in his theory of economic oppression. Plantinga argues that "if Christian belief is true, then it is also warranted."[31]

He proposes what he calls the Aquinas/Calvin, or A/C model as one possible approach to showing that Christian belief is warranted. Aquinas accepted something close to Calvin's *sensus divinitatis*, which is essentially Plantinga's answer to the de jure objection. But as Christianity teaches, humans are fallen, and thus the inner sense of God is blocked or distorted. To overcome the effects of sin and bring a person to salvation, Plantinga proposes the extended A/C model,[32] according to which the Holy Spirit gives the believer the conviction that "the main lines of Christian belief are true,"[33] including belief in Christ as Savior. The Spirit affects not only beliefs but also the will and affections. This is done apart from the *sensus divinitatis* and any natural equipment humans have for gaining knowledge. It is distinctly supernatural.

The faith generated by the Holy Spirit constitutes knowledge because it satisfies the conditions for warrant. Belief in Christianity is not the conclusion of an argument, although arguments can play a role in its acceptance, especially as a way to answer objections ("defeaters"). Divinely generated faith is not based on evidence, nor do we believe it because it is a good explanation of things. Neither is it based on a religious experience in the sense that the experience is the evidence for the conclusion that Christianity is true. Rather, the religious experience immediately gives rise to belief, like seeing a desk immediately gives rise to the belief that there is a desk. Seeing the desk is not evidence for the conclusion that it is there. We simply see it and know it is there. Knowledge of God, like seeing a desk, is "basic" and not an inference.[34]

In general, Plantinga's approach is externalist but includes at least one aspect of internalism: there must be no defeaters to belief, which requires some coherence within a person's beliefs. James Beilby points out that in Plantinga's view, warrant is relative to both the individual and the situation. A belief may be warranted for one person but not another, and in one set of circumstances but not another. Yet Beilby also clarifies that the approach is not relativism because (1) the criteria for warrant are not relative to the person or the situation, (2) the design

---

[31]Plantinga, *Warranted Christian Belief*, p. xii.
[32]Ibid., chap. six.
[33]Personal email correspondence with the author, Sept. 9, 2013.
[34]Plantinga, *Warranted Christian Belief*, p. 258.

plan is common to all humans and is not relative to individuals, and (3) in Plantinga's view truth is not relative to "persons, conceptual schemes, or cultures."[35]

Plantinga quips that his approach is a type of radical naturalism: "Striking the naturalistic pose is all the rage these days, and it's a great pleasure to be able to join the fun. . . . Here I follow Quine (if only at some distance)."[36] But he insists that "naturalism" is misnamed because it works best under theism, especially a theistic view of human beings. Naturalistic epistemology emphasizes the psychological means by which we grasp the outside world, making epistemology more like a science than like the traditional philosophical quest for justified belief. Quine regarded skepticism as a pseudoproblem but also rejected the traditional quest for objective, provable knowledge about reality. He preferred instead to turn epistemology over to psychology as the means of examining and perfecting the way we understand the world, and he was more comfortable with describing how we get beliefs and hold them than with claiming that some authoritative view of reality could be constructed.

Like Quine, Plantinga is not optimistic about our ability to arrive at a full and final understanding of truth simply by examining the world around us and reflecting on it. It is the *sensus divinitatis* that rescues us, as does the supernatural action of God, creating belief in us regarding Christianity.

Consistent with his view that we are not able to arrive at ultimate spiritual truth as the sure conclusion of a rational investigation, Plantinga does not claim to be able to demonstrate the truth of theism or Christianity.

> I don't know how to do something one could sensibly call "showing" that either of these is true. I believe there are a large number (at least a couple dozen) good arguments for the existence of God; none, however, can really be thought of as showing or demonstration. As for classical Christianity, there is even less prospect of demonstrating its truth. Of course this is nothing against either their truth or their warrant; very little of what we believe can be "demonstrated" or "shown."[37]

It is clear that he sets the bar for the support required for belief much higher than Richard Swinburne, who holds that we are justified in believing *p* as long as it is more likely true than untrue. For Plantinga, that is "nowhere nearly sufficient for

[35]Beilby, *Epistemology as Theology*, pp. 88-89.
[36]Plantinga, *Warrant and Proper Function*, p. 46.
[37]Plantinga, *Warranted Christian Belief*, p. 170.

belief that p."[38] To clarify from my personal conversations with Swinburne, he believes that we have at least some justification for a belief if it is more likely true than untrue. But of course we are far more justified when a belief is well confirmed, at least .9 on a scale of 0 to 1. He aims to show that Christianity can be confirmed to a high level, and he believes he can do just that. Regardless, there is still distance between Plantinga and Swinburne on how much confirmation it would take to rationally confirm belief. (Note that Plantinga calls two of Swinburne's books "perhaps the major work of natural theology of the century.")[39]

The difference between the two thinkers is grounded in several crucial and related issues in apologetics, and epistemology generally. How much evidence must we have to claim that we know something? What is the relationship between evidence and certainty? And what is the value of induction?

As to the first question, if we set the bar so high such that we need a very great amount of evidence for knowledge, the result will likely be either skepticism or fideism, depending on whether we choose to take a leap of faith in the absence of adequate evidence. An alternative is to accept some type of experience, which we take as evidence for a conclusion (i.e., experientialism, which Plantinga rejects) or as direct apprehension of the truth (Plantinga's view). And as we have seen, Van Til proposes another alternative, that the conclusion be accepted as an assumption that we cannot do without.

As to the gap between evidence and certainty, the fideist makes certainty entirely a matter of faith, rendering evidence irrelevant. Plantinga makes the object of faith a basic belief, thus showing it is acceptable without having to prove it. However, it is a direct apprehension of reality, and it can be rationally supported with reasons, so Plantinga—contrary to the conclusion of some people—is no fideist.

It is not surprising that Plantinga has far less confidence in induction than Swinburne, calling probability, a closely related topic, "a confusing and ill-understood morass."[40] The result, as we noted that he said, is "very little of what we believe can be 'demonstrated' or 'shown.'"[41]

Although Plantinga's goal is to show that belief in Christianity is not ir-

---

[38]Ibid., p. 271 n. 56.

[39]Alvin Plantinga, "Christian Philosophy at the End of the 20th Century," in Sennett, *The Analytic Theist*, p. 339. He was referring to Richard Swinburne's *The Coherence of Theism* (Oxford: Clarendon, 1977); and Swinburne, *The Existence of God* (Oxford: Clarendon, 1979). Plantinga also acknowledges the work of George Mavrodes and Robert Adams on the moral argument.

[40]Plantinga, "A Christian Life Partly Lived," p. 279 n. 15. In context he was referring to the difficulty of dealing with the probabilistic problem of evil.

[41]Plantinga, *Warranted Christian Belief*, p. 170.

rational even in the absence of support from arguments, he also believes that arguments have their place and that more should be done to develop them.

> There are arguments from the existence of good and evil, right and wrong, moral obligation; there is an argument from the existence of horrifying evil, from intentionality and the nature of propositions and properties, from the nature of sets and numbers, from counterfactuals, and from the apparent fine-tuning of the universe. There is the ontological argument, but also the more convincing teleological argument, which can be developed in many ways. There is an argument from the existence of contingent beings, and even an argument from colors and flavors. There are arguments from simplicity, from induction, and from the falsehood of general skepticism. There is a general argument from the reliability of intuition, and also one from Kripke's Wittgenstein. There is an argument from the existence of a priori knowledge, and one from the causal requirement in knowledge. There are arguments from love, beauty, play, and enjoyment, and from the perceived meaning of life. There are arguments from the confluence of justification and warrant, from the confluence of proper function and reliability, and from the existence, in nature, of organs and systems that function properly. . . . These arguments are not apodictic or certain; nevertheless they all deserve to be developed in loving detail.[42]

Plantinga believes not only in so-called positive apologetics, which seeks to support belief with arguments for God's existence and the like, but also in negative apologetics, which attempts to answer attacks on belief. He rejects the common Reformed idea (which he finds in Kuyper and Herman Dooyeweerd) that all thought has religious roots, including attacks on Christianity. It is thought therefore that Christians need not answer the attacks, since "faith cannot reason with unbelief: it can only preach to it." But on the contrary, says Plantinga, answers to attacks can benefit doubting Christians, as well as non-Christians who are seeking, and even those who are hostile.[43]

One of the arguments for which Plantinga is best known is his shaping[44] of

---

[42]Plantinga, "Christian Philosophy at the End of the 20th Century," pp. 339–40. He developed these themes somewhat more in class notes that circulated for years and were eventually published as "Appendix: Two Dozen (or so) Theistic Arguments," in *Alvin Plantinga*, ed. Dean-Peter Baker (Cambridge: Cambridge University Press, 2007).

[43]Plantinga, "Christian Philosophy at the End of the 20th Century," p. 336.

[44]He is sometimes credited with inventing the freewill defense, but as he would say, "I developed the free-will defense—or rather, since it can be found (at least in embryonic form) as far back as Augustine, redeveloped and restated it in a contemporary idiom." Plantinga, "Afterword," p. 355.

the freewill defense, which defends the orthodox view that God can indeed be loving, just and all-knowing despite the existence of evil in the world. Opponents had argued that the presence of any evil was incompatible with the orthodox view. They set up their argument deductively, as if the conclusion were completely certain and not merely likely.

Plantinga counters that for such an argument to succeed it must be constructed from propositions that are "necessarily true, essential to theism, or a logical consequence of such propositions."[45] The critic must show that the claim that "if evil exists, it is unjustified" is nothing less than a necessary truth.

Plantinga argues that it is at least possible that God is unable to create free moral beings who never choose evil; that is, it is possible that if beings are to be free to do good, then God cannot make them always do good so that there will be no evil in the world. If that is the case, then he is justified in making a world that contains evil (because without it there could be no freedom and thus no moral good). The opponent is defeated if it is at least possible that God cannot make a world in which there is freedom but no sin.

Plantinga's freewill defense is a remarkable achievement, with virtually everyone in the debate admitting that Plantinga has defeated the deductive argument that the orthodox God cannot exist because of evil in the world. (Opponents have since shifted to the inductive argument, that it is unlikely that God exists because of the amount or type of evil in the world.)

Plantinga now sees two very broad and general contemporary challenges that must be answered. Because the task far exceeds what can be done in a single lifetime, he calls on the community of Christian scholars to take up the challenge. In the sciences, it is common to believe that only the physical world exists—no God, soul or afterlife. Religion, morality, love, mathematics, propositions, properties and more are understood in strictly physical terms. One of the many problems of this naturalism is the difficulty of accounting for intentionality, that is, how we can intend, believe and think "about" things if only physical things exist. How can atoms be *about* anything?[46] Another problem is that naturalism has no room for right and wrong, good and bad—what could be called "normativity."[47]

He works to demonstrate that any fit between science and naturalism is su-

---

[45]Quoted in Michael L. Peterson, "The Problem of Evil," in *A Companion to Philosophy of Religion*, ed. Philip L. Quinn and Charles Taliaferro, Blackwell Companions to Philosophy (Malden, MA: Blackwell, 1997), p. 394.

[46]Plantinga, "Christian Philosophy at the End of the 20th Century," pp. 342–43.

[47]Plantinga, "Afterword," p. 356.

perficial, whereas there is a deep fit between science and religion.[48] His best-known argument challenges the idea that evolution unguided by God can reliably give us equipment that produces truth. What evolution gives is structures that are adapted to the environment, or more precisely, that allow the organism to reproduce. But that is different from truth. The creature may have equipment that indicates the presence of a predator, but such an indication is not a belief. We humans have indicators for our blood pressure, blood sugar and many other things that produce reactions in us—but those are not beliefs. We have no reason to conclude that blind evolution has produced cognitive equipment that gives us truth. (We could add that in some cases a false belief could advantage survival of a group, if for example its warriors are more brave because they believe that dying in battle will guarantee them a place in heaven.)[49] But don't true beliefs help a creature survive better than false beliefs? Certainly, however, that is irrelevant because that fact describes our present situation, not how we supposedly evolved. Plantinga takes naturalism to include materialism about human persons, and materialism is the warrant[50] for the fact that if naturalism were true, only the neurophysiological content of our brains would matter, not the beliefs associated with them. If naturalism does not really require materialism, then his argument is against the conjunction of naturalism, evolution and materialism.[51]

Different beliefs could cause the right neurophysiological response, that is, the one that helps the creature. Suppose one of our ancient ancestors associated tall grass moving on a windless day with danger and learned to run away. His life-saving behavior was associated with the untrue belief that tall grass is dangerous. Actually, it was the presence of a predator moving the grass that is dangerous, but the untrue belief allowed him to survive and reproduce. If evolution is an unguided process, we have no assurance that our mental faculties give us truth.

Plantinga then finishes turning the tables. If naturalism is true and we have no assurance that our minds give us truth, then we have no assurance that naturalism itself is true, since it came from our (faulty) mental processes.

The second broad and widespread contemporary challenge is more common

---

[48] Alvin Plantinga, *Where the Conflict Really Lies: Science, Religion, and Naturalism* (New York: Oxford University Press, 2011). On p. 310 n. 4 he traces the ancestry of his argument to C. S. Lewis and Charles Taylor. He also notes his other publications where it appears, and the fact that he has repeatedly revised it, adding, "The version presented here is the official and final version (I hope)."
[49] Pojman mentions a suggestion along these lines (*What Can We Know?*, p. 176).
[50] Alvin Plantinga, personal email correspondence with the author, Sept. 9, 2013.
[51] Ibid.

in the humanities, what he calls "creative antirealism," which was found in basic form as far back as the Greek Protagoras. As Immanuel Kant developed it, the fundamental categories by which we understand the world originate with us, being imposed by our minds on the world. They are not necessarily "out there" to be discovered as objective realities. The most we can be sure of is that they are in our minds as constructs by which we understand the world. The view is contrary to traditional thought, in which God creates the structures of the world, which are thus objective. In creative antirealism, which goes beyond Kant, it is we who give structure to the world. Even God is a construct of our minds. The notion that we create him is a "stunning reversal of roles."[52]

Taking this type of relativism even further, we do not all inhabit the same world, there being no single objective world out there. Truth is different for each of us. What is true for you might not be true for me. It sometimes takes the form of an argument that, because there are enough differences among thinking people that no amount of effort and goodwill can guarantee we will come to the same conclusions about disputes, therefore there is no objective reality to be had. Plantinga points out that this conclusion in no way follows.[53] If this postmodern theme, suggested by people like Richard Rorty, were correct, we could simply think away problems like war, poverty and disease.

Giving positive reasons for belief and answering objections are only part of the task. Plantinga believes that Christians must also engage in a vast constructive effort to give account for things like morality, ethics, responsibility, freedom, the nature of humans, causation, science and "a thousand other topics."[54] He sees a major theme of his own work as filling out the Christian view of knowledge, but there is much to be done.

Summary

Plantinga rejects philosophical evidentialism (the view that our degree of belief should be no higher than our degree of proof) as self-defeating and unworkable. In daily life we rightly believe things we would have trouble proving, such as that the world is more than a few minutes old, that people are not just complex robots and so on. He also rejects classical foundationalism, according to which we can accept without support from other beliefs (i.e., as "properly basic") only

---

[52]Plantinga, "Christian Philosophy at the End of the 20th Century," p. 332.
[53]Ibid., pp. 332–33.
[54]Plantinga, "Afterword," p. 357.

those beliefs that are self-evident, incorrigible or evident to the senses. He believes we should broaden foundationalism to include belief in God as properly basic. So that means that a person can be rational in believing in God even without being able to produce supporting arguments.

Awareness of God, the *sensus divinitatis*, comes from how we were created plus, typically, some catalyst in our experience. The more detailed belief in Christianity is also a divine gift. The former is part of our created nature, producing a knowing not unlike perception. The latter, the internal testimony of the Holy Spirit, is not.[55]

Both theism and Christianity can be supported with arguments and evidence, and should be, though it is unlikely that sufficient support could be mustered to match the importance of this issue.

Justifying a belief is not a matter of having reasons for it (internalism), but something else (externalism). A belief has warrant when it is produced by faculties that are functioning properly, that is, the way they were designed by God, evolution or both, which fits a type of externalism related to reliabilism. They must be functioning not only in the right general environment such as we typically find on earth but also in the environment that is right for the particular situation. Our goal must be to arrive at true belief, our plan must be one that will likely give us truth, and there must be nothing that successfully defeats the belief.

CRITICISMS

Plantinga enjoys a great deal of respect, even among those who disagree with his views. His sincerity, humility and good humor have graced his responses and permeate his prodigious academic output.

Though his views are not fideistic, they do fit more comfortably on the left side of the chart we've been referencing throughout this book, since he contends that belief in God depends not on rational support but on immediate awareness (the *sensus divinitatis*), and belief in Christianity is a supernatural deliverance rather than a conclusion. To the left of Reformed epistemology on the chart is presuppositionalism, which uses no direct support, but makes Christianity an assumption that is necessary for there to be knowledge of any kind. To the right on the chart is experientialism, since those in this view typically use experience as evidence to support Christianity as a conclusion. In their case only one type of evidence, experience, is useful or necessary.

---

[55]Alvin Plantinga, personal email correspondence with the author, Sept. 9, 2013.

Plantinga's views raise questions about the very nature of apologetics as it relates to epistemology, or how we know. Is knowing x primarily a matter of having right reasons for believing x? If so then we are looking for adequate reasons a person has for believing something, which is a process internal to their minds (internalism), and we are thus looking for justification. On this view it is typically thought that we have at least some obligation to find and believe what is true, which implies we have at least indirect control over what we believe (we can decide, for example, to expose ourselves to evidence). However, if knowing x is a matter of being confident that we arrived at x in a way that normally gives us truth, then we are focused on the origin and processes of getting beliefs (externalism), and we are looking for warrant—as Plantinga does. Externalists don't think justification, a mental process, is the issue; however, some internalists are happy to have not only some mental basis for a belief but also some assurance that they acquired it in a reliable way, that is, that our belief is warranted as well as justified. (Some think that coming to a belief in the right way helps guard against unusual Gettier-type problems.) Some internalists do not insist that to know x we must have reasons for believing x (justification), but they would say we need to look at evidence, be impartial and so on.

We can ask ourselves if the Bible indicates that people have at least some responsibility for what they believe. Does God hold people responsible for their beliefs and their unbelief? Note that Christ rebuked two towns he visited for their unbelief in spite of his performing many miracles (Mt 11:21; Lk 10:13). He even reproved his followers for being slow to believe what was written of him (Jn 20:31). Could character ever have a part in forming beliefs, and could we ever have at least some influence, however indirect, over the beliefs we form? Christ confronted some for failing to believe because they were more interested in respect from peers (Jn 5:44). Is there any indication that belief can come from having the right evidence, or reasons for a belief as a conclusion from other beliefs? John says he recorded selected miracles in his Gospel "so that you may believe that Jesus is the Christ" (Jn 20:31). Again, some common themes in internalism include that we have at least some responsibility for beliefs, we can have at least very indirect control over our beliefs and that beliefs have at least something to do with our reasons.

But few are absolutely pure internalists or pure externalists. Plantinga himself requires coherence among beliefs, which is an internalist theme. But before we go to extreme internalism, it may be advisable to give at least some consideration to how we came to beliefs (an externalist consideration), since unusual situations can pose problems of the sort pointed out in Gettier-type examples.

As far as Plantinga's departures from reliabilism (including his views on proper function, design plan and congenial environment), William Alston sees them as unnecessary.[56] What it means to function properly is not all that easy to determine. James Beilby notes that Plantinga's examples are highly contrived, involving brain lesions, cosmic rays and demons. Such cases "convey a specious sense of clarity about what exactly constitutes proper function."[57] Perhaps proper function tells us more about why our beliefs are properly formed and not so much about the nature of warrant.[58] If so this may show us that proper function is partly a matter of warrant but is not sufficient for warrant. Something more is needed.

With regard to proper function, can we really say that we function properly even though as humans we have many inadequacies? Even some animals can hear and see better, and our human emotions sometimes get in the way. Furthermore, couldn't we function properly even if we were not designed?[59]

Perhaps the most persistent concern about Plantinga's overall approach is that it seems it could be used to justify a broad array of beliefs, even that the "Great Pumpkin" returns every Halloween—an objection Plantinga himself anticipated. To evaluate the objection we have to recall the nuances of Plantinga's views regarding evidence and belief. Like Calvin, he holds that our minds have been affected by sin such that we do not perceive much of the evidence for God that is around us. Evidence is not necessary for belief, though it can help us decide whether Christianity is true. But, as Jonathan Edwards said, we have to go beyond merely acknowledging that Christianity is true if we are to have saving faith. That faith is a gift of God, not a mere deliverance of the mind. Complicating the relationship between knowledge, evidence and faith is Plantinga's suspicion, following Abraham Kuyper, that there is really no such thing as true neutrality or objectivity: arguments, including much of philosophy, are ultimately rooted in a person's theological assumptions and commitments. And since he sets the bar very high for proving anything, in the end those assumptions and commitments largely determine where we end up as far as belief. We

---

[56]Beilby, *Epistemology as Theology*, p. 159 n. 51, cites others with the same critique; Adrian Bardon, "Two Problems for the Proper Functionalist Analysis of Epistemic Warrant," *Southwest Philosophy Review* 15, no. 2 (July 1999): 97–107; Richard Feldman, "Proper Functionalism," *Nous* 27, no. 1 (March 1993): 34–50; and John Calvin Wingard, "Is Proper Function Necessary for Epistemic Warrant?," *Southwest Philosophy Review* 16, no. 2 (July 2000): 133–41.

[57]Beilby, *Epistemology as Theology*, p. 160.

[58]Beilby makes this point in ibid., p. 161, and he also cites William Alston, "Epistemic Warrant as Proper Function," *Philosophy and Phenomenological Research* 55, no. 2 (June 1995): 402.

[59]Two questions suggested by Pojman, *What Can We Know?*, pp. 172–73.

can see this entwining of commitments and conclusions when he says that Christianity has warrant given that it is true.[60]

Note that the question of how independent "facts" and arguments are from our assumptions, commitments and worldview is one of the most pivotal issues in apologetics. It is one of the key differences between the left side of our chart, which includes fideism, presuppositionalism and Reformed epistemology; versus the right side, which includes combinationalism, classical apologetics and evidentialism. If there is no such thing as independence (the view held by those on the left side of the chart), then there is no such thing as objectivity, and our beliefs are largely a product of our assumptions and commitments—or perhaps our experiences, since they can cut through a certain amount of our thinking. But if there is some independence (the right side of the chart) there can be some useful common ground among views, and faith can be to a greater extent a conclusion from facts. Typically, on the right side, the bar for proof is set lower and induction is accepted in religious arguments.

Because of Plantinga's overall approach, he is not trying to begin from premises that even the skeptic will agree to and to produce arguments that compel faith (an approach more typical of the right side of the chart). Rather, he is defending the idea that Christianity could have warrant if belief in God is crucially a matter of the *sensus divinitatis*, and Christian faith is ultimately a divine gift. He intends his argument that Christianity can have such warrant (i.e., in light of the *sensus divinitatis* and gift of Christian faith) to be convincing to nearly everyone, and that his argument need not be accepted by faith.

Like Van Til, he favors critiquing opposing viewpoints, but where Van Til has essentially the same approach to every view (e.g., that it can't account for its claim to have knowledge, and is built on mere human authority), Plantinga is more nuanced, focusing on non sequiturs, unsubstantiated claims and doubtful conclusions.

Though he cannot be criticized for failing at something he is not trying to do, some would say that the apparatus Plantinga has painstakingly set up could probably be used to defend other beliefs.[61] While that would disturb most traditional apologists, for Plantinga it may be the unavoidable consequence of the human condition, the nature of faith and the limits of proof. Whatever the case, he does not see it as a problem in any way.

---

[60]Plantinga, *Warranted Christian Belief*, p. xiv. In "Afterword," p. 355, Plantinga says, "The real question, so it seems to me, is whether Christian and theistic belief can have warrant. But a little reflection reveals that if Christian or theistic belief is in fact *true*, then, very likely, anyway, it does have warrant" (emphasis original).

[61]Beilby, *Epistemology as Theology*, pp. 130–34.

KEY TERMS

Evidentialist. Plantinga uses the word in its epistemological sense. To be rational a belief must have sufficient evidence, and our beliefs must be proportioned to the amount of evidence. The view appears in Locke and is classically stated in W. K. Clifford. Plantinga has steadfastly challenged it.

Coherentism. A view of the structure of knowledge in which there are no "basic" propositions, those that can be known without support from other propositions (the foundationalist view). Unlike foundationalism, according to which propositions are known either by themselves (basic beliefs) or by their relationship to basic beliefs, coherentists typically hold that propositions are known by their relationship to other propositions.

Coherence theory of truth. A theory of truth in which a proposition is true if it "coheres" (roughly, fits) with certain other beliefs. What it means to "cohere" depends on the particular type of coherentism.

Externalism. The view that at least some of what makes a belief knowledge is outside our thought process and is not a matter of having reasons.

Foundationalism. We can rightly hold some beliefs that are not inferences from other beliefs. These are called "basic" beliefs, or "properly basic" beliefs. Thus not every belief has to be supported. For Plantinga, the existence of God can be properly basic. That does not mean it is groundless, or that belief should not be supported with evidence and proofs. However, he holds that theists are not irrational even if they are unable to demonstrate their beliefs conclusively from premises accepted by opponents. Nonbasic beliefs are connected to basic beliefs by deduction, induction or abduction.

Gettier problem. In 1963 Edmund Gettier posed a challenge for the traditional view that knowledge is justified true belief. Simply put, one of the problems he raised was that a person could correctly believe *a* on grounds that "either *b* or *c* is true." But the problem is, the person could think it's *b* that is true, when actually it's *c*. So the grounds were correct because it's correct that "either *b* or *c* is true," but, being wrong about what made it true (*c* rather than *b*), did the person really "know" *a*? Plantinga is among those who concluded there is a fundamental problem with holding that knowledge is justified true belief.

Internalism. The view that a belief is knowledge if we have reasons for holding it.

Justified true belief. The traditional view that someone knows something only if they believe it, if it is true and if they have a good reason to believe it. It was challenged by the Gettier problem.

Proper function. Plantinga's modification of reliabilism in which, briefly put, belief-forming faculties must function the way there were designed, in the right environment, with the goal of producing true belief, with a substantial probability that a belief of that sort formed under those conditions is true, and with nothing that successfully contradicts the belief.

Reliabilism. A form of externalism according to which knowledge is a matter of the way a belief was formed, whether the processes that formed the belief are reliable (memory, introspection, senses, testimony from others, reasoning) and were functioning properly in the context. Plantinga's proper-function approach is a modification of reliabilism.

Sensus divinitatis. An awareness all humans have of God that can arise through interaction with such things as nature and conscience. We are born with a capacity rather than actual content (like the ability to do arithmetic), and our experiences stimulate that awareness of God. The factors that cause it to well up differ from person to person. It is an awareness, not evidence for a conclusion.

Warrant. Plantinga's term for what must be added to belief to make it knowledge. It is akin to the traditional term *justification*, except that Plantinga emphasizes the property of beliefs rather than persons.

THINKING IT OVER

1. What objections does Plantinga raise against evidentialism (i.e., the view that beliefs must be supported by evidence and be proportional to evidence)?

2. Plantinga believes that we have no cognitive duties. Why is that important to his approach?

3. Describe traditional foundationalism. How does Plantinga's form differ, and why is it important that Romans 1:19-20 be interpreted as our intuitive awareness of God arising when we see creation, not about a reasoning process whereby we come to a conclusion that God exists; for example, a conclusion that the universe must have been caused, or its order must come from a mind and not an accident?

4. Explain Plantinga's views of the *sensus divinitatis*. Is it grounds for a conclusion that God exists?

5. Describe coherentism and its metaphor of a web versus a foundation. What criticisms do foundationalists offer?

6. What is strong coherentism? Weak coherentism?

7. Explain internalism. Externalism. Which is Plantinga's stance, and why?

8. Explain the Gettier problem and how it has affected Plantinga's views.

9. Explain reliabilism and Plantinga's proper function view.

10. What is the extended A/C model, and how does it relate to the *sensus divinitatis*? What aspect of internalism does Plantinga include?

11. What level of proof is needed to confirm theism or Christianity? Must the conclusion be merely more likely than not (i.e., over .5 on a scale of 0 to 1)? Beyond reasonable doubt? Beyond any doubt? If we have an inner sense (intuition) that God exists, is it necessarily beyond doubt? How does Plantinga differ from Swinburne?

12. How does an intuition differ from a presupposition?

13. Do you think Plantinga's views could be used to support other, non-Christian beliefs? Do you think it matters?

14. How is Plantinga not a fideist?

15. With what common Reformed idea found in Kuyper and Dooyeweerd does Plantinga disagree?

16. How does Plantinga answer the problem of evil? Unguided evolution?

17. Do you favor internalism or externalism?

18. Do you think there are things people ought to believe?

19. What is the "Great Pumpkin" objection? Do you think it is a problem for Plantinga's view?

20. How does Plantinga agree, at least somewhat, with Kuyper regarding the ultimacy of theological assumptions and commitments?

Going Further

Baker, Dean-Peter. *Alvin Plantinga*. Cambridge: Cambridge University Press, 2007.

Beilby, James. *Epistemology as Theology: An Evaluation of Alvin Plantinga's Religious Epistemology*. Aldershot: Ashgate, 2005.

Kvanvig, Jonathan, ed. *Warrant in Contemporary Epistemology: Essays in Honor of Plantinga's Theory of Knowledge*. Lanham, MD: Rowman & Littlefield, 1996.

Plantinga, Alvin. "A Christian Life Partly Lived." In *Philosophers Who Believe:*

The Spiritual Journeys of Eleven Leading Thinkers, edited by Kelly James Clark, pp. 45–82. Downers Grove, IL: InterVarsity Press, 1993.

———. *God and Other Minds: A Study in the Rational Justification of Belief in God.* 2nd ed. Ithaca, NY: Cornell University Press, 1990.

———. "Is Belief in God Rational?" In *Rationality and Religious Belief,* edited by C. Delaney. Notre Dame, IN: University of Notre Dame Press.

———. *Warrant and Proper Function.* New York: Oxford University Press, 1993.

———. *Warrant: The Current Debate.* New York: Oxford University Press, 1993.

———. *Warranted Christian Belief.* New York: Oxford University Press, 2000.

———. *Where the Conflict Really Lies: Science, Religion, and Naturalism.* New York: Oxford University Press, 2011.

Plantinga, Alvin, and Nicholas Wolterstorff, eds. *Faith and Rationality: Reason and Belief in God.* Notre Dame, IN: University of Notre Dame Press, 1983.

Pojman, Louis. *What Can We Know? An Introduction to the Theory of Knowledge.* 2nd ed. Belmont, CA: Wadsworth, 2001.

Pollack, John L., and Joseph Cruz. *Contemporary Theories of Knowledge.* 2nd ed. Lanham, MD: Rowman & Littlefield, 1999.

Sennett, James F., ed. *The Analytic Theist: An Alvin Plantinga Reader.* Grand Rapids: Eerdmans, 1998

– 6 –

E. J. CARNELL, GORDON LEWIS AND FRANCIS SCHAEFFER

Christianity is logical, factual and viable

The church in the early twentieth century struggled to deal with a culture adrift from its Christian heritage. For more than a century the Bible had been subjected to the same critical methods used to study ordinary secular texts, which produced doubts about its supernatural authority. The success of the scientific method had become a challenge to the Bible as a source of knowledge, and the growing momentum of Darwin's theory was eroding a literal interpretation of the Bible.

Liberalism resolved the challenges by accepting science as the more reliable source of truth about the world. The resulting worldview left little place for the supernatural, and in the process it blurred the distinction between religious and secular, between church and world. Religion was reduced to a subjective matter, limited to the realms of feelings (Schleiermacher) and ethics (Ritschl), especially social ethics (Rauschenbusch).

Those who rejected this trend banded together across denominational lines to reaffirm the "fundamentals" of the faith, the main five being inerrancy of Scripture, the virgin birth, substitutionary atonement, Christ's bodily resurrection and the historicity of miracles. The defining publication of the movement was *The Fundamentals: A Testimony to the Truth*, published in twelve volumes between 1910 and 1915.

As sectarian lines were drawn and the cultural tide turned against them (notably in the Scopes trial in 1925), these fundamentalists began to be pushed out of denominations and their institutions of higher learning. They responded by forming their own denominations and schools, which further distanced them from mainstream culture. They turned inward, working to refine their doctrinal distinctions, a move that inevitably brought strife to a movement that was so theologically diverse. By the 1940s some members became dissatisfied with what they regarded as the movement's isolationism and anti-intellectualism. Among them was Edward John Carnell (1919–1967).

E. J. CARNELL

Carnell grew up to share the disdain that his father, a Baptist pastor, had for the denominational strife of the era. As Edward came to see it, the commitment to interpret the Bible literally and supernaturally had led to a movement that looked more like a cult than historic Christianity.[1] His life's passion became one of bringing a movement he judged to be theologically correct back into engagement with the broader culture. It entailed that it be academically respectable, a task that made Carnell a lifelong apologist.

Carnell attended Wheaton College (1937–1941), where he became one of many who were profoundly influenced by Gordon Clark. Clark's emphasis on the principle of noncontradiction as a test for truth became a permanent part of Carnell's thinking. But where Clark held that testing for contradictions is sufficient to decide truth, Carnell held that it is necessary but not in itself sufficient; after all, a fairy tale could be free of contradictions. A theory that is found to be free of contradictions could be true (whereas one with contradictions cannot), but to know if it is true we have to take the additional step of seeing whether it fits with facts in the real world.

At Westminster Seminary (1941–1944) Carnell encountered Cornelius Van Til, who was also shaping young apologists. Unlike many who came into Van Til's orbit, Carnell felt no personal attraction to him. Years later he told a fellow student that when you asked Clark a question, you would go home and mull over his answer and benefit a great deal; but when you asked Van Til a question he would merely repeat himself and you'd be sorry you'd asked.[2] In a comment to

---

[1] Edward John Carnell, "Orthodox: Cultic vs. Classical," *The Christian Century*, March 30, 1960, pp. 377–79.

[2] Rudolph Nelson, *The Making and Unmaking of an Evangelical Mind: The Case of Edward Carnell* (New York: Cambridge University Press, 1987), p. 45. Another student, John Frame, noted the same tendency in Van Til. John Frame, *Cornelius Van Til: An Analysis of His Thought* (Phillipsburg, NJ:

another student about ideas he approved and disapproved of, Carnell spoke of Van Til and said that he had "rejected him."[3] The main disagreement was that, by denying common ground between believer and nonbeliever, and denying the right to test the truth of Christianity, Van Til was denying both believer and nonbeliever the right to a rational faith. Van Til, however, regarded the willingness of Carnell and others to test biblical truth as "blasphemous."[4] In spite of their differences, it seems Carnell did benefit from Van Til's thinking. His emphasis on presuppositions likely came from Van Til. Both of them agreed that the starting point in apologetic reasoning should be the God of the Bible. We shall see, however, that those starting points functioned quite differently. Van Til regarded a presupposition as a mental commitment that controls all thinking. We cannot prove it directly with evidence, yet it can be known for certain because we cannot think without it. Carnell regarded Christianity as a hypothesis that can compete with others, and that can be confirmed as highly probable.

While working on his PhD at Harvard University (1944–1948), Carnell gained from professor Elton Trueblood the view that a theory can be tested by how well it explains why things are the way they are. Abduction, as it is sometimes called, begins with a theory and then checks that theory against the data. His dissertation, on Reinhold Niebuhr, convinced him of the pervasiveness of sin and the necessity of love—a theme that would grow in his thinking over the years.

His second doctorate, at Boston University (1945–1949) with Edgar Brightman, convinced him of the importance of empirical data, which affirmed his conviction that religious emotions do not determine truth.[5]

Early in his career Carnell emphasized that Christianity is rationally acceptable because it is the most self-consistent theory and fits all the relevant facts. (Though he retained this view, he came to emphasize more subjective aspects of the case for Christianity.) Fundamentalism was disconnected from the world, it seemed to him, largely because it lacked intellectual rigor. Carnell thought at the time that people would accept its message of the gospel if the case

---

P & R, 1995), p. 30.

[3]Letter of E. J. Carnell to James Tompkins, April 29, 1953; quoted in Nelson, *Making and Unmaking of an Evangelical Mind*, p. 45. Tompkins was a fellow student at Wheaton and Westminster. Carnell wrote, "Like yourself, I rejected Van Til; but unlike yourself, graduate studies presented no option superior to that which Clark taught me."

[4]Van Til's response to Gordon Lewis in *Jerusalem and Athens: Critical Discussions on the Theology and Apologetics of Cornelius Van Til*, ed. E. R. Geehan (Phillipsburg, NJ: P & R, 1971), p. 368.

[5]Gordon Lewis, "Edward John Carnell," in *Handbook of Evangelical Theologians*, ed. Walter A. Elwell (Grand Rapids: Baker, 1993), p. 324. From pp. 321 to 325 is a discussion of influences on Carnell.

for it could be made on a more intellectual level.

Systematic consistency. During this time he wrote *An Introduction to Christian Apologetics* (1948). He began the book with the human predicament, that all humans suffer from "soul sorrow" arising from the conflict between the "insatiable desire for self-preservation" and "the realities of a death-doomed body and an impersonal universe."[6] Man seeks a worldview that he can be confident is true and that assures him of immortality. Such a worldview could close the gap between the world of a man's ideals and reality as he knows it. It would, Carnell believed, thereby solve the age-old philosophical problem of finding the unity and meaning behind the many particular things we experience, known as the problem of "the one and the many" (a view he seems to have gotten from Van Til).[7]

What process will give us the truth that people seek? The view that knowledge can be gained purely from our senses (called empiricism) Carnell regarded as inadequate because it provides no higher authority than the senses. This being the case, there is no way to decide even something simple, such as whether it is the person with normal vision or the person with colorblindness who sees the dotted chart correctly. Carnell says that with no way to get at changeless truths we are left with subjectivism, and ultimately skepticism.[8]

He rejects traditional proofs for God's existence on the grounds that they are dependent on empiricism. From sense impressions one can never rise to the level of what is immutable, universal and necessary. In the end all you have, thought Carnell, is a disjointed string of perceptions. And similar to eighteenth-century skeptic David Hume (1711–1776), Carnell insists that we cannot infer the existence of anything greater than is required to explain what we have perceived;[9] otherwise, people could claim that from seeing a watch they know not only that there is a watchmaker but also that he has a certain color of hair and takes walks on Sundays. So because the things we perceive are finite, we can infer the existence of no more than a finite God. Moreover, we need not infer from our evidence that just one God exists; why not several, or thousands? Those like Aquinas who think that the world points to a Christian God are merely reading their beliefs back into the evidence.[10]

---

[6]Edward John Carnell, *An Introduction to Christian Apologetics: A Philosophic Defense of the Trinitarian-Theistic Faith* (Grand Rapids: Eerdmans, 1948), p. 23.

[7]Ibid., p. 41 n. 22, "The perfect pattern for the solution to the relationship between unity and diversity is found in what Van Til calls 'the eternal one and many.'"

[8]Ibid., pp. 35–37.

[9]This idea goes back to William of Ockham (1288–1347), and is known as "Ockham's razor."

[10]Carnell, *Introduction to Christian Apologetics*, pp. 129–34.

Carnell is pointing out the limits of a strict form of empiricism, one that does not allow the mind to contribute any information to the data or provide any structure. This classical form reached its high point in Hume but dwindled after Immanuel Kant's (1724–1804) objection that to have knowledge our minds must contribute something to the information we get from our senses. The necessity of this contribution is illustrated by the fact that under a strict empiricist view (such as Hume's), we cannot legitimately infer that one thing caused another, even after, for example, seeing for the hundredth time a light come on after flipping a wall switch. This is because the idea of "cause" goes beyond what we have observed. In response, Kant argued convincingly that we *can* legitimately bring in the idea that one thing caused the other, and that we *must* do so if we are to have knowledge about the world.

In any case, today there are few pure empiricists, so for Carnell to disprove the extreme empiricist view does not necessarily disprove more moderate views that allow the mind to contribute some part to the knowing process.

Carnell concluded that if the ideas the mind must contribute to the knowing process cannot come from our senses, then we must be born with them. "We are born with a clear knowledge both of God and of His law"[11] as part of our being made in the image of God. We should note that the view that our brains could be born with actual information has been regarded as philosophically suspect since Locke,[12] and remains problematic in light of modern research into the physiology of learning. But just as Carnell does not consider more moderate forms of empiricism, he does not seem to consider the possibility that we may be born with certain capacities that are triggered by our experiences (a view advanced, for example, by Noam Chomsky to explain the language ability of young children).

The upshot is that according to Carnell we cannot build up the knowledge of God's existence from our experience. Instead we must bring it to experience. Because the image of God provides that our minds think in certain ways as well as contain certain content, we do not have to begin with an empty mind and build up the knowledge that God exists. When Romans 1:20 says that people know God exists "through what has been made," Carnell insists it does not mean that we start with nothing and conclude from sense experience that God exists. It means that "because we know God's existence and nature in our heart, we recognize Him in His handiwork."[13]

---

[11]Ibid., p. 151 n 20.
[12]John Locke, *An Essay Concerning Human Understanding* (London, 1690).
[13]Carnell, *Introduction to Christian Apologetics*, p. 169.

Like Van Til, Carnell broke with the commonsense epistemology that had provided the foundation of much of the traditional apologetics in the nineteenth and early twentieth centuries.[14] Both B. B. Warfield and Charles Hodge had grounded their apologetic approach on the views of Scottish realist Thomas Reid (1710-1796), who held that we are mentally equipped by God to recognize certain truths immediately, by common sense and without having to conclude them by reason or prove them. With the common sense view on the wane after Kant's claim that the mind is active in the knowing process, many looked for another explanation for knowledge. Van Til had sought a new grounding for apologetics in the Dutch Reformed approach of Abraham Kuyper, whose Calvinism emphasized faith and left no room for common ground between believer and nonbeliever.

Carnell by contrast sought his epistemological grounding in the Augustinian view that knowledge is possible because we are made in the image of God—our minds share something of the mind of God himself.[15] It is by this endowment that we know, for example, that a contradiction cannot be true (the principle of noncontradiction) and that a claim must be either true or false but cannot be both (the principle of the excluded middle); we also know the essentials of right and wrong, and true beauty.[16] So, contrary to Reid's view, we do not know things intuitively and by common sense; we have to use the mental equipment and content God has given us. Knowledge is fundamentally based on the reasoning process, not the intuition of common sense.[17]

This connection between God's mind and ours ensures that we have real knowledge. Showing that our minds know things as they really are is no small accomplishment in modern times, especially since Kant. While Kant recognized that our mind must add something to sense data to give us knowledge, he gave little guarantee that what our mind supplies is linked to reality. We are left to infer that the categories our minds use to think actually do interpret the world as it really is. This means we can have no guarantee that our minds are justified in thinking, for example, of objects as either existing or not existing, or as existing in numbers, or as has having causes. When it comes to God, we have to assume his existence in order to make sense of our experiences, but this does not con-

---

[14]Steven Arthur Hein, "The Nature and Existence of Man in the Apologetic Mission of Edward John Carnell" (PhD diss., St. Louis University, 1987), pp. 98–100.

[15]Ibid., pp. 83–84, 109–10.

[16]Carnell, *Introduction to Christian Apologetics*, pp. 162–68.

[17]Hein, "Nature and Existence of Man," pp. 98–100.

stitute an argument that he exists outside our minds—he might or he might not exist. The closest Kant can come to a guarantee of God's existence is that we have a sense that moral living must be connected to happiness, and God's existence is the only way to ensure that one leads to the other. (He said God's existence also ensures that there is a heaven since morality and happiness do not necessarily connect in this life.) So in the end, Kant guarantees only that we can know our experience, not things as they are. His philosophy left the modern world agnostic about God and our ability to have the final truth about anything.

Carnell's image-of-God solution set him against those who were fighting liberalism's tendency to blur the sacred and secular, those who would make God so much a part of creation that he is no longer transcendent and entirely different from it. Leading the fight was Karl Barth and the growing neo-orthodox movement, which sought to restore God's transcendence by making him so different from creation that there is no point of contact between God and humanity and no one can discover God by looking at the world around them. God is also so far above humanity that there is no useful similarity between his mind and ours. Furthermore, Barth claimed (at least early on) that revelation is not propositional (i.e., revelation does not take the form of assertions about the way things are). As such revelation does not give us information about the world. Supposedly to do so would put revelation under human control, which would be inappropriate for God's Word. In this respect Barth shared the post-Kantian agnosticism about knowing the world as it is.

While Kant left our knowledge in doubt, he did not deem our feelings and motives opaque and twisted by inner subterfuge, as they would later seem under the theories of Sigmund Freud. And for Barth and Emil Brunner, while revelation is not information about reality, it is an encounter with, an experience of, God. As Brunner put it, "Revelation is something that happens."[18]

By contrast, Carnell held staunchly to the traditional view that revelation is indeed propositional. He held that the propositions of revelation are true in every respect, that they are inerrant. Our ability to grasp revelatory language is another aspect of our knowledge grounded in the connection we have with God by virtue of our having been created in his image. Therefore, our being created in the image of God ensures our knowledge of the world, God and his Word.

In Carnell's view, language can effectively bridge the gap between God and

---

[18]Emil Brunner, *Revelation and Reason*, trans. Olive Wyon (Philadelphia: Westminster Press, 1946), p. 8; quoted in Hein, "Nature and Existence of Man," p. 80.

creation. This is because what we say about God and what we say about other things share some identical meaning—that is, they are "univocal." If it were not so we could know nothing of God.

This contrasts with Thomas Aquinas's view that our descriptions of God are analogical; that is, they are neither exactly the same (univocal) nor entirely different (equivocal). In "the lamb is in the pasture" and "Christ is the lamb of God," the word "lamb" is used analogically because its meanings are related but not identical. The issue gets more complex when we notice that the meaning of "x is powerful" depends on the nature of x. If x is a tractor, then "x is powerful" entails moving a lot of dirt, but if x is an atom bomb then it means destroying a lot of things. Therefore, one knows the meaning of statements about x *only insofar as one knows the nature of x*. But since there are limits to our knowledge of God there is a limit to our knowledge of the meaning of statements such as "God is powerful."[19]

Carnell believed that this analogical solution leaves us without knowledge of God. If we are to understand anything whatever about God, then descriptions of him and other things we know of must be univocal.[20]

Carnell believed that by demonstrating our inability to know by means of analogy he was denying empiricists the ability to bridge the gap between the knowledge of ordinary things that we obtain through our senses and the knowledge of God. This is because if we cannot know by analogy, then we cannot build knowledge of God by means of our sense knowledge. For example, we cannot arrive at a knowledge of God by observing order and concluding that God must be an orderer.[21]

Carnell concluded that if we cannot begin with the world and move to a knowledge of God, then we must begin with God and move to our knowledge of the world. So rather than begin with nothing but the senses and build up to Christianity as a conclusion (as an empiricist apologetic would do), Carnell proposed that we begin with Christianity and test it. This method could be called verificational. Carnell believed that this is the only type of reasoning we can use in a case for Christianity. Induction and deduction, the other two forms of reasoning, are inadequate.

We cannot use deduction, the form of logic that offers complete certainty for the conclusion. Deduction works for two reasons: first, all the information needed to assure the conclusion is contained in the premises; second, it proceeds by as-

---

[19]Carnell, *Introduction to Christian Apologetics*, pp. 148–49.
[20]Ibid., pp. 149–51.
[21]Ibid., p. 148.

suming that if the premises are true then the conclusion follows. Deduction applies the principle of noncontradiction such that it would be inconsistent to hold that certain premises are true but the conclusion is false. This way of operating, claims Carnell, makes deduction suitable only for fields like mathematics and formal logic, where it can be assumed both that everything relevant to the conclusion is known and that the information in the premises is true. But in other fields—and in real life—we cannot be so sure.[22] Deduction, he concludes, is insufficient to deal with real life problems such as verifying Christianity.

On a deeper level, deduction and the principle of noncontradiction are insufficient because the facts of the world are not as they are by logical necessity. The number of goats on a mountain and the depth of the Atlantic Ocean are not as they are because they logically had to be that way—God could have made the world any way he wanted and was not forced by logical necessity to make it any certain way. The point is that if the world is not the way it is by logical necessity then there is no way to prove the way it is by logic alone. So we cannot get truth by mere logic. Instead we have to check the world to see what God actually chose to do.[23] Nevertheless logic (especially the principle of noncontradiction) is helpful since truth is self-consistent because the Creator is self-consistent. But it is not by itself sufficient to give truth because there is no way to know which one of the many logically consistent possibilities God chose to make actual by bringing it about (there being no logical reason why he chose one over the other). Consequently we have to go beyond self-consistency to facts.[24]

Induction is also inadequate for the challenge in another way. Its form of reasoning claims only that the conclusion probably follows from the premises (whereas deduction claims the conclusion certainly follows). It can deal with real life; however, it can do no better than offer that the conclusion is probably true.[25]

Carnell believes that his verificational method of testing a hypothesis joins the strengths of deduction and induction. It works by the broadest application

---

[22]Ibid., pp. 103-5.

[23]Ibid., p. 61.

[24]Though Carnell does not develop the connection, his view is close to that of Duns Scotus, who challenged the medieval emphasis on logic by making God's will primary over his reason. Because God's will is completely free, Scotus argued, he could have made the world any way he chose and was not under logical compulsion to make it any particular way. That being the case, there is no way to know by mere logic what God chose and thus what is true; we must examine the world to see what he actually chose. Though Scotus never intended it, his view eventually had the effect of favoring empirical examination (and thus science) over rationalism (and the medieval emphasis on philosophy and religion).

[25]Carnell, *Introduction to Christian Apologetics*, pp. 105-6.

of the principle of noncontradiction: first, test the hypothesis for self-consistency; then test for consistency between the hypothesis and everything we know. Strictly speaking we have one test, that of consistency, but practically speaking the second test is to see whether our hypothesis fits all the facts as we know them. As Carnell sees it, joining the two dimensions of consistency and factuality gives the power to adequately prove a hypothesis about the real world. If we do not demonstrate that the hypothesis is free from contradictions, then we cannot claim that it rises to the level of universal and necessary truth. However, if we do not deal with facts we cannot claim that our hypothesis is relevant to the real world. When we put them together, we have a coherent view of the real world.[26] He called the process of testing a hypothesis "systematic consistency."

Carnell regarded systematic consistency (i.e., broad consistency, lack of contradictions) as the best way to check whether a view corresponds with the real world. A true proposition is one that corresponds with the real world, which is to say it corresponds with the mind of God, who knows the world perfectly.[27] We judge those beliefs true that make a "smooth, systematically consistent picture" out of experience.[28] Experience includes the "total breadth of human consciousness, which embraces the entire rational, volitional, and emotional life of man, both within and without."[29] We judge Christianity true because it makes the best sense of external experience, including history, both ancient and recent. Thus on the one hand Carnell holds to the correspondence view of truth, according to which a proposition is true if it corresponds to the way the world is; a link to the real world makes a proposition true. But on the other hand he holds a coherence view of justification: the way we know a proposition is true is by checking whether it coheres (contradicts or does not contradict) with other things we believe. So what does it mean to say x is "true"? It means it corresponds with the way things are. How do we know x is true? We know by coherence, or consistency, specifically, (1) the hypothesis does not contradict itself, (2) it fits with the facts and (3) it has existential viability (i.e., it can be lived out without hypocrisy; "existential" is composed of the "ethical, axiological, and psychological").[30]

Gordon Lewis summarizes Carnell's method of justifying beliefs as inte-

---

[26]Ibid., pp. 106-7.
[27]"Truth for the Christian, then, is defined as *correspondence with the mind of God*" (ibid., p. 47).
[28]Ibid., p. 56; cf. 175, "Any hypothesis is verified when it smoothly interprets life."
[29]Ibid., p. 56.
[30]The first two in this description were suggested to me by Gordon Lewis in personal email correspondence, Aug. 24, 2013. The last one was adapted from Lewis, "Edward John Carnell," p. 327.

grating "the emphases of Clark on logic, Van Til on presuppositions, Machen on historical facts, Brightman on empirical givens, and existentialists like Niebuhr and Kierkegaard on internal data."[31]

Carnell admits that the entire case for Christianity is less than flawless. Nevertheless, when it comes to confirmation from history, for example, archaeology "is remarkably confirmatory of the Bible accounts, not hit or miss; this is what we should expect if Scripture has been inerrantly preserved by God."[32] Furthermore, only the hypothesis that God has indeed revealed himself in Scripture can explain the life of Christ, especially his influence on Western culture, the quality of his ethical teachings and his effect on the growth of the church.

Carnell sums up the breadth of Christianity's power to explain the external world.

> It explains the nature of man, the frailty of his body, the sin in his heart, and his quest for life and peace. Christianity can account for our three social institutions, the state, the church, and the family, for it orders their founding and directs their purpose and prerogatives. Christianity embraces explicit or implicit solutions to every conceivable social problem: labor and race relations, divorce and infidelity, equity in business, standards of jurisprudence. It explains the universality of religion and the bloody sacrifice. It accounts for the actions of both those who commit war atrocities and live in debauchery and drunkenness, and those who wait in fear and trembling for the judgment of God.[33]

While the case is not flawless (for example, the creation account and age of the earth do not fit modern science), "a rational man settles for that position which is attended by the fewest difficulties, not one which is unattended by any."[34]

As to confirmation from internal experience,

> The Bible accurately describes man—body and spirit—as a unit endowed with rationality, a moral nature, and an insatiable desire for self-preservation. Christianity accounts for the universality of the fear of God and of the knowledge of right and wrong. Christianity explains why men tremble and fear before they go to the gallows: they know God's judgment awaits them, their conscience bearing witness. Christianity explains man's quest for hope; and it meets this hope by providing personal salvation and immortality.[35]

---

[31]Lewis, "Edward John Carnell," p. 325.
[32]Carnell, *Introduction to Christian Apologetics*, p. 110.
[33]Ibid., p. 111.
[34]Ibid., p. 111; cf. p. 121.
[35]Ibid., p. 112.

All this confirms Christianity as highly probable even if not logically certain. Absolute certainty is not available when proving things in the real world, only in proofs within strictly formal disciplines such as mathematics and logic. Christianity is not a formal discipline but is founded on historical events and deals with moral values.[36] The fact that its truth can be demonstrated to a high level of probability rather than logical certainty Carnell regards as a strength:

> This admission that Christianity's proof for the resurrection of Christ cannot rise above probability is not a form of weakness; it is rather an indication that the Christian is in possession of a world-view which is making a sincere effort to come to grips with actual history. Christianity is not a deductively necessary system of thought which has been spun out of a philosopher's head, wholly indifferent to the march of human history below it; rather it is a plan of salvation, a coherent solution to the persistent problem of man.[37]

High probability is all we need, and is sufficient to verify belief. Carnell insisted that faith must be rationally connected to the real world. On the one hand, those like French existentialists and neo-orthodox theologians who boast that their views do not square rationally "simply peacock their deficiency in objective truth."[38] On the other hand, those who base faith on nothing more than a mystical feeling "fall back upon some mystical, ineffable, esoteric, subjective faith-leap, in which case the voice of God cannot be distinguished from the voice of the devil."[39] The person basing faith on feeling alone and the person basing faith on evidence both have internal assurance, but the one with evidence also has a rational faith that is connected to the world.

The fact that the evidence renders the conclusion highly probable instead of logically certain does not lessen our certitude, that is, our internal sense that it is true.[40] We can be just as sure that George Washington lived as that $2 + 2 = 4$ even though we cannot prove it to the same degree. In that sense the Christian does not believe and pray to a God who is only probably true.[41] As with so many things in life, we can be fully assured of what we can prove only 99 percent.

---

[36]Ibid., pp. 113–16.

[37]Ibid., p. 114.

[38]Ibid., p. 108.

[39]Ibid., p. 119. "Faith without objectively verifiable truth is comparable to the sort of certainty which goes along with snake-handlers, sun-adorers, and esoteric faith-healing cults of sundry species" (ibid., p. 117).

[40]Ibid., p. 120. "Certitude" is modern and widely used; Carnell calls it "moral certainty."

[41]Ibid., pp. 119–21.

Reformed epistemologists make a similar point when arguing that it can be rational for our degree of faith to exceed our level of proof; we can even be sure of things we would have difficulty proving, such as that the world was not created five minutes ago with apparent age.

Carnell is more cautious, however. He raised a few Reformed eyebrows with his suggestion that a genuine commitment to rational principles entails that we must be willing to give up Christianity if it is shown to be untrue. To say otherwise would be to "betray" all he said about faith and rationality and "to remove our only basis for telling the word of God from the suggestions of the devil."[42] He holds to this even though he affirms that the Holy Spirit provides the believer with a subjective witness within his heart that Christianity is true.[43] He is trying to be consistent with the idea that we should believe the most reasonable view and that Christianity is demonstrably just that. Accordingly, he believes that it would be inconsistent to advocate that the Christian keep believing in Christianity if in the end it turns out not to be the most reasonable view. To be rational, our faith must ultimately be responsive to reason, and that means being willing go where it ultimately leads, even if realistically it is difficult to imagine evidence sufficient to disprove it. No one should continue to propagate a belief they have ultimately concluded is false

Others resolve the issue differently. For classical apologist William Lane Craig the Spirit's internal witness to the believer provides direct awareness that is so crucial and compelling that it defeats external rational challenges to faith.[44] Similarly, veridicalist Mark Hanna insists that our sense that the essentials of the faith are true is "given" to the believer by the Spirit intuitively, such that faith is not dependent on our reasoning.[45] This internal witness means that, for the believer at least, Christianity is much more than a hypothesis to be tested. It also means that the Christian would not give up Christianity because of evidence against it.[46] For presuppositionalists, the question of what to do in the face of contrary evidence would never come up—at least not in theory—since everything is viewed in the light of the determined conviction that Christianity is the only rational view.

---

[42]Ibid., p. 120.
[43]Ibid., p. 68.
[44]William Lane Craig, "Classical Apologetics," in *Five Views on Apologetics*, ed. Steven B. Cowan (Grand Rapids: Zondervan, 2000), pp. 33–37.
[45]Mark Hanna, *Crucial Questions in Apologetics* (Grand Rapids: Baker, 1981), p. 103. His view, veridicalism, "begins with the reality of God as a universal given and with the constitutive content of the Christian faith as a special given."
[46]Personal conversations with Mark Hanna, Los Angeles, 1979–1983.

Perhaps we should view Carnell's position in the light of Basil Mitchell's observation that rationality on any level—including the sciences—demands that we continue to hold to our belief in the face of a certain amount of contrary evidence. If we gave up our views at the first sign of trouble we would never hold them long enough to verify or falsify them, and that goes for any view, even a scientific one.[47] Imre Lakatos agrees with the practice, calling it the "principle of tenacity."[48] If Carnell's point was more than a theoretical concession it is hard to imagine him, a veteran of two secular doctorates, encountering a level of disproof sufficient to give up his belief in Christianity. He no doubt held on to his own faith despite many personal challenges. What Carnell seems to have in mind is our discovery—however we reach the conclusion and however unlikely we currently judge the possibility to be—that our beliefs are factually incorrect. In that case we ought not to continue to say it is true if we know it is not. To some extent critics have focused on how difficult it would be to reach such a point, and how unlikely such an event would be. Carnell wants to focus on the principle behind what our response should be if it were to happen.

It seems that if such rational inertia has any proper limits at all for the believer, reaching that limit ought to be a distant possibility indeed. Job is given in Scripture as an example of righteously holding to faith in spite of extreme and persistent challenges. And although in John 20:29 Christ gives Thomas the evidence he needs after doubting his faith, he praises those who will believe without it.

Common ground. The hallmark of Carnell's approach to apologetics is to find and use common ground between the Christian and the nonbeliever. After pointing out Augustine's tendency to do the same, he looked back on his own life's work: "In my own books on apologetics I have consistently tried to build on some useful point of contact between the gospel and culture."[49] Christians who are theologically conservative do not do this more, he said, because they assume that "everything worth knowing is in the Bible. This has the dreadful effect of

[47]Basil Mitchell, *The Justification of Religious Belief* (New York: Oxford University Press, 1981), p. 130 (on the general issue, see his chap. seven).

[48]Imre Lakatos, "Falsification and Methodology of Scientific Research Programs," in *Criticism and the Growth of Knowledge*, ed. I. Lakatos and A. Musgrave (Cambridge, MA: Cambridge University Press, 1970), pp. 91–196. Cited in Louis Pojman, "Can Religious Belief Be Rational?," in *Philosophy of Religion: An Anthology*, ed. Louis P. Pojman, 2nd ed. (Belmont, CA: Wadsworth, 1994), p. 513. Pojman notes that C. S. Peirce rejects the practice.

[49]Edward John Carnell, *The Kingdom of Love and the Pride of Life* (Grand Rapids: Eerdmans, 1960), p. 6.

separating the gospel from culture."[50] Theologically, it is the mistake of forcing too great a distance between common grace (which is God's grace to all humans and includes the ability to know truth from error and right from wrong) and special grace (which is God's grace to believers and includes the ability to accept the gospel). To divorce them "is an offense to both culture and the gospel."[51]

By contrast, Abraham Kuyper—and following him, Van Til—held that the regenerate and unregenerate are in completely separate cognitive worlds, there being "an abyss in the universal human consciousness across which no bridge can be built."[52] Carnell regarded this exaggerated difference between believer and nonbeliever as an unseen prop holding up Van Til's claim that Christianity is the only acceptable worldview and not just the best one—allowing Van Til to illegitimately avoid appealing to probabilities. He wrote, "Dr. Van Til is anxious to negate truth in unbelievers in order that Christianity's reality may appear in absolute contrast. The fear is that if unbelievers have any truth, Christianity will only be 'better' than non-Christianity—a matter of degrees in which absoluteness is destroyed."[53] Rejecting the idea that there is extreme intellectual distance between believer and nonbeliever, he added, "May the sad day never come when Christians no longer look for truth in Pericles' *Funeral Oration* or Mill's 'Essay on Liberty.'"[54] So as Carnell saw it, he himself had a much more positive view of common grace than Van Til and thus, on theological grounds, of unbelieving humanity's ability to find truth.

A crucial philosophical difference also divides the two apologists. For Van Til, there is no separation between meaning and fact: everything is a matter of interpretation. Our presuppositions so completely overshadow everything we know that there are no facts independent of interpretation because a person's worldview completely determines how facts are viewed. This is why for Van Til there can be no useful common ground between the believer and nonbeliever from which to argue toward Christianity as a conclusion. We cannot agree, for example, that there is order and proceed to argue for a divine orderer.[55] But crucially for Carnell,

[50]Ibid., p. 9.
[51]Ibid.
[52]Abraham Kuyper, *Principles of Sacred Theology* (1898; repr., Grand Rapids: Eerdmans, 1968), p. 152; quoted in Kenneth D. Boa and Robert M. Bowman Jr., *Faith Has Its Reasons: An Integrative Approach to Defending Christianity* (Colorado Springs, CO: NavPress, 2001), p. 259.
[53]Review of *Defense of the Faith* by Cornelius Van Til, in *The Christian Century*, January 4, 1956, pp. 14–15; quoted in John A. Sims, *Edward John Carnell: Defender of the Faith* (Washington, DC: University Press of America, 1979), p. 62.
[54]Ibid., p. 62.
[55]Recall that Van Til rejected traditional formulations of theistic arguments on grounds that they reinforced a person's sinful sense of "autonomy." For a discussion of his transcendental reformulations

there is some epistemic distance between facts and interpretation. Our worldview does not overshadow literally everything we know. This explains why the Christian and non-Christian agree on so many things—but only as long as they do not deal with them on a metaphysical level. There is agreement on the nature of physics, for instance; Christians do not have to rewrite physics books from a Christian perspective. There is common ground in science because "scientific conclusions as such do not depend for their meaning upon one's logical starting point."[56] The logical starting point is "the highest principle which one introduces to give unity and order to his interpretation of reality."[57] For the Christian it is the triune God.

Common ground ends as soon as the "almost invisible"[58] line is crossed, when we go from "impersonal, nonmetaphysical"[59] descriptions to questions of ultimate meaning. On this level even a plant means something different to the Christian and non-Christian. To one it is made and sustained by God; to the other it is not. Such questions of meaning are not far from any nonmetaphysical description. Yet properly practiced, science does not deal with such questions. It "is confined to an impersonal description of the phenomenal universe."[60] This is why Christians and non-Christians can collaborate perfectly on a non-metaphysical level even though their metaphysical views clash at every point.

Van Til explained the non-Christian's possession of truth as the result of un-acknowledged and illicit borrowing from the Christian's worldview, whereas Carnell explained it in terms of a level of meaning that exists at a functional distance from the highest level (the metaphysical level) of a person's worldview. Carnell's philosophical view of meaning and his theological view of common grace thus made room for common ground and a point of contact between the Christian and non-Christian.

Point of contact. Carnell's characteristic point of contact is the felt needs of the nonbeliever. If believers do not show nonbelievers how Christianity meets his or her needs, they will conclude that the gospel is irrelevant.[61]

In his first book Carnell sees the nonbeliever as searching for a solution to "soul sorrow" and to the desire for the most consistent worldview that will bring

---

of them, see Greg Bahnsen, *Van Til's Apologetic: Readings and Analysis* (Phillipsburg, NJ: P & R, 1998), pp. 612–27.
[56]Carnell, *Introduction to Christian Apologetics*, p. 214.
[57]Ibid., p. 124.
[58]Ibid., p. 215.
[59]Ibid., p. 216.
[60]Ibid., p. 217.
[61]Carnell, *Kingdom of Love*, p. 9.

meaning to the otherwise unconnected details of life (the problem of the "one and the many"). Here the specific point of contact between believer and non-believer is the recognition that the principle of noncontradiction is the right instrument for finding truth.

Several years after his first book, Carnell's many personal struggles drove him to explore other points of contact more fully. Insomnia had been a problem for him since high school, and he admitted how much it tempted him to be irritable, and at one point "even suicide took on a certain attractiveness."[62] His presidency of Fuller Theological Seminary from 1955 to 1959 was also something of a burden. Not only did it take him away from his academic interests, but he also had to deal with controversy over fundamentalism and personnel issues. He found relief in long walks, long hours and a growing dependence on sleeping pills. He resigned in order to return to academics and the classroom, but that by no means resolved everything. In June 1961 a breakdown put him in the hospital for several weeks. He underwent electroshock therapy, which seems to have caused memory loss that brought long, awkward pauses during his teaching.[63]

Even before his troubles became so severe he thought of apologetics in terms of the total person. He affirmed that "man is not simply a *nous* [mind]. . . . He happens to be a complexity of intellect, emotions, and will—plus a lot more." As a result, "The heart knows a depth of insight which, *while it may never be separated from rational consistency*, is yet not univocally identified with such consistency."[64]

In his first book, Carnell said that apologetics can make use of internal experience that is "effable," or describable. It is different from "ineffable" experience, which is inward assurance that cannot be described and which gets its persuasive power from its immediacy (like the experience of the mystic). Unlike ineffable experience, effable experience can be connected to other types of knowledge so it can be subjected to the test for coherence, that is, against other things we know.[65]

Carnell became more convinced over the years that to reach the nonbeliever we need to do more than offer intellectually satisfying answers. He continually sought the right apologetic balance between the intellect and the other aspects of human nature. Increasingly, he emphasized those other aspects as points of

---

[62]Edward John Carnell, *Christian Commitment: An Apologetic* (New York: Macmillan, 1957), p. 11.

[63]Nelson, *Making and Unmaking of an Evangelical Mind*, p. 114. Regarding the treatment, see also pp. 113, 116–17, 161, 172, 189, 226.

[64]Carnell, *Christian Commitment*, pp. 38–39 (emphasis original).

[65]Carnell (*Introduction to Christian Apologetics*, p. 125) cites Brand Blanshard, *The Nature of Thought* (London: Allen & Unwin, 1939), 2:224 (cited in Carnell as *The Nature of Truth*).

contact between the believer and nonbeliever. As he developed the breadth of possible points of contact, he developed his view of how subjectivity functions in the apologetic task.

His next apologetic book, *The Philosophy of the Christian Religion* (1952), developed values as a point of contact with the nonbeliever. A value is what we "prize or esteem," something we hold to in order to increase our happiness.[66] Those who value what will not bring happiness in the long run are foolish, and the consequence is regret. Wisdom is a matter of choosing the right value, just as rationality is a matter of choosing what is consistent.[67]

Carnell sought, then, to show that Christianity is the right choice for true and lasting happiness. He assumed that the driving motivation of all humans is self-interest. We cannot stop at showing that Christianity is rational because we give the nonbeliever no motivation to accept it. By showing that it satisfies the most completely and that it satisfies on the highest level, we provide the desire to embrace it. This he saw as Christ's way: "When offering the gospel, therefore, Christ *appeals* to the ego. He promises men that by giving up one type of self-ishness (before men) they will gain a new and higher selfishness (before God). If we follow him, we receive peace in heart and treasures in heaven. All of this appeals to self-love."[68] Thus the apologist works on more than one level, showing that Christianity is both rational and desirable, and that the alternatives are neither—that the choice is between Christianity and despair.[69]

Inadequate solutions neglect part of the soul, leaving it unsatisfied and under-developed. Hedonism, which values pleasure above all, leads to boredom, frustration and a deep sense of exhaustion.[70] Materialism, which puts the physical above the spiritual, is best exemplified in communism. While many reject communism they accept material things as supremely valuable as well as communism's core idea that history is controlled by human initiative.[71] Communism strives for a better world but undermines the spiritual and moral foundations that make such a world possible. The individual and all sense of morals are smothered by the will of the party. Besides, communism undermines all rationality by sup-

---

[66]Edward John Carnell, *A Philosophy of the Christian Religion* (Grand Rapids: Eerdmans, 1952), p. 16.

[67]Ibid., p. 21.

[68]Ibid., p. 243-44 (emphasis original). I am grateful to Hein ("Nature and Existence of Man," p. 174) for leading me to this reference.

[69]Ibid., pp. 44-45.

[70]Ibid., chap. three, "The Siren Voice of Pleasure," pp. 49-82.

[71]Ibid., pp. 84-85.

posing that history determines what is true, which leads to the irrational notion that contradictory things can be true. By contrast, Western culture is founded on the correct idea that history is an outworking of changeless truth.[72] Logical positivism caricatured the scientific method by accepting as knowledge only what is "scientifically" verifiable. That eliminated metaphysics and ethics, but failed to realize that even science itself depends on at least some beliefs in both fields. Humanism cannot help a person "close the gap between what man is and what he ought to be,"[73] nor does it have an answer for sin and guilt.

The God of deism (who creates the world but thereafter never interacts with it) on the one hand is too transcendent to be relevant to humans. The God of pantheism on the other hand is not sufficiently distinct from humans to interact with them. Liberal theology's God is also too immanent to be relevant, since humanity must have a God who is both distinct from history and Lord of it. Universalism does not account for clear biblical teaching that some will be unsaved; furthermore, having unlimited time to repent will not ensure a different outcome, nor is it an advantage over withdrawing the offer of mercy upon person's death. Roman Catholicism is inadequate because it confuses grace and works.

Carnell finds in Christianity the way to have all that is lacking in competing views. This includes, for example, a pleasure that, being born of love, truly satisfies, timeless values that control the material realm, a metaphysical basis for science, a way to deal with guilt and so on.

At this stage of his thought, Carnell still held that we must use rationality to first test our options. Rationality is the gatekeeper, and knowledge by inference (reasoning to a true conclusion) is fundamental. But it is the servant of a higher way of knowing, knowledge by acquaintance, by which we know things immediately (akin to the way God knows), apart from having to draw conclusions in order to know. In this kind of knowing itself there is a hierarchy: acquaintance knowledge of things is the servant of acquaintance knowledge of people, which in turn is the servant of acquaintance knowledge of God.[74] Perfection of knowledge is not knowledge of rational connections but a relationship, and the highest relationship is one with God. In this way of knowing God, "when spirit clasps spirit in the intimacy and mutuality of fellowship, the heart is able to

---

[72]Ibid., pp. 103–4, 109, 123, 127.
[73]Ibid., p. 261.
[74]Ibid., pp. 181–83.

perceive conclusions so directly that the need for minor premises is ruled out."[75] Though rational consistency remains important,[76] it is only a step to higher knowing. And when it comes to God, stopping at mere inferential knowledge such that we fail to form a relationship constitutes a kind of idolatry.[77]

In *Christian Commitment* (1957) Carnell appeals to the common ground of our sense of justice and personal dignity. He notes that apologetics must be sensitive to the times since what has worked in the past will not necessarily work now. So because the modern mindset is "existential" we should appeal to the human ability to know moral as well as rational truth.[78] Awareness of God is implicit in every individual's moral self-consciousness, though people remain unaware of it "until worldly pride yields to spiritual humility."[79]

He first realized how our moral and spiritual condition affect our knowledge after he had a severe bout with insomnia that distorted his view of virtually everything. There must be an aspect of knowing that is affected by this broader aspect of our life; there must be a "third way" of knowing.

Things that exist (i.e., ontological truth) can be known immediately by "acquaintance." To know x in this way requires that we experience x. However, propositions about truth can be known by inference and require that we reason correctly.[80] Most of philosophy stops at these two kinds of truth and their two corresponding ways of knowing (a few like Kierkegaard venture further). The third way has a twofold apologetic advantage in that it does not require that we experience anything or infer anything, but only that we be human; and since it deals with a person's moral and spiritual condition, it includes the motivation a person needs to actually embrace the truth rather than merely contemplate it. Dealing with moral and spiritual reality is inescapable insofar as everyone must act,[81] and these realities get to the core problem of humanity, which (Carnell came to believe) is not lack of knowledge but lack of the will to act on the knowledge one already has (also a theme in presuppositionalism). Furthermore, a person's morals reveal what they actually believe. Scripturally, Carnell regarded the third way as part of the truth that God has made known to everyone (Rom 1:19-20).[82]

---

[75]Ibid., p. 179.
[76]Ibid., pp. 183–84.
[77]Ibid., p. 182.
[78]Carnell, *Christian Commitment*, p. viii.
[79]Ibid., p. ix.
[80]Ibid., pp. 14–17, 25.
[81]Ibid., p. 36.
[82]Ibid., p. 27.

To function as moral beings we must be aware, for example, that we are not the authors of our own existence, that we are bound by moral duties and that violations of duty are culpable before an administrator of justice who transcends humanity. If there were no such transcendent administrator (i.e., God) all moral judgments would be meaningless. Carnell believed that conclusions of this sort need not be proved in a traditional sense, since "realities to which we are committed by existence itself need only be impressed, not proved."[83] Nevertheless, his reasoning here is reminiscent of what has come to be known as the moral argument, which reasons that at least some moral obligations are objective in that they transcend human choice; if so, they must be grounded in a higher moral being (i.e., God). Therefore God exists. Of course Carnell's third way is much broader in that it also deals with a person's moral and spiritual state and doesn't just reason to the ground of moral obligation. He reasons in many ways and at length that the Christian worldview is implied in our moral life.

Gordon Lewis of Denver Seminary, once a student of Carnell's as wells as an able advocate of his views, observes that Carl F. H. Henry takes a view of ethics similar to Carnell's. Henry, the former editor in chief of *Christianity Today*, holds that only Christianity can account for the universal recognition of right and wrong, human inability to do right and attempts to justify self while rebelling against God.[84]

In *The Kingdom of Love and the Pride of Life* (1960), Carnell develops love as a point of contact with the non-Christian. His eyes were opened to love's apologetic significance by reading Freud, he admitted. Furthermore, Freud's emphasis on "the natural zest and unconditional faith of childhood" were in harmony with Christ's appeals for a childlike faith. Carnell added that a child knows that "he is not sufficient unto himself, nor does he pretend to be. Jesus says we should go and do likewise. We must learn to rest in the sovereignty of God."[85]

Simply put, the solution to our human need is love, which is "an act of un-

---

[83]Ibid., pp. 102–3.

[84]Carl F. H. Henry, *Christian Personal Ethics* (Grand Rapids: Eerdmans, 1957), p. 151; cited in Gordon Lewis, *Testing Christianity's Truth Claims: Approaches to Christian Apologetics* (1976; repr., Lanham, MD: University Press of America, 1990), pp. 269–70; on Henry's views, see Lewis, *Testing Christianity's Truth Claims*, pp. 269–81. Chaps. 7–10 of Lewis give a detailed explanation of Carnell's views. Lewis said that while a student at Gordon College he took all the courses he could "from the stimulating young professor" (Lewis, "Edward John Carnell," p. 325). Lewis's *Testing Christianity's Truth Claims* is a helpful source for understanding Carnell, and it is fortunate to have it back in print.

[85]Carnell, *Kingdom of Love*, pp. 6–7.

conditional acceptance."[86] Humility is the way to the healing power of love, whereas pride hinders it. The goal of the book "is to show how the gospel can further man's search for a happy, integrated life."[87]

Lewis notes that Vernon Grounds, former president of Denver Seminary, develops a similar psychological apologetic for Christianity. Christianity explains the inner life of the Christian and non-Christian, and it offers a basis for a sound mental life.[88]

GORDON LEWIS

From 1958 to his retirement in 1993, Gordon R. Lewis was professor of systematic theology and philosophy of religion at Denver Conservative Baptist Seminary. He founded Evangelical Ministries to New Religions and has written on cults and theology. In *Testing Christianity's Truth Claims*, he examines competing apologetic methodologies and concludes that Carnell's is the most realistic and able to stand up against real-world challenges. In the book he says that after studying other worldviews, "I failed to find a non-Christian interpretation of the world with greater consistency fit more facts."[89] Lewis draws his conclusion from a deep knowledge of alternative beliefs, especially cults, and extensive crosscultural experience.

Lewis seeks to establish that not all meaning is dependent on context, especially social context, which is claimed in some postmodern views. "Cognitive assertions may be context-related without being context-determined," he says.[90] If our basic categories are socially determined, we would not be able to change religions or philosophies, nor would we have a sufficiently transcendent perspective from which to appeal to a society to make it better. Postmodernists themselves, he says, assume that the meanings of their own statements transcend their cultural context. Furthermore, there are common values to all distinctively human life: (1) human rights, (2) justice, (3) love, (4) empirical data and (5) logical noncontradiction. These are not established by induction, de-

---

[86]Ibid., p. 7.

[87]Ibid., p. 10.

[88]Vernon Grounds, "Christian Perspectives on Mental Illness," *The Journal of the American Scientific Affiliation* 14 (December 1962): 108–12; cited in Lewis, *Testing Christianity's Truth Claims*, p. 246. Lewis also cites a series of articles by Grounds in *His*, January 1963 to February 1964. Lewis discusses Grounds in *Testing Christianity's Truth Claims*, pp. 245–50.

[89]Lewis, *Testing Christianity's Truth Claims*, p. 295.

[90]Gordon Lewis, "An Integrative Method of Justifying Religious Assertions," in *Evangelical Apologetics*, ed. Michael Bauman, David W. Hall and Robert C. Newman (Camp Hill, PA: Christian Publications, 1996), p. 70. He makes the point in the context of arguing for commonalities in any context.

duction or abduction (i.e., inference to the best explanation), but by "an existential analysis of what is essential for distinctively human life."[91] Working from the list, true statements are those that are noncontradictory (no. 5) and have empirical fit (no. 4) as well as existential authenticity (nos. 1–3, human rights, justice and love). This is essentially what E. J. Carnell referred to as systematic consistency: "By that he meant a logically noncontradictory account of the relevant lines of external (sensory) and internal (ethical, axiological and psychological) data."[92] Francis Schaeffer used them as the three tests for truth: "Logical noncontradiction, factual adequacy and existential viability."[93] Lewis sometimes simplifies it as coherence and authenticity. Ethical absolutes are rooted not in the Enlightenment but in "our divine likeness to the Creator," and can be learned from general revelation and common grace. To deny these is to lose points of contact with the world.[94]

While some argue that there can be no objectivity because perspectives differ, differences in perspectives do not necessarily contradict and disprove each other. Differences can be weighed, data tested and converging lines of data recognized in order to identify the most accurate account.[95]

So essentials for human life are the same from person to person and culture to culture. These form common ground as well as point us to true statements.

As we saw above, Lewis says that this method of justifying beliefs "integrates the emphases of Clark on logic, Van Til on the content of presuppositions, Machen on historical facts, Brightman on empirical givens, and existentialists like Niebuhr and Kierkegaard on internal data."[96] The logical starting point is not objective evidence or a presupposition but a hypothesis, which acknowledges that there is some subjectivity in a decision about what is ultimately real and good.

Verificational, or abductive, reasoning used by Carnell and Lewis differs from empiricism (the view that knowledge comes from the senses) as held by John Locke (1632–1704). Locke believed that the mind is like a blank slate and sense impressions are formed on it. For Lewis this is unrealistic in that no one can be that objective. We all come to the data with preunderstandings. All sides should

[91]Ibid., p. 74.
[92]Ibid., p. 77.
[93]Ibid., p. 69.
[94]Ibid., pp. 75–76. He says, "We know it is morally wrong to abuse another's human rights, flout justice, live dishonestly, be selfishly uncaring, distort facts and contradict our own word."
[95]Ibid., pp. 73–74.
[96]Lewis, "Edward John Carnell," p. 325.

acknowledge their views as hypotheses to be tested. Furthermore, working strictly from induction, we cannot arrive at infinite attributes of God. We cannot, for example, observe examples of power and conclude that God is omnipotent. The truths of the Bible could never be established from limited observations.

Deduction of the presuppositional sort fairs no better. We cannot start from an unchallengeable presupposition because such an approach assumes what it is supposed to prove, and, philosophically speaking, "no presuppositions are self-attesting."[97] A presupposition is considered above confirmation or disproof, whereas a hypothesis is subject to confirmation or disproof. From an outreach standpoint, it is much easier to dialogue with someone about a hypothesis than to allege that nothing makes sense until the person assumes "my presupposition of the God of the Bible."[98] The content of the hypothesis is not that different from presuppositionalism: "The existence of the God disclosed in creation, in the Jesus of history and in the teaching of Scripture."[99] So, if the God of the Bible exists, then we can account for the order and magnificence of creation, persons and values, the history of the first century, and even data from the sciences. We can also account for the "amazing unity and power of the Bible."[100] The witness of the Spirit has its place, but not as a substitute for evidence.

Testing a hypothesis using the verificational approach includes experience, but since experience is more than sensory, "hypotheses are tested by their coherence also with numerous converging internal lines of data such as the demand for ethical justice, the psychological need for love and the dynamic of religious experience. In other words, both an entire worldview and the doctrines within it are verified when they offer a coherent and viable account of the relevant data (of general and special revelation)."[101] Because we are finite and sinful, we cannot have absolute intellectual certainty. But it is sensible to accept the view with the fewest difficulties, and we can have confidence in it. He emphasizes the distinction between belief, which is assent to true information, and faith, which is a total commitment to the truth.

Lewis considers the verificational method a form of critical realism, which goes beyond simple appearances (i.e., "naive realism," which would believe that

---

[97]Lewis, "An Integrative Method," p. 81.
[98]Ibid., p. 82.
[99]Ibid.
[100]Ibid.
[101]Ibid., pp. 84–85.

the oar in the water is actually bent[102]) to discern the truth about a reality that exists independently of us. It differs from commonsense (Scottish) realism in that "not all the intuitions or 'natural judgments' of 'common sense' are true even though our minds have been made by God to know and govern reality."[103] Those intuitions have to be examined and verified.

The verificational approach can be extended to theology in a sixfold method Lewis calls "integrative" theology: define the topic for inquiry, examine historical views, examine and summarize the relevant biblical passages, formulate a cohesive doctrine and relate it to other doctrines (the systematic-theology step in the sixfold method), defend the view (the apologetic step), and apply the resulting convictions to life and ministry.[104] This avoids the temptation to read into the text an illegitimate organizing principle, because it "seeks coherence at the end of its investigation, not by eisegesis, but by exegesis. The methodology of integrative theology does not start with indefensible presuppositions or axioms. The logical starting point in verificational research discovers alternative hypotheses to be tested."[105]

This approach affirms the role of basic logic as an expression of God's mind. Principles of basic logic include the classical laws of thought, namely, the principles of identity (*a* is *a*), noncontradiction (*a* is not non-*a*) and the excluded middle (either *a* or non-*a*).[106]

The verificational approach thus forms a grand synthesis of the human condition, common human needs, the way to identify truth and a method for constructing a cohesive and expansive view of truth by which we can live.

---

[102]Lewis uses the apparent bending of an object in the water, a common illustration for the difference between how things appear versus the way they are. See, e.g., Plato (*Republic* 10), and David Hume (*Three Dialogues Between Hylas and Philonous*, third dialogue; it was well-known enough by Hume that he called the oar in the water a trite topic, "employed by the skeptics in all ages," *An Enquiry Concerning Human Understanding* 12.1). Direct realism is the general view that perception is a direct awareness of things as they are. Naive realism is the simplest form of it, "and is usually alleged by philosophers to be an innocent prejudice of the plain man that has to be overcome if philosophical progress is to be made." R. J. Hurst, "Realism," in *The Encyclopedia of Philosophy* (New York: Macmillan, 1967), 7:78 (the article includes a discussion on the different types of direct realism). Lewis's discussion on critical realism, commonsense (Scottish) realism and idealism is in Gordon R. Lewis and Bruce A. Demarest, *Integrative Theology*, three vols. in one (Grand Rapids: Zondervan, 1996), 1:36 n.

[103]Lewis and Demarest, *Integrative Theology*, 1:36–37 n.

[104]Ibid., 1:26.

[105]Ibid.

[106]Lewis and Demarest (ibid., 1:32) explain the excluded middle as "A is not non-A," and the principle of noncontradiction as "a thing cannot be both A and non-A."

Lewis gives brief examples of how other views are inadequate. David Hume's empiricism, for example, could not even affirm the existence of the self, which led to a loss of "inner dignity and responsibility."[107] Secular humanism sought to restore human worth but destroyed "the self-determining, personal agent who was to have dominion over his environment rather than be determined by it."[108] Existentialists addressed empiricism's loss of the self by giving priority to the individual, affirming that there are no constraints on freedom because there is no God, and no constraints on an individual's nature—or any other nature. Sartre said, "Existence precedes essence"; each thing is an individual and not determined by a category of which it is a part. Lewis says this entails that "no essences can be known."[109] The broader implication of Sartre's philosophy is that there can be no objectively valid statements about anything. But, concludes Lewis, that means Sartre's own statements can have no objective validity! Two major forms of Eastern thought are self-contradictory. Hinduism affirms that Brahman is ultimate reality, yet it is also said that no true statements can be made about it. On some forms of Buddhism, things in themselves cannot be known, yet Buddhist writer Alan Watts has published many books on an unspeakable experience, Lewis says.[110]

FRANCIS SCHAEFFER

Pastoring and evangelism were Francis Schaeffer's (1912–1984) primary interests, and dialogue[111] rather than writing was his preferred means of communication. As a result, he was fifty-six years old before his first book came out. He had a love for young people, who eventually came in a steady stream seeking answers at L'Abri ("The Shelter"), a ministry based out of a cluster of houses in Switzerland. Denver Seminary philosophy professor Douglas Groothuis sums up Schaeffer's focus: "He was not interested in academic apologetics per se, but wanted souls to know the God revealed in Holy Scripture."[112] As a practitioner of apologetics

---

[107]Ibid., 1:41.

[108]Ibid.

[109]Ibid.

[110]Ibid., 1:42.

[111]Francis Schaeffer, "Schaeffer on Schaeffer, Part 2," *Christianity Today*, April 6, 1979, pp. 25–26. I was led to this quote by Scott R. Burson and Jerry L. Walls, *C. S. Lewis and Francis Schaeffer: Lessons for a New Century from the Most Influential Apologists of Our Time* (Downers Grove, IL: InterVarsity Press, 1998), p. 45.

[112]Douglas R. Groothuis, Review of *Francis Schaeffer and the Shaping of Evangelical America*, by Barry Hankins, and *Francis Schaeffer: An Authentic Life*, by Colin Duriez, January 15, 2009, Denver Seminary website, http://www.denverseminary.edu/resources/news-and-articles/francis-schaeffer-and-the-shaping-of-evangelical-america-and-francis-schaeffer-an-authentic-life/.

rather than a theoretician of methodologies, he is like other popular apologists: C. S. Lewis, Josh McDowell and Ravi Zacharias.

His practical focus also led him to emphasize not only right beliefs but also spiritual living—and to join the two. Jesus said that believers should love each other so that the world will know that "you are My disciples" (Jn 13:35). And he prayed that they would be "one" so that "the world may believe that You sent Me" (Jn 17:21). Schaeffer concludes,

> If the world does not see this down-to-earth practical love, it will not believe that Christ was sent by the Father. People will not believe only on the basis of the proper answers. The two should not be placed in antithesis. The world must have the proper answers to their honest questions, but at the same time there must be a oneness in love between all true Christians. This is what is needed if men are to know that Jesus was sent by the Father and that Christianity is true.[113]

He further encouraged the church to fill out its worldview and engage culture rather than avoid it. He sought engagement on such things as the arts and ethics, including the materialism of the day, racism, abortion, infanticide and euthanasia.

Looking more closely at culture, he concluded that in modern times the West had given up the concept that truth is absolute and embraced relativism, with effects going through philosophy, art, music, general culture and theology. The culture also shifted from reason to "faith" as a way of knowing truth. The result is a kind of "despair." He generally sought to show that the Christian's worldview "presuppositions" fit reality and the non-Christian's do not, resulting in tension. The Christian can find those points of tension in an individual's thought and show where his or her presuppositions actually lead.[114]

Schaeffer's lack of interest in debating apologetic methods has led to disagreement about his approach, which has been variously identified as presuppositional,[115] empirical[116] and verificational.

Gordon Lewis outlines a substantial case for Schaeffer as verificational in his

---

[113]Francis A. Schaeffer, *The Mark of the Christian* (Downers Grove, IL: InterVarsity Press, 1970); repr. in *The Complete Works of Francis A. Schaeffer: A Christian Worldview*, vol. 4 bk. 2, 2nd ed. (Westchester, IL: Crossway, 1982), p. 191. Page numbers are those of the complete works.

[114]For a summary of Schaeffer, see Ronald W. Ruegsegger, "Schaeffer's System of Thought," in *Reflections on Francis Schaeffer*, ed. Ronald W. Ruegsegger (Grand Rapids: Zondervan, 1986), pp. 25–41.

[115]Thomas V. Morris, *Francis Schaeffer's Apologetic: A Critique* (1976; repr., Grand Rapids: Baker, 1987). Cited in Gordon R. Lewis, "Schaeffer's Apologetic Method," in Ruegsegger, *Reflections on Francis Schaeffer*, p. 69.

[116]Robert L. Reymond, *The Justification of Knowledge* (Nutley, NJ: P & R, 1976; repr., Darlington, England: Evangelical Press, 1984). Cited in Lewis, "Schaeffer's Apologetic Method," p. 69.

approach. Lewis briefly characterizes the inductive method as objectively using observations to reach conclusions that are probable. The deductive method starts with assumed premises, or presuppositions, and arrives at certainty if the premises are true. The verificational, or scientific, method starts with a hypothesis that is confirmed or disconfirmed by its coherence with relevant data. Lewis believes that verification is neither inductive nor deductive.

Lewis says apologetic methods are defined by what they say about (1) logical starting point, (2) common ground, (3) criteria of truth, (4) the role of reason and (5) the basis of faith.[117] According to verificationalism, (1) the starting point is a hypothesis to be confirmed or disconfirmed. (2) Though Christians and non-Christians differ in their metaphysical presuppositions, they have common sensory and personal experiences that can be used to derive agreement on criteria of truth. (3) The criteria for truth include noncontradiction, factual adequacy ("conformity to external or sensory data of human experience") and existential viability.[118]

Lewis points to Schaeffer's use of the word *verification* and to his statement that "scientific proof, philosophical proof and religious proof follow the same rules."[119] Schaeffer then talks about the criteria by which to test proposed answers.

As a logical starting point Lewis says Schaeffer allows for "the infinite God, the personal God, the triune God, the propositional revelation in Scripture, the fallenness of humanity, or Jesus Christ the God-man, Savior, and risen Lord."[120] Everyone has presuppositions behind how they see the world and deal with it, and these "should be chosen after a careful consideration of what world view is true."[121] Lewis argues that by presuppositions Schaeffer does not mean beliefs that are too ultimate to be verified, which he sees as Van Til's view. (Of course, Van Til would allow for indirect verification, according to which Christian presuppositions must be assumed if there is to be any knowledge.)

Lewis believes Schaeffer's use of common ground fits best with a verificational approach. Christians share with non-Christians the image of God, which gives us common qualities and experiences, such as love, beauty, rationality (inductive and deductive), longing for significance, fear of nonbeing and scien-

---

[117]Lewis, "Schaeffer's Apologetic Method," p. 72.

[118]Ibid., p. 74.

[119]Francis A. Schaeffer, *He Is There, and He Is Not Silent* (Carol Stream, IL: Tyndale House, 1973), p. 109; cited in Lewis, "Schaeffer's Apologetic Method," p. 78.

[120]Lewis, "Schaeffer's Apologetic Method," p. 79.

[121]Francis A. Schaeffer, *How Should We Then Live? The Rise and Decline of Western Thought and Culture* (Wheaton, IL: Crossway, 1983), p. 20; cited in Lewis, "Schaeffer's Apologetic Method," p. 79.

tific data. The "mannishness of man" separates us from animals and machines, and entails that we are troubled by a sense of meaninglessness. Lewis finds further affinities for verificationalism over an inductive method in that Schaeffer emphasizes not just empirical data but also inner, existential values. Unlike presuppositionalism, he uses factual and personal data to confirm a hypothesis.

As far as criteria for truth, Lewis finds in Schaeffer an appeal to what is non-contradictory, gives an answer to the phenomenon in question and can be lived out. This threefold emphasis differentiates it from pragmatism. Unlike pragmatism, it begins not with a mere methodological hypothesis, but with the Christian hypothesis of the God of the Bible.

Reason (no. 4 above) has an important role for Schaeffer, preceding faith and identifying what and why we believe. "You cannot have a personal relationship with something unknown. That something must be understood and defined," he said; and, "Then having understood who it is with whom I am to have a personal relationship and how I may have it, comes the actual step of entering into that relationship."[122]

The object of faith (no. 5) is God, and as Lewis describes Schaeffer, "The basis of faith is the coherent and viable biblical account supported by visible, verifiable evidences."[123]

Lewis critiques the conclusions of those who find Schaeffer something other than a verificationalist, including Thomas Morris,[124] Kenneth Harper,[125] Robert Reymond,[126] E. R. Geehan[127] and David L. Wolfe.[128]

SUMMARY

Carnell begins with Christianity as a hypothesis to be tested. He does not arrive at it through induction because that would wrongly assume that the mind can

---

[122]Francis A. Schaeffer, *The God Who Is There* (Downers Grove, IL: InterVarsity Press, 1968); quoted in Lewis, "Schaeffer's Apologetic Method," p. 84.

[123]Lewis, "Schaeffer's Apologetic Method," p. 85.

[124]Morris, *Francis Schaeffer's Apologetic*. Briefly put, Lewis says that Morris relies uncritically on Schaeffer's embrace of the word *presupposition*, does not sufficiently account for what Schaeffer actually does and ends up offering an alternative apologetic approach that is not far from what Schaeffer does in less technical terms.

[125]K. C. Harper, "Francis A. Schaeffer: An Evaluation," *Bibliotheca Sacra* 133 (April 1976): 138.

[126]Reymond, *Justification of Knowledge*.

[127]E. R. Geehan, "The 'Presuppositional' Apologetic of Francis Schaeffer," *Themelios* 9, no. 1 (1972): 10–15.

[128]David L. Wolfe, *Epistemology: The Justification of Belief* (Downers Grove, IL: InterVarsity Press, 1982).

begin as a blank slate (whereas Carnell believes it must operate with convictions and assumptions) and arrive at universal truth (which it cannot because generalizations from observations can never be universal). Deduction is inadequate because it functions by assuming that the premises of an argument are true, an approach that would be circular if it went no further.

Though Carnell's starting point, the God of the Bible, is very similar to Van Til's, the latter would never allow Christianity to be tested to see if it is true since that would allow the creature to question the Creator.

Carnell proceeds much like Swinburne does with theism, demonstrating that Christianity is the best explanation (though not the only explanation, as Van Til would hold). He first tests the hypothesis for self-consistency (as Swinburne does in *The Coherence of Theism*), then he checks it with the relevant facts (as Swinburne does in *The Existence of God*). He finds Christianity to be the best view when tested rationally (for consistency), empirically (for its fit with the facts) and existentially (for its livability).

Because Carnell allows for epistemic distance between facts and their interpretation, he leaves room for common ground, which forms a central feature of his apologetic approach. He finds common ground in the principle of non-contradiction, values, ethics and the need for love.

Our chart shows Carnell near the middle because he begins with Christianity yet he tests its truth. He is to the right of veridicalism, which begins with givens that are corroborated (which is vaguely reminiscent of presuppositionalism, which confirms but does not test Christianity). To the right of Carnell is classical apologetics, which (like Carnell) begins on a worldview level by proving theism. Classical apologetics then moves on to prove Christianity, which is a more detailed view than theism.

CRITICISMS

Though Carnell, like Francis Schaeffer, was regarded by some as a presuppositionalist, Van Til[129] and Greg Bahnsen[130] have been at pains to show that his

---

[129]See Van Til's review of Carnell's *An Introduction to Christian Apologetics* in *Westminster Theological Journal* 11 (1948): 4–53; Van Til, *The New Evangelicalism* (Philadelphia: Westminster Theological Seminary, 1960); Van Til, *The Case for Calvinism* (Philadelphia: P & R, 1963), chap. three; Van Til's response to Gordon R. Lewis in Geehan, *Jerusalem and Athens*, pp. 361–68; Van Til, *Defense of the Faith*, 3rd ed. (Phillipsburg, NJ: P & R, 1979), p. 206.

[130]Greg Bahnsen, *Van Til's Apologetic*, pp. 537–50. He gives seven principles of traditional apologetics and quotes both apologists on most of them.

apologetic method was traditional and therefore unacceptable. Bahnsen sees no evidence that Carnell "ever grasped the transcendental character of Van Til's presuppositional apologetic," and neither, he adds, have Gordon Lewis or Ronald Nash (1936–2006), proponents of Carnell's views.[131] Ronald Nash was a prolific scholar and professor at Reformed Theological Seminary who subjected world-views to three tests: reason (the principle of noncontradiction), experience (outer and inner) and practice (livability). Inner experience includes such things as moral awareness and a sense of guilt—the sort of thing C. S. Lewis also empha-sized.[132] Practice, the ability to live by one's worldview, was also emphasized by Francis Schaeffer.[133] Like Carnell, Nash concludes that Christianity is highly probable, a level of certainty that he believes is appropriate for a worldview.

Van Til blasted Carnell's method, saying that it "requires the destruction of Christianity" and that he "uses the idea of common grace to encourage the evil principle of human autonomy in his desire to adulterate Christian teaching so as to make it palatable to the natural man."[134] While Van Til appreciated Carnell's statements that the Word is self-authenticating and that Christianity alone makes the world intelligible,[135] he rejected Carnell's willingness to then "submit the ab-solute authority of the living Redeemer-God of the Bible to an examination admin-istered by Mr. Natural Man." The "fatal mistake" of all traditional apologetics, Van Til said, is its willingness to express *"areas of ultimate agreement"* with unbelievers.[136]

Like Van Til, Carnell held that only a Christian worldview properly inter-prets the world, yet he also held that facts can have meaning, albeit limited, apart from a person's worldview. Furthermore, his view of common grace allowed the nonbeliever some God-given ability to recognize truth. Typical of non–Van Tillian apologists, Carnell seeks to separate what is true from how we know that truth. So in terms of ontology (what is true) Christianity is the only correct view,

---

[131]Ibid., p. 547 n. 58.

[132]Ronald Nash, *World Views in Conflict: Choosing Christianity in a World of Ideas* (Grand Rapids: Zondervan, 1992), pp. 60–61. He cites C. S. Lewis, *Mere Christianity* (New York: Macmillan, 1960), especially book 1.

[133]Nash (*World Views in Conflict*, pp. 62–63) cites Morris, *Francis Schaeffer's Apologetics*, pp. 21–22. For a proper understanding of Schaeffer Nash recommends his own article, "The Life of the Mind and the Way of Life," in *Francis Schaeffer: Portraits of the Man and His Work*, ed. Lane T. Dennis (Westchester, IL: Crossway, 1986), chap. three; and Lane Dennis, "Schaeffer and His Critics," in the same volume.

[134]Van Til, *Case for Calvinism*, chap. three, sec. 2A(1), Logos Bible Software Library CD-ROM, The Works of Cornelius Van Til.

[135]Van Til's response to Lewis, *Jerusalem and Athens*, p. 362. He cites Carnell, *Introduction to Christian Apologetics*, p. 212.

[136]Van Til, *Jerusalem and Athens*, pp. 362, 365 (emphasis original).

but epistemologically it has to be shown to be true. But for Van Til what is true must be affirmed as such without testing. The central proof is that Christianity is the sole basis for rationality.

The question of the validity of Van Til's criticisms of Carnell amounts to the question of the validity of his critique of all traditional apologetics.

Norman Geisler finds Carnell inconsistent in that he criticizes apologetic approaches that begin with historical or empirical data on grounds that they cannot rise above probability. As Carnell sees it, the conclusion might not be the case. However, Geisler points out that Carnell later defended the use of probability when it came to his own method, pointing out that with real-world things like history, logical certainty cannot be had.[137]

Carnell indeed acknowledges the limits of induction, that conclusions can be known only probabilistically (it is at least *possible* that the conclusion is not the case). He also acknowledges that deduction ("pure demonstration"[138]) operates only within formal systems like formal logic and mathematics, not real world applications like history. So he advocates integrating both, in systematic consistency: "Perfect coherence always involves two elements: the law of contradiction[139] to give formal validity, and concrete facts of history to give material validity. Without formal validity we have no universality and necessity in truth, and without material validity we have no relevance to the world in which we live. This is proof by coherence."[140] He also integrates experience: "A coherent hypothesis, let us recall, is one which can smoothly lead us into the totality of our experience, inside and outside."[141] So while Carnell acknowledges the limits of induction, he shows how it fits into his broader approach to verification.

Geisler also challenges the validity of more than one test for truth. By his reckoning, Carnell says that empiricism is not an adequate test for truth, rationalism is not adequate, nor is existentialism; but taken together they are adequate. The problem, in Geisler's view, is that if one test does not make up for the weaknesses of the other, then adding them up will not help.[142] If one leaky bucket

---

[137]Norman Geisler, "Carnell, Edward John," in *Baker Encyclopedia of Christian Apologetics* (Grand Rapids: Baker, 1998), p. 119. He cites Carnell, *Introduction to Christian Apologetics*, p. 105, contra 198.

[138]Carnell, *Introduction to Christian Apologetics*, p. 104.

[139]"Law of contradiction" is another way of saying "law of noncontradiction." Logicians use both expressions.

[140]Ibid., p. 106.

[141]Ibid., p. 114. For more on coherence, see p. 107.

[142]Geisler, "Carnell, Edward John," p. 120. Also, Norman Geisler, *Christian Apologetics* (Grand

can't carry water, adding more leaky buckets won't help. Lewis says that even though analogies prove nothing, a more appropriate one than leaky buckets would be checks and balances among the branches of government.

Carnell could reply that reaching the truth about anything complex typically requires more than one test. Scientific theories are compared on the basis of such things as explanatory power, scope, fit with other things regarded as true and simplicity. Criminal guilt involves such things as means, motive and opportunity. Reformed epistemologist Nicholas Wolterstorff has even made the suggestion that the search for just one merit that beliefs must have in order to be considered true is misguided; there are a large number of such merits. So as he sees it, while philosophers have thought that they were arguing about different aspects of the one merit they have really been arguing for distinct merits.[143]

Lewis offers a more detailed defense of Carnell's threefold criterion. The three tests integrate logic, fact and value to achieve systematic consistency. They do not function separately but together, in combination. Each is adequate for the aspect of reality it tests. They are distinguishable but interrelated: "Logic continues to help clarify our view of matters of fact and value. Understanding of empirical experience needs the direction of logical and ethical principles. Ethical values ought to govern uses of logic also."[144]

Geisler says that multiple tests bring problems: there is no guidance for resolving conflicts (when, say, "the love criterion conflicts with the law of non-contradiction"[145]), and it is possible that facts will not fit with the theory. Lewis replies that conflicts among the three can indeed remain but that such conflicts may actually indicate the failure of a particular belief to meet the criterion and achieve genuine systematic consistency.

Geisler says that non-Christian worldviews can be free from contradictions, conflicts with data and hypocrisy. But Lewis answers that further investigation would reveal the best view, just as a thorough investigation would not leave all murder suspects equal as to fit with all the evidence (e.g., means, motives and opportunity).

Lewis adds that Geisler himself accepts the threefold criteria within a worldview (just not to choose a worldview; more about this in the chapter on Geisler). He

---

Rapids: Baker, 1976), p. 129 (most of his criticisms of Carnell are developed in pp. 129–31).

[143]Nicholas Wolterstorff, "Epistemology of Religion," in *The Blackwell Guide to Epistemology*, ed. John Greco and Ernest Sosa (Malden, MA: Blackwell, 1999), p. 304.

[144]Lewis, "An Integrative Method," p. 78.

[145]Geisler, "Carnell, Edward John," p. 119.

uses it to determine what is true after the worldview of theism has been chosen, for example, to choose Christianity rather than Islam. Lewis wonders why Geisler would use it at all if he finds it inadequate.[146]

As far as the problem of conflicts between more than one criterion, Geisler's specific example would not arise since Carnell requires that the subjective criteria pass the test of the principle of noncontradiction.[147] Regardless, Geisler sees other potential conflicts, for example, between our values and our needs. Carnell would answer that he strove to connect the subjective elements of his argument so they appear as a coherent whole. For example, what we should want is what we genuinely need, which is the same as what will fulfill us.

Carnell allowed that not all facts would support the accepted worldview, suggesting that evolution and origins are such examples for Christianity (as mentioned above). But he advocated that we accept the worldview with the fewest problems. We have to recall, too, that Carnell is not suggesting that his argument will lead to the only worldview (as if it possessed total support), but the best worldview, an approach that is out of line with Van Til but in line with traditional apologetic reasoning. So if more than one view seems coherent and fits with what we know, we should take the view that best explains the broadest array of facts—which is why Carnell made his case so expansive.

Geisler also argues that one cannot begin with a worldview and test it with facts since it is the worldview itself that gives meaning to facts. His objection illustrates once again the crucial relationship between theory and fact. For Van Til, theory so dominates fact that there is no common ground and thus no way to argue toward a worldview. For Carnell, epistemic distance between theory and fact allows common ground and the possibility of seeing which theory is best supported by the facts. Geisler sees a worldview as too all-encompassing to be tested by specific facts, because the meaning of all facts is dependent on the worldview. For example, we cannot claim that the resurrection is a fact and that it proves theism because only within a theistic worldview is there a resurrection; an atheist would grant only that a corpse resuscitated.[148] On Geisler's view, then, we first must prove the theistic worldview and then prove Christianity—the way of classical apologetics.[149] For the evidentialist, facts such as the resurrection can

---

[146]Lewis, "An Integrative Method," p. 78.

[147]See, e.g., Carnell, *Christian Commitment*, p. 269: "Evangelical encounter is man's whole-souled response to rationally objective evidences."

[148]Geisler, "Carnell, Edward John," p. 119; Geisler, *Christian Apologetics*, pp. 128–29.

[149]Geisler, "Apologetics, Types of," in *Baker Encyclopedia*, p. 42.

go so far as to point reliably to Christianity in one step (rather than the classical apologist's two).

Stylistically, Carnell's method of reasoning (especially after his first book) often appealed to generalities based on common experience. Sweeping statements, offered as axioms of human experience, are given with little or no support: "A man will never knowingly reveal things to his own hurt";[150] "Wisdom is characterized by wholeness";[151] "People are complete only when they are understood, noticed, and appreciated."[152] The method was no doubt founded on his determination to work from common ground without dependence on appeals to special revelation or religious experience. Such grand style was also common in philosophy before the more cautious analytic movement of the later twentieth century (in the English-speaking world at least) emphasized clarity and logical rigor. In contrast to Carnell and earlier apologists, those trained in the analytic tradition tend to be more methodical and precise. Going across the apologetic spectrum, these would include Alvin Plantinga, Richard Swinburne and William Lane Craig (and J. P. Moreland[153]).

In a sense, Van Til and Carnell begin at the top of the circle of a person's cognitive world—the place of interpretive beliefs, especially one's worldview. Van Til argues that Christianity alone provides a basis for all rational beliefs in the circle (and rational beliefs alone, since personal experiences have no apologetic value). Carnell shows that Christianity is self-consistent and can best account for all beliefs and experiences in the circle. Evidentialists begin near the bottom of the circle (the place of beliefs and experiences that are interpreted by beliefs higher up in the circle). Classical apologists begin toward the upper part of the circle and construct theistic arguments from such things as observed order (the teleological argument) and beliefs about sufficient causes (the cosmological argument). These establish theism as part of the upper-level beliefs, then these are used to establish the truth of Christianity from facts, which we could conceptualize as at the bottom of the cognitive circle.

---

[150]Carnell, *Christian Commitment*, p. 54.

[151]Carnell, *Philosophy*, p. 39.

[152]Ibid., pp. 213–14.

[153]J. P. Moreland's influence on apologetics has been enormous, and it is regrettable that the length restrictions of this book do not allow more attention to his work. His writings have not focused on apologetic methods, and based on conversations with him, his interests have been elsewhere. He has, however, applied his approach with depth and rigor.

KEY TERMS

Coherence. The fit between one idea and another such that they are consistent and do not violate the principle of noncontradiction.

Empiricism. The view that truth is known through the senses.

Rationalism. The view that at least some truths do not come through the senses. The most common candidates are necessary or universal truths, that is, those that must be true or those that are always true.

Systematic consistency. Property of a hypothesis by which it is self-consistent (does not contradict itself) and is consistent with all relevant facts (both internal to us and external).

Knowledge by acquaintance. Knowing directly, by experiencing a thing. Knowledge not dependent on logical inference. We know a house is ours, for example, not because of a reasoned argument but because we see it and recognize it.

Knowledge by inference. Knowing by the process of reasoning. If we know that Jones was born in the United States, then we know that he is a citizen because we have inferred it from something else, specifically the premise that all those who are born in the United States are citizens.

Third way of knowing. Knowing by reflecting on our moral and spiritual condition.

THINKING IT OVER

1. How did events of the twentieth century shape Carnell's interest in apologetics and his motivation?

2. What did Carnell's various teachers contribute to his views?

3. What role does the principle of noncontradiction play in Carnell's thinking? How does it regulate subjective apologetic considerations?

4. What were Carnell's criticisms of (extreme) empiricism?

5. On what two contrasting foundations did Carnell and Van Til build after each rejected the commonsense approach of Thomas Reid?

6. How did Carnell seek to overcome Kant's limitation of our knowledge of the world as it is?

7. Why, in Carnell's view, are deduction and induction insufficient for constructing a case for Christianity? Why is even the principle of noncontradiction by itself not sufficient? What method does he accept?

8. How do Carnell and Van Til differ on common ground, and what does that difference have to do with common grace?

9. How do Carnell and Van Til differ on the relationship between fact and theory?

10. How did Carnell use values apologetically? Justice and personal dignity? Love?

11. In your own words, define knowledge by inference, knowledge by acquaintance and the third way.

12. Summarize the criticisms of Carnell's views. What do you think of his approach?

GOING FURTHER

Carnell, Edward John. *The Burden of Søren Kierkegaard*. Grand Rapids: Eerdmans, 1965.

———. *Christian Commitment: An Apologetic*. New York: Macmillan, 1957.

———. "How Every Christian Can Defend His Faith." *Moody Monthly*. Part 1: January 1950, pp. 312–13, 343. Part 2: February 1950, pp. 384–85, 429–31. Part 3: March 1950, pp. 460–61, 506–7.

———. *An Introduction to Christian Apologetics: A Philosophic Defense of the Trinitarian-Theistic Faith*. Grand Rapids: Eerdmans, 1948.

———. *The Kingdom of Love and the Pride of Life*. Grand Rapids: Eerdmans, 1960.

———. "Orthodoxy: Cultic vs. Classical." *The Christian Century*, March 30, 1960, pp. 377–79.

———. *A Philosophy of the Christian Religion*. Grand Rapids: Eerdmans, 1952.

———. "Post-Fundamentalist Faith." *The Christian Century*, August 26, 1959, p. 971.

Geisler, Norman. "Carnell, Edward John." In *Baker Encyclopedia of Christian Apologetics*, pp. 114–20. Grand Rapids: Baker, 1999.

———. *Christian Apologetics*. Grand Rapids: Baker, 1976.

Hein, Steven Arthur. "The Nature and Existence of Man in the Apologetic Mission of Edward John Carnell." PhD diss. St. Louis University, 1987.

Hustad, L. Arnold. "Rationalism and the Third Way of Knowing in the Apologetics of Edward John Carnell." PhD diss. New York University, 1988.

Lewis, Gordon. "An Integrative Method of Justifying Religious Assertions." In *Evangelical Apologetics*, edited by Michael Bauman, David W. Hall and Robert C. Newman, pp. 69–88. Camp Hill, PA: Christian Publications, 1996.

————. "Edward John Carnell." In *Handbook of Evangelical Theologians*, edited by Walter A. Elwell, pp. 321-37. Grand Rapids: Baker, 1993.

————. "Schaeffer's Apologetic Method." In *Reflections on Francis Schaeffer*, edited by Ronald W. Ruegsegger, pp. 69–104. Grand Rapids: Zondervan, 1986.

————. *Testing Christianity's Truth Claims*. Chicago: Moody Press, 1976. Reprint, Lanham, MD: University Press of America, 1990.

————. "Van Til and Carnell—Part I." In *Jerusalem and Athens: Critical Discussions on the Theology and Apologetics of Cornelius Van Til*, edited by E. R. Geehan, pp. 349–61. Phillipsburg, NJ: P & R, 1971.

Nash, Ronald, ed. *The Case for Biblical Christianity*. Grand Rapids: Eerdmans, 1969.

————. *Faith and Reason: Searching for a Rational Faith*. Grand Rapids: Zondervan, 1988.

————. *World Views in Conflict: Choosing Christianity in a World of Ideas*. Grand Rapids: Zondervan, 1992.

Nelson, Rudolph. *The Making and Unmaking of an Evangelical Mind: The Case of Edward Carnell*. New York: Cambridge University Press, 1987.

Ramm, Bernard. *Types of Apologetic Systems*. Wheaton, IL: Van Kampen, 1953.

Sailer, William S. "The Role of Reason in the Theologies of Nel Ferre and Edward John Carnell." STD diss. Temple University, 1964.

Sims, John A. *Edward John Carnell: Defender of the Faith*. Washington, DC: University Press of America, 1979.

Van Til, Cornelius. "Response by C. Van Til." In *Jerusalem and Athens: Critical Discussions on the Theology and Apologetics of Cornelius Van Til*, edited by E. R. Geehan, pp. 361–68. Phillipsburg, NJ: P & R, 1971.

Williams, David Alan. "Toward a Postcritical Evangelical Apologetic: A Reappraisal of the Apologetic Work of Edward John Carnell." PhD diss. Drew University, 1998.

– 7 –

INTRODUCTION TO CLASSICAL APOLOGETICS

Prove theism, then Christianity

Classical apologetics advocates a two-step approach: first prove theism, then prove Christianity. In a more general sense, it first sets up the worldview, then proves the more detailed beliefs of Christianity. Of course, if a person already holds to some form of theism (e.g., Jehovah's Witness, Muslim) then it is unnecessary to prove it to them.

Reasoning about a broad array of topics to prove God and Christianity has been used for a long time, for example by Justin Martyr (100–165), though classical apologetic themes were expressed in a bit more focused way by Thomas Aquinas (1225–1274). He said that we could know something of causes by examining their effects, and thus we can know some basic things about God through creation. He added that reasoning backwards from causes does not yield much knowledge, so we need revelation to give us important details, such as the nature of the Trinity, and the gospel.

There are many classical apologists, to name a few, R. C. Sproul, Arthur Lindsley, John Gerstner, J. P. Moreland, Norman Geisler and, it seems, C. S. Lewis. Lewis would use theistic arguments when talking to atheists,[1] though later in life he re-

---

[1]Norman L. Geisler, "Lewis, C. S.," in *Baker Encyclopedia of Christian Apologetics* (Grand Rapids: Baker, 1999), pp. 420–25. A brief but helpful summary of Lewis's thought.

marked that they are difficult to produce on a popular level, and "fortunately, though very oddly, I have found that people are usually disposed to hear the divinity of Our Lord discussed before going into the existence of God."[2] But for him this appears to be simply a rhetorical strategy.

The classical view agrees with presuppositionalism (against evidentialism) that the worldview framework is essential to proof. The presuppositionalist emphasizes that the presuppositions that make up the worldview framework are as broad as can be, encompassing the very nature of thought, predication (roughly, making claims about reality) and proof itself. Because the presupposition in question is so broad that it grounds thought itself, there is no way to reason to it; you must assume it. Therefore, those like Bahnsen who emphasize Van Til's transcendental argument insist that all attempts to reason apart from first presupposing the (Reformed) Christian God are futile and absurd because they have no (transcendent) basis for reasoning. Nevertheless, the proof for the presuppositions is deductively certain and airtight, since if we do not assume it, we have no (transcendent) basis for rationality and everything is absurd.

Classical apologists do not hold that we must presuppose the Christian God in order to know anything. We can operate with a more modest set of assumptions, such as that it is possible to know the past, that most of the time our experience of the world is accurate, that we cannot affirm and deny the same statement and be correct, and so on. The nonbeliever can have many of the same assumptions, so we can have intellectually common ground, not just the common ground that we live in the same world. That is, we can see some things in substantially the same way. I see that there is a chair in the room; so can the atheist and the Muslim. We can both see the order in DNA, we can both believe that eyewitness testimony is better than a rumor. So what is common between us can be useful for apologetics. We can, for example, reason from the order in the world to an orderer. We can agree on the best ways to discover history, and reason to the conclusion that Christ resurrected.

On the view that is typically held by classical apologists (and others, such as Carnell), belief in the Christian God does not affect all beliefs to the same degree. If a Christian, an atheist, a Muslim and a Jew all go hiking and look over the same mountain vista, they can agree on many things, such as the altitude, that the sun is setting, that there are pine trees in the valley and so on. Our views do not diverge until we start to discuss things like the ultimate origin of the world and its regu-

---

[2]C. S. Lewis, "Christian Apologetics," in *Essay Collection: Faith, Christianity, and the Church*, ed. Lesley Walmsley (London: HarperCollins, 2002), p. 157.

larities, and the place of humanity in universe. We would have more common ground with the Muslim than the atheist with regard to creation, the origins of order and humanity's role in the universe. We would have those same things in common with the Jew, plus belief in the authority of the Hebrew Scriptures.

Because God does not have to be assumed from the start, an argument can be made that uses ideas shared by the believer and the particular nonbeliever. For example, both the Christian and the atheist may agree that complex order for some apparently beneficial purpose is best explained by the action of an intelligent being. The Christian can extend this from the order in the cosmos to the existence of a divine orderer.

The presuppositionalist, however, would emphasize that the atheist has no foundation for the order that he or she knows exists in the universe. Only (Reformed) Christianity has an ultimate basis for order because only it believes in a God who foreordains and controls all things. So while the atheist verbally denies God's existence, he covertly has to assume it in his thinking. However, using a traditional argument with premises about order to infer a conclusion about a divine orderer is improper because it fails to acknowledge the real problem: the nonbeliever's foundation for knowledge. To allow nonbelievers to think they can reason apart from God, such as by reasoning from premises that do not contain God to a conclusion that God exists, is only to make the problem worse. Reasoning without presupposing the (Reformed) Christian God is intellectual rebellion. The problem is thus not so much a lack of information, which could be addressed by means of an argument, but a problem with the whole person. Instead of basing reasoning on the authority of their own intellect, nonbelievers need to base their reasoning on the assumption of God's Word as truth. Anything less than acknowledging the Bible as the Word of God fails to give him his proper place. So in a sense trying to directly prove God's existence using premises that do not acknowledge him dishonors him by perpetuating reasoning apart from him. Only presupposing him gives him his proper place and addresses the ultimate problem of disbelief. Testing his Word, the Bible, only dishonors him by implying (1) that there is some higher standard by which to prove its truth, (2) that we are in a position to judge whether his Word is true (when his Word should be judging us) and (3) that we have the right to think apart from God—who is the sole determiner of truth and the only grounds for knowledge about anything.

Classical apologists do not see the need to presuppose the truth of Christianity in order to make any sense out of the world, have meaning to history and science, or even communicate. However, Geisler says that theism is necessary "to view life as meaningful and coherent." Without God (as he puts it, in a "closed system"),

> there is no ultimate meaning, no ultimate values, and no "miracle" happens that cannot be accounted for by natural phenomenon (cf. John 3:1-2; Acts 2:22; Heb. 2:3-4). But it is not necessary to presuppose that the God is triune, has a Son incarnate as Jesus of Nazareth, and has revealed himself in the sixty-six inspired books of Christian Scripture. One can make sense of the world by assuming less than the whole truth of Christianity.[3]

As far as the presuppositionalist's insistence that the non-Christian not test the Bible directly, classical apologists (and many other nonpresuppositionalists) think that the view may come from noble intentions but is unscriptural and intellectually muddled. It is possible for people to be unsure of which prophetic voice or Scriptures is the Word of God (especially if they were raised in a sect or another religion). That is why God tells his people in Deuteronomy 18:22 to test prophets by checking their predictions against observed events, and uses the language of a court proceeding in the general context of evidence that he is the true God (e.g., Deut 41:21-26; Is 43:26).[4] In 1 Kings 18:21-39 Elijah conducts a test to demonstrate which God is real. In John 10:37-38 Christ invites his hearers to observe him and see that he is the fulfillment of prophecy, and if they do not believe him—who is speaking the words of God—then they can believe the works he does. When John the Baptist doubts in Matthew 11:2-5, Christ directs his emissaries to reassure him with their observations of events that fit prophecy. If it is objected that the biblical audiences already presupposed the God of Israel (and Elijah's audience was merely wavering), then it can be pointed out that in Acts 14:17 Paul is addressing those outside the Judeo-Christian tradition, saying that God provided a witness of his existence in the form of rains and fruitful seasons. In other words, providential order is a type of evidence. People can observe the beneficial order and conclude that God exists. So as far as respect for the Bible as the Word, God allows, and even invites, examination of evidence to see that it is indeed his Word.

Classical apologetics assumes that a nonbeliever's mind functions well enough to process the evidence, under the grace and influence of the Holy Spirit. When the person realizes which of all the claimed revelations in the world is

---

[3]Norman L. Geisler, "Classical Apologetics," in *Baker Encyclopedia*, p. 156.
[4]Edward J. Young, *The Book of Isaiah: The English Text, with Introduction, Exposition, and Notes* (Grand Rapids: Eerdmans, 1972), 3:163, "i.e. submit to a trial in which the case may be considered."

really God's Word, then whatever respect and submission is due can be rendered. The offer of proof that God has spoken is pervasive in the Bible, from Moses being given signs that he has met with God (Ex 4:1-9) to the supernatural abilities of the two witnesses in Revelation (Rev 11:5-6).

For the classical apologist, evidences of various types point to the existence of God as the best explanation. Other explanations may work to some extent; they may explain some things, but not nearly as well. Many classical apologists (and evidentialists) believe the case for God and Christianity is a strong inductive one. By contrast, for the presuppositionalist, Christianity is the only explanation. Other explanations (religions, sects, worldviews) are absurd because they offer no transcendent foundation for knowledge. They believe the case for God and Christianity is a deductive one, that is, airtight, since nothing absurd could possibly be true. To most nonpresuppositionalists, other beliefs are not absurd, but they do not explain as well as biblical Christianity. We should note that Bahnsen would, for example, point to what he believes are internal inconsistencies in Islam such as its belief in a just God and its lack of atonement for sin.[5]

---

[5]Greg Bahnsen, "Presuppositional Reasoning with False Faiths," *Penpoint* 7, no. 2 (February-March 1996), http://www.cmfnow.com/articles/pa208.htm.

– 8 –

RICHARD SWINBURNE

Theism and Christianity are highly probable

Richard Swinburne (1934–) has produced an innovative way to demonstrate that theism is the best explanation for the existence of the universe and for the way we find the world.[1] He ties his case together using a theorem of probability familiar in science. He then shows that Christianity is indeed the best understanding of God.

His primary focus is the nonbeliever, including the person who is not already predisposed to accept theism or Christianity. No higher compliment can be paid to him than that his work helped Antony Flew, perhaps the best-known academic atheist of modern times, to become convinced of the existence of God. It is not surprising that Swinburne is one of a few whose rigorous work has brought academic respect to Christianity in recent decades. (Alvin Plantinga and William Lane Craig are also among those few.)

Swinburne argues probabilities from both ends, in a mode inspired by Bayes's theorem: we expect x (e.g., that God is loving), and if x is the case we would expect y; and we have evidence that y is indeed the case. And conversely, y being the case, it is difficult to explain unless x is the case.

Swinburne is Emeritus Nolloth Professor of the Philosophy of the Christian Religion at Oxford, where he taught and supervised doctoral studies in phi-

---

[1]His publications are listed on his Oxford University faculty page, http://users.ox.ac.uk/~orie0087 /framesetpublications.shtml.

losophy of religion. He is a prolific author whose works establish the rationality of Christian doctrine and examines its implications. For him, Christianity is no mere academic conclusion. He sees his faith as a personal relationship with God and his intellectual work as a form of spiritual service.

Though his parents were not religious, he came to personal Christian faith at an age too young to remember. For his military service he was trained in Russian and worked as a translator. He did his undergraduate education at Oxford, and during this time Christianity was the highest priority in his life. He planned to become an Anglican priest, but his interest in life's big questions drew him to philosophy. He was appalled that in an age of unbelief that so many in the church advocated a mere leap of faith without even interacting with ideas of the day. He concluded that this "head-in-the-sand" mentality was born of a "lazy indifference" founded on the past two centuries of Continental philosophy. Fideists like Barth and Kierkegaard, and those who had influenced them such as Hegel, Nietzsche, Heidegger and Sartre, made vague and unsupported statements that were more characteristic of literature than science.[2]

He took as his model the work of Thomas Aquinas (to whom he has been favorably compared), who began with the observable world rather than religious experience or the Bible, and who interacted with the best thinking of his day. Using the linguistic and logical rigor of analytic philosophy, Swinburne laid a foundation for theism in a trilogy, then in a number of books he supported the philosophical implications of Christian theology, showing its inductive strength.[3] His approach has been to start from an area of secular thought, especially in philosophy and science, develop his own philosophy of it, then show "how that philosophy leads to a Christian understanding of things in some respect."[4] For example, in *Responsibility and Atonement*, he begins from nonreligious views of obligation and supererogatory goodness, and argues to "a conclusion about our moral status in relation to God." He explains his rationale as follows: "There is no other way to proceed in the

---

[2]Richard Swinburne, "Intellectual Autobiography," in *Reason and the Christian Religion: Essays in Honour of Richard Swinburne*, ed. Alan G. Padgett (Oxford: Clarendon, 1994), pp. 2, 8. Most of the essay appears in "The Vocation of a Natural Theologian," in *Philosophers Who Believe*, ed. Kelly James Clark (Downers Grove, IL: InterVarsity Press, 1993), which was updated in "Natural Theology and Orthodoxy," in *Turning East: Contemporary Philosophers and the Ancient Christian Faith*, ed. Rico Vitz (Crestwood, NY: St. Vladimir's Seminary Press, 2012), pp. 47-77.

[3]See "Further Reading" at the end of this chapter and "publications" on his Oxford University page http://users.ox.ac.uk/~orie0087/framesetpublications.shtml.

[4]Swinburne, "Natural Theology and Orthodoxy," p. 71.

philosophy of religion if its results are to be made rationally acceptable to those who are initially non-religious."[5]

He has "no wish to worship a God who does not exist," but also believes "there is a significant balance of evidence in favor of Christian theism."[6] In all, "Worshipping our Creator is the first human duty."[7]

FOUNDATIONS OF THE CASE FOR GOD

In *The Coherence of Theism*,[8] Swinburne begins his case for theism by showing that its doctrines do not contradict themselves or other things rational people commonly believe.

Theism holds to the existence of what we might call a generic God, one without the sort of theological details that distinguish between Christianity, Judaism and Islam. Accordingly, theism holds that God is a spirit who is omnipresent, creator and sustainer of the universe, a free being, omnipotent, omniscient, perfectly good, a source of moral obligation, immutable, eternal, existing necessarily (i.e., he does not just happen to exist, he would exist in all possible worlds), holy and worthy of worship.[9] After showing that theism is a viable belief (i.e., being coherent, it could be true) Swinburne sets out to show that it is the most rational belief. He defends its claim that we can use language to describe God even though he is very different from the things language normally describes. To show that theism does not contradict itself, he shows for example that it is possible for God to be a spirit without a body, that he can be omniscient and can infallibly know our next choice while we are yet free to make it, and that he is immutable even though his knowledge changes as the world around him changes.

After demonstrating that the hypothesis of theism is self-consistent, Swinburne (like Carnell) then moves to a second level of testing. Whereas Carnell tests the more detailed hypothesis of Christianity, Swinburne does his first and second level of testing on theism. Having first tested theism for consistency, his approach to the

---

[5]Ibid.

[6]Ibid., p. 73.

[7]Ibid., p. 75. In 1995 he ended his lifelong association with the Anglican Church because it no longer seemed to care about the totality of commitment demanded of Christians nor the importance of teaching true doctrine (e.g., as found in the Nicene Creed), especially by their priests (p. 75). His desire for identity with a body that he believed represented the broadest possible unity of Christianity, as well as a connection to Christianity's ancient roots, led him to the Orthodox Church. This made him the logical choice to head a concerted apologetic outreach to Russia by the Society of Christian Philosophers, funded by the Templeton Foundation (ibid., pp. 76–77).

[8]Richard Swinburne, *The Coherence of Theism*, 2nd ed. (Oxford: Clarendon, 1991).

[9]Ibid., p. 2.

second level is summed up in Bayes's theorem of probability, which he explains in *The Existence of God*.[10] He lays the foundation for his case by showing why he uses induction rather than deduction, why pieces of evidence in the case for theism can be considered together rather than separately, and why it is valid to explain something in terms of a person's actions (God's actions, in the case for theism).

Swinburne focuses on inductive arguments because deductive ones start from premises "which are far from generally accepted."[11] And after many thinkers have expended much effort to develop deductive arguments for God's existence, "relatively few philosophers today would accept that there are good deductive arguments to be had here."[12] (Recall that deductive arguments are those that claim logical certainty for their conclusion while inductive arguments claim only that their conclusions are probable.)

While some try to show that theistic arguments must stand or fall individually (e.g., antitheists Alasdair MacIntyre, and Antony Flew before he converted to theism), Swinburne maintains that arguments can be added together to form a cumulative case, and that both deductive and inductive arguments can have a cumulative force. For example, there is no valid deductive argument from the premise "all students have long hair" to the conclusion "Smith has long hair." Neither is there a valid deductive argument from "Smith is a student" to the conclusion "Smith has long hair." But it is deductively valid to argue that because "all students have long hair and Smith is a student" that "Smith has long hair."[13] Likewise, there is no inductively strong argument to the conclusion that Smith murdered Mrs. Jones if we consider evidence separately. That Smith had a motive is not by itself sufficient; that he was near the scene of the crime is not by itself sufficient; nor is the fact that he had blood on his hands sufficient. But taken all together the evidence is convincing that Smith indeed murdered Mrs. Jones.[14] So it is that separate arguments for God's existence (arguments from the existence of the universe, from its order, from religious experience and so on) can add up to a strong case even if each argument taken separately is less than conclusive.

In contrast to the modern tendency to explain everything in physical terms (forces, particles and the like) Swinburne argues that we can validly explain some things in terms of persons. While physical explanations use natural laws and the

---

[10]Richard Swinburne, *The Existence of God*, 2nd ed. (Oxford: Oxford University Press, 2004).
[11]Ibid., p. 13.
[12]Ibid., p. 14.
[13]Ibid., p. 12.
[14]Ibid.

like, "personal explanations" (those that invoke a person) use such things as intentions and purposes. So it is valid to explain things in terms of God's action, for example, that an orderly universe exists because God created it.

It is widely recognized, especially in science, that a theory's simplicity is a crucial factor in judging whether it is probably true. Swinburne suggests that simplicity as it pertains to a personal explanation is a matter of whether the person in the theory has constant intentions, continuing capacities and simple ways of acquiring beliefs. Explanatory power in personal explanations is a matter of being able to predict or explain the facts we observe.[15] So in the case of theism we must judge how well the existence of God explains, for example, the existence and order of the universe.

Bayes's Theorem and Prior Probability

Swinburne then constructs his inductive, cumulative case, which argues that a personal being is the best explanation for the universe as we find it. He ties the strands together using a theorem of probability developed by Thomas Bayes, an eighteenth-century clergyman who was also a first-rate mathematician. It shows that a theory[16] is likely to be true if it is a good theory given other things we know (which is called the theory's prior probability), and if it can explain things that are otherwise unexplainable (called its explanatory power).

Prior probability is important because for anything that needs explaining, an infinite number of theories will do the job. But some of those theories are outlandish. To eliminate them we have to rely on something other than their explanatory power. That is because they do have explanatory power; the problem is with how they explain. Our judgments about how they explain—about the theory itself—is called the theory's prior probability, which is based on several things.

To illustrate the importance of prior probability and how we intuitively evaluate it, consider that an infinite number of hypotheses can explain why a window is broken and a baseball is lying on the rug. We could suppose that a Martian spacecraft dropped the ball and it broke the window; that a hummingbird picked it up and threw it into the window; or that children were playing baseball and accidently threw the ball through the window. Obviously, the last theory fits better with our background knowledge, specifically, what we know about baseballs and their tendency to break windows when children play

---

[15]Ibid., p. 65.
[16]For our purposes we will not distinguish between "theory" and "hypothesis."

with them. But we don't know anything about Martian spacecrafts (unless we read a lot of tabloids on the fringe), and what we do know about hummingbirds makes us think that they can't even pick up baseballs much less throw them. So even though all three theories explain the broken window, we choose the child theory over the others because it fits our background knowledge.

Besides fit with background knowledge,[17] Swinburne says that prior probability is assessed on scope and simplicity. The broader the scope of a theory the less likely it is to be true. That is because the more things it claims to tell you about, the more likely it is to be wrong; in other words, the more you assert the greater the chance for error.[18] But the broader the scope of a theory the simpler it tends to be. That is because, typically, broad theories explain a lot of things using few entities and few rules that apply to those entities. For example, Newton's theory of gravity has very broad scope in that it applies to everything from tides to planetary motion. Yet it also greatly simplifies our explanation of the universe. And we know from centuries of study in many different fields (especially science) that simpler theories often turn out to be true. A complex notion can be artificially reduced to something simple merely by substituting one symbol or word for many symbols or words. But Swinburne, as well as most philosophers of science who invoke simplicity as an indicator of truth, means something more fundamental. It is a matter of "few laws, each connecting few entities, few kinds of entity, few properties, few kinds of property, connected by a mathematically simple formula."[19] A theory "will be supported by the evidence only if it postulates few entities, which leads us to expect the diverse phenomena that form the evidence."[20]

While broader theories gain scope, they also gain simplicity. As a theory, theism has a high prior probability in that it explains everything using only one entity, God. And that entity is a simple being in the sense that God has no limits to explain (or rules that apply to him) because he is infinite in his power, knowledge and freedom.[21] Worldviews generally have to be evaluated on their simplicity rather than their fit with our background knowledge, Swinburne says. That is because worldviews affect everything, so there is nothing unaffected to form a

---

[17]Swinburne recognizes that the division between the evidence for the hypothesis and the background knowledge can be somewhat arbitrary (ibid., p. 65).
[18]Ibid., p. 55.
[19]Swinburne, "Natural Theology and Orthodoxy," p. 53.
[20]Ibid., p. 53.
[21]Swinburne, *Existence of God*, pp. 97, 150–51.

background with which to fit.[22] Consequently, Swinburne concludes, the extreme simplicity of theism counts strongly in its favor.

As we saw, explanatory power is the ability of a theory to explain what cannot otherwise be explained. A theory has explanatory power if it makes us expect (i.e., makes more probably) what has actually happened. The more things that have happened, and the more diverse they are, the more explanatory power the theory has.[23] A theory has low explanatory power if the thing it explains would happen whether we assume the theory is true or not. So, for example, if money is stolen from a bank safe one night and the police find the bank manager's fingerprints on the safe, the theory that he stole the money has no explanatory power. His fingerprints would be there whether or not he stole the money. But if the fingerprints of one John Jones are found and he doesn't work there or bank there, the theory that he stole the money explains what cannot otherwise be explained, namely, that his fingerprints are on the safe. Expanding on the illustration, it is even more likely that John Jones stole the money if it fits with our background knowledge, in this case what we know of Mr. Jones. If he has a record of stealing, and if he had an opportunity to steal from the bank (for example, if it is known that he was in the area) then it is very likely that Mr. Jones is our man.

We could add an example from the famous O. J. Simpson murder trial. Polling data revealed that by a large majority the African American community believed in Simpson's innocence while an equal majority within the white community believed in his guilt. Some analysis indicated that the issue turned on the believability of a background issue, whether a number of law-enforcement people would spontaneously conspire together to frame a man solely because he was African American. Based on what they took to be past personal experiences of prejudice, African Americans generally found the idea believable. Such a conspiracy would lower the explanatory power of the evidence because, having been unjustly created by the racist conspirators, that evidence would be there whether or not Simpson committed the murder. Whites rejected the conspiracy theory as implausible since members of the alleged conspiracy did not even know each other, and as law-enforcement personnel they would know that they each risked the death penalty for framing a person for a capital crime. In terms of Bayes's theorem, then, for whites the prior probability of the conspiracy theory was very low, which meant that the explanatory power of the evidence was very high, pointing to his guilt.

---

[22]Ibid., pp. 59–60.
[23]Swinburne, *The Existence of God*, 2nd ed., p. 56.

Bayes's theorem itself formalizes the kinds of things we have been considering about testing theories. It shows how probability (*p*), hypothesis (*h*; same as a "theory"), evidence (*e*) and background knowledge (*k*) relate to each other (see table 1).

probability of the explanatory hypothesis	=	posterior probability: explanatory power of the hypothesis	×	prior probability: how good a hypothesis it is considering other things we know
$p(h/e.k)$	=	$\dfrac{p(e/h.k)}{p(e/k)}$	×	$p(h/k)$

Table 1

In words, it says that the probability of the hypothesis equals its explanatory power times its prior probability. Notice that the explanatory power $p(e/h.k)$ / $p(e/k)$ compares how likely the evidence would be assuming that the hypothesis (*h*) is true ($p(e/h.k)$) versus how likely the evidence would be without assuming that the hypothesis is true ($p(e/k)$). That is why the *h* appears in the top part but not in the bottom. This "posterior probability" is probability given the evidence *e*.

As to the application of the theorem, Alvin Plantinga points out that where we have many items of hypothesis, and we keep the total available evidence constant and add more items of the hypothesis, the probability gets smaller and smaller, becoming too small to support belief.[24] Swinburne replies that "if we add each new bit of evidence at the same time as we add each new element of hypothesis, the probability may well increase"[25]—and he believes in this case it does increase. The "many items of hypothesis" in the case he is considering are "the more and more detailed claims about God made by Christian creeds."[26] He adds that if we do as Plantinga suggests, we could get the (counterintuitive) result that a lot of historical evidence—for any event, not just a religious one—makes the event less likely than a smaller amount of evidence for the same event.[27]

[24]Alvin Plantinga, *Warranted Christian Belief* (New York: Oxford University Press, 2000), pp. 272–80. He assumes for argument's sake that probabilities can be assigned to such things. See also the extended note in Richard Swinburne, *The Resurrection of God Incarnate* (Oxford: Oxford University Press, 2003), pp. 215–16 n. 4.
[25]Richard Swinburne, personal email correspondence with the author, Oct. 17, 2013.
[26]Ibid.
[27]Richard Swinburne, *Revelation: From Metaphor to Analogy*, 2nd ed. (Oxford: Oxford University Press, 2007), p. 356. In n. 7 he gives details of how he regards probabilities relating to theism. There he references his *The Resurrection of God Incarnate*, p. 30 n. 12.

The Evidence for Theism

Having used simplicity to judge the prior probability of theism to be "high relative to any alternative hypothesis which is available to explain the data fairly well,"[28] Swinburne then tests theism's explanatory power using six arguments in favor of theism and one argument against it (the existence of evil).

He first considers how well theism can account for the existence of the universe (cosmological argument). Theism has a high explanatory power because if God exists it is very likely that he would create a universe; whereas without God it is hard to explain why the universe exists. He adds, "There is a complexity, particularity, and finitude about the universe that cries out for explanation, which God does not have."[29] By contrast, the supposition that there is a God is a very simple one.[30] Furthermore,

> the existence of the universe is less simple, and so less to be expected a priori than the existence of God. Hence, if there is no God, the existence of a complex physical universe is not much to be expected; it is not a priori very probable at all—both because (it may well seem) it is vastly improbable a priori that there would be anything at all; and because, if there is anything, it is more likely to be God than an uncaused complex physical universe.[31]

He concludes, "There is quite a chance that, if there is a God, he will make something of the finitude and complexity of a universe. It is very unlikely that a universe would exist uncaused, but rather more likely that God would exist uncaused."[32] Hence the argument from the existence of the universe to God is a good one.[33]

Next to be explained is the order of the universe (teleological argument). Swinburne insists that there can be no valid deductive argument from order in the universe to a divine designer. That is because it is not logically necessary that order be brought about by a person.[34] However, it is very probable that order be brought about by a person. Therefore, there can be a good inductive argument from order to an orderer.[35]

---

[28]Richard Swinburne, personal email correspondence with the author, Oct. 17, 2013.
[29]Swinburne, *Existence of God*, p. 150.
[30]Ibid., pp. 96–109, 150–51.
[31]Ibid., p. 151.
[32]Ibid., p. 152.
[33]He considers it a good "C-inductive" argument (ibid., p. 152), that is, one "from premises known to be true by those who dispute about the conclusion" (pp. 6–7).
[34]Ibid., p. 155.
[35]Ibid., p. 166.

Swinburne argues that theism is a better theory than polytheism because it is simpler: we do not have to explain why there is a particular number of gods, what their limits are and so on. Furthermore, because the universe is uniform throughout, it is much more likely that it is the work of one God. If there were many gods we would expect that gravity would work in one part of the universe but not in others, and so on.[36]

Though Swinburne does not go nearly as far as Carnell in considering subjective elements of human experience, he here assesses some of its features: humans are unique in their capacities to worship God, appreciate his creation and act morally. These require assets of free will, power and knowledge.[37] God would have good reason to make a world where humans have these things, where they are free moral beings. (He would also have reason to make a world where animals have some ability to make free choices.) Furthermore, for humans to have significant choice as to their destiny, there must be temptation.[38] Swinburne therefore concludes that the human condition fits well with the existence of God.

Swinburne accepts that humans evolved, but argues that the precise and sophisticated connection between mind events and brain events defies scientific explanation: "The most novel and striking features of animals and above all of humans (their conscious life of feeling, choice, and reason, causing connected to their bodies) seems to lie utterly beyond the range of successful scientific explanation."[39] We are justified in thinking these are "footprints of the divine."[40]

He defends the view that the mind and body (specifically the brain) are different substances. The view is known as "substance dualism," and holds that a "mind" is not merely another way of talking about the brain and its chemistry. If the mind were nothing more than the physical brain, it would be hard to defend doctrines essential to Christianity, especially the existence of the soul in a future life. If one thing happening does not entail another thing happening, if one thing is not part of another but something additional, then we have two things, not one[41] (i.e., a mind and a body, or a soul and a body).

---

[36]Ibid., pp. 146–47.

[37]Ibid., pp. 122, 130, 211.

[38]Ibid., pp. 218, 237, 241.

[39]Ibid., p. 209, see also p. 210.

[40]Ibid., p. 211.

[41]Richard Swinburne, *The Evolution of the Soul*, rev. ed. (Oxford: Clarendon Press, 1997), p. x. For a concise argument for substance dualism, see J. P. Moreland, *Scaling the Secular City* (Grand Rapids: Baker, 1987), chap. three, "God and the Argument from Mind," pp. 77–103. For a more extensive

The word *soul* designates what is essential to a person, the survival of which after death is the survival of that individual.[42] The "mere continued existence of the person's body is neither necessary nor sufficient for the continued existence of the person."[43] A common objection to the view that the mind is more than the physical brain is that we cannot explain how one affects the other. Swinburne replies that "it is no objection to a theory that it cannot answer all questions."[44]

Also at stake in the mind-body question is free will. If our minds are nothing more than our physical brains, it would be difficult to see how we can make genuinely free choices that are not determined by our bodies. Swinburne concludes that nothing in science or neuroscience shows that interaction does not take place between the mind and brain. Our intentions can cause brain events; in fact, conscious events and brain events are so different that it would be impossible to establish a scientific theory that could predict what an individual would do in, say, a moral conflict. In all, he concludes that we are responsible for our actions, and they are not determined by our bodies.[45]

Swinburne sees two potential arguments from morality. First is the mere fact that humans have moral awareness. He believes that arguments from moral awareness have some confirmatory force.[46] Second, there is a potential argument from morality itself: if there are moral obligations then there must be a God for their source. But Swinburne believes that this would not make a convincing argument for those who do not already accept God's existence. That is because people will either deny that certain moral acts are obligatory or they will deny that moral acts contribute to greater good in the universe. So because the premises would not be accepted by the disputing parties, an argument from the fact of morality would have no practical value.[47]

What is traditionally called "providence" provides another argument for theism: our type of world is likely to exist if there is a God but unlikely if there is not. If there were no God to create our world, many other types of worlds would be just as likely as this one, so there is no scientific explanation as to why our particular type of world came about. This provides some evidence that our world

---

discussion, J. P. Moreland, *Consciousness and the Existence of God: A Theistic Argument* (New York: Routledge, 2008).

[42]Swinburne, *Evolution of the Soul*, p. x.

[43]Ibid., p. xiii. Part two of the book argues this.

[44]Ibid., p. xiii.

[45]Richard Swinburne, *Mind, Brain, and Free Will* (Oxford: Oxford University Press, 2013), pp. 228-29.

[46]Swinburne, *Existence of God*, pp. 215-18. He changed his view from the first edition of the book.

[47]Ibid., pp. 212-15.

is the product of God. Specific providential features of our world include the following: that we can provide for ourselves what we need to sustain our lives, that we have opportunities to make right choices but not infinite opportunities to correct bad ones (which would entail that our choices really would not matter) and that we can benefit one another and must work together to accomplish good things (note that this freedom entails that we are also able to harm each other, which helps explain why there is pain and evil). Even death has value in that, for example, it provides grounds for courage and ultimate sacrifice, it eventually allows the young a chance to be influential and it prevents a person from having unlimited time to harm others.

History and miracles also point to the existence of God. Though detailed assessment of specific events of history are beyond his scope, Swinburne does offer some reasons to think that the Christian tradition is compatible with what we know of God and history. Assuming that the human race is far less than what it should be, God could be expected to do something about it. He could send a person to teach moral and spiritual principles and even to make atonement for evil. Atonement would have to be made by someone who was not himself immoral. And since atonement would result in death, God could not require anyone else to make it; but he could make it himself. God would attest to such a person being his messenger by enabling the person to violate natural laws (i.e., do miracles), and God would have reason to resurrect him, while leaving behind a community to carry on his work and message. Yet God would not make the work of the messenger so overwhelmingly obvious as to remove the freedom of each individual to choose to believe and follow him.[48] All of this we may have some reason to find, and it is what we do find in Christianity.

In a later book, *Revelation: From Metaphor to Analogy*,[49] Swinburne shows that historical arguments are important to the case for Christianity and that when reasonable standards are applied there is sufficient historical evidence for the resurrection. Justifying the claim that particular propositional revelations are from God, as Christianity claims for its Scriptures, is made easier if natural revelation shows that God exists. In that way general revelation (what can be known without Scripture, such as the existence of God) supports special revelation. And historical arguments, such as for the resurrection, also help justify claims for those events made in propositional revelation (i.e., special revelation

---

[48]Ibid., pp. 288–91.
[49]Swinburne, *Revelation*.

as found in the Bible). Swinburne argues in the same book that such devices as metaphors, analogies, parables and poetry do not prevent Scripture from communicating eternal truth and moral principles.

Miracles figure prominently in many claims for religious truth, including in the Bible. While they are violations of natural law that would almost by definition be highly unlikely, that is no reason to necessarily dismiss a claim that such violation has occurred (as Hume famously proposed that we do).[50] Swinburne rightly points out that certain types of evidence can count for the occurrence of a miraculous event. Evidence includes memory, testimony, physical evidence[51] and our background knowledge of the rest of the world. Furthermore, if there is evidence besides miracles that God exists, then it makes it more likely that miracles have occurred in the past. This is because if there is a God he would have the ability and motivation to perform miracles.[52] Furthermore, God has reason to intervene some of the time, for example, in response to prayer, but if he intervenes too much then it removes the consequences of good or bad actions. God also has reason to become incarnate and to prove it by miracles.

Religious experience is another common but controversial argument for theism. Swinburne bases his argument on a very simple but powerful assumption, which he believes weakens the challenge of skepticism and supports belief in God. His "principle of credulity" assumes that things are as we experience them unless we have a specific reason to think otherwise. It is remotely akin to Reformed epistemology's claim that beliefs are not guilty until proven innocent and that we need not proportion our degree of certainty to the strength of the case we can make (as is claimed, for example, by philosophical evidentialism, which is not the same as apologetic evidentialism; see chap. five, on Plantinga). A view of experience that competes with Swinburne's is held, for example, by epistemologist Roderick Chisholm.[53] Chisholm contends that we are justified in believing that x is what it appears to be only when x is something we can perceive. So if we perceive that a table is brown, then we are justified in believing that it is brown. But where x is not perceivable we need further inductive support for believing it. So, for example, we need more support for the claim that the table we see is Victorian.

---

[50]David Hume, *An Enquiry Concerning Human Understanding* (1748), sec. ten, "Of Miracles."
[51]Swinburne, *Resurrection of God Incarnate*, p. 9.
[52]Swinburne, *Existence of God*, p. 287.
[53]R. M. Chisholm, *Perceiving: A Philosophical Study* (Ithaca, NY: Cornell University Press, 1957), p. 83; quoted in Swinburne, *Existence*, pp. 307-8.

This distinction matters a great deal if we want to consider an experience of God as evidence that he exists. On Swinburne's view an experience of God should be taken as evidence that God is there (unless there is some good reason not to believe it). But on the competing view an experience of God is not evidence for his existence unless there is further support for it. That a person is experiencing God is only his interpretation of what is happening; thus there must be additional evidence to support that interpretation.

Swinburne of course recognizes that a perception might be mistaken. This is the case when (1) it is made under conditions or by a person known in the past to be unreliable, such as under the influence of a hallucinogen; (2) the claim is to be able to perceive an object of a kind that in circumstances in which similar perceptual claims have been made have proved false; (3) background evidence shows that very probably the perceived object was not present; and (4) it can be shown that a person's experience did not have the cause they thought it did.[54]

Swinburne insists that objections from background evidence (no. 3, above) must be very strong to challenge experiences otherwise we would be "imprisoned within the circle of our existing beliefs."[55] If, for example, our background belief is that a friend is in another city yet we think we see him on the street, then our experience overrides our background belief. But if our background belief is that our friend is dead, then it is indeed very improbable that it is him on the street; we need more evidence to support our experience.

Caroline Franks Davis clarifies Swinburne's views[56] and develops her own views along similar lines. Against the charge that the principle of credulity leaves us gullible, she points out that challenges to certain types of experiences (such as dreams) and things (such as elves and "auras") "are so widely successful and so well known that claims based on such experiences have come to be regarded by adults initially with suspicion rather than with credulity."[57] Furthermore, when the vast majority of people reject some claim, we assume that some successful challenge is available even if we don't know what it is. But where successful challenges are not available, "perhaps it is not such a bad thing if the principle of credulity forces us to treat the claims as innocent until proven

---

[54]Swinburne, *Existence of God*, pp. 310–14.

[55]Ibid., p. 312.

[56]She bases her views partly on conversations with him.

[57]Caroline Franks Davis, *The Evidential Force of Religious Experience* (Oxford: Clarendon Press, 1989), p. 101.

guilty."[58] Furthermore, the principle does not entitle us to believe strongly in some important claim just because a challenge is not currently available—"that would be blind faith, not an argument from religious experience."[59]

Another reason the principle of credulity does not leave us gullible is that it makes religious experiences only "probable" and not "very likely." It merely ensures that an argument from religious experience is not dismissed out of hand such that it is never taken seriously enough to be investigated.

Swinburne concludes, "The point here is that the onus of proof is on the atheist; if he cannot make his case the claim of religious experience stands."[60]

EVIL AS AN ARGUMENT AGAINST THEISM

Swinburne then considers what is widely acknowledged as the most persistent and serious argument against theism: the existence of pain and evil.[61] This includes moral evil, which is the harm that people intentionally do to each other, as well as natural evil, which is evil of all other types (earthquakes, disease, accidents, animal pain and so on).

He points out that some evil is unavoidable. The nerves that protect a person from harm also produce pain. The free will that enables us to choose good also makes it possible for us to choose evil. And the more significant the freedom and possibility for good, the more potential there is for evil. It would be logically impossible for God to "give us the freedom to hurt each other and at the same time ensure that we won't."[62]

A major theme in Swinburne's theodicy is that "God wants to give us deep responsibility for ourselves and each other," and he wants us to exercise that responsibility in the right way.[63] Yet "only if agents have the power to do bad do they have significant responsibility."[64] Temptation offers the opportunity to choose good, and by doing so over time, we can develop good character. If the effects of other people's choices were the only source of challenge against which we can form our character, for many individuals that would not be enough of an opportunity to form character. Disease and old age provide further opportunities,

---

[60]Swinburne, *Existence of God*, p. 315.

[61]Swinburne develops his views more in more detail in *Providence and the Problem of Evil* (Oxford: Clarendon, 1998).

[62]Richard Swinburne, *Was Jesus God?* (Oxford: Oxford University Press, 2008), p. 21.

[63]Ibid., p. 20.

[64]Swinburne, *Providence and the Problem of Evil*, p. 154.

for example, "to be patient and cheerful, or to be gloomy and resentful." When we see others in need, we can choose to be compassionate and giving—or not.[65]

Swinburne comments on three traditional explanations for natural evil.[66] Natural evil cannot solely be punishment for sin because that would not account for suffering of babies or animals. It cannot solely be punishment for sins of ancestors.[67] Such punishment would be useful only if humans were aware of it, and most of them are not. And finally, natural evil cannot be explained as the action of fallen angels because we have no independent evidence for such beings. If belief in fallen angels were added merely to save theism from falsification then it would be ad hoc, which means that it is added for this special purpose only and has no further usefulness. That would make it an artificial addition. Since ad hoc additions detract from the simplicity of a theory, in this case theism, they reduce the theory's prior probability[68] (which, recall, is its probability as a theory based on background evidence, apart from specific evidence for it).

Why does natural evil exist? Swinburne argues that in order to exercise their freedom people must know how to bring about the results they desire—and this includes evil results as well as good since freedom entails both. Furthermore, the closer that knowledge is to personal experience the better. So seeing specific types of harm caused by nature and accidents enables humans to manipulate their world and thus exercise their freedom. Seeing that poison causes harm, for instance, shows us how to prevent or cause harm to others.

Evil can also be explained by the fact that certain types of good things can exist only where there are types of evil. For example, tolerance requires something irritating, courage requires danger, forgiveness requires sin and so on. God could not have gained the consent of those who would suffer since his decision to create the world as it is had to be made before there were any people. Besides, as Creator he knows how people will suffer and what effects it will have. But in any case, as Creator, he has rights over us that we do not have over each other.

We must not forget that God does limit the amount of pain people suffer. People do not live forever, and there are physical limits to how much pain people can suffer.

In all, there are good reasons for God to bring about or allow a world such as ours—and there is more to human well-being than "tingles of pleasure."[69]

---

[65]Swinburne, *Was Jesus God?*, p. 21.
[66]Swinburne, *Existence of God*, pp. 238–40.
[67]Ibid., p. 239.
[68]Ibid., p. 240.
[69]Swinburne, "Natural Theology and Orthodoxy," p. 74.

Therefore there is no convincing argument from evil to the nonexistence of God. Swinburne observes that readers will agree with his conclusion insofar as they think that what people do is more important than how good they feel.[70]

Evil and suffering provide a bridge from theism to the more specific views of Christianity in that if God caused humans to suffer (albeit for good reason) "he should suffer with them."[71] In the person of Christ, we find just such suffering.

CHRISTIANITY AND THE BALANCE OF PROBABILITY

Based on all the evidence for and against the existence of God, Swinburne concludes that it is more likely that God exists than that he does not.[72] He believes that one reason the case for theism is not even more convincing is that the existence of God is compatible with so many different types of worlds that God could have created. But insofar as our world is not clearly incompatible with theism (where, for example, there is great evil that is random and pointless) it supports God's existence. In favor of theism is the fact that it need not be highly probable but only the most probable hypothesis available. The main competing alternative is that there is simply no explanation for the universe. However, Swinburne adds, it is not a good alternative since we expect things to have explanations.

Having shown that theism is coherent, and having established a strong inductive argument that God exists, Swinburne then sets out to show that Christianity is the correct understanding of theism. He gives a priori reasons for believing the central doctrines of Christianity, such reasons as the nature of God and the "general condition of the human race."[73] He then argues that, granting only a moderate probability on other evidence that God exists, and the a priori evidence, "the historical evidence about the life and Resurrection of Jesus and the subsequent teaching of the Church makes it very probable that these doctrines are true." The historical evidence provides a posteriori reasons. (A priori

---

[70]Swinburne, *Existence of God*, p. 267: "The reader will sympathize with my verdict in so far as he believes that it is more important what an agent does (the choices he makes, the changes he produces in the world and the effects of his life on others) than what happens to him (the sensations and disappointments he experiences)."

[71]Swinburne, "Natural Theology and Orthodoxy," p. 68.

[72]In *The Resurrection of God Incarnate* (p. 201) he notes that he has argued the case for theism elsewhere, and says, "I do not wish to exaggerate the strength of the evidence, and so I have claimed merely that the evidence makes it as probable as not that there is a God." Then as to the case for the incarnation, "Again, I do not wish to exaggerate the strength of this plausibility and I suggested that it is as probable as not that God will be come [sic] incarnate" (p. 201).

[73]Swinburne, *Was Jesus God?*, p. 5.

reasons exist in the mind prior to or independent of experience; a posteriori reasons do not and entail examining evidence.)

The evidence for theism also makes Christianity more likely to be true, because of course Christianity cannot be true unless theism is true. (The evidence for theism counts more for theism than for Christianity.) So the posterior evidence for theism provides the prior evidence for Christianity, since if theism is true then Christianity fits with the background knowledge (i.e., of theism). The stronger the prior evidence (that God exists), the weaker the posterior evidence (historical arguments for Christianity) can be and still result in Christianity being confirmed overall.[74]

He links the case for the resurrection to the case for theism (which is typical of classical theists like Norman Geisler): "It is simply not possible to investigate whether Jesus rose from the dead without taking a view about how probable it is that there is a God likely to intervene in human history in this kind of way."[75] So, "If the background evidence leaves it not too improbable that there is a God likely to act in the ways discussed, then the total evidence makes it very probable that Jesus was God Incarnate who rose from the dead."[76]

Swinburne explores the a priori evidence that the God of the Nicene Creed (put in final form in A.D. 381) exists. God, being perfectly good, must also be perfectly loving. Perfect love is love of an equal, and God thus eternally generates the Son. Love between two can be selfish, and God would have reason to share love with another equal, which is the Holy Spirit.

The "whole Trinity is ontologically necessary because nothing else caused it to exist."[77] A loving God would respond to human suffering and wrongdoing by himself living as a human (the incarnation), and he would probably use that life to make atonement as well as to teach us how to live.[78] It is not improbable that the incarnation would take place through a process that was supernatural, in a way that would show that Jesus is both human and divine, that is, through a virgin birth.[79] It is fitting that he would ascend after death, and an ascension is a priori highly probable. Atonement was made by God, the wronged party, making payment for sin. At some point this stage of creation will end, and the

---

[74]Ibid., pp. 23, 25.
[75]Swinburne, *Resurrection of God Incarnate*, pp. 202–3.
[76]Ibid., p. 203.
[77]Swinburne, *Was Jesus God?*, p. 31.
[78]Ibid., p. 39.
[79]Ibid., p. 50.

second person of the Trinity will come to judge the living and the dead. Those who desire God and good will be blessed in heaven, while those who have continually chosen what is bad, or do what is good from purely selfish motives, will be away from God in hell. God gave them opportunity in life to choose him and good, but having continually refused, there is no point in allowing them to continue to make harmful choices. Having made their choice persistently and knowingly,[80] he cannot simply impose on them good desires and character.

Swinburne finds initial reason to regard as credible the writers of the Bible and principal people involved in the Gospels. His principle of testimony (related to the principle of credulity) suggests that we should start by giving the benefit of the doubt to the Gospel records of Christ. (John Warwick Montgomery makes a similar point.) The principle of testimony does not function as "an independent epistemic principle dependent only on a fundamental assumption."[81] There is complex interaction between our initial assumption and evidence for the credibility of the source.[82] Initial acceptance of central Christian doctrine[83] is confirmed by diverse layers of evidence. For example, a number of early Christians died for their beliefs, which is evidence of their sincerity. The biblical account of the life and teaching of Jesus "is such as it is quite probable we would find if Jesus lived a perfect life with much suffering, claimed to be God Incarnate and to be making atonement for human sins, gave plausible teaching (as a revelation) on morality and God, and founded a Church."[84] Conversely, so much is very improbable if he did not.

Of course much more evidence is needed, and Swinburne explores the biblical support for the resurrection. The accounts are by eyewitnesses, and any differences in their reports are reconcilable. No argument for the empty tomb is offered and none is needed because even the Jewish opponents admitted it was empty (Mt 28:15). The celebration of the Eucharist on Sunday provides crucial and normally unrecognized evidence because, first, the custom must have arisen very early, before the Christian community dispersed from Jerusalem, within three or four years after the Passion. If it originated after the dispersion, the custom would not have been uniform and uncontroversial. Second, Sunday is

---

[80]Swinburne acknowledges that those who die young have not persistently formed their character, and he suggests some ways in which God may deal with them (ibid., pp. 80-81).

[81]Richard Swinburne, *Epistemic Justification* (Oxford: Clarendon Press, 2001), p. 125.

[82]Ibid., pp. 125–28.

[83]Clarified for me by Richard Swinburne, personal email correspondence with the author, Oct. 17, 2013.

[84]Swinburne, *Was Jesus God?*, p. 113.

not the most natural day for the Christians to meet, so the best explanation is the supernatural events of Easter Sunday.[85] The resurrection itself was unexpected by first-century Jews and would not be the sort of event they would have made up. Alternative explanations to the resurrection all have "massive difficulties."[86] The resurrection fits the prophetic pattern of faithfulness to the Lord (Deut 13:1-3), and the prophet's prediction coming true if he made one (Deut 18:22).[87]

The amount of eyewitness testimony needed to believe a claim depends on the prior probability of the claim, that is, how believable it is based on our background knowledge. A claim to have seen someone fifteen feet tall needs much more evidence than a claim to have seen someone ten feet tall. Swinburne says that there is modest prior probability provided by evidence of God's existence, as well as the fit between what we find in history and what we would expect to find if Jesus did the things the Bible claims. Furthermore, there is a lack of fit between what we find and the idea that Jesus did not live and do what the Bible claims. In other words, it is easy to explain the evidence if the Bible is correct, but it is hard to explain it if the Bible is incorrect.[88] All of this means that a bit less proof is needed to show that Jesus in fact rose from the dead. That is provided by the significant historical evidence about him. Christ is the only "serious candidate in human history" about whom we have evidence (1) of the right kind of life, who had "a perfect life with much suffering, claimed to be divine, claimed to be making atonement, gave plausible moral and theological teaching,[89] and founded a Church to continue his work," and (2) "that his or her life ended with a miracle recognizable as a divine signature."[90] (By "plausible" he means "not very improbable."[91]) A church would "continue his work, report his actions, and interpret his teaching for new cultures and generations."[92] Mohammed and Buddha and others do not qualify because "they did not give the right sort of teaching"; for example, they did not claim to be God incarnate, and "their lives

---

[85]Ibid., pp. 119–20.

[86]Swinburne, *Was Jesus God?*, p. 122. Swinburne, *Resurrection of God Incarnate*, chap. eleven, "Rival Theories of What Happened," pp. 174–86.

[87]Swinburne, *Was Jesus God?*, pp. 123–25.

[88]Ibid., pp. 126–27.

[89]For Swinburne's view of how to interpret some biblical statements (which differs from most of the other apologists in this book), see "The Bible," chap. eleven in *Was Jesus God?*, pp. 144–60.

[90]Swinburne, *Was Jesus God?*, p. 132.

[91]Ibid., p. 135.

[92]Ibid., p. 161. The message of the church must be an accurate interpretation of the original one, and "plausibly true." More about the church in ibid., chap. ten, "The Church," pp. 134–43, and p. 161. And Swinburne, *Resurrection of God Incarnate*, "Jesus Founded a Church," chap. eight, pp. 127–41.

ended in altogether non-miraculous ways." The fact that historical evidence for both the right kind of life and the right kind of death come together in Christ alone provides some evidence that Christian claims about him are true.[93]

Swinburne concludes that Christianity is true, entailing that Jesus was God, and, "since no divine person can cease to be divine, that *Jesus is God.*"[94]

SUMMARY

Swinburne first tests theism for coherence (in *The Coherence of Theism*) and then finds it to be far more probable than not (in *The Existence of God*) according to the two criteria formalized by Bayes's theorem. According to Bayes, a theory is confirmed if it is (1) a good theory according to everything we know that is relevant (i.e., it has high prior probability), and (2) it makes evidence likely that otherwise would not be (i.e., it has explanatory power). He shows that theism has a high prior probability primarily because it is simple in that it explains everything by means of one being who is as simple as can be (e.g., his capacities have no limits to explain).

Then theism's explanatory power is checked with respect to a number of positive arguments. The cosmological and teleological arguments confirm theism. Consciousness does too, because it would not have appeared from evolution alone. The argument from moral awareness has some confirmatory force. Providence forms a good argument because the world supports the existence and development of free creatures. History and reports of miracles support the Christian message. As to religious experiences, an experience of anything should be taken as evidence for that thing, and experiences of God are no exception. This shifts the burden of proof to the atheist. Evil does not form an effective argument against theism since there are good reasons why God would allow it. On balance, then, theism is well confirmed and not merely the most probable hypothesis available.

He sums up his case in *Is There a God?*

> The basic structure of my argument is this. Scientists, historians, and detectives observe data and proceed thence to some theory about what best explains the occurrence of these data. We can analyse the criteria which they use in reaching a conclusion that a certain theory is better supported by the data than a different theory. . . . Using those same criteria, we find that the view that there is a God explains everything we observe, not just some narrow range of data. It explains the fact that there is a universe at all, that scientific laws operate within

---

[93]Swinburne, *Was Jesus God?*, pp. 132-33.
[94]Ibid., p. 170 (emphasis original).

it, that it contains conscious animals and humans with very complex intricately organized bodies, that we have abundant opportunities for developing ourselves and the world, as well as the more particular data that humans report miracles and have religious experiences. In so far as scientific causes and laws explain some of the things (and in part they do), these very causes and laws need explaining, and God's action explains them. The very same criteria which scientists use to reach their own theories lead us to move beyond those theories to a creator God who sustains everything in existence.[95]

The evidence makes theism as probable as not, so the additional evidence of religious experience makes theism overall a "substantial probability," and "quite likely." The evidence for theism interfaces with the evidence for the life, death and resurrection of Jesus.[96]

CRITICISMS

The most fundamental criticism of Swinburne's case is his use of Bayes's theorem for a subject area in which it is difficult to assign numbers. Assigning numbers is a straightforward matter when we are dealing with such things as parts coming off an assembly line or insurance data. But how to assign numbers to such things as the likelihood of an uncreated universe's being orderly is much less clear.

In Swinburne's favor, however, he assigns only very general numbers to elements of his case, and that procedure seems quite plausible. It is not hard to see how general numbers can be had. Where, for example, there is complete uncertainty, the number would be .5 on a scale of 0 to 1 (where 0 represents no possibility that something is the case and 1 represents certainty that it is the case).[97] We could say in general terms that .9 is very certain, .8 less so; .6 would be only slightly better than uncertainty, and so on. It seems that we can make use of Bayes's theorem as long as we do not try to assign much more accurate numbers (such as .785) where there is no numeric basis for doing so, and as long as we realize that our final probability cannot be more accurate than the estimates we used to get it.

Whether we can use probability in even this general way in an environment where numbers are assigned rather than observed depends somewhat on our underlying theory of probability. According to the subjectivist view, probability is

---

[95]Richard Swinburne, *Is There A God?* (Oxford: Oxford University Press, 1996), p. 2.

[96]*The Existence of God*, pp. 341-42; *The Resurrection of God Incarnate*, p. 30.

[97]We could say that deduction operates at the extremes of zero and one whereas probability and induction operate between zero and one.

essentially a matter of degree of one's belief, so assigning numbers in a case for theism is clearly acceptable. On a logical view (the view Swinburne accepts) probability is a matter of the relationship between propositions and the world, and assigning numbers in this type of case is also acceptable. But assigning numbers in a case for theism on a relative-frequency view of probability is more problematic. According to this view, probability is nothing more than a calculation, a matter of deriving numbers from observable numbers. It is not surprising that much of the criticism of Swinburne's case assumes this stricter view. Certainly, however, there are uses for probability that do not demand numbers in order to get numbers. We could say, for example, that there is a very low probability (.1 or less) that a high school football team ranking at the bottom of its league could beat this year's Super Bowl champions. Yet we have no frequencies of past games between high school teams and Super Bowl teams because such numbers do not exist.

Besides showing in a general way the probability of theism, Bayes's theorem has the advantage of showing how explanatory power and prior probability work together to confirm a theory. We can see that either high explanatory power or high prior probability can confirm a theory. If a theory has high prior probability (if it is a good theory) then it is confirmed even if it does not have a lot of explanatory power. But opponents are prone to view theism as having a low prior probability; that is, they are likely to think that God's existence is unlikely on grounds that it does not fit what we already hold in our background beliefs, or that we have no independent reason to think that a being such as God could exist, and the like. But even with a low prior probability, theism could be confirmed if it has high explanatory power, that is, if it makes likely what is otherwise unexplainable. This makes it important for the theist to insist on reasonable explanations for things, such as the Big Bang and sophisticated, beneficial design.

There are two main objections to an argument from religious experience as evidence for God: religious experiences conflict, and they can be explained without supposing God exists.

The fact that religious experiences are of such different beings—from Allah to Zeus—seems to count against their being veridical, that is, really there as opposed to something imaginary or mistaken. Swinburne answers, in part, that the same God can be known under different names in different cultures, a view he believes is supported by two biblical verses. One is Exodus 6:3, where God tells Moses that he has appeared to "Abraham, Isaac, and Jacob, as God Almighty, but by My name, Lord, I did not make Myself known to them." However, on a contrary interpretation, the name LORD (Yahweh) was known very early, and to the patriarchs (Gen 4:26; 9:26; 12:8; 22:14; 24:12), so God is actually saying (Ex 6:4-8) that his power had already been revealed but his faithfulness to keep his covenant with Israel would only now be revealed.

Swinburne defends his view of religious experience with a second verse, Acts 17:23, in which Paul addresses the religious authorities of Athens. One of their altars has the inscription "TO AN UNKNOWN GOD," and Paul tells them, "What you worship in ignorance, this I proclaim to you." However, again on a contrasting interpretation, Paul is filling in details the Athenians felt they lacked. Having erected many altars to various gods, they erected one to a god they may have overlooked and thereby offended. The altar was there precisely because they had no experience of the deity, not because they had experienced that deity.[98]

The contrasting interpretations of these biblical passages do not necessarily count against Swinburne's point. If the views contrasting with Swinburne's interpretation are correct, the verses simply would not support his view. The general problem with Swinburne's view that veridical experiences of the same God can be had within different religious traditions is that experiences are so closely related to beliefs about those experiences. To take an admittedly extreme example, an experience of Molech in ancient times was an experience of the fire God who desired child sacrifice, whereas an experience of Yahweh was of a God who detested that very thing (Lev 18:21; Jer 7:31). Furthermore, the biblical Yahweh objects to being confused with the interpretations of deity offered by the religions of the indigenous peoples. Only a distinct separation between an experience and the interpretation of it could allow devotees with conflicting beliefs to each have a veridical experience of God. However, it seems Swinburne would generally discourage separating an experience from its interpretation (judging from his criticism of Chisholm, above) because an expe-

---

[98]Others have used another verse to make a similar point. John Sanders refers to Melchizedek to make his argument for inclusivism, the view that God can save a person through the atoning work of Christ but without that person's knowledge of the gospel (in places where the gospel is not known, for example). Though Melchizedek was a pagan priest-king, he was called a priest of "God Most High" (Gen 14:18). Sanders concludes that he worshiped the same God as Abraham but without any special revelation. A problem with this view, however, is that Melchizedek calls God by the very same name as Abraham, "God Most High, Possessor of heaven and earth" (Gen 14:19, 22). General revelation (what can be known about God apart from special revelation, such as Scripture) alone would not account for the identical wording. Therefore it is likely that the two communicated, and this fact entails the possibility that Melchizedek did not get his information about God solely from general revelation. So this case does not show that the same God can be experienced within two different religious traditions (in this instance, Melchizedek's supposed paganism and Abraham's belief in Yahweh). It seems likely that both substantially believed in Abraham's God.

rience would require further evidence to show that it is an experience of God.

The second main objection to arguments from religious experience is that such experiences can be completely accounted for without supposing that they are caused by God. Of course it is important to realize that even if religious experiences could be accounted for without God, that alone would not disprove God's existence. It would disprove only that the argument from religious experience has no force.

Though Swinburne does not explore the second objection, Davis does, and shows that attempts to explain religious experiences as pathological mental states have so far been unsuccessful. Some studies even show that believers are better adjusted than nonbelievers. Natural histories of religion have also been unsuccessful. These seek nonreligious explanations as to how religion in general arose. An example would be Freud's view that God is a projection of one's father that serves to make the universe seem personal and manageable to unscientific minds. Nonpathological explanations of religious experiences have also been unsuccessful.

So in the end, Davis concludes, the case for theism depends a lot on the success of a cumulative case for God, that is, a case based on many different types of evidence. In such a case religious experience would play a crucial part.[99] And that would be Swinburne's conclusion as well.

COMPARISONS WITH OTHER APOLOGISTS

Both Swinburne and Carnell seek to compare beliefs as whole explanations for a broad range of phenomena. Both check first for internal consistency. Carnell then checks how well the theory fits all relevant facts. Swinburne checks the self-consistency ("coherence") of theism, then its prior probability (how good a theory it is, based mostly on its simplicity) and explanatory power (how well it explains what can not otherwise be explained).

Carnell, on the one hand, is eager to show that Christianity fits with highly subjective aspects of human experience, such as the fear of death, the need for a sense of meaning and the need to be loved. Swinburne, on the other hand, is reluctant to use more subjective experiences, no doubt because they can be interpreted in nontheistic ways.

Carnell assumes that there is a level on which facts are simply there, available to us without their interpretation being determined by theory. As such, facts can be checked as to whether they fit with the theory. People fear death, for example,

---

[99]Davis, *Evidential Force of Religious Experience*, chap. eight, "The Reductionist Challenge," pp. 193–238.

and Christianity can explain why. In his view, discourse is not necessarily constrained by a worldview as long as the discourse is about what some would call objective matters, for example, if it does not entail such issues as morals and ultimate questions. Such areas of discourse that are not influenced by the theory in question form common ground between the Christian and non-Christian.

Van Til, by contrast, sees no such ground that is free of the influence of theories that could be classed as worldviews. Thus he considers the influence of such broad theories to be pervasive. In his view, the theory determines even what we see as a fact as well as how we interpret every fact. In this sense he is closer to what is sometimes called hard perspectivism, the view that the influence of theories is so pervasive that each theory is locked up within itself because its holders are unable to really communicate with those who hold other theories. Thus Van Til's view entails that there is no common ground between the Christian and non-Christian. He explains any interaction by claiming that the non-Christian covertly, inconsistently and illegitimately uses pieces of the Christian's worldview. Carnell, by contrast, sees common ground existing on a level of discourse that is unaffected by the theory.

Carnell's view seems to account for why Buddhists, atheists and Christians, for example, can agree on so much—such as the number of chairs in a room, whether the lights are on, whether DNA shows complexity and order, and so on for much of what we can say we know.

By assessing a theory in terms of its simplicity and not just its fit with the facts, Swinburne reduces the problem of circularity whereby a theory will appear to fit "facts" because the theory has already determined what those facts are. That a worldview determines everything within it forms part of Geisler's argument against approaches like Carnell's. As we shall see, Geisler solves the problem by judging worldviews according to principles of thought so fundamental that they must be affirmed by every worldview.

Swinburne, like Carnell, believes that there is also plenty of apologetically useful common ground between believer and nonbeliever.[100]

Swinburne's writing has benefited a great deal from the emphasis on clarity and precision found in the analytic movement in philosophy. Then too, he shares the movement's more empirical orientation, by which he (unlike Carnell) favors objective evidence and (unlike Van Til) emphasizes common ground.

Van Til rejects regarding beliefs as hypotheses to be tested on grounds that it

---

[100]Taped personal conversations with Swinburne in Los Angeles, ca. 1990.

is improper (even blasphemous) to subject God's truth to some supposed higher standard. Others, like William Craig, would place more value than Swinburne and Carnell on the possibility of divinely caused intuition within the believer, that is, that the believer can have confidence that is not dependent on evidence. On Craig's view, the believer knows the essentials of his faith simply because God makes it known internally, yet the believer also has access to evidence. We will see Craig's view of intuition along with the classical apologetics view that once we prove God's existence by theistic arguments we can use other means to prove the more specific truths of Christianity.

KEY TERMS

Bayes's theorem. A theorem with a wide variety of uses, it shows that a theory is likely to be true if it is a good theory given other things we know (called the theory's prior probability) and if it can explain things that are otherwise unexplainable (called its explanatory power).

Prior probability. Simply put, the probability of an event is its probability before the consideration of new or specific data. If 1 percent of the population has a disease, then the prior probability that Jones will have it is 1 percent. But if Jones is tested and found to be positive for the disease, then the (posterior) probability that he has it will go up. (The precise amount depends on the accuracy of the test.) In assessing the prior probability of a theory, Swinburne emphasizes its fit with background knowledge, scope and simplicity.

Explanatory power. The ability of a theory to explain what cannot otherwise be explained. If the theory offers the only explanation for something, then the theory has a lot of explanatory power. But if the truth of the theory does not make what is to be explained more likely, then it has no explanatory power. So if Jones gets a contagious disease, the theory that he was in contact with someone who had the disease has a lot of explanatory power. If such contact did not take place, it is difficult to explain how he came down with the disease. But the theory that Jones recently got a phone call from a relative has no explanatory power in this case, since even if he did, it wouldn't make it more likely that he would come down with the disease.

Background knowledge. "The knowledge that we take for granted before new evidence turns up."[101]

---

[101]Swinburne, *Existence of God*, p. 16.

Principle of credulity. A fundamental principle of rationality that things are as they seem unless there is a specific reason to think otherwise. If it seems x is present, then it is likely x is present, absent a good reason to think otherwise. So if a wall seems blue, then it is blue unless, for example, we know it is a white wall being illuminated with a blue light.

Principle of testimony. People's experiences are probably as they report them, unless we suspect, for example, that they have misrepresented them, are exaggerating or are lying.[102]

Logical theory of probability. The view that probability represents the relationship between propositions and the world.

THINKING IT OVER

1. What apologetic approach does Swinburne flatly reject? Which does he accept, and what philosopher is his model?

2. What common ground does Swinburne use?

3. What role does coherence have in Swinburne's approach?

4. How does Swinburne use probability?

5. What is prior probability, and how does theism measure up?

6. What is explanatory power?

7. Which arguments does Swinburne use to support theism?

8. Why is the problem of evil not decisive against theism?

9. What is Swinburne's conclusion about the case for theism?

10. How does Swinburne compare with other apologists?

GOING FURTHER

Davis, Caroline Franks. *The Evidential Force of Religious Experience.* Oxford: Clarendon, 1989. In chapter four and elsewhere she examines Swinburne's argument from religious experience.

Padgett, Alan G. *Reason and the Christian Religion: Essays in Honour of Richard Swinburne.* Oxford: Clarendon, 1994.

Quinn, Philip L., and Charles Taliaferro, eds. *A Companion to Philosophy of Religion.* Blackwell Companions to Philosophy. Malden, MA: Blackwell,

---

[102]Ibid., p. 322.

1997. Mentions many aspects of Swinburne's thought (e.g., design argument, pp. 342–44; natural theology, pp. 176–78).

Swinburne, Richard, *The Christian God*. Oxford: Clarendon, 1994.

———. *The Coherence of Theism*. Oxford: Clarendon, 1977. Rev. ed., 1993.

———. *The Existence of God*. 2nd ed. Oxford: Clarendon, 2004.

———. *Faith and Reason*. 2nd ed. Oxford: Clarendon, 1981.

———. "Intellectual Autobiography." In *Reason and the Christian Religion: Essays in Honour of Richard Swinburne*, edited by Alan G. Padgett, pp. 1–18. Oxford: Clarendon, 1994.

———. *Is There a God?* Oxford: Oxford University Press, 1994.

———. "Natural Theology and Orthodoxy." In *Turning East: Contemporary Philosophers and the Ancient Christian Faith*, edited by Rico Vitz, pp. 47–77. Orthodox Christian Profiles. Crestwood, NY: St. Vladimir's Seminary Press, 2012.

———. *Providence and the Problem of Evil*. Oxford: Clarendon, 1998.

———. *Responsibility and Atonement*. Oxford: Clarendon, 1989.

———. *Revelation: From Metaphor to Analogy*. Oxford: Clarendon, 1992. 2nd ed., 2007.

———. *Simplicity as Evidence of Truth*. Aquinas Lectures. Milwaukee: Marquette University Press, 1997.

– 9 –

WILLIAM LANE CRAIG

God Is proved by theistic arguments, and Christianity by evidences

One of the most prolific and respected scholars in the classical camp is William Lane Craig (1949–). With depth and precision that has brought respect even from secular scholars, he has authored or edited over thirty books and one hundred scholarly articles. "New atheist" Sam Harris paid him a high compliment when he said that Craig is "the one Christian apologist who seems to have put the fear of God into many of my fellow atheists."[1]

He came to Christ in a nonevangelical home[2] at age sixteen and later enrolled at Wheaton College, full of enthusiasm and faith. He said at the time, however, the school was a "seedbed of skepticism and cynicism," and he was dismayed to see intelligent students give up their faith in the name of reason. Doubt was touted as a virtue of the mature Christian life, and in classes he heard none of the arguments for God's existence or the reliability of the Gospels. He briefly toyed with Kierkegaardian fideism[3] but gave it up for its lack of engagement with the intellect.

---

[1]Nathan Schneider, "The New Theist: How William Lane Craig Became Christian Philosophy's Boldest Apostle," *The Chronicle of Higher Education*, July 1, 2013, http://chronicle.com/article/The-New-Theist/140019/. Quoted from a debate on April 7, 2011, with Craig at the University of Notre Dame, "Is the Foundation of Morality Natural or Supernatural?," *Reasonable Faith*, http://www.reasonablefaith.org/media/craig-vs-harris-notre-dame.
[2]William Lane Craig, "Classical Apologetics," in *Five Views on Apologetics*, ed. Steven B. Cowan (Grand Rapids: Zondervan, 2000), p. 26. Described further by Craig in Schneider, "The New Theist."
[3]Craig, "Classical Apologetics," pp. 26–27.

He was not attracted to philosophy when he was exposed to it in the required introductory class, but later he picked up the book *The Resurrection of Theism*,[4] by his philosophy professor Stuart Hackett. At Wheaton the main apologetic he had heard in his theology classes was, "If theism is not true, then human life is absurd and culture goes down the drain."[5] So Craig was "stunned" by Hackett's rigorous defense of traditional arguments for the existence of God. That book led him into philosophy, and to later write the dissertation for his first doctorate, at the University of Birmingham, on a largely forgotten form of the cosmological argument that claims, "It is rationally inconceivable that the series of past events be infinite; there must have been a beginning of the universe and therefore a transcendent cause which brought it into being."[6] He termed it the kalam cosmological argument, and his defense of it has inspired more articles than any other philosopher's formulation of an argument for the existence of God.[7]

Craig went on to get master's degrees in philosophy of religion and church history, as well as doctorates from both Birmingham and the University of Munich. He has become well known for debating high-profile scholars who are hostile to a conservative Christian viewpoint. For Craig, an important reason to engage in apologetics is to influence the culture so that Christianity is an "intellectually viable option"[8] and Christians are not regarded as mere "emotional fanatics and buffoons."[9] He believes it is especially important to engage the academic world. In this he agrees with J. Gresham Machen that ideas need to be answered before they diffuse through the culture, when it is then largely too late to effectively counter them.[10] Craig is clear, however, that people do not become Christians because of

---

[4]It was out of print at the time, but is now in a second edition, Stuart C. Hackett, *The Resurrection of Theism: Prolegomena to Christian Apology*, 2nd ed. (Grand Rapids: Baker, 1982). He also benefited from E. J. Carnell, *An Introduction to Christian Apologetics: A Philosophic Defense of the Trinitarian-Theistic Faith* (Grand Rapids: Eerdmans, 1948).

[5]William Lane Craig, "In Memoriam: Stuart Cornelius Hackett (1925–2012)," Evangelical Philosophical Society website, www.epsociety.org/library/articles.asp?pid=140.

[6]William Lane Craig, "Stuart Hackett," *Reasonable Faith*, www.reasonablefaith.org/stuart-hackett; see also Craig, *On Guard: Defending Your Faith with Reason and Precision* (Colorado Springs, CO: Cook, 2010), p. 67. The book puts Craig's ideas on a high school, or even middle school, level.

[7]Quentin Smith, "Kalam Cosmological Arguments for Atheism," in *The Cambridge Companion to Atheism*, ed. Michael Martin (Cambridge: Cambridge University Press, 2007), p. 183. Craig points to this quote in Craig, "Stuart Hackett."

[8]William Lane Craig, *Reasonable Faith: Christian Truth and Apologetics*, 3rd ed. (Wheaton, IL: Crossway, 2008), p. 16.

[9]Craig, *On Guard*, p. 18.

[10]J. Gresham Machen, "Christianity and Culture," *Princeton Theological Review* 11, no. 7 (1913): 7; quoted in Craig, *Reasonable Faith*, p. 17.

intellectual arguments. Ground is being regained, he believes, after a long period of isolation following the fundamentalist controversies of the twentieth century.[11]

Some say that postmodernism's rejection of traditional ideas about logic, rationality, truth and rational argumentation makes apologetics useless. On this view, "we should simply share our narrative and invite people to participate in it." But Craig believes that this "could not be more mistaken" and that "the idea that we live in a postmodern culture is a myth."[12] No one can ignore that texts have objective meaning. No one is postmodern when they differentiate between a bottle of medicine and a bottle of rat poison. With science, engineering and technology they are not postmodern—only with regard to religion and ethics. What we really have, Craig concludes, is old-fashioned modernism that still accepts positivism and verificationism: if you can't verify something with your five senses then it's a matter of "individual taste and emotive expression."[13] Accepting the notion that society is postmodern and then laying aside reason and the case for Christianity would be catastrophic, even suicidal.

Christians then—especially young people—need to be educated so they can engage the culture. If we do not, we may find ourselves in an "intellectual backwater, unable to deal with the well-read man across the street."[14] Apologetics also helps the believer through difficult times, and also produces maturity so that Christians can have more than an "immature, superficial faith," with minds that are "going to waste."[15]

Despite his devotion to apologetics, he is clear about its limits and proper role.

> Apologetics is therefore vital in fostering a cultural milieu in which the gospel can be heard as a viable option for thinking people. In most cases, it will not be arguments or evidence that bring a seeker to faith in Christ—that is the half-truth seen by detractors of apologetics—but nonetheless it will be apologetics which, by making the gospel a credible option for seeking people, gives them, as it were, the intellectual permission to believe. It is thus vitally important that we preserve a cultural milieu in which the gospel is heard as a living option for thinking people, and apologetics will be front and center in helping bring about that result.[16]

[11]Craig, *Reasonable Faith*, p. 18.
[12]Ibid., p. 18.
[13]Ibid.
[14]Ibid., p. 20.
[15]Ibid.
[16]Ibid., p. 19.

KNOWING CHRISTIANITY IS TRUE

Craig has found it useful to distinguish between knowing Christianity is true and showing it is true. He believes that the difference has been confirmed in the work of some recent epistemologists, especially Alvin Plantinga. For both apologists, their religious epistemology has been shaped by their inner, nearly unshakeable sense of God. For Craig, reason and rational arguments have a major role in showing truth, but only a secondary role in knowing truth. He says, "The proper ground of our knowing Christianity to be true is the inner work of the Holy Spirit in our individual selves; and in our showing Christianity to be true it is his role to open the hearts of unbelievers to assent and respond to the reasons we present."[17] Rational arguments can confirm what we know, but not defeat it.

Craig points out that the believer's confidence in the bare essentials of Christianity (i.e., the belief that one has been reconciled to God through Christ) is described in one verse as the witness of God's spirit with our spirit (Rom 8:16). If we have assurance of salvation, then we have assurance of other truths as well, especially the existence of God and Christ's role in salvation. But we can hinder the work of the Spirit in our lives (1 Thess 5:19, quenching; Eph 4:30, grieving), and thereby come to doubt those essential truths, so we must walk in the Spirit's fullness (Gal 5:16-17, 25; Eph 5:18). Those who walk in the Spirit have an assurance that is unmistakable. Craig sees elements of the broader ministry of the Spirit as relevant to the believer's inner knowing, such as Christ's promise to the disciples that the Spirit would teach them all things (Jn 14:26), the Spirit's anointing that teaches them all things (1 Jn 2:20, 26-27), Jesus' promises to send the Spirit to abide in the disciples so they can know that they are in Christ and he is in them (Jn 14:16-17, 20) and John's statement that "we know that we abide in Him and He in us, because He has given us of His Spirit" (1 Jn 4:13). Where John says we have from the Spirit a testimony greater than man's (1 Jn 5:6-10), this means, Craig believes, that the inner witness of the Spirit is even greater than the testimony of the apostles—as important as that is (Jn 20:31). "Although John is eager to present evidences for the truth of Christ's claims, it is apparent that he does not consider such evidence necessary for knowledge of those claims."[18]

The witness of the Spirit is not an experience that is taken as evidence for a conclusion, but is an immediate awareness. In terms that remind us strongly of Plantinga, Craig calls the witness of the Spirit "properly basic," in that it "is not

---

[17]Craig, "Classical Apologetics," p. 28.
[18]Ibid., p. 32. For other points about the role of the Spirit, see pp. 30–32.

derived inferentially from any more foundational belief but which is rationally justified by being formed in appropriate circumstances. Belief in the Christian God is properly basic when formed in the circumstances of the witness of the Holy Spirit. It is only due to sin that persons under such circumstances do not form this belief."[19] The person whose belief is grounded in the witness of the Spirit is not merely being rational to believe as they do; they actually know that Christianity is true. Craig notes that whatever must be added to true belief to make it knowledge is what Plantinga calls warrant. He agrees that, in the end, our belief is knowledge: "Whether Plantinga's specific analysis of warrant proves successful or not, he is surely in line with the teaching of the New Testament that our belief in the biblical God is not merely rational, but warranted, and therefore knowledge."[20]

Craig regards the Spirit's witness as self-authenticating in the sense that our inner awareness overwhelms arguments that may challenge belief. The witness does not provide a counterargument; it simply provides "more warrant" than any challenge. He recalls Plantinga's illustration of a person unjustly accused of a crime who is rationally justified in believing in his innocence despite not being able to refute the evidence against him.[21] His inner awareness is not a rational argument, but it trumps the rational argument. And the man is being rational. Plantinga points out that the witness of the Spirit is available to all believers regardless of their intellectual ability or how well equipped they are to answer challenges. Craig says that the believer has an intellectual right—even an obligation—to believe in God.[22]

There is a slight difference between Plantinga's *sensus divinitatis* and Craig's witness of the Spirit. Plantinga regards the awareness of God as partly due to how we are made and partly due to the action of the Holy Spirit,[23] whereas awareness of Christianity is not a matter of how we are made but only the action of the Spirit.[24] Craig does not mention how we are made, and awareness of both God and Christianity he regards as the action of the Spirit.

The Spirit's action is effective regardless of the claims of people who say they have an immediate awareness that some other religious belief is true. For one, the witness of the Spirit is self-authenticating in that the believer simply knows

---

[19]Ibid., p. 32.

[20]Ibid., p. 33 n. 3.

[21]Alvin Plantinga, "The Foundations of Theism: A Reply," *Faith and Philosophy* 3, no. 3 (1986): 310; cited by Craig, "Classical Apologetics," p. 34.

[22]Craig, "Classical Apologetics," p. 35.

[23]Alvin Plantinga, *Warranted Christian Belief* (New York: Oxford University Press, 2000), pp. 173-75. How we are made can include action of the conscience.

[24]Ibid., chap. 6.

what is true. Second, it is possible that in some cases a nonbeliever actually is experiencing something of God, such as that he is the ground of all being, or the moral absolute, or the loving Father of humankind.[25] Third, the witness of the Spirit is very different from non-Christian religious experiences, such as those of Hindus or Buddhists, so would be distinguishable from them.[26]

What about the possibility of a neuroscientist artificially inducing a religious experience by stimulating some portion of the brain?[27] Those experiences that have been induced, says Craig, have been more like pantheistic experiences of the All rather than a personal and loving God. Besides, inducing an artificial experience of God would do no more to undermine the possibility of a real experience of God than inducing artificial sights and sounds would undermine the confidence that we can have sights and sounds of real objects.[28]

For Craig, then, rational arguments and evidence therefore play a subsidiary role in knowing that Christianity is true. He finds it helpful to use Martin Luther's distinction between the magisterial and ministerial roles of reason. Some see reason as a magistrate, standing over the gospel, judging it to be true or false without the benefit of the work of the Spirit. But that approach would deny faith to those who cannot understand and formulate proper arguments, furnish an excuse to those who choose to disbelieve and put intellectual elites in control of what others believe. Depending on changes in evidence, Christianity could conceivably be rational for one generation but irrational for the next, whereas faith founded on the witness of the Spirit "secures a firm basis for faith."[29]

Craig follows Luther in seeing reason as having a ministerial role, submitting to the gospel and serving it, helping us to understand and defend faith. He believes this fits the Augustinian-Anselmian tradition of faith seeking understanding. For

---

[25]Craig, "Classical Apologetics," p. 36, cites William Alston, "Response to Hick," *Faith and Philosophy* 14, no. 3 (1997): 287-88.

[26]Craig, *Reasonable Faith*, pp. 49-50.

[27]The classic experiment, done in the 1980s by Michael Persinger of Canada's Laurentian University, was challenged in 2004 by Pehr Granqvist of Uppsala University in Sweden. Persinger defended his results and pointed to what he claimed were confirming results by other researchers. Todd Murphy and Dr. Michael A. Persinger, "Debate Concerning the God Helmet," 2011, www.innerworlds.50megs .com/The_God_Helmet_Debate.htm. The article includes links to similar research. For a brief overview of the debate between them, see Roxanne Khamsi, "Electrical Brainstorms Busted as Source of Ghosts," *Nature*, December 9, 2004, www.nature.com/news/2004/041206/full/news041206-10 .html. Michael J. Murray, "Belief in God: A Trick of Our Brain?," in *Contending with Christianity's Critics: Answering New Atheists and Other Objections*, ed. William Lane Craig and Paul Copan (Nashville: B & H, 2009), pp. 54-57.

[28]Craig, *Reasonable Faith*, p. 50.

[29]Craig, "Classical Apologetics," p. 37.

the believer, "What he knows immediately and unmistakably via the work of the Sprit, he may also know inferentially and defeasibly via argument and evidence. But the latter obviously will be of less importance to him than the former. If, due to the contingencies of one's life situation, confirmation by argument and evidence is unavailable, the basis of one's faith remains secure."[30] If evidence seems to turn against Christianity, the believer will not immediately lose faith but will wait for further evidence. In an ideal world, the rational case and the witness of the Spirit would never conflict, but they sometimes do, and for that we have the testimony of the Spirit. So, "The proper basis of faith is the witness of the Holy Spirit, not rational argumentation and evidence, though the latter may serve to confirm the former."[31] Rational arguments confirm the faith; they are not the basis of faith.[32]

Ultimately, the nonbeliever is without excuse, but not on the basis of rational arguments. If that were so, says Craig, lack of adequate rational arguments would provide an excuse. "Even those who are given no good reason to believe and many persuasive reasons to disbelieve have no excuse, because the ultimate reason they do not believe is that they have deliberately rejected God's Holy Spirit,"[33] and the Spirit's drawing of his heart.[34] So, "No one in the final analysis really fails to become a Christian because of lack of arguments; he fails to become a Christian because he loves darkness rather than light and wants nothing to do with God."[35] Christ said that if a person is truly seeking, he will know that Christ's teaching is truly from God (Jn 7:17). The Spirit convicts the nonbeliever of his own sin, of God's righteousness and of his condemnation before God (Jn 16:7-11). The convicted nonbeliever knows those things.[36]

So for the believer and nonbeliever the self-authenticating work of the Holy Spirit supplies knowledge of Christianity's truth. A belief can be rational in the sense that a person has good reasons to believe it even though it might actually be false. However, something is known when it is not only rationally justified but also true. Because the belief in Christianity "is formed in response to the self-disclosure of God himself, who needs no external authentication, it is not merely rational for us, but constitutes knowledge."[37]

---

[30]Ibid.
[31]Ibid., p. 38.
[32]Craig, *Reasonable Faith*, p. 48.
[33]Ibid., p. 50.
[34]Ibid., p. 47.
[35]Ibid.
[36]Ibid., p. 46.
[37]Ibid., p. 47.

Craig's emphasis on the witness of the Spirit is a bit greater than that of many classical apologists and evidentialists, who see a stronger role for confirming evidence and rational argument. Gary Habermas does not see knowing and showing as separate categories, so there is no reason why a believer could not stand on either the Spirit's testimony or evidence. In John 14:10-11 Jesus invites people who do not believe his words outright to believe because of his miracles, and in Luke 7:18-28 he uses evidences to convince John the Baptist when he is doubting.[38] Having struggled with doubt himself over a period of time years ago, Habermas, unlike Craig, sees the causes of doubt as more complex than just sin.

Habermas observes that, although he agrees that the witness of the Spirit confers knowledge (especially of one's salvation), there are many technical issues around the word *know*. Absent much clarification, it would be easier to talk in terms of assurance and conviction.[39] As far as Craig's distinction between knowing and showing, Habermas remarks that apologetics has mostly to do with the latter anyway. Where Craig says that 1 John 5:6-10 validates the Spirit's witness even over the testimony of the apostles, Habermas says that the verse requires nothing more than placing the witness of the Spirit above that of human beings in general.[40]

Paul Feinberg wonders about the wisdom of putting so much emphasis on the witness of the Spirit—unaided by evidence—as grounds for belief within the Christian. If Christians can be mistaken about the Spirit's leading them or assuring them of something like surviving cancer, then how can we say that the Spirit's witness can override all defeaters? Certainly those mistaken cases of his leading or surviving were defeated by evidence. How could the Christian challenge someone of another religion if there could be no challenge to an inward sense of truth revealed by divinity? There seems to be no reason why the working of the Spirit should be beyond defeat in the case of testimony but not in other matters.[41]

John Frame points out that witness of the Spirit of God is always to the Word of God. That does not fit with the idea of the claim in 1 John that the witness of the Spirit supersedes the apostolic message. Rather, the Spirit assures us that the apostolic witness is true.[42]

---

[38]Gary Habermas, "An Evidentialist's Response," in Cowan, *Five Views on Apologetics*, pp. 64–65.
[39]Ibid., p. 62.
[40]Ibid., p. 63.
[41]Paul D. Feinberg, "A Cumulative Case Apologist's Response," in Cowan, *Five Views on Apologetics*, pp. 70–71.
[42]Ibid., p. 75.

SHOWING CHRISTIANITY IS TRUE

When it comes to showing others that Christianity is true, the roles of the Spirit and rational argument are almost completely reversed. Argument and evidence are primary, and the Spirit's role is not in demonstration but in opening the nonbeliever's heart.

When the non-Christian believes he or she has an experience that confirms their belief, and the Christian believes the same, what can be done? Craig cites philosopher William Alston,[43] who says the Christian should search for common ground and a noncircular argument to adjudicate their differences. Common ground may include "sense perception, rational self evidence, and common modes of reasoning."[44]

Apologetics can then use deduction, or induction, including Bayes's theorem and inference to the best explanation. The problem with using Bayes's theorem is the difficulty of calculating the probabilities. And while we can pick the best explanation for something, there is no universal agreement on what makes an explanation the best. Common criteria include how well it explains what cannot otherwise be explained, how many different things it can explain and whether the explanation was invented to account for just the phenomenon in question or if it is used for other things. The drawback to an inference to the best explanation is that we have no guarantee that the best explanation is true; it might be only the best of the options we have considered.[45]

Those who reject the use of induction in apologetics need to remember, first, that almost all our conclusions are inductive, including that smoking is linked to lung cancer, and that it is now safe to cross the street. Second, convictions we have that are basic (because they are not inferred from any other belief) can be weak, as when we barely remember what we had for lunch a week ago.

To be as convincing as possible whatever form of logic we use, we should try to develop a cumulative case (in the sense of using many different arguments rather than just one), and we should use premises that are widely accepted or intuitions that are commonly shared (i.e., common sense). If we cannot appeal to those, we will need to appeal to expert testimony. The expert should be unbiased, and if possible, even anti-Christian. It is not just the content of what we say. We cannot neglect interpersonal factors that make

---

[43]William Alston, "Religious Diversity and Perceptual Knowledge of God," *Faith and Philosophy* 5, no. 4 (1998): 442–43; cited in Craig, *Reasonable Faith*, p. 51.

[44]Craig, *Reasonable Faith*, p. 51.

[45]Ibid., pp. 54–55.

argumentation more persuasive, such as "courteousness, openness, genuine concern for the listener, and so forth."[46]

The absurdity of life without God. This line of reasoning arose very recently, being popularized by Francis Schaeffer (1912–1984). It is cultural and practical, not concerned with epistemology or justification, but with the implications for society and the individual if the God of Christianity does not exist. Craig sees its value as helping a person to realize the alternatives and the need for the gospel, in order to arouse interest in the broader case for Christianity. The idea is to drive the person to the logical conclusion of his or her atheistic or agnostic position, which has no basis for meaning, value or purpose.[47] (This is a line of argument that presuppositionalists like John Frame would approve of, though they would insist it be used in a presuppositional framework.[48]) In Craig's extensive experience, even university students who espouse relativism quickly see that objective moral values must exist. The Holocaust, ethnic cleansing, apartheid and child abuse can be condemned only if there is a God to provide a transcultural basis for moral values.

Encouraging people to draw back from the unacceptable implications of atheism has a rich history in Western writing. Blaise Pascal (1623–1662) wrote of the contradictions and paradoxes of the human condition. We are faced with uncertainty all around, an infinitesimal speck in the universe facing a life of inconstancy, boredom and anxiety—but at least we know our predicament. Yet people refuse to seek answers; rather, they amuse themselves to avoid coming to grips with their situation. We must wager. Even if there were no rational way to know God exists, it would be prudent to believe in him. If we are right, we gain all. If we are wrong we lose nothing. But if we bet there is no God and we are right, we gain nothing. If we are wrong, we lose all. No gambler would accept the atheist's bet.[49]

Craig points to Russian novelist Fyodor Dostoevsky (1821–1881), who offered a twofold defense of theism in the face of the problem of evil. Positively, innocent suffering may perfect a person's character and bring them closer to

---

[46]Ibid., p. 56.

[47]Ibid., pp. 86–87.

[48]John M. Frame, *The Doctrine of the Knowledge of God* (Phillipsburg, NJ: P & R, 1987), p. 354. Note that he regards a wide variety of apologists as "evidentialists": "McDowell, Montgomery, Hackett, Pinnock, Gerstner, and Sproul" (ibid., p. 353).

[49]Blaise Pascal, *Pensées* 343. For more by Craig on the wager, see "Pascal's Wager," *Reasonable Faith*, http://www.reasonablefaith.org/pascals-wager.

God. Negatively, if there is no God we are left with moral relativism, and no act, no matter how wretched, can be condemned. No one can consistently live with such a destructive consequence.

The Danish existentialist philosopher Søren Kierkegaard (1813–1855) said that life can be lived on three levels, or stages. On the lowest level a person lives for himself. On this "aesthetic" stage there is no meaning or happiness. This may bring someone to more or less leap to the ethical stage, where they are committed to moral principles. But moral striving and failure leads only to guilt and despair. Another leap is possible, to the religious stage, where forgiveness and a personal relationship with God brings true fulfillment.

Craig summarizes Francis Schaeffer's view that Western culture has trended toward despair, largely owing to the acceptance of German philosopher G. W. F. Hegel's (1770–1831) view that there are no absolutes. For Hegel, everything is changing, so nothing is always true or always wrong. Without this mooring, human existence drifts toward meaninglessness and absurdity, which can be seen in literature and the arts, for example, in the theater of the absurd, a form of drama that ignores conventions of plot and theme to portray life as meaningless and irrational. God having been abandoned, life itself becomes meaningless, and abortion and infanticide become acceptable. If the culture fails to return to God and his moral absolutes, there is nothing to stop a further drift toward population control and even human breeding. So modern humanity lives in a two-story universe, on the bottom of which is a finite world without God where life is meaningless. Unhappy and unable to live with such a reality, people try to leap to the upper story to find meaning, value and purpose—but with no God there can be none of these things.[50] The atheist existentialist philosopher Jean-Paul Sartre concluded that "it amounts to the same thing whether one gets drunk alone or is a leader of nations."[51]

Craig echoes these themes, adding that if there is no God, then even the universe and its eventual death have no meaning. And with no ultimate grounds for ethics, there is no ultimate difference between genocide and self-sacrifice.

The alternative is biblical Christianity, according to which there is a God to whom we can meaningfully relate forever. Craig hastens to clarify that contrasting the alternatives does not prove Christianity, but "if the evidence for these two options were absolutely equal, a rational person ought to choose

[50]Craig, *Reasonable Faith*, pp. 70–71, 78.
[51]Jean-Paul Sartre, *Being and Nothingness*, trans. Hazel E. Barnes (New York: Washington Square Press, 1993), p. 797.

biblical Christianity. It seems to me positively irrational to prefer death, futility and destruction to life, meaningfulness and happiness. As Pascal said, 'we have nothing to lose and infinity to gain.'[52]

Though not spearheaded by Craig, there has been a recent response to the modern charges that Christianity has had a negative effect on culture. The famous atheist Bertrand Russell (1872–1970), in *Why I Am Not A Christian*, identified two types of objections to religion in general, intellectual and moral. Of religion he said, "I regard it as a disease born of fear and as a source of untold misery to the human race."[53] Christopher Hitchens, the late outspoken atheist, detailed what he felt were moral failings of religion in two chapters of his book *God Is Not Great: How Religion Poisons Everything*.[54] In his various attacks, Christianity attracts special attention.

Christians would not want to defend the ethics of all religions and their devotees; in fact, a good amount would be deemed indefensible. Even some actions in the name of Christianity would be condemned (e.g., marginalization and persecution of Jews in Europe, and treatment of the Anabaptists), namely, those that are ignorant of Christian ethical teachings or unfaithful to them.

What remains is the question of the overall influence of Christianity on civilization. Showing that it has had a favorable influence does not prove its claims are true; however, it diffuses objections that it is unworthy of consideration, or that because of its morals it must be false. Jonathan Hill has written on a wide variety of contributions made by Christianity, and sociology professor Alvin J. Schmidt has extensively documented Christianity's beneficial effects. (In another book he contrasts the societal influence of Christianity versus Islam.)[55] He describes the morals of the existing Greco-Roman world into which Christianity was born (and some other non-Christian cultures around the world), then shows how Christianity gave birth to the unique ethics we in the West now accept as moral—though few realize its origins. Claiming that humans are made in the image of God and that individual lives are valued by their maker (e.g., Gen 9:6), Christianity condemned infanticide and abortion, wanton violence such as the gladiatorial games,

---

[52]Craig, *Reasonable Faith*, p. 86.

[53]Bertrand Russell, *Why I Am Not a Christian and Other Essays on Religion and Related Subjects* (New York: Simon & Schuster, 1957), p. 24.

[54]Christopher Hitchens, *God Is Not Great: How Religion Poisons Everything* (New York: Twelve, 2007), chap. two, "Religion Kills," pp. 15–36; chap. thirteen, "Does Religion Make People Behave Better?," pp. 173–93.

[55]Alvin J. Schmidt, *The Great Divide: The Failure of Islam and Triumph of the West* (Salisbury, MA: Regina Orthodox Press, 2004).

human sacrifice and suicide. It promoted heterosexual monogamy, condemning what we now call child molestation (which has not been condemned in many cultures). Women had the status of slaves in the ancient world and have little better in some cultures today. Though related to a barbaric notion of sexual restraint rather than status, sexual mutilation of girls is still practiced in twenty-six African and some Middle Eastern countries, mostly within Islam, affecting 125 million women worldwide.[56] To the astonishment of people in his day, Christ treated women seriously and with respect, accepted them as followers and instructed them as he did men; moreover, women were the first witnesses of the empty tomb. In an effort to exemplify divine compassion, Christians cared for the dispossessed, including orphans, widows, the poor, the elderly, the sick, the blind and the insane. To the classical mind this was foolish; you should help only those who can pay you back. Christianity emphasized education, and eventually gave birth to universities. Public education was pioneered by the Reformers.

Knowledge of God: inference or immediate awareness? Craig briefly explores a controversy he admits may be unresolvable: the relation between general revelation and natural theology. Paul says that the knowledge of God is evident to everyone: "For since the creation of the world His invisible attributes, His eternal power and divine nature, have been clearly seen, being understood through what has been made, so that they are without excuse" (Rom 1:20). Is Paul referring to an inference, from features of the world to the conclusion that God exists? As Craig says, it could be "that the inference from creation to Creator is so evident at any level of inquiry, from the observations of the primitive savage to the investigations of the scientist, that the nontheist is inexcusable in failing to draw this inference."[57] But he adds that others (as we have seen in the case of Plantinga) regard the creation as the context that occasions belief in the Creator as properly basic. We see the creation and we simply become aware of the Creator without forming any inference. We do not, for example, see the order and design and conclude there must be a God. We do not think, *a* is true (premise), so therefore *b* must also be true (conclusion). We could add to what Craig said by borrowing a classic example: we see a watch and simply become aware of the watchmaker; but on the view that it is an inference, we see the watch and conclude there must be a watchmaker. Or it may be like the difference between being out in the rain

---

[56]World Health Organization, fact sheet no. 241, updated February 2014, World Health Organization website, www.who.int/mediacentre/factsheets/fs241/en/index.html.

[57]Craig, "Classical Apologetics," p. 39.

and simply being aware that it is raining versus being indoors and concluding it is raining because we hear the rain and see wet people coming in from outdoors.

If the knowledge of God is an inference from creation then it would seem that inferential reasoning is endemic to apologetics. But if the knowledge of God is an immediate awareness, then it would seem that inferential reasoning from creation to God is at the very least not pervasive.

We cannot settle the matter by saying that because everyone is without excuse the knowledge of God must be properly basic, because not everyone could be held accountable for drawing a conclusion. Some individuals might be incapable of drawing an inference, but everyone is capable of a basic belief. Yet as Craig points out, this would confuse proper basicality with degree of belief. As we mentioned, our grasp of a basic belief may be weak and prone to error, such as our memory of what we had for lunch a week ago. (It is properly basic because we simply remember it, it is not a conclusion from other beliefs.) On the other hand, an inference can be obvious and easily formed by anyone, with very little chance we are wrong.[58] We could suggest the example of looking out a window and seeing bright sunlight on the street, and we conclude that there are no dark clouds blocking the sun.

Craig points out that in favor of the view that Romans 1:19 is talking about an inference that God exists is the fact that inferential thinking was characteristic of both Greek and Hellenistic-Jewish thought. The biblical language of the verse is strongly reminiscent of that influence, and the wording of the passage even sounds a great deal like the Hellenistic-Jewish Wisdom of Solomon 13:1-9, where inferential thinking is clearly in view. Furthermore, a reference to an inferential process would fit pervasive biblical rhetoric. In Acts 14:17 Paul says that God provided a witness to himself in the beneficial order. In Luke 11:20 Jesus appeals to miracles and fulfilled prophecy and even exorcism as evidence. Near the beginning of John's Gospel Nicodemus reasons that Jesus must be from God because of the miraculous signs he can do (Jn 3:2), and near the end John says that he wrote of the signs so that people would come to saving faith (Jn 20:31). Miracles and appeal to prophecy come together in Jesus' response to John the Baptist's doubts (Mt 11:5-6; cf. Is 35:5-6; 61:1). When talking to Jewish audiences, the apostles appeal to fulfilled prophecy, miracles and the resurrection (Acts 2:22-32). This seems to have been Paul's approach.

---

[58]In ibid., p. 39; Craig cites George Mavrodes, "Jerusalem and Athens Revisited," in *Faith and Rationality*, ed. Alvin Plantinga and Nicholas Wolterstorff (Notre Dame, IN: University of Notre Dame Press, 1983), pp. 214-15.

Craig has come to have a very positive view of theistic arguments. He says, "After years of study and reflection, I have come to share Leibniz's conviction that 'nearly all of the means which have been employed to prove the existence of God are good and might be of service, if we perfect them.' My experience of debating these arguments orally and in print with atheists and agnostic philosophers has only served to confirm this conviction in my mind."[59]

Ontological argument. A distinctive of classical apologetics is the use of theistic arguments, though not everyone outside the classical view is categorically opposed to them. For example, Plantinga is known for revitalizing the ontological argument, and some evidentialists like Habermas and John Warwick Montgomery are willing to make use of them, but do not require the arguments be used to set the stage for evidences for Christianity.

Each type of argument has many variants, so each type really identifies a category of arguments. And of course the entire subject of theistic arguments is a large, complex and ever-changing field. Only a brief summary can be given here, but there are books and countless articles on each variant.

Without doubt the most controversial theistic argument is the ontological, first conceived by Anselm of Canterbury (1033–1109), a churchman and philosopher, as a one-argument proof for God as the most perfect possible being. Unlike the others, it is an a priori argument; that is, it uses only concepts and definitions, in this case, of God. It does not use the things that we learn from examining the world around us, which are used to form what are called a posteriori arguments.

According to the most common characterization of his argument,[60] Anselm starts out with the premise that God is the greatest possible being. This has to be true because it is the definition of God. So God exists at least in the mind. But something that exists only in the mind and not in reality is not the greatest possible being. That would be a contradiction, so God must exist in reality. If the argument is successful, Anselm has proved not merely the existence of a creator or designer but also the greatest possible being.

Objectors have replied that the same argument could be used to prove the existence of any number of imaginary things, like the "best possible island." But

---

[59]Craig, *Reasonable Faith*, p. 106. Gottfried Wilhelm Leibniz, *New Essays on the Understanding*, trans. Alfred G. Langley (New York: Macmillan, 1896), p. 505.

[60]For various characterizations, and whether Anselm was making one argument in *Proslogion* 2 and another in 3, or whether they are the same argument, see Graham Oppy, "Ontological Arguments," in *The Stanford Encyclopedia of Philosophy*, ed. Edward N. Zalta, winter 2012 ed., http://plato.stanford.edu/archives/win2012/entries/ontological-arguments/.

the reply is that other things do not have an intrinsic maximum; there is no "best possible" island. However, a maximally powerful being is an omnipotent being, a maximally knowledgeable being is omnipotent, and a maximally good being is morally perfect. Descartes added that existence is a predicate that something can be said to have or not have, and that a supremely perfect being necessarily has the attribute of existence, just as a triangle necessarily has three sides. Immanuel Kant (1724–1804) later objected that even supposing we cannot separate God from existence such that if we affirm the most perfect being we have to accept that being's existence, we could still reject the whole idea of an existing all-perfect being. He added (largely echoed by Bertrand Russell) that in effect there is no way to describe something such that it has to exist. We describe it, and then we have to see whether it exists.

Charles Hartshorne, Norman Malcolm and Alvin Plantinga have revived the argument in modern times. Plantinga recasts it in terms of possibility and necessity. In simplified form (adapted from Craig),[61]

1. It is possible that a maximally great being exists.

2. If it is possible a maximally great being exists, then it exists in some possible world.

3. If a maximally great being exists in some possible world, then it exists in every possible world.

4. If a maximally great being exists in every possible world, then it exists in the actual world.

5. Therefore, God exists.

At first Plantinga did not think the ontological argument was sound because of the key premise stating that it is possible a maximally great being exists. But he later thought that he had set the bar too high, and decided that the ontological argument was as good an argument for God's existence as any serious philosophical argument for any important philosophical conclusion.[62]

---

[61]Adapted and simplified from William Lane Craig, "Two Questions on the Ontological Argument," *Reasonable Faith*, http://www.reasonablefaith.org/two-questions-on-the-ontological-argument.

[62]Alvin Plantinga, "Reason and Belief in God," typescript dated Oct. 1981, pp. 18–19, quoted in J. P. Moreland and William Lane Craig, *Philosophical Foundations for a Christian Worldview* (Downers Grove, IL: InterVarsity Press, 2003), p. 497. The authors explain that the quotation was accidently omitted in the published version, but a similar statement appears in Alvin Plantinga, "Self Profile," in *Alvin Plantinga*, ed. James E. Tomberlin and Peter van Inwagen, Profiles 5 (Dordrecht: D. Reidel, 1985), p. 71.

In a text coauthored with J. P. Moreland, Craig says that the main issue is the key premise. To evaluate it, we have to distinguish between metaphysical possibility (whether it is possible for something to exist) and epistemic possibility (whether we can imagine something existing). The important point is that if God is a maximally great being, then his existence is either metaphysically necessary or impossible. It has to be one or the other, even if we are not sure which.

In the end Plantinga suggests, and Craig accedes, that if we consider the key premise in light of other propositions that we personally accept or reject, we may find that we have reason to accept the premise in question. If so, we are within our rational rights to accept it. So we may come to accept the key premise not on a priori grounds (i.e., on the basis of the concepts alone), but on a posteriori grounds (because we have added information from a source other than concepts).

It may seem that considerations like these make acceptance of the ontological argument something like circular reasoning, where our reason for accepting a premise of an argument is that we already accept the conclusion. But Craig says that perhaps this is seeing theistic arguments in too linear a fashion, like a chain, which is no stronger than the weakest link. Instead we should see them like links in a coat of chain mail, where they strengthen each other so that the whole is stronger than any one link.[63]

There is no doubt that an ontological argument requires at least one significant assumption in the premises. Some, like theologian Karl Barth, believe its importance lies in reminding believers that God is the greatest possible being. As John Hick concludes, the argument is perennially fascinating because it "employs such fundamental concepts, operates so subtly with them, and professes to demonstrate so momentous a conclusion."[64]

Cosmological argument. A cosmological argument assumes that something exists and argues to the existence of a first cause or sufficient reason for the cosmos. Its list of supporters is long and distinguished, reaching back to antiquity.

The Islamic thinker al-Ghazali (1058–1111) argued that every being that begins to exist has a cause; the world is a being; therefore it has a cause. Part of his argument claimed that the universe must have had a beginning because an actually infinite number of things is impossible. Craig's also uses this in his revived cosmological argument.

---

[63]Moreland and Craig, *Philosophical Foundations*, pp. 498–99.
[64]John Hick, "Ontological Argument for the Existence of God," in *The Encyclopedia of Philosophy*, ed. Paul Edwards (New York: Macmillan, 1967), 5:540.

Thomas Aquinas based his argument on the impossibility of an infinite regress of simultaneous causes. He is not arguing for God as the first agent in a string of causes, where the first agent causes something, then stops because the effect is set in motion. Rather, he has in mind a cause that continually has an effect, making movement, or change, possible. For example, a pen moves because a hand continually acts. In the first of his five ways to prove the existence of God, he argues from motion to the existence of an unmoved mover. We cannot have an infinite series of causes of motion with no unmoved mover as the first cause any more than you could have an infinite number of boxcars and no engine to pull it.[65] If the cause of motion goes back to a person or animal as a self-moving being, we have to realize that they came into being at some point. So ultimately motion in the universe remains unexplained. God must exist as the Unmoved Mover.

In the second way, the same basic reasoning leads us back not to a cause of motion but to a cause of existence. Something has to cause a thing to come into being, and something had to cause that, and so on backwards—not to infinity because that would be impossible—but to a first cause, which is God. In the third way, we see in the world things that might have existed or might not have existed. We say they are contingent. There must be something that has to exist, that is, whose nature includes existence, to uphold everything. If the past were infinite, then all possibilities would eventually have occurred, which means that at some point all things would have gone out of existence— and nothing would now exist.

Gottfried Wilhelm Leibniz (1646–1716) begins by asking why there is something rather than nothing. He assumes that nothing happens without a sufficient cause, and there must be a reason why one state of affairs came into being rather than another. So then, why does the universe exist? The answer must lie outside the universe since everything in it is contingent; that is, everything might or might not have existed; all of it happens to exist. He points out that even if the world is eternal there must be a sufficient cause for it, something that is its own sufficient reason for existing, whose existence can be explained only by reference to himself. This self-explanatory being is God. He does not argue to a being who is "self-caused," since God is uncaused. He simply does not need a cause. Thomas argues to an uncaused cause; Leibniz, to a self-explanatory being (neither argues to a self-caused being).[66]

---

[65]Craig uses the boxcar example in Craig, *Reasonable Faith*, p. 97.
[66]William Lane Craig, *Apologetics: An Introduction* (Chicago: Moody Press, 1984), p. 66.

Craig formulates Leibniz's argument as follows:[67]

1. Anything that exists has an explanation of its existence, either in the necessity of its own nature or in an external cause.

2. If the universe has an explanation of its existence, the explanation is God.

3. The universe exists.

4. Therefore, the universe has an explanation of its existence. (from 1, 3)

5. Therefore, the explanation of the existence of the universe is God. (from 2, 4)

Since the logic is valid, the remaining question is, are the three premises more plausible than their denial? The wording of premise one rules out things existing inexplicably. Some things may exists by their nature, such as numbers, and so do not have causes (although we could add that numbers are not things in the way physical objects are things). Aside from those, we expect things to have explanations for how they came to be, and anyone who wants to claim otherwise needs to justify the exception. It won't help if the thing in question is big, even very big, like an entire universe. There is an objection[68] that because explanations are about what happened before the existence of the thing we are trying to explain (e.g., to explain how a horse came to be, we have to go back to the time before the horse existed, when its parents bred) it will do no good to try to explain the universe by going back to the time when there was nothing; it is absurd. According to the objector then, the universe is an exception to the rule that things need an explanation (if the thing doesn't exist by nature, like numbers). But as Craig points out in reply, this merely begs the question, that is, assumes what it is supposed to prove. The very question at issue is whether there is some nonphysical cause of the universe, that is, God.

Premise two seems to claim a lot, but ironically, says Craig,[69] the atheist is implicitly claiming the same thing. The atheist claims that the universe simply exists without explanation as a brute contingent thing—there being no God to explain its existence. Thus, says the atheist (contrary to Leibniz), it is false that everything has an explanation, because the universe is just such an inexplicable thing. Craig says that the atheist's claim is in effect logically equivalent to

[67]For the inspiration for the formulation of the argument, Craig (*Reasonable Faith*, p. 106) credits Stephen T. Davis, "The Cosmological Argument and the Epistemic Status of Belief in God," *Philosophia Christi* 1 (1999): 5-15.

[68]Craig, *Reasonable Faith*, p. 107, cites Crispin Wright and Bob Hale, "Nominalism and the Contingency of Abstract Objects," *Journal of Philosophy* 89 (1992): 128.

[69]Craig, *Reasonable Faith*, p. 108.

premise two because it is its contrapositive.[70] A contrapositive is formed by denying both terms and switching them, so the contrapositive of "If *a* then *b*" is "If not *b* then not *a*." A statement and its contrapositive are logically equivalent because if one is true the other has to be true, and if one is false the other has to be false. So premise two, "If the universe has an explanation of its existence, that explanation is God," is in effect implicitly held because of the atheist's own affirmation of the contrapositive, roughly, because the existence of the universe is not explained by God, it has no explanation.

Craig adds that the atheist could say the universe has an explanation for its existence, but it is not explained by anything external to itself (i.e., God). Instead it is explained by the necessity of its own nature; in other words, the universe is a necessary being. Then premise two would be false. Craig replies that we have a strong intuition that the universe does not exist necessarily but contingently; that is, it does not have to exist because of its nature; rather, it could have existed or not existed. Since we normally trust our intuition as to whether or not something has to exist, the atheist owes us an explanation why we shouldn't trust our intuition regarding the universe.

In any case, premise two is quite reasonable. Since the universe includes all physical reality, the cause of the universe must not be physical. That leaves only two candidates. One is abstract objects, like numbers—but they cannot cause anything. The other is a mind, which would be God.

Typically, variants of the cosmological argument are considered separately, but Craig points out how another form, the kalam argument, could strengthen the Leibnizian form. An essential property of something that exists "necessarily" (such that it needs no explanation for its existence) is that it must be eternal, having no beginning or end. If the kalam argument is successful, it shows that the universe came into being. Simply put, the argument is as follows:

1. Whatever begins to exist has a cause.

2. The universe began to exist.

3. Therefore, the universe has a cause.

It then draws conclusions about the nature of the cause of the universe.

Premise one certainly seems more plausible than its denial. Our intuition that nothing just pops into existence is constantly confirmed by our experience. But if something—the universe in this case—did just pop into existence, then why doesn't

---

[70]Moreland and Craig, *Philosophical Foundations*, p. 467.

anything and everything do so as well? Can anyone seriously think, asks Craig, that it is possible that a raging tiger pop into the room uncaused, out of nothing, right now? Furthermore, we have to remember that before the universe existed there was absolutely nothing, no space or time, and according to the atheist, no God. So how could the universe come about? The theist says it couldn't.

There have been a number of attacks on the argument. Craig says that Daniel Dennett misstates the first premise as, everything that *exists* must have a cause. Then he asks, what caused God?[71] But the premise says, whatever *begins* to exist must have a cause. The theist claims that God is eternal so does not need a cause.

Others look to experiments in quantum physics that seem to show events coming about uncaused on the subatomic level, in a vacuum. But Craig notes that there are a number of interpretations of quantum physics and there is disagreement about the experiments. Also, whatever is happening, no one is claiming that particles are coming into existence but rather that there are spontaneous fluctuations in energy. And the "vacuum" is far from nothing, "but is a sea of fluctuating energy endowed with a rich structure and subject to physical laws."[72] So nothing is happening *ex nihilo*, or out of nothing, as it would have to in order to mimic the origin of the universe. The same problem undermines the quantum creation model of Alexander Vilenkin. He envisions a small, closed universe, the radius of which collapses to zero. Quantum physics allows it to "tunnel" into a state of expansion rather than collapse. He claims that collapsing to zero is a state of nothingness, and tunneling to something with size shows that something can come from nothing. But Craig notes that not even Vilenkin regards that zero state as truly nothingness, so it is really about tunneling from something to something.[73]

The next premise claims that the universe began to exist. This claim matters because if the universe began to exist and had a cause, then the nature of that cause can be shown to have some of the qualities associated with God.

Premise two is supported by both philosophical and scientific arguments. The first philosophical argument is that it is impossible to have an actually infinite number of things. If that can be shown, then it is impossible that the universe be infinitely old, since that would require an infinite number of things, such as

---

[71]Craig, *Reasonable Faith*, p. 114.
[72]Ibid., p. 115.
[73]Ibid., p. 116.

events (an event is "any change"[74]). An actual infinite is different from merely referring to infinity, such as in a mathematical equation,[75] and it is different from a potential infinite, such as dividing a line in half a limitless number of times. You can keep dividing it forever, but you would never reach an actually infinite number of divisions, it is claimed. The paradoxes of infinity are illustrated by mathematician David Hilbert's (1862–1943) hotel that has an infinite number of rooms. If all the rooms are taken, and an infinite number of new guests arrive, the manager can accommodate all of them by moving existing guests into rooms whose number is double the number of their original room. So a guest from room one moves to two, two moves to room four, three moves to six, and so on. Since doubling any number results in an even number, all the odd numbered rooms are vacated, and available for the new guests. Thus an infinite number of new guests can be accommodated in the hotel that had no vacancies—and the process can be repeated an infinite number of times. Craig suggests Hilbert's scenario also be reversed. If the guests from the odd-numbered rooms check out, the hotel would be half full. Yet the number remaining is the same, namely infinite. Suppose the manager then shifts around all the remaining guests so that all the rooms are full, but then after that all the guests leave, except those in rooms one, two and three. The hotel would be completely empty except for guests in the three rooms. The departures would reduce the number of guests from infinity to just three, yet the same number departed as when the guests in the odd-numbered rooms checked out, leaving behind an infinite number of guests in the hotel.[76] If an actual infinite is possible, Craig argues, then the hotel is possible; but if the hotel is impossible, then so is an actual infinite. This does not undermine the mathematics of infinity, since that deals only with theoretical infinites, as many mathematicians themselves would stress. If we insist on affirming that actual infinites are possible, we enter an *Alice in Wonderland* world.

The second philosophical argument, following al-Ghazali, claims that since events of the past happened one after another, and since you can never reach infinity by adding one thing at a time, then an infinite past would be impossible. It

[74]William Lane Craig, "The Kalam Cosmological Argument," in *Blackwell Companion to Natural Theology*, ed. William Lane Craig and J. P. Moreland (Malden, MA: Blackwell, 2009), p. 106.

[75]Craig points out that "mathematical existence" is often understood as synonymous with "mathematical legitimacy," not actual existence. Craig, "The Kalam Cosmological Argument," p. 105. He also notes that Cantor, who did the pioneering work on mathematical infinity, differentiated between a potential infinite (which he called a "variable infinite"), identified with the symbol ∞ (called a lemniscate), and $\aleph_0$ (read aleph-naught, aleph-null, or aleph-zero).

[76]Craig, *Reasonable Faith*, p. 118; Craig, *On Guard*, p. 82.

would be like counting up from zero, you can never reach infinity, but only a very large number. But if you cannot count up to infinity (0, 1, 2, 3 . . .), then you cannot count down from it either (. . . -3, -2, -1, 0); hence you cannot have an infinite past and reach today. Coming from an infinite past, today would be the end point of infinity. We could add that the reason we are comfortable with counting up to infinity is that we think of the process of counting going on forever; however, never stopping the process of counting is different from reaching a number that is infinite. We never get to the point where we add one more number and finally enter infinity. It will not solve the problem to say that we can have a beginningless past because every event in the past will be only a finite distance from us; even an event a trillion years ago is a finite distance from us. Craig says this commits the logical fallacy of composition, mistakenly attributing what is true of the parts (that they are a finite distance from today) to the whole (that the whole infinite series is a finite distance from us). To use an illustration inspired by al-Ghazali, if for every one orbit Saturn makes around the sun, Jupiter makes two, then the more time that passes the more orbits Jupiter would make, even if this went on forever. But if they had been orbiting from eternity past, the number of both is infinite. If someone says that counting events backwards from infinity can indeed work if we have an infinite amount of time, Craig responds that if the past is truly infinite, then prior to any point in the past an infinite amount of time had already elapsed. Why should it take until now to finish?

Some object that if we disprove that an actual infinite can exist then we have also disproved God, because he is also infinite. But God is infinite in a different way. He is not an infinite number of things or an infinite succession, but an infinite being, one with no limits. For example, he has infinite knowledge and power, and he is everywhere present. The arguments against an actual infinite set of things or an infinite regress simply do not apply to an infinite being.

In addition to the philosophical problems of a beginningless past (that is, one that could be explained without God), there are also some scientific problems. The age-old view that the universe is unchanging has been replaced in modern times with the Big Bang theory, according to which matter is not simply expanding inside existing space, but space itself is expanding. The point is that if we project the expansion backwards, we come to a beginning point of the universe.[77] This is a scientific confirmation of the kalam argument's second premise.

---

[77]Craig, *Reasonable Faith*, pp. 126–27, 140.

The red shift of light from distant objects,[78] the abundance of light elements like helium and the discovery of background radiation in the universe all fit the Big Bang theory.[79] Dozens of alternate models have come and gone, but nothing has yet unseated the eighty-year-old theory that the universe had a beginning.

A second scientific argument comes from the second law of thermodynamics, an implication of which is that given enough time, energy will disperse evenly throughout a closed system (that is, an environment where no new energy is introduced). We could suggest the illustration that if we put an ice cube in a bowl of water, eventually all the water will be the same temperature. The problem is, if the universe is infinitely old, why has that not yet happened such that the universe has the same energy and temperature throughout? Alternate theories do not avoid the general problem. If the universe is expanding rapidly enough to avoid an even distribution of energy, that energy will eventually run down, resulting in a cold, dark universe. Even the oscillating universe theory, which proposes that the entire universe has been expanding and contracting, points to a beginning of the universe. Nor will we escape the second law if our universe is only one bubble in a "multiverse" of universes.

Since we cannot say that the universe caused itself (contrary to philosopher Daniel Dennett), then its cause must transcend it. That transcendent cause must itself be uncaused, because as has been shown there cannot be an infinite series of causes backward. It must also be immaterial, transcend the space and time that it created and be enormously powerful. And it must be a person. That is because, as al-Ghazali reasoned, if a cause is sufficient to produce an effect, then as soon as the cause is there, the effect is brought about. But if the cause was always there because it is timeless, why isn't the universe timeless as well (since we saw that it is not)? So creation had to be a decision by a personal being, which we call God. As Craig concludes, "The kalam cosmological argument thus gives us powerful grounds for believing in the existence of a beginningless, uncaused, timeless, spaceless, changeless, immaterial, enormously powerful Personal Creator of the universe."[80]

---

[78]Ibid., p. 126. The observation that distant objects appear redder than we would expect seems to help confirm the view that the entire universe continues to expand. Light that is moving away would stretch out and appear redder because red is a longer wavelength, just like sound waves coming from a car horn or siren sound deeper as they move way from us because longer waves sound deeper.

[79]Ibid., p. 129.

[80]Craig, On Guard, p. 100.

Teleological argument. Craig brought the kalam argument into prominence in philosophy using reasoning backed by current science. Recent discoveries in science have also heightened interest in a form of the teleological argument suggested by Aquinas. The inference from design to a designer focused on living things as the best examples of design until Darwin theorized that design was only apparent and was actually a product of natural forces. That seemed to weaken the inference, or at least embroil it in controversy. Recent discoveries revealing the complexity of cells and multicellular organisms have challenged the adequacy of mutation and random selection to explain the origin of life and biological diversity. Theories that life could have originated from a primordial soup of chemicals exposed to energy now seem far less likely, and there is no nontheistic consensus as to an alternative.[81]

Besides the growing debate over the origin and diversity of life, discoveries in recent decades have revealed the astounding ways in which the universe is fine tuned for life, both in regard to the constants of nature and arbitrary physical qualities. The probabilities are staggering. It is as if more than twenty dials, most of which are independent of each other, have to be set perfectly for there to be life. If any were off, in some cases by the smallest possible measures, life would be impossible.

Craig points out that the fine-tuning argument should be regarded not as an argument from analogy, wherein it is claimed that because "things are alike in some ways, they will probably be alike in others."[82] Rather, it should be regarded an inference to the best explanation, because it gives the best account of the data.[83] (By contrast, other ways of drawing a conclusion first reach the explanation, then use it to explain.)

William Dembski says we infer design on three conditions. The phenomenon in question has to be contingent, that is, not produced automatically such that it was not designed. It has to have complexity, so that it cannot be easily explained by chance. And it has to have specification in that it shows the type of pattern characteristic of intelligence.[84]

---

[81]Craig, *Reasonable Faith*, p. 157.

[82]Simon Blackburn, "Analogy," in *The Oxford Dictionary of Philosophy* (Oxford: Oxford University Press, 1994), p. 14.

[83]Moreland and Craig, *Philosophical Foundations*, p. 483.

[84]William A. Dembski, *Intelligent Design: The Bridge Between Science and Theology* (Downers Grove, IL: InterVarsity Press, 1999), p. 128. He says (p. 290 n. 12) that this complexity-specification criterion is the same as his "specification/small probability" developed in his *The Design Inference* (Cambridge: Cambridge University Press, 1998).

The most general constraints determine the universe on the broadest level. The force of gravity is crucially weak, so that its force is negligible for small objects like molecules, but becomes powerful for large objects like planets and stars. But if it were weaker, large bodies like planets and stars would not form (from weakest to strongest: gravity, the weak force, electromagnetism, the strong force). Masses greater than Jupiter are crushed by their own gravity, unless their center is hot enough to balance the pressure, as is the case with the sun and other stars.[85] The strength of the force of gravity determines how large bodies can be, including insects, birds and humans. (The mass of a human is midway between the mass of atoms and the mass of stars.[86]) Gravity is weaker than forces in the micro world by a factor of 10^{36}. If that were stronger or weaker by a mere factor of 1 in 10^{40}, life-sustaining stars like the sun could not exist. That's one click off on a dial with 10^{40} markings.[87]

The so-called strong force is the main force in the micro world. It determines how strongly atomic nuclei are held together, and therefore how much energy is released when atoms break apart and reform in the process of nuclear fusion, which fuels stars. It is quantified by Einstein's equation $E = MC^2$ and harnessed in the mass destruction caused by a hydrogen bomb. The strong force also determines how stars turn hydrogen into all the elements that exist. That force is calculated at .007, but if it were a mere one-thousandth off, .006 or .008, we could not exist. Carbon, on which all life is based, forms only because of a unique "resonance," which depends on an even finer tuning of the strong force. A shift of only 4 percent would drastically hinder the amount of carbon produced.[88]

Astrophysicist Hugh Ross lists twenty-nine finely tuned characteristics of the universe and forty-five of the solar system, a list that is constantly growing.[89]

---

[85]Martin Rees, *Just Six Numbers: The Deep Forces That Shape the Universe* (New York: Basic Books, 2000), pp. 32–33. In this section on fine tuning I add to some of Craig's fine material.

[86]Humans are made of between 10^{28} and 10^{29} atoms. It would take about as many human bodies as there are atoms in each of us to equal the mass of the sun. Ibid., p. 7.

[87]Calculation by Brandon Carter, cited in Paul Davies, *Superforce* (New York: Simon & Schuster, 1984), p. 242. I was pointed to Davies by Robin Collins, "The Fine Tuning Design Argument: A Scientific Argument for the Existence of God," in *Reason for the Hope Within*, ed. Michael J. Murray (Grand Rapids: Eerdmans, 1999), pp. 47–75; reproduced on the Discovery Institute website, www.discovery.org/a/91. For more from Collins, see "The Teleological Argument: An Exploration of the Fine-Tuning Of The Universe," in Craig and Moreland, *Blackwell Companion to Natural Theology*, chap. four, pp. 202–81.

[88]Rees, *Just Six Numbers*, p. 56. For the calculation he cites (p. 181 n. 1), see M. Livio, D. Hollowell, A. Weiss and J. W. Truran, "The Anthropic Significance of the Existence of a Excited State of ^{12}C," *Nature*, 340, no. 6231 (27 July 1989): 281.

[89]Hugh Ross, "Big Bang Refined by Fire," in *Mere Creation: Science, Faith, and Intelligent Design*,

The particulars of the subatomic world have to be exactly right as well. For example, if the decay rate of protons were smaller the universe would not have enough matter to sustain life, but if it were greater, life would be exterminated by radiation. If the mass excess of neutrons over protons were greater, heavy elements would not be possible; but if it were smaller, proton decay would cause stars to rapidly collapse into neutron starts or black holes.[90] If neutrons were not 1.001 times the mass of protons all protons would have decayed into neutrons, or vice versa, and life would be impossible.[91]

Characteristics of the galaxy and our solar system's place in it have to be right. If supernova eruptions were too close or too frequent radiation would exterminate life on earth, but if too far or too infrequent there would not be enough material to form rocky planets.[92] If the solar system were farther from the center of the galaxy, or farther from the nearest spiral arm of the galaxy, there would not be enough heavy elements to make rocky planets; but if it were closer, incoming radiation would be too high, and the density of stars would affect the earth's orbit.[93]

The nature of the sun has to be just right. For example, if the sun had more mass it would burn too rapidly, but if it had less then the range of distance within which life could exist would be too narrow and there would be insufficient ultraviolet light to make sugars and oxygen. If the sun's color were redder or bluer, photosynthesis could not adequately sustain life.[94]

Characteristics of the earth have to be within a narrow range. To be the right temperature its distance from the sun must fall within a very narrow range. If the earth's gravity were greater the atmosphere would retain too much ammonia and methane, but if it were weaker, the atmosphere would lose too much water. If the tilt of the earth were greater or less the earth's temperatures would be too extreme. If the earth's elliptical orbit were more extreme seasonal temperatures would be too extreme. If its rotation period were too long, daily temperature differences would be too great, but if it were shorter, wind speed would be too high.[95] If the

---

ed. William A. Dembski (Downers Grove, IL: InterVarsity Press, 1998), p. 372. For his specific aspects of fine tuning, some of which appear below in this chapter, see pp. 372–80. Also, see his website www.reasons.org.

[90]Ibid., p. 374.

[91]John Leslie, *Universes* (New York: Routledge, 1989), pp. 39–40; cited in Collins, "The Fine Tuning Design Argument."

[92]Ross, "Big Bang Refined by Fire," p. 374.

[93]Ibid., p. 376.

[94]Ibid., p. 377.

[95]Ibid.

earth were farther from Jupiter, or if Jupiter were less massive, it would not protect the earth from asteroids by capturing them in its gravitational field; but if it were closer to earth, or more massive, the earth's orbit would be unstable.[96]

For earth to sustain life the ratio of oceans to continents, amount of minerals in the soil, even characteristics of specific elements and molecules, must be just right. To take one example, if the polarity of water were greater the heat of fusion and vaporization would be too great and life would not exist; but if it were smaller, liquid water would not be enough of a solvent to support chemical interaction, and ice would not float, which would cause too much freezing.[97] Even seismic and volcanic activity are necessary. They are products of the interaction of the massive plates that make up the earth's crust (plate tectonics). Earth is the only planet we know that has such plates. Plate tectonics is crucial to life for a number of reasons, such as regulating the earth's temperature (which among other things allows liquid water, and thus life itself). It also causes limestone to be subducted deep into the earth's mantle and in the process returns carbon dioxide to the atmosphere, causing the earth to warm up. But the weathering of minerals containing silicates (as found in granite, for example) takes carbon dioxide out of the atmosphere, causing the earth to cool down. The two are kept in balance because, as the temperature rises from the release of more carbon dioxide, the rate of the chemical reaction that removes it increases.[98]

One of the lesser-known features of the fine-tuning argument is that some of the already finely tuned numbers have to be in the right proportion to other finely tuned numbers if life is to be possible. So, for example, a number of factors during the Big Bang had to have been finely balanced in order for the universe to expand at the appropriate rate: too slowly, and the force of gravity would have caused it collapse in on itself; too rapidly, and stars and galaxies would not have been able to form. The initial density of all matter, the strength of gravity and the power of the explosion had to have been just right. Not only were all such conditions just right, but also it appears that they were inconceivably precise. If the universe had been so dense that it eventually collapsed back in on itself, space would be curved like a giant ball (called a "closed" universe). Had the density been low enough, the universe would have expanded forever, and space would be curved like a saddle

---

[96]Ibid., p. 379.
[97]Ibid., p. 374.
[98]Peter D. Ward and Donald Brownlee, *Rare Earth: Why Complex Life Is Uncommon in the Universe* (New York: Copernicus Books, 2000), p. 210.

(called an "open" universe). But the density of everything in the universe seems perfectly balanced with the rate of expansion (that rate is called the Hubble constant) such that the universe is "flat" and not curved (the resulting destiny of the universe is unknown—whether it will collapse, expand or have some other fate).[99] In a flat universe, parallel lines never cross, the angles of triangles always add up to 180 degrees and the sides of a cube are made of right angles.

One of the world's top physicists, Roger Penrose, puts the odds of the universe's initial low-entropy condition arising by chance, without any other constraining principles, at an astounding $10^{10^{123}}$. He adds that he cannot remember anything in physics even remotely as accurate.[100]

The probabilities add up to unimaginable numbers because the likelihood that different elements of fine tuning will occur together is the product of them occurring separately, as both Craig and Collins point out.[101] To illustrate, if the chance of getting a four on a six-sided die is 1/6, and the chance of getting a five is 1/6, then the chance that you will get both on two rolls of the die is 1/36. But when you start with the large numbers in the fine-tuning argument, their products become enormous. Just taking two numbers, $10^{40} \times 10^{100}$, their product is 10^{140}. We can get a sense of the size of that number from the estimate that there are "only" 10^{80} atoms in the observable universe. Hugh Ross illustrates the size of a much smaller number, 10^{37}. Color one dime red and hide it in a pile of dimes up to the moon (239,000 miles) covering an area one billion times the size of North America. The chance of randomly picking it out is one in 10^{37}.[102]

As could be expected, there have been a number of objections to the fine-tuning argument.

Some have criticized the assumption underlying the probability calculations of fine tuning, which is that all possibilities are equally likely. It assumes that the possibility of this universe existing is the same as for any universe existing. Absent a reason to think otherwise, we have to make that assumption, which is

---

[99]Since the results of the WMAP (Wilkinson Microwave Anisotropy Probe) we know that the universe is flat within a .4 percent error.

[100]Roger Penrose, "Time-Asymmetry and Quantum Gravity," in *Quantum Gravity 2: A Second Oxford Symposium*, ed. C. J. Isham, R. Penrose and D. W. Sciama (Oxford: Clarendon, 1981), p. 249; quoted in Craig and Moreland, *Philosophical Foundations*, p. 483. Penrose does not necessarily draw the same theological conclusions as Craig.

[101]Craig, *Reasonable Faith*, p. 163 n. 9; Collins, "The Teleological Argument," pp. 252–53.

[102]Hugh Ross, *The Creator and the Cosmos*, 3rd ed. (Colorado Springs, CO: NavPress, 2001), p. 115. See also chap. fourteen, "A 'Just Right' Universe," reproduced at *LeadershipU*, www.leaderu.com/science/ross-justright.html.

called the principle of indifference. It is the same assumption we make to calculate, for example, the possibility of heads coming up in a coin toss. Unless we have information otherwise, such as that we have a trick coin, then we assume the likelihood is one-half for heads and one-half for tails. If there is some physical reason why our particular universe has to exist, that would of course change the probabilities, just as the discovery that we have a trick coin would change our calculation that heads will turn up one-half of the time. But science knows of no reason why our universe has to exist, or even that it is more likely to exist over some other universe. So the only thing we know that can bring about some purpose (i.e., life) that is fantastically unlikely is design.

Another objection appeals to the analogy of a lottery. No matter who wins, it is fantastically unlikely that they did, but it is also unremarkable since someone had to win. But Craig points out that this misunderstands the fine-tuning argument. The issue is not that this particular universe won the lottery, but that a life-permitting universe won out over all the others. It is more like a lottery set up with billions and billions of white ping pong balls, and only one black one. If anything but the black one is randomly chosen, you would be shot. It may be equally unlikely that any particular ball is chosen, black or white—which is the point of the objector, but it is irrelevant. What matters is that it is incomprehensibly more likely that the only ball chosen will be a white one. So if the black one is chosen you should suspect that someone rigged the lottery to let you live.[103]

One objection suggests that there is some physical reason why the universe had to be this way. Some would connect that to the quest for a "theory of everything" (T.O.E.), which would effectively unify into one the four fundamental forces of nature: gravity, the weak force, electromagnetism and the strong force. It would show why each force has the value it does. Superstring theory, or M-theory, has been suggested as a candidate, which proposes that the universe has eleven dimensions. But there is no explanation as to why it should have just that number of dimensions. And as even Stephen Hawking admits, even if we accept the theory, it does not make a life-permitting universe more probable.[104] But even if it could explain why all the finely tuned constants are set at their precise numbers, it still leaves unexplained the very special starting conditions of the universe. Craig says, "It seems likely that any attempt to significantly reduce

[103]Craig, On Guard, pp. 114–15.
[104]S. W. Hawking, "Cosmology from the Top Down" (paper presented at the Davis Cosmic Inflations Meeting, U. C. Davis, May 29, 2003); quoted in Craig, Reasonable Faith, p. 162.

fine-tuning will itself turn out to involve fine-tuning."[105]

One of the more interesting challenges to the idea that the universe is designed is called the anthropic principle. Simply put, we should not be surprised by the fact that our universe seems fine tuned, because this is the only one we could observe; if it were any other way life would be impossible and we would not exist to observe it. So although the likelihood of this one is astonishingly small, we do not need to explain it. Paraphrasing Craig (and others) this confuses the idea that (1) if people exist it is highly probable that they will observe their universe as fine tuned, with the idea that (2) it is highly probable that a fine-tuned universe exists.[106] He likens this notion to a person facing a firing squad of one hundred marksmen at close range. They all fire, yet miss. The person thinks, "Well, I guess I shouldn't be surprise that they all missed because if they hadn't I wouldn't be here wondering about it; so there's nothing to explain." On the contrary, the reasonable conclusion is that they meant to miss. The outcome was not coincidence; it was by design.[107]

Another attempted answer is the many-worlds hypothesis, according to which our universe could be only one of an untold number of universes, perhaps even an infinite number, forming an "ensemble" of universes. With such a large number of them, it is not remarkable that one life-permitting universe exists. But in answer, even an ensemble of universes would have to have a beginning, so there may be only a finite number of them, which might not be enough to produce a finely tuned universe by chance alone. In terms of sheer probabilities, Roger Penrose points out[108] that it is far more likely to get an orderly universe no larger than our solar system. And it is more likely to have that smaller universe that merely has the appearance of being that huge one. It is even more likely that you exist as a brain in a vat imagining the universe around you. More significantly, it is much more likely that if there is an ensemble of universes, there is a God who created it.[109]

The many-worlds hypothesis is purely conjecture, and it is no less metaphysical than the hypothesis of a cosmic designer. It is arguably inferior because the design hypothesis is simpler, and in science, simpler theories are generally preferred. According to a principle we have encountered in previous chapters

---

[105]Moreland and Craig, *Philosophical Foundations*, p. 485.
[106]Ibid., pp. 486–87.
[107]Craig, *On Guard*, p. 116.
[108]Roger Penrose, *The Road to Reality* (New York: Knopf, 2005), pp. 762–65; cited in Craig, *On Guard*, p. 119.
[109]Craig, *On Guard*, pp. 117–20.

called Ockham's razor (after William of Ockham, 1288–1347), we should not multiply causes beyond what is necessary to explain something. Until someone suggests a simple mechanism that is plausible for producing a large number of universes, the design hypothesis should be preferred.[110]

Some object that to be a viable explanation for the universe, the designer needs an explanation; if the complexity of the universe needs an explanation, so does a complex designer. Craig answers that of course this misunderstands explanations, especially those in science. If someone digs up arrowheads they can postulate that they were made by someone without knowing anything about them or their civilization. To say that an explanation is not valid unless we have an explanation for the explanation is unworkable. It would lead to a demand for an explanation for the explanation to the original explanation—and on to infinity. We couldn't explain anything.[111]

As far as the complexity of God's mind, ideas can be complex, but a mind is simple. Furthermore, properties like intelligence, consciousness and volition are essential properties for a mind and not something a mind could lack. "Thus postulating an uncreated mind behind the cosmos is not at all like postulating an undesigned cosmos."[112]

So God is the best explanation for the cosmos.

Incidentally, although Craig has not personally emphasized it, there is a new theistic argument from reason. It was first suggested by C. S. Lewis and developed by Victor Reppert (Craig has included articles by Reppert in two of his coedited books),[113] with contributions also from Derek Barfoot, Angus Menuge and Michael Rea.[114] It takes a number of forms, each claiming that the necessary conditions of logical and mathematical reasoning, disciplines that undergird the natural sciences and human activity, cannot be found in materialist worldviews. The argument is faintly related to Van Til's transcendental argument in that both argue from the need to ground the knowing process. According to Van Til, as we have seen, only (Reformed) Christianity provides the preconditions for rationality, because it presupposes that a rational God determines all truth and is in complete control of

---

[110]Moreland and Craig, *Philosophical Foundations*, p. 487.

[111]Ibid., p. 490.

[112]Ibid.

[113]Victor Reppert, "Confronting Naturalism: The Argument from Reason," in Copan and Craig, *Contending with Christianity's Critics*, chap. 3; Reppert, "The Argument from Reason," in Craig and Moreland, *Blackwell Companion to Natural Theology*, chap. six.

[114]Reppert, "Argument from Reason," p. 362. *Philosophia Christi* 5, no. 1 (summer 2003) featured a symposium on the argument from reason.

everything. The argument from reason contends that mental realities cannot be sufficiently grounded in a materialistic world of only atoms and molecules.

Another argument, advanced in recent years by, for example, J. P. Moreland,[115] is the argument from consciousness. It notes the difficulty that naturalism has reduced certain mind events to purely brain events, and argues that theism gives a better account of their relationship and emergence.

The moral argument. The argument from objective moral values is not as well-known as the cosmological or teleological arguments, and it is often misunderstood. If it is indeed valid it can be effective because many people already accept its premises.

It turns crucially on the idea that some things are objective, that is, independent of people's opinions. For example, Canada is north of Mexico regardless of people's opinions. Something is subjective when it is dependent on someone's opinion, such as which dessert is best. Values have to do with a judgment that something is good or bad, whereas duty has to do with whether we ought or ought not to do something. So if there are objective moral values then some things are good or evil independent of what anyone thinks about them, and if there are objective moral duties then there are things we ought or ought not to do regardless of human opinion. For example, those who believe that the Holocaust was objectively wrong believe it does not matter that the Nazis approved of it, and it wouldn't matter if they had won the war and convinced the rest of the world of their views.

The moral argument is:

1. If God does not exist then objective moral values and duties do not exist.

2. Objective moral values and duties do exist.

3. Therefore, God exists.

The argument does not claim that someone must believe in God to live a moral life, or that it is impossible to formulate an ethical system without referring to God, or that a person must believe in God to recognize a moral value. The argument is not about how we know moral values (moral epistemology), but about their ultimate grounding (moral ontology). We could add that for the argument to work we do not even have to all agree on what things are objectively right or wrong. We merely have to agree (premise two) that moral values and duties exist.

---

[115]J. P. Moreland, *Consciousness and the Existence of God* (New York: Routledge, 2009); and Moreland, "The Argument from Consciousness," in Craig and Moreland, *Blackwell Companion to Natural Theology*, chap. 5.

Support for premise one comes from simply pressing the implications of atheism or naturalism (the view that everything can be explained by natural processes with no need for anything supernatural). If God does not exist, then there is nothing special about humans, and thinking otherwise is "speciesism," an unjustifiable bias in favor of your own species. Absent God, humans are no more than animals, and animals have no moral obligations. When animals kill it is not murder. When they cohabitate with near relatives it is not incest. Behavior that is socially or biologically disadvantageous to the individual or the race may become taboo, which is all that is needed to explain the behavior of a troop of baboons. The rules they develop are not morally right or wrong in any objective sense. So it is with humans, if there is no God. Many who tilt toward atheism admit and even promote this conclusion. Philosopher of science Michael Ruse says, "Darwinism points to an essential relativism about morality, thereby striking at the very core of all Christian thought on moral behavior."[116] Some atheists try to insist that actions like genocide are objectively wrong and are not merely distasteful, counterproductive or taboo. However, as Craig points out, moral values exist only in people and are not mere abstractions. It is hard to see how "justice" could exist if there were no persons.[117] Furthermore, even if values like justice and love did exist somehow in abstraction, why would we be obligated to act on them? They are just there. It is God who obliges us to act on them. For that matter, it is God who provides accountability. If there is no God and death ends everything, why does it matter how we live? A moral life may be in our self-interests much of the time, but clearly not always, especially if we are powerful enough to avoid the consequences of "bad" behavior. Self-sacrifice and other altruistic behaviors become nothing more than an adaptation of the species to perpetuate itself. We could add that, absent God, an individual has every right to question why it is "better" to perpetuate the human race. (Some believe that humans are a detriment to other life forms anyway, and that their influence should be drastically reduced, or even that it would be no loss if humans died out.) So why should a mother risk her life to save her baby from a burning building? And if she does, why should we respect her and hold her up as an example?

---

[116]Michael Ruse, abstract of his article, "Evolutionary Theory and Christian Ethics: Are They in Harmony?," *Zygon: Journal of Religion and Science,* 29 no. 1 (March 1994). This essay was reprinted with minor changes as chap. ten of *The Darwinian Paradigm: Essays on Its History, Philosophy and Religious Implications* (London: Routledge, 1989). The print version is quoted in Moreland and Craig, *Philosophical Foundations,* p. 491.

[117]Moreland and Craig, *Philosophical Foundations,* p. 492.

Premise one, then, is an implication of the view that there is no God. Premise two runs counter to some of our deepest moral intuitions and is already held by most people, including many young people who are committed to values like tolerance, open-mindedness, love and the idea that you should not force your values on others. Craig adds the "powerful" pragmatic argument of William James (1842–1910), that if theoretical arguments are indecisive regarding an important and urgent question, then we can consider practical implications. Craig adds the obvious fact that belief in God and the afterlife is a powerful incentive for moral behavior, and conversely, atheism is a powerful disincentive.

Craig is one of the most formidable proponents of theistic arguments, and is equally respected for his extensive development of evidences for Christianity. But because they overlap with evidentialism, those arguments will be left for that chapter.

Summary

William Lane Craig distinguishes between personally knowing the truth and showing it by way of demonstration. The dichotomy, which isn't necessarily shared by other classical apologists, brings one aspect of his views into conceptual kinship with Reformed epistemologist Alvin Plantinga. Nevertheless, Craig's approach to demonstration—what is normally considered "apologetics"— is straightforwardly classical.

Craig allows for some possibility that the case for Christianity can be made without first making the case for theism. As we will see, Norman Geisler does not.

Craig single-handedly brought back into public discussion what he termed the kalam cosmological argument, and has promoted other theistic arguments. He has also done extensive work on evidences for the resurrection.

Criticisms of the classical view appear at the end of the chapter on Norman Geisler.

Key Terms

Magisterial use of reason. Craig rejects, as did Martin Luther, the idea that reason judges the gospel to be true or false without benefit of the work of the Spirit.

Ministerial use of reason. Craig accepts, as did Luther, the idea that reason should be submitted to the gospel and serve it, helping the believer understand and defend faith. He believes this fits the Augustinian-Anselmian tradition of faith seeking understanding. The proper basis of faith is the witness of the Holy Spirit, not rational argumentation and evidence, though the latter may serve to confirm the former.

Witness of the Spirit. An immediate awareness—not grounds for a conclusion—granted by the Holy Spirit. In Craig's view, the proper basis of faith is the witness of the Spirit, not rational argumentation and evidence, though they may confirm belief. His view is not necessarily characteristic of all classical apologists.

Thinking It Over

1. What is Craig's view on postmodernism?

2. What is the proper role of apologetics?

3. Explain the difference between "knowing" and "showing."

4. How does the witness of the Spirit function? How is it different from Plantinga's view of the *sensus divinitatis*?

5. For Craig, rational arguments _____ the faith, they are not the _____ of faith.

6. How do Habermas, Feinberg and Frame respond to Craig's emphasis on the witness of the Spirit?

7. What are the limitations of Bayes's theorem and argument to the best explanation?

8. What is Craig's response to those who reject induction?

9. What should we do to be as convincing as possible?

10. Briefly outline the issue of the absurdity of life without God.

11. Though not Craig's answer, what has been the response to the objection that Christianity has had a negative effect on society?

12. What are Craig's thoughts on whether Romans 1:20 refers to an inference or an immediate awareness? What is it to confuse proper basicality with degree of belief?

13. Outline the ontological argument. Would you use it? Why or why not?

14. Summarize the cosmological argument. Is there a form of it you would use?

15. What is the teleological argument from fine tuning? What are some examples of fine tuning? What is Craig's answer to the anthropic principle? The many-worlds hypothesis? The objection that God needs an explanation?

16. Explain the moral argument.

GOING FURTHER

Craig, William Lane. *The Best of William Lane Craig: Debate Collection.* Vols. 1–2. La Mirada, CA: Biola University. DVD.

———. "Classical Apologetics." In *Five Views on Apologetics,* edited by Steven B. Cowan and Stanley N. Gundry, pp. 25–54. Grand Rapids: Zondervan, 2000.

———. *On Guard: Defending Your Faith with Reason and Precision.* Colorado Springs, CO: David C. Cook, 2010.

———. *The Kalam Cosmological Argument.* Reprint. Eugene, OR: Wipf & Stock, 2000.

———. *Reasonable Faith: Christian Truth and Apologetics.* 3rd ed. Wheaton, IL: Crossway, 2008.

———. *The Son Rises: Historical Evidence for the Resurrection of Jesus.* Reprint. Eugene, OR: Wipf & Stock, 2000.

Craig, William Lane, and Quentin Smith. *Theism, Atheism, and Big Bang Cosmology.* New York: Oxford University Press, 1993.

– 10 –

NORMAN GEISLER

Theism is proved by what is undeniable, and
Christianity is known from evidences

Like his former student William Craig, Norman Geisler (1932–) has had a prodigious output over his fifty years in apologetics. He has written hundreds of articles, authored or coauthored over eighty books, engaged in twenty-five debates, has taught in several major seminaries and continues to teach into his eighties. Though he has also worked in ethics and theology, the capstone verse that heads his posted résumé is Philippians 1:16, "I am appointed for the defense of the gospel."[1]

Choosing the Right Test for Truth

He begins, and spends a significant portion of, his *Christian Apologetics*[2] critiquing various approaches to truth. Thus as a classical apologist he lays a foundation on a worldview level. Better than any of Geisler's many books, this one shows the systematic nature and philosophical rigor of his approach. What follows is only a brief summary of some major points and is no substitute for getting this extensive work, which runs nearly five hundred pages.

The first methodology is agnosticism, which he divides into those who claim merely that God is not known, and those who claim God and all of reality is unknowable, the latter alone being expressly incompatible with Christianity. He

---

[1]"About Dr. Geisler," personal website, http://www.normangeisler.net/about/default.htm#BooksByNorm.
[2]Norman L. Geisler, *Christian Apologetics*, 2nd ed. (Grand Rapids: Baker Academic, 2013).

includes postmodernism as a type of agnosticism that is reacting to modernism. Postmodernism emphasizes diversity of thought rather than unity of thought, the social and psychological over the rational, hermeneutics over epistemology, uncertainty over certainty, and the reader's meaning over the author's meaning. It is pluralistic, and it rejects foundationalism as well as the correspondence theory of truth. With no God as absolute mind, it is left with no objective truth, no absolute meaning (semantical relativism) and no absolute history (reconstructionism). It is a form of "total relativism and subjectivism."[3]

Complete agnosticism is self-defeating because in effect it says that we can know enough about reality to assert that we can know nothing about reality. Geisler says that this was a problem with Hume's skepticism. Suspending judgment about all reality assumes that we know enough about reality to know that no attempts at discovering it will do any good. He asks, "Why discourage all truth attempts, unless one knows in advance that they are futile? And how can one be in possession of this advance information without already knowing something about reality?"[4] Second, Hume's insistence that all meaningful statements are either a relation of ideas or are about matters of fact is itself neither of them. Third, his contention that the self is merely a collection of sense impressions such that we have no empirical knowledge that we are a single, unified entity (i.e., a "self") is self-defeating. To make a statement like "I am nothing but the impressions about myself" assumes there truly is an "I" making the assertion.[5] Kant is equally self-defeating when he claims that the categories our minds use in our thought processes, such as unity and causality, do not apply to reality. If they did not we could assert nothing about reality, including Kant's own claim. It doesn't help for the Kantian to claim that he is merely showing the limits of our knowledge and is claiming nothing about reality itself. That is because, Geisler says, you cannot know where to draw the line between appearance and reality unless you know enough about both to know where one ends and the other begins. Wittgenstein makes a similar mistake when he claims that language cannot speak cognitively about God: "How can we know that God is inexpressible without thereby revealing something expressible about God?"[6]

The second methodology is rationalism, loosely defined as holding "that what is knowable or demonstrable by human reason is true."[7] According to the

---

[3]Ibid., pp. 9–10.
[4]Ibid., p. 12.
[5]Ibid., pp. 12–13.
[6]Ibid., p. 14.
[7]Ibid., p. 19.

view, knowledge comes through the mind, and we can have a priori knowledge, that is, knowledge that did not come from the senses. Empiricism, by contrast, says that everything we know comes through the senses.

Of course, René Descartes (1596–1650) is the classic rationalist, who developed his ideas as a way to cope with the doubt that followed in the wake of the Reformation's challenge to the Catholic Church and its authoritative claims. Baruch Spinoza's (1632–1677) rationalism brought him to pantheism, and Gottfried Leibniz (1646–1716) used his own hybrid approach to reasoning to support his idea that reality is a grouping of simple natures ("monads") brought into harmony by God. Descartes based reasoning on the undoubtable idea, Spinoza on the perfect idea and Leibniz on the sufficient idea.

Geisler summarizes the unique views of Stuart Hackett (1925–2012), who influenced William Lane Craig as an undergraduate. While Hackett believes that Kant was right that all knowledge comes from our senses and is shaped by the categories that our minds use when we think, he was wrong to say that those categories do not necessarily tell us about reality. When we think, for example, that some things cause other things, Hackett would insist that we can know that causality is a feature of the real world. Kant said we cannot know that our minds connect to the real world, so we have to be agnostic about reality. Hackett said that such agnosticism not only leads to skepticism but is also self-contradictory in that it covertly assumes we know something about reality. We could not even understand people's statements, including those made by Kant himself, if Kant were right that our minds do not necessarily connect to reality. Since we can know for sure that the mind's categories connect us to reality (i.e., that things like causality exist in the world and not just in our minds) empiricism must be wrong in its central claim that all our knowledge comes through the senses and therefore cannot be known with certainty. Contrary to empiricism, our knowledge that the mind's categories are true does not come through our senses (we know it by reason), and also contrary to empiricism, we can be sure that the mind's categories are true.[8] Hackett develops his proof for the existence of God by arguing that we cannot deny the existence of everything, because the person making the denial must exist. What exists is either an effect of something else or it is not. If

---

[8]Stuart Hackett, *The Resurrection of Theism* (Chicago: Moody Press, 1957), pp. 54, 60, 62, 65; quoted in Geisler, *Christian Apologetics*, p. 25. Geisler notes that Hackett modified his claim that these arguments are rationally inescapable to something more like the claim that they are "actually undeniable," a concept he explains in his *Christian Apologetics*, chap. eight, under "Undeniability as a Test for Truth."

it is not, then we have already arrived at the existence of an absolutely necessary being. If it is an effect of something else, then there must exist a necessary being, since an infinite regress of causes and effects is rationally inconceivable. Then there must exist an absolutely necessary being,[9] which is God.

Gordon Clark (1902–1985) held that traditional attempts to establish the truth have failed. Various systems have failed to construct a systematic, consistent set of universal principles, and do not give practical guidance on daily decisions. This means we need to adopt Christian presuppositions. Every view depends on axioms that cannot be deduced or proved from more original principles. They have to be proven another way. Clark proposes that "revelation should be accepted without proofs or reasons, undeduced from something admittedly true."[10] To judge Christian revelation adequate as an axiom, we have to ask, does it make knowledge possible, establish values and ethical norms (i.e., principles of conduct), give a theory of politics? The results must be consistent with each other because for Clark, logical consistency is the essence of truth, and contradiction is the essence of falsity. He makes the point that the principle of noncontradiction is a feature of God's thought processes, and as such it is embedded in Scripture. He famously said that John 1:1 should be translated, "In the beginning was Logic, and Logic was with God, and Logic was God."[11] This fits because the Word is the expression of God. In a sense the principle of noncontradiction is a connection between us and God. He operates on the same principle as we do, just as two plus two is four in our arithmetic as well as God's. Truth is the same for God and for humans. We can see why he clashed with Van Til over the question of whether our knowledge and God's overlap at any point.

One criticism of depending so much on coherence, or self-consistency, is the dilemma of two systems being self-consistent. But for Clark, the answer is to look further, for the widest possible consistency. We should choose the system that provides plausible answers to the most problems, gives more meaning to life and leaves the least room for skepticism. For Clark, this is a reductio ad absurdum that points to Christianity. (Recall that a reductio ad absurdum argument shows that the opposing view leads to absurdity and is therefore false.)

Geisler identifies the basic tenets of rationalism as follows: reality is rationally

[9]Hackett, *Resurrection of Theism*, pp. 194–95; quoted in Geisler, *Christian Apologetics*, p. 26.
[10]Gordon Clark, *Religion, Revelation, and Reason* (Philadelphia: P & R, 1961), pp. 59–60; quoted in Geisler, *Christian Apologetics*, p. 27.
[11]Clark, *Religion, Reason, and Revelation*, pp. 64, 67, 68; Geisler, *Christian Apologetics*, p. 27.

analyzable, there are innate ideas or principles, truth is derived by deduction from self-evident principles, rational certainty is possible in arguments for God. Also, the rationally inescapable is the real. He says this is often misconstrued as conflating the rational and the real, but what is rational is only possibly real (e.g., mermaids are possibly real because the concept doesn't contradict itself). For rationalists God is actually real because it would be contradictory to deny his existence.[12]

Though Geisler commends rationalism for its contributions, he believes that it makes an invalid move from thought to reality, from what is possible to what is actual. As many people have pointed out, logical consistency works best as a test for falsity, not truth. If a view or statement contradicts itself, it cannot be true; but if it does not contradict itself then it could be true but does not have to be true (a novel may be noncontradictory yet not true). Rationalists might agree "but insist that they are not moving merely from the logically possible to the actually real, but from the logically necessary to the ontologically inescapable."[13] In other words, they are claiming that if they can show that something is logically necessary, it has to exist. In response Geisler emphasizes the difference between logical necessity and undeniability. We could add our own illustration: "Every quark is a quark" is logically necessary (by the basic laws of logic it can't possibly be false), but it does not prove that quarks exist. Geisler says there is no way to rationally prove anything in reality, although some things may be undeniable. A person cannot, for example, deny their own existence, because they have to exist to even make such a denial. He ties this to a criticism of the ontological argument. We can show that if triangles exist they must have three sides, yet there is no way to show in any logically necessary way that triangles actually exist. He says,

> In like manner, it is logically necessary to predicate existence of a necessary Existent, and if such a Being exists, it must necessarily exist. But it is not logically necessary for a Necessary Being to exist any more than it is for a triangle to exist. Of course, if something exists, then the ontological argument takes on new strength; if something exists, it is possible that something necessarily exists. But the point here is that there is no purely logical way to eliminate the "if."[14]

Geisler sees another problem in that rationalists cannot demonstrate that all their first principles (the principles that underlie their view) are rationally nec-

---

[12]Geisler, *Christian Apologetics*, p. 30.
[13]Ibid., p. 31.
[14]Ibid., p. 32.

essary. Not all rationalists start with the same first principles, so how can we decide which ones are correct? Even Gordon Clark's weaker form of rationalism has no adequate test for truth. He himself admits that only an omniscient being could apply with certainty the logical-consistency test for truth. Geisler concludes that pure logic cannot tell us about reality. We must begin with some truth about reality, then draw logical inferences from it. We need both logic and experience to know the world.[15]

Next is fideism, the view that faith need not, or cannot, be supported. He contests the popular idea that Tertullian (d. A.D. 230) was a fideist, finds Pascal (1623–1662) more of an antirationalist than a fideist, and concludes the same for Kierkegaard (1813–1855), except that he also held to some of fideism's central claims.[16]

He considers the views of Cornelius Van Til, which he calls "revelational fideism." He quotes Van Til's assertion that "the only 'proof' of the Christian position is that unless its truth is presupposed there is no possibility of 'proving' anything at all."[17] Van Til holds that without presupposing the God of Christianity we cannot interpret one fact correctly; they are brute facts, having no intelligible relation to one another. So we cannot argue from facts to God, and traditional apologetics must fail. Proofs for God and historical evidences for Christianity make no sense apart from presupposing Christian theism. Geisler recounts that Van Til says, "I do not reject the 'theistic proofs' but merely insist on formulating them in such a way as not to compromise the doctrines of Scripture."[18] Then Geisler adds, "Of course, therein is the fideistic hitch in his whole approach, it would appear that, in an admittedly circular reasoning process, the Bible is assumed to be true by an act of faith in its self-vindicating authority. If that is the case, the 'proofs' of God and historical 'facts' of Christianity have absolutely no meaning or validity outside the fideistic acceptance of the presupposition that Christianity is true."[19]

The problem with accepting Van Til's approach as a transcendental argument (i.e., one that proves not directly as a conclusion from facts, but indirectly, as a presupposition that we cannot do without) is that this reasoning process would

---

[15]Ibid., p. 33.

[16]Ibid., pp. 35–42.

[17]Cornelius Van Til, "My Credo," in *Jerusalem and Athens: Critical Discussions on the Theology and Apologetics of Cornelius Van Til*, ed. E. R. Geehan (Phillipsburg, NJ: P & R, 1971), p. 258; quoted in Geisler, *Christian Apologetics*, p. 45.

[18]Cornelius Van Til, *Defense of the Faith* (Philadelphia: P & R, 1955), p. 256; quoted in Geisler, *Christian Apologetics*, p. 47.

[19]Geisler, *Christian Apologetics*, p. 47.

have the same problem that Van Til says all human reasoning has; namely, it is fallen and ineffective. If human reasoning is so affected by sin, why is transcendental reasoning exempt? Second, since nonbelievers can and do use transcendental reasoning, why is it not a form of common ground between believer and nonbeliever, something Van Til insists does not exist? Third, even if we grant that it is rationally necessary to posit a theistic God in order to make sense of the world, it is a leap of faith to say we know that God is triune and is the author of the Bible. Van Til said we can know that God is triune because only a Trinity can solve the problem of the one and the many (the age-old problem of how individual things, like a particular table, relates to the category it is in, like all tables). But Geisler says it fails because the divine persons are not three beings in one being. That aside, why should there be three rather than two or four persons? He says that Van Til gets the idea of a Trinity by faith, not by any transcendental argument. Furthermore, special revelation is not necessary to make sense of the world, but even if it were, there is no way to show how the entire Bible is necessary. What if we took out the book of 3 John? Consequently, "this too is a matter of faith for Van Til, so in the final analysis there is a fundamental fideism" at the core of Van Tillian apologetics.[20]

Geisler wonders if Alvin Plantinga (1932–) is correct that Calvin saw the *sensus divinitatis* as removing any need for proofs or reasons to believe. He refers to Kenneth Kantzer's doctoral dissertation at Harvard,[21] which defends the idea that Calvin found a place for natural theology and theistic proofs. In any case, Geisler sees the name "Reformed epistemology" as a misnomer, because there are plenty of Reformed thinkers who accept more traditional apologetics rather than Plantinga's ideas, among them being B. B. Warfield, Charles Hodge, John Gerstner and R. C. Sproul. He finds Plantinga's ontological argument flawed. As Geisler describes it, Plantinga claims that "modal logic demands that there be a necessary Being—namely one that exists in every possible world."[22] But even Plantinga admits a contingency: a person does not have to accept modal logic. So, concludes Geisler, "his argument was really a hypothetical one; namely, *if* you accept modal logic, then a necessary Being must

---

[20]Ibid.

[21]Kenneth Kantzer, "John Calvin's Theory of Knowledge of God and the Word of God" (PhD diss., Harvard University, 1950); cited in Geisler, *Christian Apologetics*, p. 48.

[22]Geisler, *Christian Apologetics*, p. 48. See Alvin Plantinga, *Nature and Necessity* (Oxford: Clarendon, 1974).

exist."[23] Plantinga was asked if "no world at all was a possible world," and he said no. The argument then assumes that some world must exist in order to prove that something exists necessarily, which Geisler finds to be circular. In general, Geisler says there must be some rational justification for what we accept as basic, and he is not satisfied with Plantinga's response to the Great Pumpkin objection, which says that if we can accept God as properly basic, there is nothing to stop those who hold clearly inadequate views from claiming them as basic as well.[24]

Geisler summarizes fideism's central claims: faith alone is the way to God, truth is not found in the purely rational or objective realm, evidence and reason do not definitely point to God, tests for truth are existential and not rational, and divine revelation is the source of all truth. Though he admits that fideism has some merits, he has several criticisms: (1) it confuses epistemology with ontology. We have to distinguish between the fact that God exists, and how we know that God exists. If God is what we are attempting to prove, we cannot begin by assuming that he exists. A related criticism is that (2) fideists fail to distinguish between belief in God and belief that there is a God. And (3) fideists do not differentiate between belief in God and the support, or warrant, for that belief. (4) Fideists often overlook the need for propositional support and focus on the personal. (5) They fail to see the difference between the unavoidable and the unjustifiable. We may grant that presuppositions are unavoidable in that we cannot think without them. But the real question is, can we justify our presuppositions? How do we decide between beliefs? What is the proper test for truth? Geisler says, "Fideists do not face these questions squarely, or if they do, they tend to provide nonfideistic answers, such as that to believe otherwise is contrary to one's experience, to reason, or to one's hope for the future, or that it brings undesirable results."[25]

Experientialism comes in many forms, and Geisler summarizes some influential cases. Plotinus (d. A.D. 270) finds God inexpressible and beyond our knowing, because he is beyond knowledge, being and personality. Since God cannot be known, he must be felt or intuited in a mystical experience. Friedrich Schleiermacher (1768–1834) centered his interpretation of religion on the experience of absolute dependence, which all humans share. So science is a way of thinking, ethics is a way of living and religion is a way of feeling. While ethics is about self-control, religion is about surrender. In religion, feeling is primary and theological statements are only secondary reflections. Since re-

---

[23]Geisler, *Christian Apologetics*, p. 48.
[24]Ibid., p. 49.
[25]Ibid., p. 53.

ligion is not about ideas, truth and falsity do not apply. This fits with Schleiermacher's view that religious feelings are not a direct apprehension of reality, but only the way nature operates in us. These religious feelings are different from our mere awe of the physical side of the universe. Rudolf Otto (1869–1937) explored the nature of religious experience and found what he believed was a common element: a religious experience of the "Holy" that is awe-inspiring, "uncanny" and of a being that is "wholly other." Experientialism has some common elements, though not every form of it will share each of them: the core of religion is experience, not theological constructs; experience, not propositions and the like, is the highest court of appeal for all things religious; religious experience is self-verifying; and God, or ultimate reality, is in the final analysis indescribable.[26] Despite positive features,[27] experientialism confuses truth and experience, according to Geisler. Experiences are neither true nor false; one simply has them. Truth is what we express in words about our experiences. Geisler says, "The basis of truth rests in the experience, but not the support of that truth. Truth finds its source in primary experience, but not its substantiation."[28] "As a source and basis of truth, the experientialist's claim may be correct, but as a test or warrant for the truth of that claim, it is decidedly lacking."[29] This leads to the standard criticism of experientialism, that experiences are not self-interpreting. Geisler cites John 12:28-29, in which the experience of a noise in the sky is interpreted in three different ways, as the voice of God, as an angel speaking and as thunder. Conversions and claims to have experienced a miracle are interpreted differently by various people of different worldviews. Experiences as such, then, have no meaning; they must be described, which is a serious problem for those who claim to have had encounters with God that are indescribable. Mysticism is a private, noncognitive religious experience that is by nature subjective and untestable. The mystic usually regards the experience as informative only as to what God is not. This amounts to a type of agnosticism and has two problems. First, to know what something is not requires some knowledge of what it is. Second, a relationship, including a relationship with God, requires at least some positive knowledge. In any case, as far as providing grounds for a belief, since mystical experiences are claimed by people with contradictory beliefs, they effectively cancel each other out.[30]

Evidentialism is not far from classical apologetics, and Geisler both defends

---

[26]Ibid., p. 66.
[27]Ibid.
[28]Ibid., p. 67.
[29]Ibid., p. 70.
[30]Norman L. Geisler, "Mysticism," in *Baker Encyclopedia of Apologetics* (Grand Rapids: Baker, 1999), pp. 516–17.

principles that allow for a historical case and critiques the view that such a case can be made without first establishing the background view of a theistic universe. History (as many would acknowledge) includes interpretations about the context and meaning of events, and even which events are selected as worthy of focus in the first place. History is objective as far as being "an accurate and adequate presentation that reasonable human beings should accept," and can be as objective as some of the sciences.[31] It does not deal with repeatable events, but not all sciences do; paleontology and archaeology are examples. The criticism that history cannot be objective the way a science can is invalid, since disciplines like paleontology and geology also work with less than complete records. Contrary to some objections, history can contain value judgments, "if events are given the value they had within their original context. . . . The question is not whether value language can be objective, but whether value statements objectively portray the events the way they really were. Once the worldview has been determined, value judgments are not undesirable or merely subjective; they are essential and objectively demanded."[32] The charge that history cannot be objective because historians are merely products of their times, which determines their views, assumptions, perspectives and the like, is invalid. That very charge would itself be a product of the times, and thus invalid. And if the charge can rise above the times and be valid, then so can history.[33] The very rewriting of history assumes that objectivity is possible. Perfect objectivity may not be possible, but that is true of most, if not all, disciplines. Furthermore, less than perfect objectivity in no way justifies relativism (the notion that objectivity is impossible and that truth is relative to the observer). Neither does the necessity of the historian's having to select a limited number of facts threaten objectivity. Jurors consider only the limited facts before the court, and even scientists have to work with limited knowledge. What matters is that no important fact is overlooked.

Geisler turns to aspects of historical cases that relate to the difference between classical and evidential apologetics. There is a charge that objective history is impossible since it is inevitable that the historian has a worldview, and the historian necessarily interprets everything through that grid. Here Geisler makes common cause with the presuppositionalist by making the (somewhat common) claim that historical events have meaning only within worldviews. "Meaning is system de-

---

[31]Marc Bloch, *The Historian's Craft*, trans. Peter Putnam (New York: Random House, 1953), p. 50; cited in Geisler, *Christian Apologetics*, p. 76.
[32]Ibid., p. 78.
[33]Ibid., p. 79.

pendent"; thus, "within another system, an event may have a very different meaning."[34] Facts can be arranged in at least three ways, chaotic, cyclical and linear; and it is the worldview that determines which. But the fact that worldviews determine interpretations does not make objectivity impossible, "since there are objective ways to treat the question of worldviews."[35] Van Tillians, especially of the Bahnsen stripe, would agree, but for them the choice is determined by their view that the only the (Reformed) Christian presupposition grounds things like rationality, the possibility of discourse and ethics. However, for Gordon Clark, the choice of a worldview is a starting point that can be justified by extensive use of the principle of noncontradiction. For Geisler as a classical apologist, there is limited, though useful, common ground between the theist and the nontheist, which can be used to show that the universe is indeed theistic.

Geisler parts company with evidentialists by insisting that since historical facts have meaning only within a worldview, there is no way to argue from an event like the resurrection to the entire worldview of Christianity. Without theism as a worldview, a resurrection could be interpreted as a mere freak event, likewise for any miracle. Furthermore, the historical method is based on uniformity, the assumption that the past is like the present. If there are no miracles in the present then there is no basis for claiming them in the past. And we cannot claim one in the present because that would presume there is a God who could perform them. The answer, says Geisler, is to establish on independent grounds that there is a creator beyond the world who can intervene in it. A resurrection, or any miracle, is a special act of God only if there is a God. Without theism, there is no reason why a person coming back to life even matters. Geisler says the evidentialist cannot argue that it matters because it is so unusual, since only in the context of theism would it have great significance. In Geisler's view even a fantastically unlikely event does not demand a supernatural explanation.

Pragmatism rose to challenge traditional thinking, and the view exists in a number of forms. Simply put, it emphasizes workability over epistemological abstractions. Most properly, C. S. Peirce (1839–1914) offered pragmatism as a theory of meaning rather than as a test for truth: "He was not concerned with theory verification as such but with clarification of thought."[36] He shifted the focus from attaining truth to being free from doubt, and proposed four

---

[34]Ibid., p. 80.
[35]Ibid.
[36]Ibid., p. 90.

ways in which people attempt that.[37] Sheer tenacity is simple, but as soon as people realize that the opinions of others are as good as their own, they are back to doubt.[38] Authority will not work because no institution can regulate everything effectively. A priori rationalism attempts to reach certainty by agreeing with reason, but it ends up making it a matter of taste so is subject to what is fashionable. Only science is sufficient to fix belief in a way that removes doubt. For Peirce, "The opinion which is fated to be ultimately agreed to by all who investigate, is what we mean by the truth, and the object represented in this opinion is the real. That is the way I would explain reality."[39] Peirce seems to know God by direct experience: "As to God, open your eyes—and your heart, which is also a perceptive organ—and you see him." We cannot be totally deceived about the reality of God, even if we may misunderstand God's precise nature.[40]

William James (1842–1910) categorizes our choice of hypotheses as living or dead, and a live option is one in which each alternative makes some appeal to our beliefs. Options may be forced or avoidable, the forced ones being unavoidable. They are also momentous or trivial, trivial ones being insignificant or reversible. So a genuine option is forced, living and momentous. The question of God is just such a decision. In reality, however, we do not have enough evidence to make the decision objectively. But we must make it. The impulse to wait until there is sufficient information will not work for religion. He quotes one of his contemporaries, FitzJames Stephen,

> We stand on a mountain pass in the midst of whirling snow and blinding mist, through which we get glimpses now and then of paths which may be deceptive. If we stand still we shall be frozen to death. If we take the wrong road we shall be dashed to pieces. We do not certainly know whether there is any right one. What must we do? "Be strong and of a good courage." Act for the best, hope for the best, and take what comes.... If death ends all, we cannot meet death better.[41]

---

[37]Charles S. Peirce, "The Fixation of Belief," *Popular Science Monthly*, November 1877, pp. 1–15, www.peirce.org/writings/p107.html.
[38]Geisler, *Christian Apologetics*, p. 91, summarizes it in terms of unworkability within a community.
[39]Charles S. Peirce, "How To Make Our Ideas Clear," *Popular Science Monthly*, January 1878, pp. 286–302, www.peirce.org/writings/p119.html. I added this; it is not quoted or referred to by Geisler.
[40]C. S. Peirce, "Concept of God," in *Philosophical Writings of Peirce*, ed. Justus Buchler (New York: Dover, 1955), chap. 28; quoted in Geisler, *Christian Apologetics*, p. 93.
[41]James FitzJames Stephen, *Liberty, Equality, Fraternity*, 2nd ed. (London, 1874), p. 353; quoted in William James, *The Will to Believe and Other Essays in Popular Philosophy* (New York: Longman's, Green, 1912), p. 31, available at *Project Gutenberg*, www.gutenberg.org/files/26659/26659-h/26659-h.htm. I added this quotation; it does not appear in Geisler, *Christian Apologetics*.

In *Pragmatism*, James develops more of his unique ideas. For instance: "Truth happens to an idea"; ideas are not true or false. The true "is only the expedient in the way of our thinking, just as 'right' is only the expedient in the way of our behaving."[42] Pragmatism's "only test of probable truth is what works best in the way of leading us, what fits every part of life best. . . . If theological ideas should do this, if the notion of God, in particular, should prove to do it, how could pragmatism possibly deny God's existence?"[43]

Geisler acknowledges a pragmatic element to apologetics. When a person retells their testimony and those of others, they are employing a type of pragmatic approach. He notes that Francis Schaeffer includes the following as a test for truth: "The theory must be non-contradictory and must give an answer to the phenomenon in question," and "we must be able to live consistently with our theory." Schaeffer made the point that no one can live with a philosophy of pure materialism and chance.[44]

The pragmatic test for truth has several characteristics that are found in most types of pragmatism: human experience is the testing ground of truth (the results in the life of a person); collective experience over the long haul, rather than current experience of an individual, is the best way to determine truth in religion; conclusions about truth are not absolute or final but always subject to revision.[45]

As with all the methods he examines, Geisler finds a number of contributions. Pragmatism considers the outworking of ideas, which has a place in claims to have religious truth: "Any theory that offers itself as a world and life view must be applicable to life. Human experience is the proving ground where many beautiful theories have been ruined by brutal gangs of facts. If a view is actually unlivable, how can it be considered a true perspective on life? Certainly religious truth, with its life-transforming claim, must be applicable to life or else must be disqualified as a claimant of truth."[46] The view also reminds us that as humans we have a limited grasp of truth. And there must be more than an intellectual response to truth; it requires faith, which is in part volitional.[47]

---

[42]William James, *Pragmatism, and Other Essays* (New York: Washington Square Press, 1963); quoted in Geisler, *Christian Apologetics*, p. 97.

[43]James, "What Pragmatism Means," in *Pragmatism*, p. 38; quoted in Geisler, *Christian Apologetics*, pp. 97-98.

[44]Francis Schaeffer, *The God Who Is There* (Downers Grove, IL: InterVarsity Press, 1968); cited in Geisler, *Christian Apologetics*, p. 99.

[45]Geisler, *Christian Apologetics*, pp. 99-100.

[46]Ibid., p. 100.

[47]Ibid., pp. 100-101.

On the problematic side, it confuses what works with what is true—a common criticism of pragmatism. If something works we can still ask, is it true? Of course we would expect that what works will help point us to what is true, but they are still different, and success may be accidental. It is a well-known fact that placebos "work" for some people, making them feel better, and at times even slightly improving cure rates. But it is not true that they are a cure for the medical condition. Believing a relative put us in his will might "work" in that it encourages us and keeps us happy, but it may turn out to be untrue.[48] Josiah Royce (1855–1916) criticized the idea that what works or is expedient is the same as what is true. He said he doubted his Harvard colleague William James would be satisfied with putting a witness on the stand under the oath, "I swear to tell the expedient, the whole expedient, and nothing but the expedient, so help me future experience."[49] Other problems with pragmatism include that it is impossible for us to know how a view will work over the long run, and that commitment to a view cannot decides its truth. Consider too the fact that those seeking nirvana want the eventual cessation of all desire, whereas Christians want a future in heaven. Heaven would not be a place of extinguished desires, nor would nirvana satisfy the Christian. So although each destination works for those desiring it, their actual existence cannot both be true (at the same time and in the same sense).

Like a number of critics, Geisler emphasizes the difference between a pragmatic theory of truth and a pragmatic test for truth. While pragmatism cannot work as a theory of truth because what works is not the same as what is true, it can be part of a test for truth because we can expect that what is true will likely work in experience. But we cannot use what works as the only test for truth, Geisler says, because we will end up with relativism, fideism or experientialism, none of which can establish truth.[50]

Combinationalism proposes more than one test for truth. Frederick Ferre (1933–2013) has five tests for the theistic model: no contradictions in its key statements, external consistency with all bodies of knowledge, applicability to human experience, applicability to feeling and perceptions, and usefulness in coping with the total environment of human experience.[51] E. J. Carnell (1919–1967) pro-

---

[48]The illustrations are mine, not Geisler's.

[49]Joseph L. Blau, in introduction to James, *Pragmatism*, p. xiv; quoted in Geisler, *Christian Apologetics*, p. 102; full quote in *One Hundred Twentieth-Century Philosophers*, ed. Stuart Brown, Diane Collenson and Robert Wilkinson (London: Routledge, 1998), p. 170.

[50]Geisler, *Christian Apologetics*, p. 103.

[51]Kent Bendall and Frederick Ferre, *Exploring the Logic of Faith* (New York: Association Press,

poses we use a lack of contradictions within the theory and fit with both the external facts of human history and internal facts of experience.[52] To this Carnell later added what Geisler calls "existential relevance."[53] Geisler summarizes combinationalism as typically testing truth by means of "consistency, factual adequacy, and moral or religious relevance."[54] They usually presuppose their starting point, and regard starting points as crucial and non-self-justifying. There are no necessarily true starting points, and they hold that "formal logic is empty, and sense experience alone needs structure and meaning."[55] Testing truth can follow the scientific approach, which first tests a theory for inner consistency, then the ability to fit the facts of experience.

Positive contributions include recognizing that facts need an interpretive framework and do not have meaning in themselves, an attempt to comprehensively test an entire worldview, and that combinationalism is indeed adequate in some contexts, such as testing scientific theories.

But for Geisler, we cannot presuppose the very worldview we are testing, as for example is done by those who use the resurrection to prove Christianity. Unless we have already proved there is a God, what happens cannot be a miracle, an act of God. Note that the presuppositionalist would say something similar but take it another major step: that classical apologists like Geisler are assuming within their theistic proofs conditions that can exist only within a theistic worldview, including such things as the consistency of the universe, by which we know that the past and future resemble the present, the applicability of the rules of logic and so on. Presuppositionalists further claim that these assumptions do not form common ground with the non-Christian but were covertly taken from the (Reformed) Christian worldview, so it is illegitimate to argue from supposed neutral premises to the conclusion that God exists.

Geisler objects to using more than one test for truth. If one test will not work, adding another will not help. A rational test for truth such as checking to see if the central beliefs of a system contradict each other (i.e., application of the principle of noncontradiction) at best will determine only if a view is false, because

---

1962); cited in Geisler, *Christian Apologetics*, p. 108.

[52]Edward J. Carnell, *An Introduction to Christian Apologetics* (Grand Rapids: Eerdmans, 1950); cf. Geisler, *Christian Apologetics*, p. 108.

[53]Edward J. Carnell, *Christian Commitment* (New York: Macmillan, 1957), pp. 22, 29; cited in Geisler, *Christian Apologetics*, p. 110.

[54]Geisler, *Christian Apologetics*, p. 113.

[55]Ibid., p. 114.

if a view contradicts itself, it cannot be true. But there may be many systems that are noncontradictory. Empirical fit will not work, says Geisler, because fit is a matter of fitting a worldview, which is the very question at issue. Because combinationalism works in science does not mean that it will work in metaphysics.

The reason these tests for truth do not work, Geisler says, is that they are testing a particular aspect of reality, not reality itself, which is being. He explains, "The only way to understand being or reality as such is by the first principles of being, for all thought about reality is based on and is reducible to the first principles of reality. These principles must be self-evident since everything else is evident only in terms of them." So we do not need to give reasons for the principles, and they are not conclusions: "We just 'see' that they are truth once we know what they are saying."[56] Here Geisler points out the difference between reductive foundationalism and deductive foundationalism. The latter (also called geometric deductivism) is found in Spinoza, begins with pure thought and attempts to deduce other truths from it. But Geisler, like Aquinas, is proposing reductive foundationalism, which "begins with reality and proceeds to reduce what we know intuitively about it to self-evident first principles."[57] These first principles apply to all of reality, are self-evident and are undeniable in that any attempt to deny them must use them.

Geisler's first principles are not new; they have been regarded by some in history as indispensable foundations of thought. He emphasizes that they are about reality and not just the way we talk about reality.

1. Being Is (the principle of existence). Something exists. This cannot be denied since anyone who tries is admitting they exist.

2. Being Is Being (the principle of identity). Something is identical to itself.

3. Being Is Not Nonbeing (the principle of noncontradiction). Opposites cannot be true at the same time and in the same sense.

4. Either Being or Nonbeing (the principle of the excluded middle). Something must either be or not be. The denial of this is a contradiction.

5. Nonbeing Cannot Produce Being (the principle of causality). It takes something to cause anything. Nothingness cannot be a cause.

6. Being Causes Being Similar to Itself (the principle of analogy). Like produces like.

---

[56]Ibid., p. 128.
[57]Ibid. See also Norman L. Geisler, "The Bible: Truth and/or Error?," *Journal of the American Scientific Affiliation* 32 (March 1980): 55–58, www.asa3.org/ASA/PSCF/1980/JASA3-80Geisler.html.

There is for Geisler a crucial distinction between establishing the truth of a worldview and establishing truth within a worldview. He uses the above criteria to establish theism as the correct worldview (we'll see how below). Once theism is established, then he establishes the truth of Christianity using combinationalism, by showing that Christianity explains all the known facts in the most consistent way (i.e., systematic coherence).

Undeniability does not work within a worldview since it cannot be had in the historical and experiential matters that are required to prove a view like Christianity. No truth of history or experience is undeniable; it might be the case or it might not. We have to figure it out. We cannot, as with first principles, know them on the grounds that it is impossible to deny them. Only God knows everything and thus knows with 100 percent certainty all claims about history or experience. For us nonomniscient humans, we know (almost all) things probabilistically. But probability can definitely give us a decisive level of certainty.

CONSIDERING ALTERNATIVE WORLDVIEWS

There are a limited number of conceivable worldviews, and they are mutually exclusive; that is, if you hold one, you cannot logically hold another.

Like theism, deism holds that God created the world but that he did not intervene after that; it runs by itself. So there are no miracles, including the incarnation of Christ, and no supernatural revelation, such as an inspired Bible. And there is no Trinity. The movement, which takes various forms,[58] was popular in the seventeenth and eighteenth centuries, and died out in the nineteenth, though its influence lives on in some liberal thinking. It is difficult to reconcile deism's view that God created the universe from nothing, a colossal event, with his apparent inability to do lesser miracles like walking on water. If he is unwilling to do them, why would he care enough about humanity to create but then never intervene? Also, deism is built on an outdated view of the universe as mechanistic. Furthermore, it seems that the universe, once created, must be upheld by divine power (Col 1:7; Heb 1:3). Doesn't that constitute supernatural action toward the universe? Also, some deists like American Revolutionary Thomas Paine (ca. 1737–1809) aggressively attacked the Bible as supernatural revelation; however, their arguments have since been weakened by archaeology and biblical studies. The arguments that deists use against God's

---

[58]Four types are briefly described in Norman L. Geisler and William D. Watkins, *Worlds Apart: A Handbook on World Views*, 2nd ed. (Grand Rapids: Baker, 1989), pp. 148–49.

continuing supernatural intervention in the world would also work against his creation of the world.[59]

Finite godism, which holds that God is a limited being, was held by Plato (ca. 427–ca. 347 B.C.), John Stuart Mill (1806–1873) and Harold Kushner (1935–, who wrote *When Bad Things Happen to Good People*[60]). A God who is limited cannot be uncaused or a necessary being, and as such cannot explain the universe. He would himself need a creator and would not be the standard of perfection. It is hard to see how such a being would even be the standard and source of morals. Would such a being even be an object of worship? Would he even be capable of defeating evil?

Where deism views God as apart from the universe and above it, pantheism claims that God is the same as the universe. According to absolute pantheism (Parmenides and Shankara Hinduism), there is only one being in the universe and all else is nonbeing or illusion. The emanational type (Plotinus) holds that everything flows from God, whereas the developmental type (Hegel) holds that God unfolds over time. Modal pantheists (Spinoza) consider finite things to be modes or moments of a single infinite substance. There are manifestational or multilevel types of pantheism in forms of Hinduism, and permeational pantheism (Zen Buddhism and the film *Avatar*), which claims that a life force permeates all things.[61]

Geisler says that stricter forms of pantheism are unaffirmable because no finite reality exists that is separate from God or the "Absolute," which would entail that we cannot be a finite self. But then how can we affirm that we do not exist? Most pantheists, however, allow for finite humanity but still consider humans as aspects of God. But the critic would ask, why we do not experience ourselves as such? We seem to be separate beings. If we are deceived into thinking we are separate beings, we could be deceived about pantheism being true. Some forms of pantheism try to avoid this dilemma by saying that the individual is one with God such that they can say, "I am God." But they came to realize at some point in time that they are God, so how did God not know something and then know it? Additionally, if there is no finite self and we are part of God, then we cannot have a relationship with God as another being. Any experience of God is really God experiencing himself.

Both Plotinus and philosopher and former president of India Sarvepalli Radhakrishnan attempted to argue that humans are an emanation from God, which

---

[59]Geisler, *Christian Apologetics*, pp. 155–56.
[60]Harold Kushner, *When Bad Things Happen to Good People* (New York: Schocken, 1981).
[61]Geisler, *Christian Apologetics*, p. 179; Geisler and Watkins, *Worlds Apart*, pp. 77–79.

despite their being such only temporarily would still make them in some sense a "self." Geisler responds that this will not solve the problem because according to pantheism, only what is part of God is fully real, and therefore "there is no reality in the finite individual that is the individual's own."[62] Other pantheists like Alan Watts try to solve the problem of the self using the analogy of the Trinity, in which there is more than one person yet one being or essence. But this will not work either, says Geisler, since unlike the Trinity, humans are finite, so their persons are not one but are a collection of changing essences.

One of the central assumptions of pantheism is monism, according to which there is only one kind of thing and everything is a variation of it. So, for example, if everything is consciousness, then the rock is a lowly manifestation of it while the guru is a high manifestation of it; but they are both forms of consciousness. Geisler points out that it might be that things are only similar, not identical. If so, there is no basis for pantheism.

Pantheism has a particularly difficult time explaining evil. If all things are one such that God is everything and everything is God, then where does evil come from? It cannot be separate from God because he is everything. So God is evil and good? One solution is that evil is an illusion, but if it is an illusion, why is it so persistent and real? Those who hold that it is an illusion (the majority of pantheists) would add that God, or the Absolute, is beyond good and evil because it is beyond all categories and logic. On this view of ultimate reality there is no difference between good and bad, right and wrong, true and false, you and me, God and the universe. So ultimately, the statement "X is bad and you shouldn't do it" is the same as "X is good and you should do it." A being that is beyond all categories is not personal, not kind or beneficent, "but an impersonal force driven by metaphysical necessity and not by volitional and loving choice. . . . A personal God—if there is one—is at best a lower manifestation or appearance of the highest impersonal reality."[63] Furthermore, a pantheistic God is incomplete without creation and needs creation to work out the perfections that are latent within.

Pantheists stress that God is unknowable, but that itself is a problem. If the claim cannot be understood in an intellectual way then it is meaningless. If it can be understood then it is self-defeating, because it is claiming to know something about God. It is like someone saying, "I cannot speak a word of English." Additionally, the pantheist's claim that "God is all," including good and evil,

---

[62]Geisler, *Christian Apologetics*, p. 195.
[63]Ibid., p. 197.

finite and infinite, and so on (which, we could add, is related to the claim that God is beyond all categories). This claim is hard to distinguish from saying nothing about God at all. Normally when we say what something is, it distinguishes it from something it is not. If we say John is tall, that means he is not short, if we say the mountain was small, that means it was not big. But in claiming that God is "all" and above categories, making a statement is indistinguishable from an opposite statement, or any other statement. Why do pantheists try to tell us about God at all? Ironically, some, like Alan Watts, would admit that their writings about God tell us nothing about God.[64] This is further undermined by the insistence of stricter pantheists that sense experience is unreliable in that it misleads us to think reality is divided into different things and is material, instead of being undivided and immaterial. But to read what they have written, or hear what they have said, don't we have to trust our senses?

Whereas pantheism is the view that all is God, panentheism (all-in-God; the most common form being process theology) is the view that God inhabits the world the way a soul inhabits a body. He is intimately connected with the world and not separate from it (as in theism), but as a mind is more than a body, God is more than the world. God, then, has two "poles," an actual pole that is the physical world and a potential pole that is beyond the world. He does not create the world out of nothing, since matter is eternal, but he directs the world, not as one sovereign over it but as one who cooperates with it. Thus God and the world are interdependent like a mind and a body. The world depends on God for its grounding, and God depends on the world as his manifestation. Since God envelops the world, he is enriched by what goes on within it, such as human achievement. Because he is not infinite there can be no assurance that he will overcome evil, though he will overcome it as much as possible because he will get help from human cooperation.

Geisler says panentheism's dipolar concept of the divine is inadequate because it leaves God to actualize his own potentialities. But potentialities cannot actualize themselves; it must be done by something outside. Creativity has been suggested as a solution, but it will not fit into the system.[65] Furthermore, panentheism's God is not ultimate, not absolute and unchanging. Whatever has potential can change, but it needs something to act on it to actualize that potential. Therefore there must be something beyond panentheism's God that is pure

---

[64]Ibid., p. 198.
[65]Ibid., p. 216.

actuality and can provide the grounding. As to the problem of evil, the God of panentheism is not adequate to achieve a better world, and it is not clear why he would try. How can he bring about a better world through human cooperation when most humans are unaware of such a God and his intentions? The supposed increase in value achieved does not even seem worth so much human suffering. Furthermore, "panentheists confuse God's unchanging attributes with his changing activities. Thus what God *is* reduces to what God *does*." In the end, God is reduced to a being who is "finite, limited in knowledge, goodness, and power."[66] Despite claims to the contrary, he is not the God of the Bible. Panentheism's view of divine interaction with the world is based on the mistaken idea that God cannot interact with the world unless he reacts to it. The biblical God, however, interacts yet is still in total control. The view of change held by a process-theology form of panentheism is incoherent, says Geisler. It has change, but nothing changes. Process theologian Shubert Ogden (1928–) alleges there are antinomies in traditional theology, but Geisler calls them "ungrounded." Ogden's antinomy of creation, for example, is based on the mistaken idea that a necessary being must necessarily create (that is, he is not free to either create or not create).

It is natural to assume that today polytheism is relevant only to regions far from Western culture, but Geisler points out that it has influence here, and not just on the fringe. He characterizes Mormonism as polytheistic, from its view of the Trinity to its concept of humans. In a view known as tritheism, God is not a traditional Trinity, but three separate beings, a "plurality of Gods" to use the words of founding prophet Joseph Smith.[67] According to the Mormon theologian Bruce McConkie, "Each God was begotten by a previous God in an endless series of gods, which is a serial polytheism."[68] God has a heavenly wife, who is our heavenly mother, by whom we were all begotten. Our Heavenly Father was once a man much like us, who became our God. Our goal is to someday become gods ourselves over our own planets, populating them by procreating in heaven with the spouse we married in this life, in a Mormon temple.

Though polytheism acknowledges a religious reality and our need to interact with it, the various forms of it have one or more problems. It sets aside ratio-

---

[66]Ibid., p. 217.

[67]Joseph Smith, *Teachings of the Prophet Joseph Smith*, ed. Joseph Fielding Smith, 4th ed. (Salt Lake City: Deseret News, 1938), p. 370; quoted in, Geisler, *Christian Apologetics*, p. 224.

[68]Bruce McConkie, *Mormon Doctrine*, 2nd ed. (Salt Lake City: The Church of Jesus Christ of Latter-day Saints, 1959), sec. 130.22; quoted in Geisler, *Christian Apologetics*, p. 224.

nality, a move which can entail that opposites are affirmed, which is self-defeating (e.g., "rationality is not a reliable guide to truth" would be equal to "rationality is a reliable guide to truth"). Many forms are relativistic, yet relativism is presented as a nonrelative truth. If we affirm a number of gods, it is hard to see how physical reality could be as unified as we know it to be from science. Natural laws and constants, for example, seem to operate all over the universe. The universe does not seem to have fiefdoms, or to be the product of warring gods. We could add that if the gods submit to a higher power—or come from a higher power—which produces harmony, it begins to look like monotheism.[69] It is difficult to explain the origins of everything if there are a number of ultimately less-than-infinite gods. If every finite thing has a cause, where did they all come from? Mormonism holds that there are an infinite number of gods going back in time, but Geisler says that has the problems of every infinite regress (see, for example, Craig's explanation of the problems in the kalam argument, or of Aquinas's cosmological argument). Besides, the consensus in current science is that the universe had a beginning. If the gods emerged from nature, how does something impersonal cause a person? If we are told that we should accept polytheism because it is inclusive of all beliefs, it actually is excluding everything but itself, since every form of monotheism (one God) is being rejected. Geisler adds that their protestations notwithstanding, polytheists such as neopagans do have creeds and seek converts.

Of course atheism gets more attention these days, due to aggressive efforts by several high-profile proponents. There have been a few attempts to disprove the existence of God. Bertrand Russell (1872–1970) said that if everything needs a cause, then so does God; but if God does not need a cause, then neither does the world.[70] But of course theists are not arguing that everything needs a cause. Aquinas said only what is finite, changing and dependent needs a cause, from which he and others have concluded there must be an uncaused cause of all finite things. Atheists who object to an uncaused cause need to realize that many atheists themselves believe the universe had no cause. Jean-Paul Sartre (1905–1980) said that if God does not need a cause then he must be self-caused, which is impossible. He's right that it is impossible, but theists claim that God is uncaused, not self-caused. J. N. D. Findlay (1903–1987) attempted an ontological

---

[69]Geisler, *Christian Apologetics*, p. 236.
[70]Bertrand Russell, *Why I Am Not a Christian* (New York: Simon & Schuster, 1957); cited in Geisler, *Christian Apologetics*, p. 242.

disproof: God must be conceived as a necessary being, but necessity applies only to statements not to things that exist, therefore, God cannot exist.[71] But Geisler points out that the argument turns on the claim, "No statements about existence are necessary." If the statement is true, then it applies to that very statement, making it self-defeating: "It is a necessary statement about existence claiming that no necessary statements about existence can be made."[72]

There are of course arguments from pain and evil, which often form the basis of attempts to disprove God's existence. According to one classic argument, if God were all-powerful he would be able to eliminate evil, and if he were all-good he would want to eliminate evil; but evil persists, therefore either God is not all-powerful or he is not all-good. There are many ways to answer the argument, but Geisler simply points out the faulty implied premise that if God has not defeated evil by now he never will. But there is no way for the atheist to know if God will defeat evil in the future. God alone knows his plans.[73] There are positive reasons why God allows some evil, such as that some goods exist only where there is evil, such as long-suffering patience, forgiveness and the like. In some cases, then, permitting some evil is the way to the best possible world. If the atheist insists that God should not do his best if it entails evil, then there is no longer any grounds for the atheist to object that this is not the best world.[74]

Bertrand Russell attempted another argument based on morals. If there is a moral law, it could be the result of God's sovereign decree whereby he could have arbitrarily made anything moral (e.g., lying, cruelty, torture). In this case God would not be good. Or it could be that God merely recognizes what is good, in which case he is not ultimate. So either he is not good or he is not ultimate because he is subject to something higher. But Geisler points out a third option that was not considered (and which is the most common understanding of God's relationship to moral guidelines): the moral law is based on God's good nature. It is neither arbitrary, nor is it above him.[75] In his novel *The Plague*, Albert Camus (1913–1960) set up a dilemma in which one must either join the doctor and fight a plague that God sent on a sinful city, or join the priest and refuse to fight the

---

[71]J. N. D. Findlay, "Can God's Existence Be Disproved?," in *The Ontological Argument*, ed. Alvin Plantinga (Garden City, NY: Doubleday, 1965), pp. 111–12; cited in Geisler, *Christian Apologetics*, pp. 243–44.

[72]Geisler, *Christian Apologetics*, p. 244.

[73]Ibid., p. 245.

[74]Ibid., p. 259.

[75]Ibid., p. 246.

plague since that would be fighting God. The implied claim is that if humani-tarianism is right, theism is wrong. But Geisler says this is a false dichotomy in that the right solution may be to fight the plague as a way of working for God. If the theist believed that stubborn human sin brought on the plague, then the only way to deal with it is to encourage repentance. Part of that may entail demon-strating love by fighting the plague. Furthermore, there is no reason why we cannot lovingly help heal the wounds that were the result of sinful behavior.

One example of an objection regarding God's power asks, can God make a stone so big he cannot lift it? If he cannot create such a stone, he is not omni-potent; or if he can create it but not lift it, then he is not omnipotent. Geisler says that some activities are incompatible with his omnipotence but that does not disprove his existence. He cannot sin, go out of existence or do the logically contradictory (e.g., make a married bachelor). So it is not a limitation on God that he can lift any stone he can create.

Geisler turns the tables and criticizes atheism for having no adequate expla-nation for basic metaphysical questions. It is untenable that persons arose from impersonal forces—as even the famous atheist Antony Flew had to admit when he eventually came to believe in God: "It is simply inconceivable that any ma-terial matrix or field can generate agents who think and act. . . . The world of living, conscious, thinking beings has to originate in a living Source, a Mind."[76] The atheist proposes that all the potential of the universe, including human achievement, came from the mere swirling of atoms, but "potentials do not actualize themselves any more than steel forms itself into skyscrapers."[77] The atheist cannot even answer why there is something rather than nothing.

Geisler mentions the very interesting research of psychologist Paul Vitz,[78] who has found that history's outspoken and famous atheists were raised with absent or dysfunctional fathers, and that they struggled with the experience. Going beyond Geisler's brief reference, we can summarize Vitz. He proposes that a person can (wrongly) connect their attitude toward their father with their at-titude toward God. He writes, "There are, of course, many ways a father can lose his authority or seriously disappoint his child: he can be absent through death or abandonment; he can be present but obviously weak, cowardly, and unworthy of

---

[76]Antony Flew with Roy Abraham Varghese, *There Is a God* (San Francisco: HarperOne, 2007), p. 183; quoted in Geisler, *Christian Apologetics*, pp. 261-62.

[77]Geisler, *Christian Apologetics*, p. 262.

[78]Paul C. Vitz, *Faith of the Fatherless* (Dallas, TX: Spence, 1999).

respect, even if he is otherwise pleasant or 'nice'; or he can be present but physically, sexually, or psychologically abusive." All these prominent atheists lost their fathers at a young age (by the age of five, except Schopenhauer): Friedrich Nietzsche (1844–1900), David Hume, Bertrand Russell, Jean-Paul Sartre, Albert Camus and Arthur Schopenhauer (1788–1860). According to Vitz, loss of a father has the most effect if it occurs between ages three, when a person becomes less dependent on their mother, and five, after which peer relations blunt the loss. Others had abusive or weak fathers: Thomas Hobbes (1588–1679), Jean Meslier (1664–1729), Voltaire (1694–1778), Jean d'Alembert (1717–1783), Baron d'Holbach (1723–1789), Ludwig Feuerbach (1804–1872), Samuel Butler (1835–1902), Sigmund Freud (1856–1939) and H. G. Wells (1866–1946). He recounts less-known atheists, as well as contemporary atheists, such as Madalyn Murray O'Hair (1919–1995), who brought the suit that ended prayer in US schools. (O'Hair so deeply hated her father that she once tried to kill him with a ten-inch butcher knife.[79])

Vitz finds the converse with twenty-one well-known theists. There were no early deaths or abandonments by their fathers, and they clearly had positive relationships with them (or in some cases, good father substitutes). While he does not expect that his hypothesis will hold in anything like every case, he believes it establishes a clear trend.

He regards his study as an argument for deciding questions on the basis of evidence, and not psychology, which seems to intrude in the case of many atheists. It seems clear, he says, that "an intense personal 'reason' lies behind the public rejection of God. If one wishes to genuinely reach such people, one must address their underlying psychology. Aside from the common, superficial reasons, most serious unbelievers are likely to have painful memories underlying their rationalization of atheism. Such interior wounds are not irrelevant and need to be fully appreciated and addressed by believers."[80]

The work of Vitz is a unique example of probing possible nonrational motives for holding atheism. He wrote the book to challenge the widespread assumption "that belief in God is based on all kinds of irrational, immature needs and wishes, whereas atheism or skepticism flows from a rational, grown-up, no-nonsense view of things as they really are."[81]

---

[79]W. J. Murray, *My Life Without God* (Nashville: Thomas Nelson, 1982), p. 7; quoted in Vitz, *Faith of the Fatherless*, p. 55.
[80]Vitz, *Faith of the Fatherless*, p. 145.
[81]Ibid., p. xiv.

THEISM AS THE RIGHT WORLDVIEW

Having set up the criteria for choosing a worldview, and applying them to the alternatives, Geisler now comes to reasons for choosing Christianity.

The problem of evil. He has worked to answer this crucial area of apologetics,[82] which is a special challenge to theism since it affirms both the existence of a good and omnipotent God and evil, whereas atheism denies God, and pantheism denies the real existence of evil. As to the origin of evil, God created beings with free will, and they alone are responsible for their misuse of it. "Free" choice could be determined by another, but that would remove their freedom and responsibility. Or it could be undetermined, but that would be irrational since every action must have a cause. That leaves the option of choices being self-determined. God creates all things, but did not create evil since evil is not a thing. Rather, it is a lack or privation of a good thing that ought to be there. In that way it is different from mere absence. (Sight may be absent from a stone, but in a blind person lack of sight is privation.) Privation can be in a substance (such as a mutilated body) or a relationship (such as blasphemy instead of worship). In a metaphysical sense privation cannot be total, because if there were no good of any kind in a thing, it would not exist, just as if a car were 100 percent rusted it would not exist. But evil can be total in the moral sense in that evil invades every part of a person.

God does not annihilate all evil because it would entail destroying free choice, since to force someone to "freely" choose good is a contradiction. And destroying free choice would eliminate the possibility of good in the form of free moral choice. But God will eventually defeat or overcome evil in a way that keeps choice intact in that those who reject him are separated to an existence in hell.[83]

God has a good purpose for evil even if we cannot see it. We do know some good purposes, as when pain warns us that we are being harmed, or warns us about some moral issue. Some evil is a byproduct of good, such as when the deaths of plants and animals provide food for humans or other animals. Not every evil must have a corresponding good; it can be simply that the overall setup is good. Water, for example, sustains life, but it also can cause drowning. God can bring good out of evil, yet this present world does not have to be the

---

[82]Norman L. Geisler, with response by John W. Wenham, *The Roots of Evil*, 2nd ed. (Dallas: Probe, 1989); Geisler and Winfried Corduan, *Philosophy of Religion*, 2nd ed. (Eugene, OR: Wipf & Stock, 1988), part 4, "God and Evil," pp. 295–385; Geisler and Ronald M. Brooks, *When Skeptics Ask* (Wheaton, IL: Victor, 1990); Geisler, "Evil, Problem of," in *Baker Encyclopedia*, pp. 219–24.
[83]Geisler, "Evil, Problem of," p. 221.

best of all possible worlds, just the best way to attain his goal of the greater good. For those who think that God could have done better than to create this world, Geisler reviews some options. Creating no world at all cannot in any way be compared to creating this or any other world because nothing cannot be compared to something; they have nothing in common. A world with no freedom would indeed contain no sin, but it would not be better because it would not be a moral world. A free world in which no one sins might be conceivable yet not achievable. A world where sin never materializes might not be the most desirable because sin can never be defeated, and higher virtues cannot be developed either (e.g., mercy, which requires the presence of suffering; justice, which requires sin to forgive).[84] Whatever the case, we cannot judge God by this present world, since he promises something far better.

Theistic arguments. Geisler offers his own cosmological argument, which he subsequently defends line by line, and he argues that most of the objections to theistic arguments do not apply to this version:[85]

1. Some things undeniably exist (e.g., I cannot deny my own existence).

2. But my nonexistence is possible, for I am not a necessary being but one that changes or comes to be.

3. Whatever has the possibility not to exist is currently caused to exist by another.

4. There cannot be an infinite regress of current causes of existence.

5. Therefore, a first uncaused cause of my current existence exists.

6. This uncaused cause must be infinite, unchanging, all-powerful, all-knowing and all-perfect.

7. This infinitely all-powerful, all-knowing, all-good being is what is meant by a theistic God.

8. Therefore, a theistic God exists.

9. This God who exists is identical to the God described in the Bible.

10. Therefore, the God described in the Bible exists.

He is not saying his conclusion proves that everything the Bible claims about God is true. (He supports the truth of the Bible by means of additional arguments.) What can be concluded is that the God described in the Bible does exist,

---

[84]Ibid., p. 222.
[85]Geisler, *Christian Apologetics*, pp. 268–79, 282–87.

and that "whatever the Bible claims for this God that is not inconsistent with his nature, it is possible that he did indeed do or say."[86] Geisler's is an example of the "vertical" type of cosmological argument, which concerns how the universe continues to be, and argues for a sustaining cause. The horizontal, or kalam, type is about how the universe came to be, and argues for an originating cause.[87] One problem with the latter type, says Geisler, is that it cannot show that God now exists or necessarily exists, which leaves it vulnerable to the claims of deists. That can be fixed by arguing that a first cause of the universe must now exist, "since the only kind of being that can cause a contingent being (i.e., one that can come to be) is a Necessary Being. A Necessary Being cannot come to be or cease to be."[88] Another problem with the horizontal type of argument is that a pantheist would not grant the premise that a finite, space-time world exists, or is running down, or that time is real and passes in succession. Since the horizontal cosmological argument depends on the vertical argument, it might be better to simply start with the vertical, Geisler says.

After reviewing various forms of the teleological argument, Geisler concludes that as arguments they are probable but not certain, and since they argue from intelligent effects in the world to an intelligent cause, they are dependent on the principle of causality. That principle states that every effect has a cause.[89] Teleological arguments thus assume the very fundamental idea that there is a cause for the order in the world.[90]

The moral argument goes back only to Kant, though he did not offer it as a proof, only as a morally necessary presupposition. Hastings Rashdall (1858–1924) argued that morals must be objective on the grounds that we generally understand morality as objectively binding, and mature minds understand it that way; if it were not we could not judge some things as better or worse, and moral ideals are practically necessary. So if an objective moral law exists independent of human minds, then it must come from a mind that is independent of finite minds. W. R. Sorely (1855–1935) argued that "since there exists a moral ideal prior to, superior to, and independent of all finite minds, there must be a supreme moral Mind from which this moral ideal is derived."[91] Geisler finds the

[86]Ibid., p. 279.
[87]Norman Geisler, "Cosmological Argument," in *Baker Encyclopedia*, p. 160.
[88]Norman Geisler, "Kalam Cosmological Argument," in *Baker Encyclopedia*, p. 401.
[89]Norman Geisler, "Causality, Principle of," in *Baker Encyclopedia*, p. 120.
[90]Norman Geisler, "Teleological Arguments, in *Baker Encyclopedia*, p. 721.
[91]Norman Geisler, "Moral Argument for God," in *Baker Encyclopedia*, p. 499.

roots of the moral argument in Romans 2:12-15, which says that humans have the law of God written on their hearts and are therefore without excuse. He argues that our moral judgments constitute strong evidence that they are objective. That is the only way we could make, and make sense of, such statements as, "The world is getting better (or worse)," and "Hitler was wrong."[92]

He also constructs an argument from religious need: humans beings really need God; what humans really need probably really exists; therefore, God really exists.[93] He clarifies that human desires are not the same as real needs, and the argument is not claiming that what people need will be found (e.g., people do die of thirst). In Scripture people indicate they really need God (Ps 42:1; Jer 29:13; Mt 4:4), and Augustine sums it up by saying that the heart is restless until it finds God. Some of history's greatest minds indicate a need for God, and even some atheists seem to pine wistfully for something godlike: "Sartre found atheism 'cruel,' Camus 'dreadful,' and Nietzsche 'maddening.'"[94] While it is logically possible that humans have real needs for which there is no fulfillment, it is "unbelievable, because it goes against the very grain of human hopes and of human history."[95]

Some have objected that even the language of theistic proofs—and all talk of the divine—cannot connect to the reality it speaks about, because that reality is too transcendent, too different from the everyday contexts in which words have meaning. Geisler uses the trifold distinction made famous by Aquinas. Some uses of language are equivocal, or completely unrelated, such as when we talk about a "chair" for sitting and the "chair" of a department. On the one hand, if all talk about God is equivocal it could have no meaning for us, yet the very statement "We cannot make any meaningful statements about God" implies that we know enough about God to say that, thus falsifying the claim that we can know nothing about God. On the other hand, talk of God cannot be univocal; that is, it cannot have exactly the same meaning as it does for other things. When we say, "John knows" and "God knows," "knows" means something different in the two instances because John and God know in different ways. So words used to describe God are neither entirely different nor identical to the way we use them when

---

[92]Norman Geisler, "God, Evidence for," in *Baker Encyclopedia*, p. 279.
[93]Ibid., p. 279; see also Geisler and Corduan, *Philosophy of Religion*, chap. four. A chapter with the same title appears in an earlier edition of the book in which Geisler does not have a coauthor, Norman L. Geisler, *Philosophy of Religion* (Grand Rapids: Zondervan, 1974).
[94]Geisler, "God, Evidence for," p. 282.
[95]Geisler and Corduan, *Philosophy of Religion*, p. 75.

talking about other things. Our talk about God, then, is analogical.[96] It is similar to an analogy as a figure of speech, such as, "He went like a lamb to the slaughter." The lamb and the person are said to be similar, for example, in that they are docile as they go into harm unaware. But of course the two are different in other ways.

CHRISTIAN EVIDENCES

As a classical apologist, Geisler insists that the theistic framework must be in place in order for arguments for Christianity to be effective. He has written extensively on those evidences, but since they overlap with the work of evidentialists, those writings will not be covered here. However, I will briefly summarize Geisler's defense of the objectivity of history, which is important because if objective history is impossible, then the case for Christianity is impossible.[97]

In explaining how objectivity is possible, he argues strongly for a classical apologetics viewpoint of the relationship between worldview and fact, that the worldview must be in place first before facts can have meaning (which is why theism must be proved before the argument for Christianity can be made, that argument being largely historical in nature). This is the crux of the difference between the classical and evidential view. Evidentialists maintain that insofar as some events fit one interpretive viewpoint (e.g., a worldview) better than others, they give some evidence for that interpretation. Virtually all evidentialists accept arguments for theism, but they do not believe that theism must be established before making the case for Christianity. Geisler insists that only theism gives the facts of history any meaning. We have seen, however, that Craig believes it is possible to make the case for Christianity without first making the case for theism, though he believes the case is stronger overall if theism is established first.

Geisler gives each prevalent objection to historical objectivity and then offers a response. (1) Although historians have only indirect access to events through such things as documents, they are no worse off than, say, the paleontologist, who must work with fossils. Furthermore, the "facts" of science must be interpreted no less than facts of history. (2) The historian has only a small, fragmentary portion of the entire scope of events, but so does the paleontologist,

---

[96]Norman Geisler, "Analogy, Principle of," *Baker Encyclopedia*, p. 22. For a broad array of topics on religious language, see Geisler and Corduan, *Philosophy of Religion*, part four, "God and Language," pp. 209–91.

[97]Geisler uses ten major objections to the possibility of objective history that are developed in William Lane Craig, "The Nature of History" (master's thesis, Trinity Evangelical Divinity School, n.d.); see Geisler, "History, Objectivity of," in *Baker Encyclopedia*, pp. 320–30.

who may have fossils of only part of an animal. Objectivity comes not from access to every fact, but "resides in the view that best fits the facts consistently into an overall theistic system which is supported by good evidence."[98] (3) It is true that historians are influenced by the times in which they live, and they cannot become neutral by stepping outside their own context. But that does not mean their work is unavoidably biased. Perfect objectivity may not be attainable, but that in no way warrants historical relativism. Continual striving for more accuracy is the goal. Besides, if no view can be accurate because it is a mere product of its time, then historical relativism itself cannot be true since it would be a mere product of its time. (4) The fact that the historian selects only some materials from all that are available does not unavoidably bias his or her judgment any more than juries are necessarily biased because they consider only selected evidence. But objectivity is not possible apart from the meaningful structure of a hypothesis or worldview into which events fit. Meaning comes from the place of a fact within a broader theory: "Objective meaning is system-dependent. Only within a given system can the objective meaning of historical events be understood."[99] (5) History necessarily interprets things like causes, but that very element of interpretation means it cannot be objective. In response, Geisler again affirms that the basic interpretation of events presupposes a worldview since events can be interpreted in at least three ways: chaotic, cyclical and linear. So "the problem of the objective meaning of history cannot be resolved apart from appeal to a worldview. Once the skeletal sketch is known, then one can know the objective placing (meaning) of the facts. However, apart from a structure the mere 'Stuff' means nothing."[100] Contrary to evidentialists, "The question of which structure is correct must be determined on some basis other than the mere facts themselves. If there were an objectivity [sic] of bare facts, it would provide only the mere 'what' of history. But objective meaning deals with the why of these events; this is impossible apart from a meaning-structure in which facts may find their placement of significance. Objective meaning apart from a worldview is impossible."[101] Since theism can be demonstrated, objectivity is possible. (6) It is said that the historian's part in arranging events makes objectivity even less likely, but Geisler responds that the arranging can follow

---

[98]Geisler, "History, Objectivity of," p. 325.
[99]Ibid., p. 325.
[100]Ibid., p. 326.
[101]Ibid.

actual events, and "as long as the historian consistently incorporates all the significant events in accordance with an overall established worldview, objectivity is secure."[102] (7) Value judgments are indeed unavoidable, admits Geisler, but "objectivity demands making value judgments, rather than avoiding them." The real question is "which value statements objectively portray the events," and "if this is a theistic world, then it would not be objective to place anything but a theistic value on the facts of history."[103] (8) Geisler agrees with those who argue that history cannot be objective since the historian must first assume a worldview; however, as we have seen, he believes that theism can be proven on independent grounds. (9) Some claim that we could never have acceptable evidence for a miracle. Geisler identifies this view with David Hume and Ernst Troeltsch (1865–1923), and responds that it gratuitously assumes a naturalistic point of view, that empirical generalizations from events of the past should not be used to counter worthy eyewitness accounts, and that if we followed that advice, we would rule out remarkable events of history (even such things as the career of Napoleon). (10) Those who claim that miracles are suprahistorical and thus cannot be known have the first part right. They are in, but not of, the natural process.

Summary

Geisler, like Richard Swinburne, is rigorously systematic and addresses broad issues that impinge on apologetics. Swinburne, somewhat like E. J. Carnell, puts more stress on the principle of noncontradiction as it relates to the coherence of Christian doctrine. Geisler rigorously applies the principle of noncontradiction to opposing arguments. He rejects various tests for truth in favor of the principle of noncontradiction and other undeniable principles of thought as transworldview criteria by which to arrive at theism. He answers crucial objections such as the problem of evil and the limits of language, then defends the possibility of finding objective truth as a foundation for considering evidences for Christianity. Unlike Gary Habermas, he focuses on the general reliability of the Bible. He consistently maintains (contrary to evidentialism) that theism as a worldview cannot be arrived at by an examination of evidences that may point to Christianity. Theism has to be decided separately, and first.

---

[102]Ibid.
[103]Ibid., p. 327.

CRITICISMS

Theistic arguments that do not proceed from initially presupposing God are rejected by presuppositionalists as an attempt to reason without acknowledging the biblical God. Rather than reasoning to God as the conclusion, we should reason from God as the presupposition. Those like Bahnsen who emphasize Van Til's transcendental argument maintain that all reasoning which does not explicitly assume the (Reformed) Christian God is futile and absurd, because it has no (transcendent) basis for rationality. Any attempt to prove the truth of the Bible directly fails to recognize that it would require some higher authority to do so, and there is none. The Bible must be recognized and respected as the Word of God, a divine document that puts humanity on trial. We cannot put God on trial by trying to test whether he is telling the truth in his Word. Besides, presuppositionalists say, any offer of supposed neutral evidence encourages people to think that they are autonomous and authorized to decide what is and is not true. What is needed is submission to God and his word, not encouraging of humans to keep rebelling in their thinking.

Classical apologists agree with presuppositionalists (against evidentialists) that the right framework for reasoning is essential. You cannot prove the Son of God rose from the dead if you do not first prove God. Absent a theistic universe, the resurrection of Jesus could lead to any number of conclusions.

Plantinga's Reformed apologetics accepts some theistic arguments as promising in principle, though their conclusions could not be compelling enough to ground belief. The *sensus divinitatis*, that inner sense of God, is a much firmer basis for belief. The *sensus divinitatis* is an immediate awareness of God, not evidence that we use to conclude anything. This is different from the type of experientialism that accepts religious experience as evidence for the conclusion that God exists.

Most evidentialists do not object to theistic proofs, and many encourage them. But they do not believe they are necessary as a first step when engaging an atheist. To them, classical apologists like Geisler miss the point when they argue that theism must be proven first because, for example, a miracle like the resurrection cannot take place unless there is a God to cause it. To the evidentialist, the issue is not what is demanded or strictly entailed, but what is more likely and therefore more reasonable to believe. An evidentialist would say that Jesus' prediction plus the extreme unlikelihood of a naturalistic explanation do point toward theism, even if an opponent could always claim that it is merely an unexplainable freak event. A freak event is not the more reasonable explanation, and to be reasonable a person should pick the better explanation. The evidentialist could also say that it is not a matter of a worldview coming out of the event, or that the worldview of theism has to already be established on independent grounds. If we use inference to the best explanation, we look at an event and determine the best explanation for it. The worldview need not come out of the facts, nor does it have to already be proved to make the interpretation of a miracle or resurrection possible. We look at the event and see which explanation fits best.

An evidentialist could also point out that even in a theistic universe a person coming back to life is not necessarily "the most important event, in the light of which all other events must be understood."[104] The idea that a resurrection is such an important event is best explained by the claims of Christianity—which shows that it can be difficult in an apologetic case to make a neat, clear separation between theism and the more specific beliefs of Christianity, such that theism has to be proved first, and only then can we start proving Christianity.

Those who disagree with Geisler that the worldview must first be proved before attempting to prove Christianity could argue that they are using an inference to the best explanation. In that approach we look at some state of affairs and figure out which hypothesis best explains it. So the hypothesis does not need to be proved beforehand since that is exactly what the process does, prove a hypothesis. The approach to proving the resurrection through the historical method would be accepted by most worldviews. We could then point to the worldview that best explains the remarkable event. The fact that it is a worldview we are checking and not a smaller theory within a worldview does not mean that we cannot use an inference to the best explanation. (Incidentally, presuppositionalists would claim they are not arguing to the best explanation, but to the only explanation.)[105]

KEY TERMS

Panentheism. The view that God inhabits the world the way a soul inhabits a body. He is intimately connected with the world and not separate from it (as in theism), but as a mind is more than a body, God is more than the world.

Reductive foundationalism. The view, advocated by Geisler, that "begins with reality and proceeds to reduce what we know intuitively about it to self-evident

---

[104]Geisler, *Christian Apologetics*, p. 81.
[105]Emphasized to me by Greg Bahnsen after he kindly guest lectured in my apologetics class at Master's College, Santa Clarita, California, fall 1993.

first principles."[106] These first principles apply to all of reality, are self-evident and are undeniable in that any attempt to deny them must use them.

Undeniability. To deny certain assertions is self-defeating, such as denying one's own existence ("I do not exist"), or denying the existence of everything (if nothing exists, who is making the denial?).

THINKING IT OVER

1. How does Geisler criticize complete agnosticism?

2. How are the claims of Hume, Kant and Wittgenstein self-defeating?

3. Summarize Clark's views.

4. How does Geisler summarize and criticize rationalism?

5. Explain Geisler's criticisms of presuppositionalism.

6. What criticisms doe Geisler make against fideism?

7. What is the problem with experientialism?

8. In what way does Geisler agree with presuppositionalists? In what way does he disagree?

9. What does Geisler find valid and invalid in pragmatism? What is the difference between pragmatism as a theory of truth versus a test for truth?

10. Why does Geisler say combinationalism is assuming the worldview it is supposed to prove? In what way do presuppositionalists say classical apologists like Geisler are doing the same thing?

11. What are first principles of being? Are they conclusions, or known intuitively? Put those six principles in your own words.

12. Geisler rejects combinationalism as a way to know a worldview, but how does he use it?

13. What are Geisler's arguments against deism?

14. What are the problems with pantheism? How does it have difficulty explaining the problem of evil, and the supposed unknowability of God?

15. What is panentheism, and how is it inadequate?

16. What are the criticisms of polytheism?

---

[106]Geisler, *Christian Apologetics*, p. 128; see also Geisler, "The Bible: Truth and/or Error?"

17. How does Geisler turn the tables on atheism? Explain the research findings of Paul Vitz.

18. What is Geisler's answer to the problem of evil?

19. Summarize Geisler's cosmological argument.

20. What are his conclusions about the teleological and moral arguments, and what is his argument from religious need?

21. How do evidentialists, Geisler and Craig differ somewhat as to the meaning of the facts of history?

22. Summarize Geisler's case for the objectivity of history.

23. What are your conclusions about the views of Geisler, presuppositionalism, Plantinga and evidentialism—or any other views we've looked at so far?

Going Further

Geisler, Norman L. *Baker Encyclopedia of Christian Apologetics*. Grand Rapids: Baker, 1998.

———. *The Big Book of Christian Apologetics: An A to Z Guide*. Grand Rapids: Baker Books, 2012.

———. *Christian Apologetics*. 2nd. ed. Grand Rapids: Baker Academic, 2013.

Geisler, Norman L., and William Watkins. *A Handbook on Worldviews*. 2nd ed. Eugene, OR: Wipf & Stock, 2003.

Geisler, Norman L., and Ronald Brooks. *When Skeptics Ask: A Handbook on Christian Evidences*. Rev. ed. Grand Rapids: Baker Books, 2013.

– 11 –

JOHN WARWICK MONTGOMERY

Facts point to interpretations, and critical facts point to Christianity

Evidentialism is the opposite of Van Tillian presuppositionalism in a number of important respects, so seeing one in the light of a review of the other makes it easier to grasp both.

Van Til held that facts are not self-interpreting so they do not point to one interpretation over another. As he would put it, there are no "brute" facts. "Facts" must always be interpreted by our presuppositions. Interpretation always goes downward, from presuppositions to facts, never upward, where independently understood facts point to presuppositions. Yet our particular choice of presuppositions is not arbitrary and fideistic, but is dictated by what is required for rational thought. For Van Til, only (Reformed) Christianity has the presuppositions that give us a rational, workable worldview.

Evidentialism, such as that represented by John Warwick Montgomery, holds that we can approach facts objectively, without bias toward one interpretation, and to some extent the facts will point us to the proper interpretation. He expects that opponents of Christianity will be riled by his approach, which "depends in no sense on theology. It rests solely and squarely upon the historical method, the kind of method all of us, whether Christians, rationalists, agnostics, or Tibetan monks, have to use in analyzing historical data."[1]

Montgomery has remarkably broad interests, which as we will see he brings to apologetics. Besides his focus on apologetics, theology and contemporary thought, he has interests in antique cars and antiquarian books, fantasy literature and Sherlock Holmes; and he holds an academic chair in a French gastronomical society. He also has a very incisive legal mind. I first met him when he was a full-time professor at a theological institution and about to take the California bar exam, having never gone to law school, but having read law under Virginia regulations. He passed the California bar—probably the most difficult in the United States—the first time. (Law school is normally three years of full-time study, and even graduation in no way assures passage of the bar exam, especially first time.) He holds ten advanced degrees, among them the PhD from the University of Chicago and the DThéol from the University of Strasbourg, France—three of his degrees being in law, including the higher doctorate in law from Cardiff University, UK, granted for his publication record. He has written or edited some fifty books in five languages, plus hundreds of articles.[2] He went on to found a law school and a graduate program in apologetics,[3] then to teach law in England (he is a practicing English barrister and an avocet à la cour, barreau de Paris), and to win important international human rights cases. A student in his Renaissance class at Trinity Evangelical Divinity School wrote that he seems to embody the idea of a Renaissance man completed by the Godward focus of the Reformation.[4] Norman Geisler has called him "one of the pioneers of historical apologetics," adding that his extensive knowledge and work are "virtually unparalleled in this field."[5] His work had a significant effect on Josh McDowell, whose 23,000 talks have reached over ten million people, and whose 108 authored or coauthored books have sold nearly 50 million copies (including *Evidence That Demands a Verdict* and *More Than a Carpenter*).[6]

---

[1]John Warwick Montgomery, *Where Is History Going? Essays in Support of the Historical Truth of the Christian Revelation* (Grand Rapids: Zondervan, 1969), pp. 53–54.
[2]For his official website: www.jwm.christendom.co.uk/.
[3]See the International Academy of Apologetics, Evangelism and Human Rights, www.apologeticsacademy.eu.
[4]David Stott Gordon, "John Warwick Montgomery: God's Universal Man," in *Tough-Minded Christianity: Honoring the Legacy of John Warwick Montgomery*, ed. William Dembski and Thomas Schirrmacher (Nashville: B & H, 2008), pp. 33–42.
[5]Norman Geisler, "An Open Letter," in Dembski and Schirrmacher, *Tough-Minded Christianity*, p. 682.
[6]See the updated edition of McDowell's book, *New Evidence That Demands a Verdict: Fully Updated to Answer the Questions Challenging Christians Today* (Nashville: Thomas Nelson, 1999); and McDowell, *More Than a Carpenter*, rev. ed. (Carol Stream, IL: Tyndale House, 1999).

For Montgomery, interpretation properly goes only one way—upward—from facts to interpretation. He surveys all manner of errors that he believes are born of speculation carried on without sufficient reference to facts, in philosophy, science, theology, the arts and law. Such epistemic irresponsibility arises "if one believes that truth depends in the final analysis on one's own stance."[7] Instead, "Philosophically, one needs to distinguish the real world from one's encounter with it."[8] The solution is exemplified in the way we should allow texts themselves to ultimately point us to their correct interpretations, and the way a scientific theory is credible ultimately by confirmation from facts: "The facts ultimately decide the value of our attempts to understand them."[9] It is tempting to speculate apart from facts because it can be done to fit one's "desires and interests," allowing the speculator to be in the center of his or her world. Interestingly, he links such practice to the same impulse that Van Til argued characterizes reasoning apart from God: "Speculation and autonomous self-centeredness go hand in hand."[10] But for Montgomery, the solution is not presupposing the Christian God and viewing all facts accordingly (which on Van Til's claim is the only way facts have meaning), but the opposite, testing theories, assumptions and biases by the facts—which will point us to the Christian God.

Though he does not propose choosing a worldview based on how well it works, Montgomery does point out that right beliefs will interface better with reality. He shows how four major thinkers whose work figured prominently in the prehistory of computers held to the truth of the Bible and essential Christian doctrines. He points out that computers are binary and thus linked to the biblically affirmed principle of noncontradiction (according to which a statement and its denial cannot be true), which fits much better with biblical thinking than with denials of propositional truth, formal logic and subject-object distinctions. "There are no neo-orthodox computers," he quips.[11]

All societies have a paradigm for reasoning from facts to larger ideas, which act as theories into which they fit (in contrast to Van Til's view that facts cannot stand alone but that we must reason from interpretive ideas to the facts). That

---

[7]John Warwick Montgomery, "Speculation vs. Factuality: An Analysis of Modern Unbelief and a Suggested Corrective," in *Christ as Centre and Circumference: Essays Theological, Cultural and Polemic*, Christian Philosophy Today 13 (Eugene, OR: Wipf & Stock, 2012), p. 32.
[8]Ibid., p. 33.
[9]Ibid.
[10]Ibid., p. 37.
[11]Montgomery, "Computer Origins and the Defense of the Faith," in Montgomery, *Christ as Centre*, p. 102.

paradigm was designed for resolving important matters of fact, especially as to what happened in the past; this is the basis for the process of legal reasoning. Since Christianity is grounded in historical events and founded on the resurrection, legal reasoning is well suited to judging whether its claims are credible. The legal method is a process of deciding truth that is familiar to everyone, and has the advantage of functioning without appealing to abstract theological or philosophical concepts and terms. It is used by societies for deciding the most significant and grave issues, including matters of life and death.[12]

Legal proof is inductive, as is historical and virtually every other type of proof (mathematics being one of the few exceptions). Though induction does not offer airtight proof, it is entirely adequate for apologetics—and in the real world, that is the best we have. All matters of fact are "limited to probabilistic confirmation," yet probabilistic confirmation is sufficient for even life-and-death decisions in both daily life and law.[13]

Van Til, by contrast, held that only 100-percent certainty is appropriate for apologetics, which is achieved through the transcendental argument. So positively, (Reformed) Christianity is certain because it is necessary for rationality, and negatively, other views reduce to absurdity because they cannot undergird rationality. If the case for Christianity were not airtight, the nonbeliever would have an excuse for rejecting it. Furthermore, faith itself requires 100-percent proof. Less than 100-percent proof could not justify 100-percent faith (the view Plantinga spends a good deal of time trying to refute).

THE ROLE OF PRESUPPOSITIONS

Criticisms of the apologetic approaches of Montgomery and Gary Habermas are sufficiently entwined that they will be addressed jointly, in a section following the explanation of Habermas's views in chapter twelve.

Those who take their inspiration from Abraham Kuyper's Calvinism emphasize the proper foundations of thought, which could be called starting points, assumptions or presuppositions (e.g., Van Til, that such presuppositions are

---

[12]These advantages are summarized and pointed out by William P. Broughton, *The Historical Development of Legal Apologetics: With an Emphasis on the Resurrection* (Maitland, FL: Xulon Press, 2009), pp. 118–19.

[13]John Warwick Montgomery, *Human Rights and Human Dignity* (Grand Rapids: Zondervan; Plano, TX: Probe Ministries, 1986), p. 153. This book, as well as Montgomery's other publications and audio lectures and debates, can now be obtained from New Reformation Press (www .newreformationpress.com).

provable; Dooyeweerd and Gordon Clark, that they are not provable in the same sense). Montgomery considers all apologetic approaches that emphasize presuppositions as ultimately circular and disconnected from effective verification. He would say that it is of course true that presuppositions have a role in our thinking, for example, as starting points for theology, but they "still require justification over and against other possible starting points for theologizing."[14] He finds no real difference between the type of presuppositionalism which claims that the Christian has as much right to start from Christian presuppositions as the non-Christian has to start from theirs, versus the type of presuppositionalism which claims that Christian presuppositions are proven because they explain reality more comprehensively or coherently than do non-Christian presuppositions. As Montgomery sees it, neither form connects Christianity to "concrete facts," or allows "evidence to arbitrate ultimate questions of religious truth."[15] They "remove Christianity's most powerful cognitive weapon in a pluralistic world—the factually attestable sword of the Spirit, the Word of God."[16]

This contrasts with Van Til's emphasis on the "self-attesting" Word of God, the impossibility of knowing facts independent of presuppositions (i.e., no "brute" facts), that (Reformed) Christianity is proved because it must be presupposed in order to have knowledge of anything and the ultimate circularity of the case for religious truth.

Montgomery implies that the Van Tillian appeal to presuppositions is not that different from fideism (a conclusion shared by Norman Geisler) except that the fideist claims that a religious view not only cannot be proved but also should not be proved.[17] He illustrates what he considers to be the problem with insisting that presuppositions so determine the interpretation of facts that there can be no neutral appeal to them, hence no common ground from which believer and nonbeliever can reason. He supposes two groups who hold contradictory worldviews where each insists the other must begin with their assumptions in order to properly interpret the facts. Each insists that theirs is the context that gives facts their true meaning, and only in that context are they compelling.[18] With each retreating to their own

---

[14]John Warwick Montgomery, *Tractatus Logico-Theologicus*, 2nd rev. ed. (Bonn, Germany: Culture and Science Publications, 2003), p. 30 (2.18211).

[15]John Warwick Montgomery, *Faith Founded on Fact: Essays in Evidential Apologetics* (1978; repr., Edmonton, AB: Canadian Institute for Law, Theology, and Public Policy, 2001), pp. x–xi.

[16]Ibid., p. xi.

[17]Ibid., pp. 33, 121.

[18]Ibid., p. 117.

framework, the discussion between them goes nowhere, and the approach borders on "invincible ignorance."[19] By contrast, Montgomery says that in Acts 17:22-34 the apostle Paul starts with common ground when talking to those on the Areopagus whose pagan worldviews are not unlike those in our secular world.[20] Modern Christians do a disservice to nonbelievers when they exclusively prefer "non-intellectual, subjective religiosity" and attempts to grow megachurches, to the rigorous study that would equip them to adequately interact with nonbelievers.[21] Effective interaction requires not just knowledge of the evidence but also skill in adjusting the unchanging message to the changing personal, social and cultural context. Montgomery identifies four strategies for interacting with the nonbeliever.

First, Christians should point to the need, challenging *"the utterly fallacious notion that one does not need Jesus Christ for a fulfilled life."*[22] Atheistic existentialists like Jean-Paul Sartre (1905–1980) and Albert Camus (1913–1960) highlight the misery of the human condition, and they can effectively be used by Christians. Second, there should be a *"frontal attack on prevailing non-Christian worldviews."*[23] Christians should not focus on peripheral issues, such as the failure of people to live up to those views, but on *"the presuppositional heart of their beliefs."*[24] He likens this "frontal attack" to destroying a building's foundation.

Presuppositionalists charge that evidentialists view nonbelievers as needing only a few adjustments to their views, yet here Montgomery says that even the nonbeliever's presuppositions must especially be confronted and demolished. However, Montgomery does differ from presuppositionalists in that they want to address the most fundamental aspects of the knowing process, claiming that non-Christians know things only because they covertly operate on the presuppositions of a Christian worldview and cannot have knowledge based on their own worldview. Non-Christians know only by epistemological theft of presuppositions that in no way fit their worldview. Thus Christianity must be a fundamental assumption, not a conclusion. The Christian must reason *from* the Christian worldview. Evidentialists, and nonpresuppositionalists generally, hold that it is possible that the non-Christian can have some knowledge of some things from

[19]Ibid., p. 69.
[20]Montgomery, "A Short History of Apologetics," in *Christ as Centre*, p. 125.
[21]Ibid., pp. 124–25.
[22]John Warwick Montgomery, "Apologetics for the 21st Century," in *Christ as Centre*, p. 132 (emphasis original).
[23]Ibid., p. 133 (emphasis original).
[24]Ibid. (emphasis original).

their own worldview, which allows the Christian to reason to some extent to the right worldview. This is also one reason why presuppositionalists argue that Christianity is the only explanation (the only one that allows for knowledge), while nonpresuppositionalists (those who reason along these lines) argue that Christianity is the best explanation. For the presuppositionalist it is all or nothing; Christianity is deductively certain, a reductio ad absurdum of other worldviews.[25] For virtually all nonpresuppositionalists, it's inductively certain (and, they would add, such arguments can be very strong and connect to the real world).

Montgomery gives several examples of confronting non-Christian presuppositions. Marxism should be confronted on its central notion that modifying the means of production will produce a "new man," and thereby a utopia. But external changes have never changed selfish human nature. The same fallacy lies at the heart of liberal Western utopian central planning, yet if you replace slums with nice buildings and put the same people back into them, unchanged, you will soon have slums again. Christianity properly identifies the problem as internal to humans, not external; people need to be made new in Christ (Mk 7:20-23; 2 Cor 5:17). The fallacious reasoning of non-Christian positions should be challenged. Of course we cannot prove our own position merely by showing that others are inadequate, since there is a near infinite number of views and no guarantee that even one of them we are considering is true.[26] So the last-man-standing approach will not work. However, we must remove the false hope offered by the fallacious reasoning of alternatives. For example, those who claim that a creator is untenable because that creator must also have a creator fail to realize the problem of an infinite regress of explanations; also, the universe cannot explain itself (nothing in it can explain itself), so a noncontingent, absolute creator is far more sensible.[27]

Third, it is not enough to offer criticisms, so a positive case must be made. We must offer reasons for our hope (1 Pet 3:15). Thus apologetics is not the same as preaching. There is no way to avoid "arguing for the soundness of the New Testament documents, the reliability of the testimony to Jesus contained therein, and the facticity of His resurrection from the dead as the final proof of His claims."[28]

---

[25]Recall that Van Til regards his argument as a reductio ad absurdum, that is, one that reduces the alternative to absurdity: the non-Christian's view is absurd because it cannot give an adequate account for how we know *anything*. Because a reductio argument is a type of deduction, Van Til believes he can therefore offer deductive proof for (Reformed) Christianity.

[26]Montgomery, *Faith Founded on Fact*, p. 119.

[27]Montgomery, "Apologetics for the 21st Century," p. 134.

[28]Ibid., p. 135.

Fourth, the nonbeliever's most difficult problems must be addressed; for instance, why God allows horrible injustice. Montgomery suggests the outline of an answer: the issue is not the quantity of evil that exists.[29] Rather, the issues are qualitative, including that God's love entails that he give creatures free will, which they have abused by committing evils. And it may be functionally impossible to create a world with free will in which no on ever falls.[30] What is significant is that God is willing to suffer undeservedly for us, and "those who have created the mess are in a particularly poor position to criticize the only One who is doing anything cosmically about it."[31]

On a practical level Montgomery recommends that apologetics be incorporated into every aspect of ministry and evangelism. The faith must not be reduced to "a cultic matter of inner experience and personal testimony."[32]

He reiterates a common criticism of presuppositionalism. Simplifying his argument a bit, he says that we must distinguish between what we believe and how we know it. We cannot start with what we believe (ontology) without considering how we know it to be true (epistemology). To start with ontology rather than epistemology is to assume what we are supposed to be proving, a logical fallacy called begging the question.[33]

Those who agree with Montgomery could add that if we begin by presupposing the more detailed content of our beliefs we run the risk of removing effective common ground between the believer and nonbeliever. When we begin with our Christian worldview and someone else begins with their Buddhist view, we each remain in our separate cognitive worlds. Montgomery proposes that instead of beginning with the content of our beliefs, we begin with methods of obtaining truth, such as the use of logic.[34] This is commonly done in fields like law and science (interpretations of Thomas Kuhn notwithstanding).[35]

Logic is a useful tool for finding truth; however, we must realize that though as a method it offers certainty, it is also removed from the world of fact. It can

---

[29]See also James Warwick Montgomery, "Pain in Theological Perspective," in *Christ as Centre*, p. 171, sec. 4.891.

[30]Ibid., p. 170, sec. 4.861.

[31]Ibid., p. 171, sec. 4.8834.

[32]Montgomery, "Apologetics for the 21st Century," p. 136.

[33]Montgomery, *Tractatus*, 2.194, p. 31.

[34]Ibid., 2.2 and following, pp. 31–32. He makes a similar point in *Where Is History Going?*, pp. 178–79; and in *Christ as Centre*, pp. 34–35.

[35]See Thomas Kuhn, *The Structure of Scientific Revolutions*, 3rd ed. (Chicago: University of Chicago Press, 1996).

tell you only that if the premises are true, then the conclusion follows. Therefore to say that a belief is logical is not to say that it is true in actual fact. To determine what is true in the world we must use an empirical method, which requires that we deal with experience.[36] And that depends on such things as plausibility,[37] likelihood and induction. While these do not give us absolute certainty, they connect us to the real world. We stake our lives on our inductive conclusions, for example, when we fly in an airplane, or even cross the street.[38] Absolute certainty is available only for analytic truths (e.g., "circles are round") and such things as mathematics.[39]

Montgomery says that the bridge between induction and deduction is ret-roduction, or inference to the best explanation (or "abduction," as C. S. Peirce calls it). We see facts and come to an interpretation that explains them. Typi-cally, the facts are not in doubt, only the interpretation. We arrive at it as a kind of gestalt, seeing the facts in a way that makes sense of them. Thus what we experience (empirical phenomena) is made intelligible by our hypothesis (em-pirical hypothesis).[40] If we hear tires screeching and then a crash, and we run outside to see a wrecked car by a tree, we conclude that the car hit the tree. The explanation makes sense of what we experience.

This brings Montgomery to two crucial insights. First, we see the facts and we form the correct hypothesis that interprets them. The hypothesis comes out of the facts. Thus, second, facts are self-interpreting. This is the exact opposite of the presuppositionalist's claim that we can interpret facts only in the light of a prior commitment to an interpretive framework. It also challenges the views of classical apologists like Norman Geisler, who say that facts have no meaning apart from a worldview, and a worldview must be decided without appeal to the facts.

Montgomery does not naively assume that everyone will look at facts objec-tively. Yet bias due to sinful self-interest can be uncovered in religious inquiry no less than in nonreligious inquiry.[41] People most strongly resist arguments that unsettle their personal beliefs or demand a change in their lifestyle, "but that is not the same as saying that such arguments cannot in principle convince. In every sphere of life, people change their beliefs in the face of overwhelming evi-

---

[36]Montgomery, *Tractatus*, 2.3 and following, p. 35.
[37]Montgomery, *Faith Founded on Fact*, pp. 126–27.
[38]Montgomery, *History, Law, and Christianity*, p. 92.
[39]Ibid.
[40]Montgomery, *Tractatus*, 2.362–2.364, p. 42.
[41]Montgomery, *Faith Founded on Fact*, p. 34.

dence against their strongly held prejudices (e.g., in the sphere of racial equality)."[42]

In most endeavors it is possible for both the Christian and non-Christian to investigate truth, including in such fields as chemistry and history. Advances in knowledge provide evidence that even unregenerate people can properly understand and interpret the world.[43]

Montgomery insists that the non-Christian need not function, overtly or covertly, on uniquely Christian presuppositions in order to come to the proper interpretation of facts (as well as presuppositions, as we just saw). So it is not a question of assuming a theistic worldview or importing Christian presuppositions into one's apologetic methodology. The essential assumptions that knowledge is possible, that the universe has structure and that our senses can be trusted must be made by the non-Christian too, or no effort to discover truth or meaning could ever be made. Without such assumptions, the Christian and non-Christian could never even carry on a meaningful discussion.[44]

For presuppositionalists the fact that non-Christians think and draw conclusions because they operate covertly on Christian assumptions points to the real issue: the nonbeliever's intellectual rebellion. Thus Van Tillians tend to emphasize what they see as the spiritual roots of the academic issues rather than debate the non-Christian regarding the details of the academic issues themselves. But for Montgomery (and typically for evidentialists), because the non-Christian can mentally function somewhat on their own worldview, seeing facts can cause them to change their viewpoint, and ultimately the presuppositions (or foundations) of their thought. If it were not so, the Bible would not present so many facts as offers of proof, such as in Elijah's showdown with the prophets of Baal, Thomas getting the evidence he had asked for and Paul recounting the eyewitnesses to the resurrection.

Both the presuppositionalists and Montgomery want to leave the non-Christian without excuse for rejecting the gospel. Van Til insists that only deductive certainty can do that, which requires an argument that all but the (Reformed) Christian view are absurd because they cannot account for how we know anything. Furthermore, their knowledge begins from themselves rather than God, who determines truth. In sharp contrast, Montgomery insists that

---

[42]Personal email correspondence with the author, Oct. 4, 2013.

[43]Montgomery, *Faith Founded on Fact*, p. 33.

[44]John Warwick Montgomery, "A Note from Our Editor: Boa and Bowman's *Faith Has Its Reasons*; the 'Open Theism' Debate," *Global Journal of Classical Theology* 3, no. 1 (March 2002): www.phc .edu/gj_jwm_intro_v3n1.php. He is referring to Kenneth D. Boa and Robert M. Bowman Jr., *Faith Has Its Reasons: An Apologetics Handbook* (Colorado Springs, CO: NavPress, 2001), pp. 241–44.

only an inductive process can leave the non-Christian without excuse because only it connects us to the world. The facts confront the non-Christian because those facts point to the interpretation that Christianity is true. A person's resistance to the true interpretation thus becomes clear, leaving them with the cross as the only offense—and without excuse because they are behaving irrationally.

Presuppositionalist Robert Reymond objects that facts cannot point to a Christian interpretation because many other interpretations are possible.[45] Montgomery replies that the issue is not what is possible but what is plausible. A person could not survive a day if he or she operated on the basis of what is merely possible (e.g., the truck about to hit us could be a figment of our imagination). Such a person would have to be "put away for his own protection."[46] Virtually all human endeavor, academic and practical, requires that we pick out the most plausible explanations. And the world over, societies use legal processes that codify the way to do that. In a closely related process, humans have a way to determine what happened in the past. It is no coincidence that God's revelation supplies the kind of evidence that is amenable to historical-legal verification.

It is important to realize that Montgomery, and evidentialists generally,[47] is not opposed in principle to proofs for the existence of God. But unlike classical apologists, they do not consider them necessary to establish a theistic conceptual framework in which evidences for Christianity are effective. So they believe a one-step argument is feasible, and a two-step argument (first prove theism, then Christianity) is unnecessary. As Montgomery says, "One does not need such a structure to understand what Jesus meant in claiming divinity for himself or to appreciate the force of the argument for the significance of his resurrection."[48]

Though he finds a place for some theistic arguments, some are flawed, he believes. He agrees with a common objection to Anselm's ontological argument that existence is not a property. Rather, it is the name of something that has properties. He also agrees with other common objections to theistic arguments, such as those made by Immanuel Kant (1724–1804). And, even if they were successful, the theistic arguments would prove only one aspect of God (e.g., creator, designer), not the "Transcendent Absolute," nor the God of Abraham, Isaac and

---

[45]Robert L. Reymond, *The Justification of Knowledge*, 3rd ed. (Darlington, UK: Evangelical Press, 1984).

[46]Montgomery, *Faith Founded on Fact*, p. 127.

[47]Gary Habermas, "Evidential Apologetics," in *Five Views On Apologetics*, ed. Steve Cowan (Grand Rapids: Zondervan, 2000), p. 98 n. 20.

[48]Montgomery, *Tractatus*, 3.812, p. 115.

Jacob, and Father of the Lord Jesus Christ.

He does accept the cosmological argument from contingency. To paraphrase his version, (1) nothing in the world can explain itself; (2) the world is the sum total of everything in it; (3) as a whole the world is contingent and requires an explanation beyond itself (i.e., a transcendent God); (4) the transcendent God must be either noncontingent or himself require an explanation; (5) if God requires an explanation then there must be a higher deity to explain him, and a yet higher deity to explain that deity, and so on to infinity; (6) but since an infinite series has no end there would be no explanation for any deity, and the world would itself be without explanation; and (7) therefore, an absolute, noncontingent, existent God must be regarded as the final explanation of the contingent world.[49]

Why don't we simply accept the world as it is, without any explanation? A world without explanation would deny the "contingent nature of the world and mythologically make it absolute—in the face of all empirical knowledge of its non-self-explanatory character."[50] But who created God? The question is nonsensical, since whatever is absolute does not require an explanation; if it did, it would not be absolute. The world is clearly contingent, but there is no evidence to suggest that God is.

God must be rational since we creatures are rational. It is obvious that we are rational, having used a rational argument for his existence. He must be personal, since persons do not come from what is impersonal (contrary to atheistic evolutionary views). He must be moral, since humans and their societies are moral, though that does not tell us which of the competing moral codes are right.[51]

Science also points to God's existence. The second law of thermodynamics requires that a closed system (one that receives no energy from outside it) eventually "runs down." If our universe were uncreated it would be infinitely old and would have run down by now, resulting in a heat death where there is no useable energy. It would not help to claim that our universe is the product of another one, since all universes would have the same problem, and besides, there is no evidence for a succession of universes. An oscillating universe, which explodes and collapses in on itself in endless cycles, would similarly conflict with the second law.

Neither does a Big Bang alone solve the problem, since "it will be incumbent

---

[49]Ibid., 3.851, p. 118.
[50]Ibid., 3.8521, p. 118.
[51]Ibid., 3.8541, 3.8542, 3.8543; pp. 123–24.

upon us to identify the 'Banger.'"[52] Claiming that the Big Bang came from a prior universe would only land us back in the same problem with the second law. On the other hand, those who claim that the Big Bang is absolute and noncontingent have arrived at the very God that is the conclusion of the argument from contingency (above).

The universe gives ample evidence of intelligent design in its specified complexity, which Montgomery accepts from William Dembski. He also accepts the evidence that the universe is remarkably fine tuned. Furthermore, we have examples of (Michael Behe's) irreducible complexity, such as the bacterial flagellum.[53] Furthermore, the human brain cannot account for the human mind.

Theistic arguments "present in other terms what is stated theologically in Romans 1:[20], 'The invisible things of him from the creation of the world are clearly seen, being understood by the things that are made, even his eternal power and Godhead.'"[54]

Though the logic of some theistic arguments is acceptable, Montgomery points out that in a practical sense they have been overemphasized. After all, salvation is not just a matter of acknowledging God, but coming to Christ as savior.[55]

Connecting theistic arguments to the case for the resurrection, Montgomery comes close to the classical apologetics position when he says, "With all its limitations, the evidence supplied by what has been traditionally called 'natural theology' is very powerful in supporting the existence of a transcendent God and in underscoring the meaningfulness of Jesus' historically attested claim to Divinity."[56]

Montgomery, citing Swinburne, believes that natural theology can be interlocked with evidence for the resurrection of Jesus using Bayes's theorem. The resulting probability for the resurrection is in the upper-90-percent range. It is so well confirmed because we would expect the evidence we have for the resurrection if Jesus indeed rose from the dead, given the reasons we already have for believing God exists. Put a little more technically, the hypothesis (h) that Jesus rose is confirmed because we would expect the evidence (e) for the resurrection if the hypothesis is true, given our background reasons (b) for believing that God exists (i.e., because of arguments for the existence of God from natural theology). We have some reason for believing in the resurrection (h) even

---

[52]Ibid., 3.8625, p. 120.
[53]Ibid., 3.8643, p. 123.
[54]Ibid., 3.871, p. 124.
[55]Montgomery, "A Short History of Apologetics," p. 125.
[56]Montgomery, *Tractatus*, 3.87, p. 124.

without the historical evidence (e) because there is evidence for God (b). There is further confirmation from the fact that we would not expect to find evidence for the resurrection if Jesus did not rise (i.e., if h is false).[57]

Although Swinburne and others have put Bayes's theorem to good use, Montgomery points to its limitations. In rough terms, it calculates the likelihood of a hypothesis being true by considering its explanatory power (i.e., how well it explains what otherwise cannot be explained), and its prior probability (how good a hypothesis it is considering background knowledge, which is everything relevant).[58] But Montgomery points out that quantifying a prior probability is notoriously difficult, especially with the resurrection or any miracle, because of the number of nonmiraculous prior events.[59] So Montgomery prefers legal analysis over Bayes's theorem for the resurrection. He frames it in terms of Wigmore juridical analysis, after John Henry Wigmore (1863–19430), which precisely classifies and charts large amounts of evidence. Typically, different symbols represent circumstantial evidence or inference, empirical data, testimony, widely accepted generalizations and an alternative explanation.[60]

Comparing the positive case for the resurrection versus the negative case, his conclusion is that "the objector to the facticity of the resurrection relies entirely, not on factual data, but on conjecture, inference, and supposed universal generalizations. This in itself places the negative case in the worst possible light."[61] On the positive side, the case for the resurrection depends on the reliability of the New Testament documents, not on "philosophical, presuppositional, or sociological argument."[62]

Despite positions that harmonize with aspects of the classical approach, Montgomery should still be considered an evidentialist since he maintains that even without theistic arguments the case for God is clear from the resurrection alone. As he sees it, facts point to the correct interpretation, so we do not need to first adopt the correct interpretation in order to properly interpret the facts—as presuppositionalists insist.

---

[57]Ibid., 3.873–3.8732, pp. 124–25. He quotes Swinburne that the probability of the resurrection is "something on the order of 97%."

[58]My summary, not Montgomery's. See Brian K. Morley, "Swinburne's Inductive Argument for Theism" (PhD diss., Claremont Graduate School, Claremont, CA, 1991).

[59]Montgomery, "A New Approach to the Apologetic for Christ's Resurrection by Way of Wigmore's Juridical Analysis of Evidence," in *Christ as Centre*, p. 188.

[60]Ibid., p. 186.

[61]Ibid., p. 193.

[62]Ibid.

APOLOGETICS FROM BELOW

Presuppositionalists insist that apologetics must begin "from above," by embracing Christian assumptions and convictions (at the very least provisionally, with the nonbeliever looking at the world through Christian glasses to see how much it makes sense of everything). Classical apologists, too, establish a theistic worldview (when talking to atheists) before proving Christianity, which is loosely a top-down approach. But evidentialists like Montgomery favor starting "from below," with Christ and the biblical record, typically focusing on the resurrection and prophecy. He looks to Luther, who preferred beginning with Christ rather than natural theology.

The approach from above seems to have support from philosophy of science; Thomas Kuhn characterized science as highly influenced by commitment to theory-laden paradigms. But Montgomery points out that working scientists take great care to construct crucial experiments that can decisively test which explanation is correct. So science is a more bottom-up process after all. Defending Montgomery's point, Angus Menuge adds, "The fact, emphasized by Duhem and Quine, that strict logic allows one to retain a hypothesis in the face of any evidence no matter how recalcitrant, because something other than the hypothesis might be to blame, does not prevent one showing a strong probability that the hypothesis is mistaken."[63] In law as well, close examination of evidence points to the correct interpretation of the case, which is a bottom-up process. Montgomery quotes Sherlock Holmes, who is apparently no presuppositionalist: "It is a capital mistake to theorize in advance of the facts."[64]

If the historical data is to be viewed through the lens of legal reasoning, which standard should be used? In civil cases it is not assumed that the defendant is innocent, so it is decided simply on which side has the more persuasive case, that is, on the preponderance of evidence. But in criminal cases the accused is presumed innocent and the prosecution has the burden to prove the charges beyond reasonable doubt. If the criminal standard is adopted, then atheism or agnosticism is assumed unless Christianity is proven, or as Plantinga disapprovingly puts it, beliefs are guilty until proven innocent. In favor of this more rigorous standard is the fact that many people demand a high standard of

---

[63] Angus J. L. Menuge, "The Transcendent Incarnate, J. W. Montgomery's Defense of a Christocentric Weltanschauung," in Dembski and Schirrmacher, *Tough-Minded Christianity*, p. 110 n. 9. Menuge's essay captures the flow of Montgomery's apologetic thought.

[64] Montgomery, *History, Law, and Christianity*, p. 11.

proof to change their minds about something as important as religion. In favor of the civil standard, however, is the fact that Christianity competes with other worldviews. It is not a choice between Christianity or no view, as if the default is no view, since everyone must operate on some view. The typical atheist, for example, assumes a materialist worldview.

Without emphasizing these theoretical implications, Montgomery affirms that the evidence rises to the level of legal proof[65] because it can "rationally exclude all other explanations,"[66] there being no other reasonable explanation consistent with the facts.[67]

He emphasizes that verdicts rely on "the ability of facts to speak for themselves,"[68] that is, to point to their correct interpretation. He cites Paul Feinberg, who suggests two interpretations of the Holocaust. One is that the deaths were murders motivated by insane anti-Semitism. The second is that Hitler loved the Jews, and feeling that their history was one of unfair persecution, wanted them to immediately enter the eternal blessedness of heaven. Only if facts to some extent point to their interpretation can we rule out the second interpretation.[69]

When Montgomery says that facts point to their interpretation he does not mean there is one and only one possible interpretation, as if there is a necessary connection between them. Rather, facts point to the most likely, or best, interpretation—an inductive process such that we stray from rationality if we do not accept where the facts point. The same is true if we regard the fit between facts and interpretation as, more precisely, one of abduction.[70]

The decision to accept or reject the New Testament claims of Christ is one of those momentous decisions that we cannot ignore. Like many important decisions, we cannot put it off on grounds that we lack 100-percent proof. Existentialists are correct that life entails decisions, and refusing to make a decision is itself a decision. So the real question ought to be, is there a better reason not to

---

[65]Montgomery, *Tractatus*, 3.665, p. 102.

[66]Ibid.

[67]Montgomery, *History, Law, and Christianity*, p. 92.

[68]Ibid., p. 97.

[69]Paul D. Feinberg, "History: Public or Private? A Defense of John Warwick Montgomery's Philosophy of History," *Christian Scholar's Review* 1 no. 4 (Summer 1971): 325–31.

[70]Feinberg (ibid., pp. 129–30) regards Nash's criticism of Montgomery as off the mark on the relationship between fact and interpretation. See Ronald H. Nash, "The Use and Abuse of History in Christian Apologetics," *Christian Scholar's Review* 1, no. 3 (Spring, 1971): 217–26. For Montgomery's rich and complex view of the interaction between theory and fact in the broader context of science and theology, see Montgomery, "The Theologian's Craft," in *The Suicide of Christian Theology* (Minneapolis: Bethany House, 1970), pp. 267–313.

make a decision for Christ?[71] For Montgomery, faith fills the gap between a high level of probability and certainty.[72] To suggest some numbers for illustration, we can prove it to a level of 95 percent, and faith makes up the remaining 5 percent, giving us certitude.

To underscore the practical side of a faith decision, Montgomery points to Pascal's famous wager. Even if the evidence were exactly balanced for and against the truth of Christianity, there would still be a strong practical (utilitarian) reason to believe. If you accept Christianity and it is true, you gain everything by going to heaven. If it is false, you lose nothing and still have a good life (e.g., one that is moral). However, if you reject Christianity and turn out to be correct, you gain nothing. But if it turns out you are wrong to reject the faith you lose everything. So the Christian has everything to gain and nothing to lose, whereas the atheist has nothing to gain and everything to lose. No gambler would accept such a bet. Montgomery quickly adds that the case for and against Christianity is by no means equally balanced.[73]

Underscoring the spiritual dynamics of the process, Montgomery points to "another way to attest Christ's claims."[74] He cites John 7:17, in which Jesus says that if anyone is willing to do God's will, he will know whether the teaching is from God; and Romans 10:17, in which Paul says that faith comes by hearing the Word of God. Montgomery concludes, "This means that if any person honestly wishes to discover the truth of Christ's claims, he need only put himself in contact with God's word in Scripture and Church, and God's word will attest itself in his personal experience. Only a suspension of disbelief is necessary" (Mark 9:24).[75]

Presuppositionalists would agree, and further emphasize that because spiritual rebellion is the nonbeliever's core problem, information and arguments are not the primary solution. Plantinga would agree with Montgomery, but would also point to the *sensus divinitatis*, which can well up in us. But where Plantinga regards the *sensus divinitatis* and work of the Spirit as the primary source of belief, Montgomery sees any such workings as subjective and secondary. He sees

---

[71]Montgomery, *Tractatus*, 3.9–39.23, pp. 125–26.

[72]John Warwick Montgomery, "God and Other Lawmakers," *Beyond Culture Wars*, special issue of *Modern Reformation* 2, no. 3 (May/June 1993): 21–25. I was led to this by Ross Clifford, *John Warwick Montgomery's Legal Apologetic* (Edmonton, AB: Canadian Institute for Law, Theology, and Public Policy, 2004), p. 51.

[73]Montgomery, *Tractatus*, 3.96–97, p. 127. Pascal sets out his "wager" in section 233 of his *Pensées*.

[74]Montgomery, *Where Is History Going?*, p. 35.

[75]Ibid., p. 36.

as unhelpful Calvin's claim that "without the illumination of the Holy Spirit, the Word can do nothing."[76] Emphasizing subjectivity can leave the impression that Scripture is "true" only for people who already believe it, as if it were a subjective matter (the error of Barth and neo-orthodoxy).[77]

He says that Calvin's inner testimony of the Holy Spirit is no substitute for evidence, as a number of sample passages indicate: Peter's injunction to always be ready to make a defense (1 Pet 3:15); Jesus' miracles, such as healing the paralytic to demonstrate his power and authority to forgive sin (e.g., Mk 2); Luke's descriptions showing that the resurrected Christ is not a spirit (Lk 24:39); Luke's inclusion of "many infallible proofs" of Christ's resurrection (Acts 1:3); and Paul's mention of the more than five hundred to whom the risen Christ appeared (1 Cor 15:6).[78] The issue is whether the Spirit works through the Scriptures, whose trustworthiness can be verified independently, or if his work is a precondition for recognizing that the Bible is trustworthy.[79]

We cannot confuse the Spirit's role in effecting salvation, where he is the sole efficient cause of the faith that results in salvation, with his role in apologetics. Put a little differently, the Spirit's role in soteriology differs from his role as it relates to bibliology. Furthermore, the Spirit does not create evidence, but "makes the gospel personally meaningful."[80] Confusion on the role of the Spirit can leave the impression that the truth of Scripture is a subjective matter, pushing its believability into the "abyss of unverifiability" with its "nonrevelatory competitors."[81]

Montgomery believes that Van Tillians have a closely related problem because of incorrectly assessing the state of the nonbeliever's mind. Since he believes that apologetics must start with the nonbeliever's needs,[82] the issue is especially important. Viewed from his theological perspective as not only an evangelical but also a Lutheran (Missouri Synod), Montgomery sees the fallen

---

[76]John Calvin, *Institutes of the Christian Religion*, trans. Ford Lewis Battles, ed. John T. McNeill (Philadelphia: Westminster, 1960), 3.2.33; quoted in "The Holy Spirit and the Defense of the Faith," in *Christ as Centre*, p. 140. Calvin also says that the Spirit is "stronger than all proof," and that "Scripture bears its own authentication." Calvin, *Institutes* 1.7.4–5; quoted in "The Holy Spirit and the Defense of the Faith."
[77]Montgomery, "The Holy Spirit and the Defense of the Faith," in *Christ as Centre*, p. 143.
[78]John Warwick Montgomery, "The Holy Spirit and the Defense of the Faith," in *Christ as Centre*, p. 140.
[79]Ibid., p. 141.
[80]Ibid., p. 142.
[81]Ibid., p. 144.
[82]Personal email correspondence with the author, Oct. 10, 2013.

mind of the nonbeliever as fully capable of using logic and processing evidence. He derives several "fundamental apologetic axioms" from the Book of Concord: (1) fallen man retains the ability to reason deductively and (2) inductively (induction enables him "to draw correct factual inferences from empirical data"); (3) logic and fact form common ground between the believer and nonbeliever by which the believer can use the nonbeliever's own reasoning against him; (4) that same common ground allows the believer to effectively reason with the nonbeliever using analogies; (5) fallen man can acquire natural knowledge of God's existence, of biblical events and of the "perspicuous Scriptural text"; yet (6) none of these capacities enable humans to mend their relationship with God—only the Holy Spirit can bring conversion.[83]

Fallen humanity can understand the voice of God and respond rationally, just as Adam did after the fall (Gen 3:9-10). "Total depravity" means that fallen man is totally cut off from God and cannot "by his own reason or strength" (see Luther's *Shorter Catechism,* third article of the creed) save himself by his own works, including intellectual argument. But the Van Tillian interpretation of Calvin removes the confidence that nonbelievers can properly process factual arguments for the truth of the faith—even though nonbelievers would have no problem with a similarly structured argument that has a nonreligious conclusion. Montgomery agrees that people resist arguments that challenge their personal beliefs and lifestyles, but the problem is not that they have difficulty reaching the proper conclusion; rather, they have a problem accepting it. He believes that Van Tillians are not sufficiently clear as to the difference. And it seems inconsistent that they do not allow positive arguments for the faith yet are confident that the nonbeliever can grasp criticisms of their views.

Montgomery concludes that offering positive arguments for Christianity neither encourages a sinful sense of autonomy in the nonbeliever nor usurps the sovereignty of God, but legitimately offers a reason for the hope within (1 Pet 3:15).

THE CASE FOR THE BIBLICAL RECORD OF THE RESURRECTION

Montgomery says that Christianity differs from other religious traditions in that it is testable and does not offer mere self-validating experience. Subjective experience cannot prove religious truth anyway.[84] Instead, Christianity "declares that

---

[83]Montgomery, "Christian Apologetics in the Light of the Lutheran Confessions," in *Christ as Centre,* pp. 159-61.

[84]He cites several works, including Kai Nielsen's, "Can Faith Validate God-Talk?" in *New Theology No. 1,* ed. Martin E. Marty and Dean G. Peerman (New York: Macmillan, 1964), esp. p. 147. Montgomery, *History, Law, and Christianity,* p. 67 n. 1.

the truth of its absolute claims rests squarely on certain historical facts open to ordinary investigation."[85] Only two other great religions claim a historical basis, but the evidence for them is insufficient. The Scriptures of Judaism date only to the first century B.C.; thus too much time elapsed between the key events and the records. If the New Testament life of Jesus can be validated, that would validate the Old Testament, but not Judaism per se, with its rejection of Jesus. Islam depends on the Qur'an, but we have only Muhammad's personal claims and no miraculous events of any kind. Though not a major religion, Mormonism claims to be historical, but Montgomery says that it lacks historical credibility.[86]

Since Montgomery examines the Gospels not just from a historical perspective[87] but also from a legal one, he considers such things as the parol evidence rule. According to this rule, certain documents, such as wills, must be considered (by a court) apart from any other documents that may claim to challenge their interpretation or claim that the document under consideration is an incomplete expression of the writer's message. He believes the Gospels must be considered in just such a standalone fashion, as "executed and complete."[88]

He also considers the hearsay rule. Accordingly, statements made out of court are not allowed into evidence because they cannot be cross-examined. Would the Gospels be admitted in spite of the fact that they cannot be cross-examined? Montgomery proposes that the hostile circumstances surrounding the writing of the Gospels reduce this problem to the "vanishing point."[89] The extreme opposition to the Gospels at the time of their writing provides a real-world cross-examination wherein misstatements, exaggerations and even delusions on the part of the disciples would have been caught.[90] New Testament scholar Craig Blomberg adds the observation that, had critics of Christianity been able to find falsehoods and distortions, they would have used them to

---

[85]Montgomery, *History, Law, and Christianity*, p. 67.

[86]Montgomery, *Tractatus*, 3.14311–3.14313, p. 73.

[87]For example, in Montgomery, *Where Is History Going?*, pp. 37–74.

[88]John Warwick Montgomery, *The Law Above the Law* (Minneapolis: Bethany House, 1975), pp. 87–88.

[89]Montgomery, *Human Rights and Human Dignity*, p. 149. He notes that there is no such hearsay rule in Continental civil law, but it is in Anglo-American common law, though exceptions to it in the United States and in English criminal trials have almost swallowed up the rule. Clifford (*John Warwick Montgomery's Legal Apologetic*, p. 81) believes Montgomery need not argue that the hostility provides the equivalent of cross-examination. It is not rigorous enough to be equivalent, and the documents stand on their own merit anyway.

[90]Montgomery, *History, Law, and Christianity*, pp. 85–86; and Montgomery, *Human Rights and Human Dignity*, p. 149.

make damaging attacks in that early stage, when the movement was "very vulnerable and fragile." But we see no such attacks, and it took root even in Jerusalem, where Christ's life was known firsthand. Later Jewish writings attacked Christ on the basis that he was a sorcerer, which acknowledges that he "really did work marvelous wonders." Only the source of the power is disputed.[91]

Regardless of whether extreme opposition functions as cross-examination, the ancient documents rule provides an exception to the hearsay rule, because an old document cannot be cross-examined, yet it can be admitted as having evidentiary value. Following Simon Greenleaf, a nineteenth-century authority on legal evidence, Montgomery says that an ancient document will be received if it shows no evidence of tampering and has been maintained in "reasonable custody."[92] Of course admitting a document into evidence does not validate its contents, so the proponent and opponent offer their arguments as to its credibility.[93] Thus, demonstrating the dates, authorship and provenance of the New Testament documents is followed by the reasons for accepting the testimony they contain.[94]

The proper place to start is examination of the biblical record to determine if it is a reliable source.

> How good are these New Testament records? They handsomely fulfill the historian's requirements of transmissional reliability (their texts have been transmitted accurately from the time of writing to our own day), internal reliability (they claim to be primary-source documents and ring true as such), and external reliability (their authorships and dates are backed up by such solid extrinsic testimony as that of the early second-century writer Papias, a student of John the Evangelist, who was told by him that the first three Gospels were indeed written by their traditional authors).[95]

---

[91]Quoted in Lee Strobel, *The Case for Christ* (Grand Rapids: Zondervan, 1998), p. 51; Clifford (*John Warwick Montgomery's Legal Apologetic*, p. 81) reminded me of this quote.

[92]Montgomery, *Human Rights and Human Dignity*, p. 137. Simon Greenleaf, *The Testimony of the Evangelists*, reprinted in John Warwick Montgomery, *The Law Above the Law*, appendix, pp. 91–140, and available at *Project Gutenberg*, www.gutenberg.org/files/34989/34989-h/34989-h.html. A defense of the ancient documents rule can be found in an online journal edited by Montgomery: Boyd Pehrson, "How Not to Critique Legal Apologetics: A Lesson from a Skeptic's Internet Page Objections," *Global Journal of Classical Theology* 3, no. 1 (March 2002): 1–9, www.phc.edu/gj _boydpehrson.php. Clifford (*John Warwick Montgomery's Legal Apologetic*, p. 59) pointed me to Pehrson. See ibid., pp. 59–72, on the ancient documents rule.

[93]Montgomery, *Human Rights and Human Dignity*, p. 139; Montgomery, *Tractatus*, 3.2912, p. 80. Clifford (*John Warwick Montgomery's Legal Apologetic*, p. 68) pointed me to these two citations.

[94]Montgomery, *Tractatus*, 3.29121, p. 80.

[95]Montgomery, *Human Rights and Human Dignity*, p. 137 (emphases original).

As to transmissional reliability, lower criticism shows that the New Testament is the most reliable document of Greco-Roman antiquity. We have far more manuscripts, and more that are closer to the actual events, than for any other ancient literature. Some fragments, quotations and lectionary readings date to the early first century, and perhaps earlier. A contrasting example is Catullus, who wrote in the first century B.C. All our knowledge of him comes from only one manuscript from the Italian Renaissance, which was lost. It is true that we do not have any originals of the New Testament, but that is true of all ancient literature. We do not have any of Shakespeare's original plays either.

There are some differences in the surviving New Testament manuscripts, but none of them affects any major doctrines. Besides, the number of variants is to some extent a consequence of the sheer number of manuscripts available. Muslims claim to have a superior manuscript tradition because the Qur'an has fewer variants, but as Montgomery points out, that is only because the third caliph, Uthman, solved the problem of variants by canonizing the manuscripts from Medina and destroying all the rest. There is now no way to determine which manuscripts were best.

Montgomery concludes that anyone who doubts the reliability of the New Testament documents but trusts anything else from antiquity is either ignorant of the facts or blindly biased.[96]

The internal test considers what a document claims for itself. Historical, legal and literary scholarship follow Aristotle's dictum, that the benefit of the doubt goes to the document itself.[97] In daily life too, we regard people as truthful unless there is evidence to the contrary. Only paranoids doubt everyone (cf. Swinburne's principle testimony).

The New Testament documents claim to be written either by eyewitnesses or their close associates. Luke opens his Gospel by saying that he used "eyewitness" sources and "investigated everything carefully" (Lk 1:2-3). John says, "He who has seen has testified" (Jn 19:35), and he proclaims what "we have seen and heard" (1 Jn 1:3). The New Testament writers recognized the value of eyewitnesses testimony (Acts 1:22; 2:22), and were careful to distinguished between quoting Jesus and speaking from their own authority (1 Cor 7:12). They faced a hostile audience that would have eagerly pointed out inaccuracies.[98]

---

[96]Montgomery, *Tractatus*, 3.241–3.258, pp. 73–76. Regarding Uthman, Montgomery cites (p. 75) A. Jeffery, *Materials for the History of the Text of the Qur'an* (Leiden: E. J. Brill, 1937).

[97]Montgomery, *Tractatus*, 3.261, p. 76. Aristotle, *De Arte Poetica* 1460b–1461b, cited by Montgomery.

[98]F. F. Bruce, *The New Testament Documents: Are They Reliable?*, 5th ed. (London: Inter-Varsity Fellowship, 1960), pp. 45–46; quoted in Montgomery, *History, Law, and Christianity*, p. 35.

Only better sources could discount the biblical record of Christ, but no such sources exist.

The external evidence looks at what outside sources have said. The New Testament is backed up by other documents (not so for Gnostic and apocryphal Gospels),[99] which is rare for ancient sources owing to the limited number of documents that have survived. Papias, bishop of Heiropolis, wrote (about A.D. 130) that the apostle John credited Peter as the source of Mark's Gospel, adding that Peter had insisted nothing be omitted or falsely included. Irenaeus, bishop of Lyons, was discipled by Polycarp, who in turn had been discipled by the apostle John. About A.D. 180 he wrote that Matthew published his Gospel when Peter and Paul were preaching, Mark wrote from what Peter had said, Luke followed Paul around and wrote from him as a source and John wrote his Gospel while living at Ephesus.

Though the Gospels were once dated quite late, which would allow for fanciful distortions, the discovery of various manuscripts pushes the dates back much closer to the time of the events. Besides early complete manuscripts like Codex Sinaiticus and Codex Vaticanus there are fragments, quotations and lectionary readings that date to the end of the first century, and perhaps even earlier. (We could add that the John Rylands fragment of John's Gospel dates to the early second century, thus refuting claims that the Gospel was written so late in the second century that John could not have written it.) Montgomery adds that Acts does not mention Paul's death in A.D. 64–65, so it must have been written earlier. Therefore Luke's Gospel (which was part one of his history, Acts being part two) was written before that. Mark must have been written even earlier, since some of his material seems to be used in Luke (and Matthew).[100] Others point out that the Gospels must have been written early because they do not mention the destruction of Jerusalem in A.D. 70, or even Nero's persecution in A.D. 67 and the deaths of Paul and Peter. John A. T. Robinson points out that Matthew contains seven warnings against the influence of the Sadducees, which was very seriously weakened after A.D. 70, as was Jewish culture in general; thus there would be no need for coexistence with Judaism, which the Gospel seems to reflect.[101]

So there is good support for the soundness of the New Testament documents, which means good support for their testimony about Christ.

---

[99]Montgomery, *Tractatus* 3.274, p. 78.
[100]Montgomery, *Tractatus*, 3.2771, p. 79.
[101]Clifford, *John Warwick Montgomery's Legal Apologetic*, p. 93.

Moving from the reliability of the records, what can be said of the witnesses themselves and the reliability of what they wrote? Drawing from perhaps the most respected work on the subject, a fourfold test can be applied. (1) Are there any defects in the witnesses? Does anything in their background indicate that they are untrustworthy or unreliable? Can they tell fact from fantasy? They seem trustworthy, straightforward and certainly able to separate fact from fiction. Peter, for example, underscores this ability when he says that they do not follow cleverly devised myths, but are eyewitnesses (2 Pet 1:6). (2) Did they have any motive to lie? Hardly. They lost wealth and social acceptability. They followed a master who taught that lying is of the devil (Jn 8:44). (3) Is the account internally consistent, or is it self-contradictory? There are four independent witnesses, who see events from different perspectives. Their accounts are not so similar that we should suspect collusion or fabrication. It adds credibility that the records present the apostolic company in a very unflattering light, "slow of heart" as Jesus called them (Lk 24:25), to name just one passage. (4) Are there contradictions between the accounts and what we know from other sources, such as history and archaeology? The Gospels are rich in verifiable, details; for example, "In the fifteenth year of the reign of Tiberius Caesar, when Pontius Pilate was governor of Judea, and Herod was tetrarch of Galilee, and his brother Philip was tetrarch of the region of Ituraea and Trachonitis, and Lysanias was tetrarch of Abilene, in the high priesthood of Annas and Caiaphas, the word of God came to John" (Lk 3:1-2).[102] With such remarkable detail, it is significant that the biblical record harmonizes so well with ancient history and archaeology. For example, critical scholars doubted that Pilate existed until the "Pilate inscription" was discovered in 1961 in Caesarea.

Deceptions are more difficult to perpetrate than is generally recognized, Montgomery points out. People living at the time a fake is produced may not see a problem, but later generations can more easily tell that it fits the style of the faker's age, not the age in which it purports to have been written.[103] A perpetrator must keep his story not only consistent with what he has already said but also in line with what he thinks someone examining his story knows. He also must not give details that could be checked against a contrary source—clearly not the strategy of the Gospel writers, as verses like Luke 3:1-2 (above) attest.

---

[102]Montgomery, *History, Law, and Christianity*, pp. 76–80. He says (p. 76 n. 16) his fourfold test draws from Patrick L. McCloskey and Ronald L. Schoenberg, *Criminal Law Advocacy* (New York: Matthew Bender, 1984), vol. 5, para. 12.01 [b].

[103]Montgomery, *Tractatus*, 3.2921, p. 80. Montgomery quotes Lord Hailsham of St. Marylebone (no publication information).

Alternate attempts to explain the resurrection have failed. Militant atheistic scholar Antony Flew (before coming to believe in God)[104] argued that Christians simply prefer the resurrection as a biological miracle over the psychological miracle of the disciples dying for what they knew was a lie. But for Montgomery this completely misses the point that it is a matter of evidence. There is no evidence that the disciples were psychologically aberrant; rather, they provide "tremendously powerful testimonial evidence" that Jesus rose from the dead.[105] Hugh Schonfield claims in *The Passover Plot* that Jesus induced his crucifixion and drugged himself, surviving just long enough to convince the disciples that he had risen. This does not fit with Jesus' moral teachings and does not explain what happened to Jesus' body. As Montgomery characterizes it, Erich Von Daniken's *Chariots of the Gods?* suggests that "Jesus was a kind of Martian cleverly dressed in a Jesus suit." While such theories may be, strictly speaking, possible, they are not probable. Montgomery likens accepting such claims to a jury finding a defendant innocent on the grounds that invisible Martians did the crime.[106]

The early church used two major themes in apologetics, Montgomery says. They appealed to miracles when interacting with the Gentiles, and prophecy when interacting with the Jewish community.[107] The two themes connected in that central miracles such as the virgin birth had also appeared in prophecy.

Today, any charismatic appeals to the miracle of "prophetic" speaking in tongues is inadequate as an apologetic since such speech "lacks the structural characteristics of language," and the unbeliever has no way of knowing what was said.[108] Apologetic appeals to end-time prophecy are also problematic because we lack the perspective to link current events to prophecy. But prophecies fulfilled in a remarkable way in history are very effective, especially those fulfilled at Christ's first coming.

The Old Testament was finished before he was born, so there is no way the prophecies could have been written to fit his life. And the Jewish leaders knew both the Scriptures and the life of Christ, so any lack of fit would have been

---

[104]Antony Flew with Roy Abraham Varghese, *There Is A God: How the World's Most Notorious Atheist Changed His Mind* (San Francisco: HarperOne, 2008). Interview with Gary Habermas, "Atheist Becomes Theist: Exclusive Interview with Former Atheist Antony Flew," 2004, Biola University website, http://www.epsociety.org/library/articles.asp?pid=33.

[105]Montgomery, *Human Rights and Human Dignity*, p. 152.

[106]Ibid., p. 152.

[107]John Warwick Montgomery, *Christ Our Advocate: Studies in Polemical Theology, Jurisprudence, and Canon Law* (Bonn, Germany: Verlag für Kultur und Wissenschaft, 2002), p. 255. He recommends Mark Edwards et al., eds., *Apologetics in the Roman Empire: Pagans, Jews, and Christians* (Oxford: Oxford University Press, 1999).

[108]Montgomery, *Christ Our Advocate*, p. 256.

loudly noted. To calculate the likelihood of two events occurring together you multiply the likelihood of them occurring separately. If the chance of rolling a two on one die is one in six, or 1/6, then the probability of rolling a two on each of two dice is $1/6 \times 1/6$, which is 1/36. If we suppose that the chances of Christ fulfilling a prophecy is one in four then the probability of fulfilling twenty-five prophecies is $1/4^{25}$, or one in a thousand trillion.[109] Such a calculation is very reasonable because one chance in four is extremely conservative, and the prophecies do not overlap in a way that fulfilling one would automatically fulfill another or make it more likely to happen. Jesus could not have deliberately fulfilled them, and any attempt by the apostles to alter the facts of Jesus' life to fit the prophecies would have been caught by hostile people who knew both the Old Testament prophecies and the details of Jesus' life.[110]

To answer some of the challenges to the historicity of the Gospel accounts of Jesus' trial Montgomery recounts samples of the work of Jean Imbert, a legal scholar at the University of Paris.[111] First, it is claimed that the legalistic Pharisees would never have permitted the violations of legal procedure portrayed in the Gospel accounts, so they are likely nonhistorical. But Imbert cites several other known breaches of justice committed in trials at the time of Jesus. Besides, the trial was intended as a "pseudo-judicial" means to reduce Jesus' prestige among Jews. Second, it is claimed that a trial could not have taken place entirely in one night and the following day because it would have been a major violation of the Mishnah. But a discovery of a "Jubilees-Qumran" calendar allows for the three-day chronology of the events. This has been supported by the discovery of manuscripts that show that the Essene festival cycle began with Passover on Tuesday evening, which confirms Tuesday as the day for the Last Supper and the trial chronology. Third, it is said that the Gospel of John has no details about the trial, and thus the Romans were solely responsible for the verdict and Jews had nothing to do with it. Imbert replies that John knew that the details were amply described by the other Gospels, written earlier. Fourth, being only a procurator, Pilate could not have handed down a death penalty; and from what

[109]Ibid., p. 262; and Montgomery, "Why Human Rights Are Impossible Without Religion," in *A Place for Truth: Leading Thinkers Explore Life's Hardest Questions*, ed. Dallas Willard (Downers Grove, IL: InterVarsity Press, 2010), pp. 275-76.

[110]Montgomery, *Christ Our Advocate*, p. 265. He also recommends his *Where Is History Going?* and *Human Rights and Human Dignity*.

[111]John Warwick Montgomery, "The Trial of Christ Defended: Jean Imbert's *Le Proces De Jesus*," in *Christ Our Advocate*, pp. 309-12; reprinted from "Jesus Takes the Stand: An Argument to Support the Gospel Accounts," *Christianity Today*, April 9, 1982.

we could guess of the personal dynamics, he probably would not have turned Jesus over to Herod nor would he have been pressured to release Barabbas rather than Jesus. In answer, the Pilate inscription, discovered in 1961, shows him to also be a "prefect," which means that he had the authority to deliver the death penalty. Also, there is evidence that Roman governors could refer the accused to a local magistrate, and there is an entire book of examples of Roman provincial governors yielding to pressure from the crowd in delivering sentences.

Anyone making a rational decision on the resurrection must see where the evidence points. We cannot accept Hume's dismissal of it on the mere conviction that this sort of thing never happens.[112] Were we to reason that way we would never accept scientific discoveries, such as that inert gases really can combine with other elements under certain conditions.

Doesn't verifying an event as unusual as a resurrection present special difficulties? No, it is as simple as verifying that a man was dead and is now alive. We are certainly competent to verify whether someone is dead or alive. And the better the individual is known the more sure is the conclusion that the person who was dead is the same as the person who is now alive. Eyewitnesses like Thomas are therefore unimpeachable.[113]

Besides evidence, there is simple logic. Montgomery recounts the argument made by Frank Morrison (who came to Christ investigating the resurrection). If Jesus did not rise someone must have stolen the body. The only people involved were the Roman authorities, the Jewish religious leaders and the disciples. But the Romans would not because they wanted no trouble in the region, and the Jewish leaders would not because they wanted to preserve their influence. Yet the disciples would not have stolen the body and then died for a lie.[114]

Some claim that there are conflicting interpretations for the resurrection, but Montgomery replies that explanations come from either the one raised or someone else. Clearly, the one raised is in a far better position to give us the proper interpretation. He adds facetiously that until Von Daniken or someone else rises from the dead, he will prefer Jesus' account of what happened.[115]

Jesus validates not only the traditional Christian view of the resurrection but also the entire Old Testament, because he regarded it as divinely authoritative.

---

[112]Montgomery, *Human Rights and Human Dignity*, p. 151.

[113]Ibid., pp. 155–56.

[114]Ibid., pp. 151–52. Frank Morrison, *Who Moved the Stone?* (Grand Rapids: Zondervan, 1987).

[115]Montgomery, *Human Rights and Human Dignity*, p. 158.

And because he said the Holy Spirit would enable his apostles to infallibly recall his teachings (Jn 14:26; 16:12-15), he validated their future teachings.[116]

The picture that emerges from the New Testament is consistent: Jesus is divine. This conclusion challenges the remarkably diverse images of him produced by a number of critical scholars.[117]

LITERARY APOLOGETICS

While Montgomery believes in the value of a legal case enhanced by natural theology, he proposes that an entirely different approach may be useful for a growing number of people. While some are "tough-minded" in that they are searching for objective facts, others are "tender-minded," seeing life in subjective and existential terms. They are not interested in things like the second law of thermodynamics, and conclude that apologetics is "an arid and irrelevant activity."[118] They may even be (unwisely) running from objectivity to seek answers that may be "hidden in the subjective depths of their own souls."[119]

Romans 1:20-21 indicates that an awareness of God can be suppressed but not eradicated. Perhaps that sense of the Creator, and such things as the lost relationship with him and the need for redemption, well up in the individual and society, resulting in their expression through enduring and pervasive themes in literature. Evidence of this may be the many studies of folklore and myth that show remarkably common themes across cultures. Mircea Eliade (1907–1986), for example, observed that there is a common yearning for paradise at the beginning and end of history.[120] Others have documented nearly universal accounts of a widespread flood and the recurrent theme of slaying "monsters." Claude Levi-Strauss (1908–2009) concludes that there is "an astounding similarity between myths collected in widely different regions of the world,"[121] a fact backed up by other researchers.

Montgomery suggests ways in which a folktale could be linked to Gospel themes. In the story of Sleeping Beauty, a princess is put into a deathlike trance

[116]Ibid., p. 159.
[117]Montgomery, *Where Is History Going?*, pp. 54–63.
[118]John Warwick Montgomery, "Neglected Apologetic Styles," in *Evangelical Apologetics: Selected Essays from the 1995 Evangelical Theological Society Convention*, ed. Michael Bauman, David Hall and Robert Newman (Camp Hill, PA: Christian Publications, 1996), p. 119.
[119]Ibid., p. 126.
[120]Mircea Eliade, "The Yearning for Paradise in Primitive Tradition," in *Myth and Mythmaking*, ed. Henry A. Murray (New York: George Braziller, 1960), p. 73; quoted in Montgomery, "Neglected Apologetic Styles," p. 128.
[121]Claude Lévi-Strauss, *Structural Anthropology* (New York: Basic Books, 1963), 1:208; quoted in Montgomery, *Tractatus*, 6.41, p. 188.

by an evil witch, and impenetrable brambles grow up around her castle. The tragedy is resolved only when, in fulfillment of a prophecy, a prince raises her up with a kiss of love. There is a marriage feast, and "they lived happily ever after." Montgomery likens the princess to humanity, the witch to the devil and the prince to Christ. The princess cannot save herself, nor can anyone in the castle; salvation must come from outside the castle, which represents the world. "Incorporated into this tale is the Fall of man, with its consequences for the entire physical world; the act of transcendent divine redemption; and the marriage supper of the Lamb at the end time," says Montgomery. Such stories, which typically begin with "once upon a time," are fulfilled by the gospel, a real event in history.[122]

What is to prevent the listener from regarding the gospel itself as just another story that itself fits the patterns of folktales? The answer is that here there is a convincing body of evidence that it is actual history.

Montgomery suggests that the Christian literary apologist can craft stories from archetypal motifs that "are sure to strike to the deep reaches of man's being and point him toward the Christ who fulfilled the myths and legends of the world."[123] He sees in C. S. Lewis and J. R. R. Tolkien[124] highly effective examples of just such writing. Montgomery's theological doctorate argues that a seventeenth-century Lutheran pastor was not heretical and syncretistic when he wrote an alchemical allegory of the gospel story. Rather, he was communicating the gospel in a creative, mythic way.[125] That Montgomery's interest in such subjective apologetics goes back so early in his academic career shows that this is no mere side interest. He sees it as a manifestation of how Christ is relevant to every aspect of life.

There is a deeper reason why such a literary approach can connect to people—we all have the same needs, which can be satisfied only by Christian truth. As humans, we all need an integrated personality, genuine fellowship, the assurance that life has purpose and ultimate purpose. Just as themes in literature point to universal human problems and solutions, so some psychology and religious phenomenology "reinforce the biblical claim that only God's way of salvation can provide the integrated

[122]Ibid., 6.42-6424, pp. 186–87.
[123]Montgomery, "Neglected Apologetic Styles," p. 129.
[124]See John Warwick Montgomery, "Tolkien: Lord of the Occult?," in *Christ the Centre*, pp. 393–99.
[125]See John Warwick Montgomery, *Cross and Crucible: Johann Valentin Andrea (1586–1654)*, *Phoenix of the Theologians*, 2 vols. (The Hague: Martinus Nijhoff, 1973). Ross Clifford notes that UC Berkeley historian William J. Bouwsma favorably reviewed Montgomery's interpretation. Clifford, *John Warwick Montgomery's Legal Apologetic*, p. 184 n. 96. (Andrea's work is titled *The Chemical Wedding of Christian Rosenkreutz*.)

personality for which we seek."[126] While not endorsing broader aspects of their varied and conflicting views, Montgomery sees some psychologists as uncovering universal needs and problems, if only in a fragmentary way. Jacques Lacan (1901–1981), for example, "saw the self-centered heart of the fallen human condition." Carl Jung (1875–1961), while rejecting what he regarded as Freud's overly simplistic view of human motivation, identified a common psychic life expressed in universal symbolic patterns, such as "the Old Wise Man (a God symbol), the Earth Mother, the Persona (the social mask behind which dwells the true ego)" and so on. Jung saw humans as fractured and in need of healing, which can come through "symbols of transformation," principally the cross (though Jung understood it psychologically).[127] It is these common motifs that Eliade and others find across cultures. For Montgomery these represent common human needs, "the very ones for which biblical religion offers a solution."[128] (Recall that E. J. Carnell incorporated into his apologetic broad human needs and experiences to which Christianity is the answer, though he made it part of his overall strategy to show that Christianity is true because without contradiction it fits empirical facts and can be lived without hypocrisy.)

CHRISTIANITY AS THE GROUNDING FOR HUMAN RIGHTS

Everyone is for human rights, even brutal dictators, notes Montgomery. But the grounding is unclear, and setting it forth provides an apologetic approach that is "vital for the effective proclamation of the Gospel in the secular age."[129]

From the Greeks to the eighteenth century the West operated under the theory of natural law. It was "natural" because it was thought that laws could be patterned according to the way things are, which in religious terms means the way God made them. The view joined human nature and the nature of the world with ethics and law. It also made ethics and law a rational thing in that we can reason from the order of things to the way we ought to act. Because laws thus followed an objective order, they could be evaluated objectively, from outside the legal system, or even from outside the nation that made them. So even kings did not have absolute power, because it was expected that their laws would conform to the objective moral order, to natural law.

---

[126]Montgomery, *Tractatus*, 6.3, p. 184.

[127]Ibid., 6.321–6.324, pp. 185-87.

[128]Ibid., 6.36, p. 186.

[129]John Warwick Montgomery, "God and Other Lawmakers," p. 21. See also Montgomery, "The Need for Epistemological Sophistication in Human Rights Teaching," in *Christ the Centre*, pp. 194–209.

A classic example of the view is the Justinian Code, constructed in the sixth century under Emperor Justinian, who put Greco-Roman law into a Christian framework. In brief, it required all to live honestly, to harm no one and to give each what is due them. But in later centuries, as the Christian worldview began to recede from dominance, there arose differing ideas of the natural order, which was supposed to ground natural law. It could be interpreted differently. This was tragically illustrated later under the Nazis, who put on the gate to the Buchenwald concentration camp a version of the third principle, to each what is due them.[130]

Natural law theory began to run into trouble about the eighteenth century, when an effort was made to describe the natural state of humanity, prior to forming any government. Thomas Hobbes (1588–1679) famously described primitive life as "nasty, brutish, and short," and that people in societies agreed to give up their individual rights to a government in order to stay safe from each other. Jean-Jacques Rousseau (1712–1778) held nearly the opposite view, that people are born free and enter a social contract to secure both their freedom and protection. John Locke, who greatly influenced the founders of the United States, believed that only some rights are given up to the state, others are inalienable, and because they are not grounded in the state, the state cannot rightly take them away (an idea reflected in the Declaration of Independence).

In the nineteenth century natural law gave way to legal positivism, which held that laws are no more than products of the state. There is no higher authority for them, and thus no way to critique them from a higher standard. But a major weakness was revealed after the Second World War, when putting Nazi war criminals on trial. The Nazis argued that they had merely acted according to the laws of their country. If legal positivism is correct that there is no higher authority by which to judge a country's laws, on what basis could the war criminals be held accountable? Supreme Court justice Robert Jackson was on the prosecution team and grounded the basis in international law and "principles of jurisprudence of philosophy of law, which are the assumptions of civilization." But Montgomery points out that there was no attempt to show where such assumptions come from, nor how they can be identified or justified.[131]

Those who held to natural law and depended on the conscience to determine right from wrong needed to realize that the conscience can be distorted and is

---

[130]*Jadem das Seine*, "to each his own." Other such camps had *Arbeit Macht Frei*, "work makes free." Criticism of natural law also appears in Montgomery, *Tractatus*, 5.3–4, pp. 167–68.
[131]Montgomery, "God and Other Lawmakers," p. 22.

somewhat dependent on culture. In the novel *Oliver Twist*, for example, Fagin trains street children to steal and makes them feel guilty if they do not bring him back things of value.

One of the best-known attempts to ground law in modern times was provided by John Rawls (1921–2002), who echoed Immanuel Kant's maxim to accept as law only what we could wish everyone would do (which Montgomery finds too vague; someone, such as a sadomasochist, might wish everyone behaved the way he does).[132] Ideally, people should be blind to their personal situation, including things such as their age, religion, wealth, abilities and the like. Then reason and self-interest would lead each to agree to the proper foundations of a state, roughly, that each has a right to as much liberty as anyone else, things should be arranged to benefit the least advantaged and all positions should be open to everyone.[133] Montgomery says, first, Rawls's attempt fails because people will always be aware of their own situation and figure out how to act in their own interests, "and there is no point in doing it in theory if in practice people will always operate in terms of their special advantages and privileges."[134] Second, even if individuals and nations agreed to follow such requirements, there is no guarantee they would. Third, the worst dictators are not going to agree to anything of the sort. Montgomery imagines Genghis Khan reacting to the suggestion that he become an enlightened ruler. He would reply that he is going to continue to terrorize those who can't stop him and that while others enjoy things like collecting stamps, he enjoys raping and pillaging. He would then proceed to bounce the person suggesting all this on his head.[135]

Two things are needed for human rights, according to Montgomery. We need absolute ethical guidelines given to us from above the human race, and we need a changed heart so that we self-centered humans can actually follow the guidelines. Christianity offers both. The objective evidence for the resurrection and the reliability of the Scriptures offer people a basis for entering into a relationship with God, and when they do, they "really are more interested in other people than they are in themselves."[136] Montgomery notes that slavery of various sorts (which continues to exist today) was not effectively addressed by natural law and neo-Kantian arguments, whereas the evangelical Christian arguments of people like Granville Sharp, John Newton and William Wilberforce were effective in

[132]Montgomery, *Tractatus*, 5.541, p. 172. He finds other deficiencies; see 5.53–5.572.
[133]My paraphrase of Rawls.
[134]Montgomery, "Why Human Rights Are Impossible Without Religion," p. 270.
[135]Ibid., pp. 270–71.
[136]Ibid., p. 278.

their day. There must be a transcendent argument—of the right kind—and a genuine change in the human heart. What is true of slavery is true of various practices that assault human dignity.[137]

A revelational philosophy of human rights corrects the deficiencies of other major approaches. Utilitarianism, which claims that we should bring about the greatest good for the greatest number, fails by leaving too much undefined. Christianity is specific; for example, it clearly defines the good. Legal positivism fails to give a transcendent basis for law, which Christianity offers. Natural law leaves human nature and the content of natural law undefined, whereas Christianity defines both. Sociological jurisprudence falls on the naturalistic fallacy (we cannot derive what ought to be by merely describing what is factually the case), and it cannot establish absolutes (what ought to be done by all peoples at all times). Christianity states what ought to be in absolute terms. The neo-Kantianism of Rawls and others cannot ground what it assumes up front, but in Christianity universal rules are proved by evidence and sanctioned by the last judgment. Marxism tries to change humans by changing their environment, offering no way to change their motives. Christianity offers personal redemption, which changes their motives and thereby their external condition. Approaches based on policy orientation cannot go beyond a sociological basis and leave the human heart unchanged. Christianity offers sound policies that are grounded in revelation, and a new heart by which to keep them.[138]

Montgomery finds that the Bible includes many of the basic principles of human rights, including impartial tribunals (Mal 2:9); a fair hearing (Ex 22:9); no double jeopardy (Nahum 1:9); and no discrimination before the law as to race, gender or condition of servitude, wealth or citizenship (e.g., Ex 12:49; Gal 3:28; Jas 2:1-7).[139]

Christians have certainly not been blameless in living out biblical morality; the problem, however, is not with the biblical guidelines, but with lack of obedience to them (unlike other religions, such as Islam, which Montgomery regards as discriminating against women and commanding cruel punishments).[140]

Montgomery uses his legal abilities to deal with a common stumbling block, the use of torture to extract confessions in witchcraft trials. The use of torture has long

---

[137]John Warwick Montgomery, "Slavery, Human Dignity, and Human Rights," in *Christ the Centre*, pp. 438-39.

[138]Montgomery, *Human Rights and Human Dignity*, p. 183. Adapted from his chart.

[139]For his complete list, Montgomery, *Tractatus*, 5.83, p. 176-77.

[140]Montgomery, *Human Rights and Human Dignity*, p. 185.

been a source of criticism of the church.[141] To put it in perspective, the number of prosecutions were much lower that is commonly alleged. Torture used to extract confessions was originally a Roman, not a Christian practice, and the church initially condemned it. It disappeared with the fall of Rome but was again practiced when Roman law was revived due to political ambitions, becoming common again by the fourteenth century. Tragically, it was adopted by the church when it accepted Roman law as a model for canon law. While torture was used in Continental law, it was never officially accepted in the common law system used in England and exported to American, though there were some lapses. Montgomery finds tragic irony in the fact that Christians had earlier endured horrific torture at the hands of Roman authorities, only to eventually adopt the same methods toward doctrinal deviants. He admits this is a failure of the church, but at least it is not a failure in Christ's teachings—merely a failure to follow his teachings.

MODERN THINKERS ON MIRACLES

The possibility of miracles and the evidentiary weight that can be given to them has been a matter of great interest to evidentialists and others, and this section adds the valuable insights of other thinkers.[142] Of course classical apologists and even some combinationalists are also interested in miracles. As Geisler puts it, "If miracles have no evidential value, then there is no objective, historical evidence to support the claims of historic, orthodox Christianity."[143] Since prophecy and the resurrection are sometimes regarded as miracles, it is easy to see the importance of the subject.

But classical apologists are less confident than evidentialists that miracles can point to proper conclusions about religion without first setting the up the worldview. It is the overall case for the theistic God, established through theistic arguments, that can show the possibility of miracles, says Geisler. But the only way to show that miracles are impossible is to disprove the existence of God (which, we could add, is a daunting task). Then, only history can show the actuality of a miracle. Geisler says further that theism makes miracles probable.[144]

In the historical investigation of biblical archaeology, prophecy and miracles,

[141]Montgomery, *The Law Above the Law*, chap. two, "Witch Trial Theory and Practice," pp. 58–83.
[142]Here we depart somewhat from the format by adding additional thinkers.
[143]Norman L. Geisler, "Miracles, Apologetic Value of," in *Baker Encyclopedia of Christian Apologetics* (Grand Rapids: Baker, 1999), p. 452. His encyclopedia has eight articles and forty pages on miracles.
[144]Geisler, "Miracles Apologetic Value of," p. 450.

classical and evidential apologists overlap and affirm each other's work. (Even John Frame, a presuppositionalist, appreciates the historical work of classical apologist William Lane Craig, evidentialist Gary Habermas and a number of others.)[145]

Gary Habermas, a prolific evidentialist, agrees that it is helpful to provide a broader conceptual context, which makes miracles more probable. He finds that the extensive testimony of those with near-death experiences provides background support for the idea of a resurrection, as does the extraordinary life and claims of Jesus Christ. He also allows that theistic arguments can provide a more congenial context, and he adds that he does not think he has ever known an evidentialist who opposes them. But whereas classical apologists often argue first for God's existence and then the resurrection, evidentialists do not think it is necessary to go in that order. In fact, "Historical evidences are not only a legitimate avenue of argument for Christian theism, but, on many occasions, they may be the best way to proceed."[146]

It is important to consider Hume's argument against miracles as found in his *An Enquiry Concerning Human Understanding* (1748), since to this day a remarkable number of discussions interact with it. Its publication turned biblical miracles from an apologetic asset to a liability. Since evidentialists and a number of other apologetic approaches deal with miracles, it is important to examine Hume's challenges.

As with many important works, there is some disagreement over exactly what he meant,[147] but we can summarize a couple of main points. According to Hume, a wise person proportions his or her level of belief to the amount of evidence. (Recall that Plantinga spends a great deal of time refuting this view.) The claim that a miracle has occurred competes with our extensive background knowledge that the laws of nature always hold. It is reasonable to believe the miracle only if it would be a bigger miracle that the report of it is false.[148] Further counting against any miracle claim is that things we have not experienced resemble those we have, and we have to prefer the claim that has the greatest number of observations supporting it.[149] He says, "There never was a miraculous event estab-

---

[145]John Frame, "Presuppositional Apologetics," in Cowan, *Five Views on Apologetics*, p. 229 n. 39.

[146]Gary Habermas, "Closing Remarks," in Cowan, *Five Views on Apologetics*, pp. 337–38.

[147]See, e.g., David Johnson, *Hume, Holism, and Miracles*, Cornell Studies in the Philosophy of Religion (Ithaca, NY: Cornell University Press, 1999).

[148]David Hume, *An Enquiry Concerning Human Understanding* 10.1: "That no testimony is sufficient to establish a miracle, unless the testimony be of such a kind, that its falsehood would be more miraculous, than the fact, which it endeavors to establish."

[149]Ibid., 10.2.

lished on so full an evidence."[150] No miracle has ever been a attested by sufficient number of people who have enough "good sense," learning and integrity so as not to be deceived or to deceive, nor have the supposed miracles been performed in a public way and in a "celebrated part of the world as to render detection unavoidable." Besides, people love to hear and tell stories, which allows bogus miracle claims to proliferate.[151]

Responses to Hume began early and have remained vigorous. First off, Hume seems to accept a version of what is called the straight rule, that the likelihood of something being the case in the future is the same as its frequency in the past.[152] So if 90 percent of *a*'s in the past have been *b*'s, then the likelihood of that being the case in the future is 90 percent. But does this guarantee that if all the cases in the past have been a certain way that all the cases in the future will be that way as well? Therein lies a problem. Two of Hume's contemporary critics were Nonconformist pastors as well as first-rate mathematicians Richard Price and Thomas Bayes (who came up with the theorem used extensively by Richard Swinburne). As modern historian and philosopher of science John Earman retells it, the upshot is that no matter how many past *a*'s have been *b*'s it does not follow that all future *a*'s will be *b*'s. So it doesn't follow that because we have never seen a natural law violated by a miracle in the past we won't see one in the future.[153]

The classic example showing that predictions can be fallible when based solely on past observation is the conclusion that all swans must be white since only white swans had been observed. But some who had argued from higher knowledge that not all have to be white were vindicated in 1697 when black swans were discovered in Australia. This kind of reasoning keeps us from concluding that our car will never break down because it never has before, or that we will never die because we have never died before. Though these examples entail no violations of natural law, they show the risk of depending on a narrow class of past observations to determine what is possible in the future.

---

[150]Ibid.

[151]Ibid.

[152]For a more modern and sophisticated form of the straight rule, see Hans Reichenbach, *The Theory of Probability: An Inquiry into the Logical and Mathematical Foundations of the Calculus of Probability*, trans. E. H. Hutten and M. Reichenbach (Berkeley: University of California Press, 1949). Note too modern criticisms of his views. For an accessible discussion, see Clark Glymour and Frederick Eberhardt, "Hans Reichenbach," in *The Stanford Encyclopedia of Philosophy* (winter 2012 ed.), ed. Edward N. Zalta, http://plato.stanford.edu/archives/win2012/entries/reichenbach/.

[153]John Earman, *Hume's Abject Failure: The Argument Against Miracles* (New York: Oxford University Press, 2000), pp. 24–30.

In a sense, the classical apologist uses knowledge from higher up in his worldview, made available by theistic arguments. The strict evidentialist is more likely to depend on the believability of the testimony that a miracle occurred.

In his quest for pure empiricism (the view that all knowledge comes from the senses), Hume did away with the idea that we can know something causes something else—precisely because it is an idea, not something we can know from our senses (i.e., we do not see that *a* caused *b*, we conclude it). So rather than argue that miracles are impossible, he claimed that they are not believable. He comes close to saying they are impossible, however, when he implies they are not believable because it is unlikely they happened. Hume argues in part one of his chapter that even if there were a report of a miracle where credibility were not an issue, a wise person would reject it because of the vast amounts of evidence that natural laws are consistent. Then in part two he argues that in fact there never has been a credible report of a miracle.

Of course Hume's argument is only one way of attacking miracles. Baruch Spinoza (1632–1677) implied that miracles are impossible, claiming that the universe is deterministic. (As a rationalist he had no qualms with making claims about the ultimate nature of the universe.) The Newtonian idea that the universe and its natural laws are deterministic was made obsolete by quantum mechanics, and especially the Heisenberg uncertainty principle (1927). According to the principle, the orbits of subatomic particles are unpredictable. Though some like Albert Einstein (1879–1955) said we merely do not yet know enough to make the predictions, by contrast most concluded that the universe is not deterministic after all. This makes it much harder to argue against the possibility of a miracle, as Montgomery emphasizes.[154]

Hume's argument that no miracle is believable leaves out the possibility of physical evidence. Often, besides direct testimony, others may also have access to, for example, the body of someone who died (e.g., Herod, Acts 12:23, was struck by worms; see Josephus, *Antiquities of the Jews* 17.6). In the case of the resurrection, no one could produce Christ's body, a kind of negative physical evidence. And Hume did not consider the force of multiple witnesses saying the same thing.

Hume's argument that we have to pit the report of a miracle against our

---

[154]Craig acknowledges the change from Newtonian determinacy to Quantum indeterminacy, but adds, "Any event that would be miraculous in Newtonian physics would be so extraordinarily improbable even in quantum physics that it would have to be regarded as miraculous if it actually occurred." William Lane Craig, "Doctrine of Creation (Part 16)" (transcript of William Lane Craig's Defender's Two class), *Reasonable Faith*, http://www.reasonablefaith.org/defenders-2-podcast/transcript/s8-16.

knowledge that such things do not happen is much too far-reaching. If in general we could not believe the report that something highly unusual has happened we would cut ourselves off from a good deal of knowledge. In science, for example, we would never believe that light could be both a wave and a particle, that an inert gas could form a compound, or that nonconductors pass electricity at very low temperatures. We would not even believe some events in the news, or history. There is a well-documented account in *Life* magazine of an explosion that destroyed a church in Nebraska in 1950. Not one of the fifteen choir members was hurt because each was late for a different reason. The odds were calculated at a million to one. Granted, their tardiness violated no natural laws; nevertheless, on Hume's account we should not believe it.[155] Hume's notion that we ought not believe the highly improbable elements of the Bible was parodied in 1819 by Bishop Richard Whately in *Historic Doubts Relative to Napoleon Buonoparte.*[156]

Hume's very calculations of the odds shows some bias. The only way he can say that miracles are so improbable is by assuming in the first place that they do not happen. He says, for example, "It is a miracle, that a dead man should come to life; because that has never been observed in any age or country."[157] But that is the very question at issue: Has it occurred? An Internet search turns up various news stories of some fourteen people who were thought dead but came back to life.[158] Hume assumes what he is supposed to prove, which is a logical fallacy known as begging the question.

When he claims that there has never been a miracle attested by a sufficient number of people who had enough "good sense," learning and integrity so that they would not be deceived or deceive, he is making a sweeping and remarkable claim that cannot be substantiated. How much learning is required to determine that someone was dead and is now alive? (Roman soldiers who performed executions were quite experience at determining whether someone was dead.) When he also demands that the purported miracle be performed in a celebrated part of the world, he is ignoring the fact that the most important miracle of Christianity was performed in Jerusalem, a major city of the ancient world. And when he says that

---

[155]George Edeal, "Why the Choir Was Late," *Life*, March 27, 1950, pp. 19–23. I was reminded of the story by Francis J. Beckwith, *David Hume's Argument Against Miracles* (Lanham, MD: University Press of America, 1989), p. 33.

[156]Richard Whately, *Historic Doubts Relative to Napoleon Buonoparte* (London: Longmans, Green, 1865); available at *Project Gutenberg*, www.gutenberg.org/files/18087/18087-h/18087-h.htm.

[157]Hume, *Enquiry* 10.1.

[158]For example, "Seven Bizarre Tales of People Coming Back from the Dead," *The Week*, http://theweek.com/article/index/228986/7.

people love to tell and hear stories, that may be true to some extent, but many religious people regard lying and even misleading exaggeration to be a sin. Colin
Brown says that Hume's requirements would "preclude the testimony of anyone
without a Western university education, who lived outside a major cultural center
in Western Europe prior to the sixteenth century, and who was not a public figure."[159]

Key Terms

Ancient documents rule. A rule stating that ancient documents are an exception to the hearsay rule, since they cannot be cross-examined. Montgomery
follows nineteenth-century legal scholar Simon Greenleaf, who says that ancient
documents will get preliminary acceptance if they show no evidence of tampering and have maintained "reasonable custody."

Apologetics from above. The method of beginning with the "higher" interpretive issues in a worldview. Presuppositionalists insist that apologetics must
begin by embracing Christian assumptions and convictions, at least provisionally, in the sense that the non-Christian should try looking at the world
through Christian glasses to see how it makes much more sense of everything.
Classical apologists believe it is necessary to begin with a theistic worldview.

Apologetics from below. The method, advocated by Montgomery, and Luther
before him, beginning apologetics with Christ and the biblical record.

External reliability. A document's trustworthiness based on evidence outside
itself.

Hearsay rule. Statements made out of court are not allowed into evidence
because they cannot be cross-examined.

Internal reliability. A document's trustworthiness based on its claim to be a
primary source and its giving evidence of being such.

Parole evidence rule. A legal principle that certain documents must be considered
by a court apart from any other documents that may claim to challenge them.

Retroduction. Another term for abduction, or inference to the best explanation. We see facts (that typically are not in doubt), and draw a conclusion to
the best explanation.

Tender-minded. Those who see life in subjective and existential terms and are
thus not interested in theistic arguments and such.

Tough-minded. Those who look for, and respond to, objective facts.

---

[159]Colin Brown, *Miracles and the Critical Mind* (Grand Rapids: Eerdmans, 1984), p. 97. Francis
Beckwith (*David Hume's Argument*, p. 50) reminded me of this quote.

Transmissional reliability. A document has been transmitted accurately from the time of its writing to our day.

THINKING IT OVER

1. How does evidentialism differ widely from the presuppositionalism of Van Til?

2. Describe how Montgomery sees facts as pointing to Christianity.

3. Why is the legal paradigm especially suited to confirming Christianity, according to Montgomery?

4. Why does Montgomery think induction is well suited to apologetics? Why does Van Til hold a different view?

5. What, in Montgomery's view, is a problematic trend in the contemporary church?

6. Illustrate how Montgomery proposes that Christianity should be destroying the foundations of false beliefs. How does his view differ from Van Til's?

7. What approach to the problem of evil does Montgomery suggest?

8. How does presuppositionalism confuse what we believe with how we know it? Montgomery proposes that instead of beginning with the _____ of our beliefs, we begin with the _____. What fields use this approach?

9. In Montgomery's view, the hypothesis comes out of the facts such that facts are self-interpreting. How is this the opposite of Van Til? How does it differ from Geisler's view?

10. How does Montgomery explain the refusal of some people to reach the proper interpretation of the facts?

11. Van Til and Montgomery agree that the non-Christian can mentally function, but they disagree as to why. What is the nature of their disagreement, and who do you think is right? Why?

12. How do Van Til and Montgomery each believe their view leaves the non-Christian without excuse?

13. How does Montgomery answer Reymond's objection that many interpretations are possible?

14. What is Montgomery's view of the various theistic arguments?

15. What does he think of Bayes's theorem? What does he prefer, and why?

16. How does apologetics "from above" contrast with apologetics "from below"?

17. Why does the case for Christianity rise to the level of legal proof?

18. If, typical of human reasoning about real-world issues, we cannot have 100 percent proof, how do we get to certainty?

19. Besides the existence of evidence, what are the spiritual dynamics of belief; that is, what is God's assurance to the sincere seeker?

20. What does Montgomery believe is the problem with making the subjective element primary, as he believes is done, for example, by Calvin and Plantinga?

21. How does Montgomery believe Van Tillians have incorrectly assessed the state of the fallen mind? What does Montgomery find inconsistent in the Van Tillian approach?

22. Which religions have a historical basis? In Montgomery's view, why is only Christianity provable?

23. What is the parole evidence rule? The hearsay rule? Why does Montgomery believe the hearsay rule is not a problem for the Gospels?

24. What is the ancient documents rule?

25. Explain external reliability, internal reliability and transmissional reliability, and how the biblical records exhibit them.

26. What can be said of the reliability of the biblical witnesses?

27. Why is deception more difficult than commonly understood?

28. What is the evidence from prophecy?

29. Who are the "tender-minded," and how might literary apologetics be of help? How can literary apologetics be used?

30. What needs are universal? How can that be used in apologetics?

31. What is natural law, and how is its ability to define right conduct limited?

32. What is Rawls's approach, and why is it doomed to fail, according to Montgomery?

33. What is needed for human rights? How does Christianity fulfill those needs?

34. What are some of the responses to Hume's view of miracles?

GOING FURTHER

Broughton, William P. *The Historical Development of Legal Apologetics: With an*

Emphasis on the Resurrection. Maitland, FL: Xulon Press, 2009.

Clifford, Ross. *John Warwick Montgomery's Legal Apologetic*. Reprint. Edmonton, AB: Canadian Institute for Law, Theology, and Public Policy, 2004.

Dembski, William, and Thomas Schirrmacher. *Tough-Minded Christianity: Honoring the Legacy of John Warwick Montgomery*. Nashville, TN: B & H, 2008.

Montgomery, John Warwick. *Christ as Centre and Circumference: Essays Theological, Cultural and Polemic*. Christian Philosophy Today 13. Eugene, OR: Wipf & Stock, 2012.

————. *Christ Our Advocate: Studies in Polemical Theology, Jurisprudence, and Canon Law*. Reprint. Bonn, Germany: Verlag für Kultur und Wissenschaft, 2002.

————. *Faith Founded on Fact: Essays in Evidential Apologetics*. Reprint. Edmonton, AB: Canadian Institute for Law, Theology, and Public Policy, 2001.

————. *Human Rights and Human Dignity*. Plano, TX: Probe Ministries, 1986.

————. "The Jury Returns: A Juridical Defense of Christianity." In *Evidence for Faith: Deciding the God Question*, edited by John Warwick Montgomery, pp. 319–41. Dallas, TX: Probe Books, 1991.

————. *The Law Above the Law*. Minneapolis: Bethany House, 1975.

————. *Myth, Allegory, and Gospel*. Minneapolis: Bethany House, 1974.

————. *The Shape of the Past: A Christian Response to Secular Philosophies of History*. Reprint. Eugene, OR: Wipf & Stock, 2008.

————. *The Suicide of Christian Theology*. Minneapolis: Bethany House, 1970.

————. *Tractatus Logico-Theologicus*. 2nd ed. Bonn, Germany: Verlag für Kultur und Wissenschaft, 2003.

————. *Where Is History Going? Essays in Support of the Historical Truth of the Christian Revelation*. Grand Rapids: Zondervan, 1969.

– 12 –

GARY HABERMAS

Christianity can be proved by widely accepted crucial facts

A number of excellent volumes have come out in recent years that advance historical apologetics, including those by N. T. Wright and Michael Licona.[1] Gary Habermas is among those who have been producing outstanding work for a long time, and he has been a steady influence on evidential apologetics since the 1970s.

Habermas chairs the Department of Philosophy at Liberty University, and has written thirty-eight books and over one hundred articles. (This chapter could easily have featured him as the main representative of evidentialism.)[2] In his dissertation and since, he has developed what he calls a "minimal facts" approach to the resurrection, which focuses on the few facts for which there is strong evidence and on which most scholars, even atheists, agree. He has composed a list of a dozen "known historical facts."[3] Even atheist Antony Flew agreed with them in his debate with Habermas. From this list he chose four to six that are so well-attested they are affirmed by the "vast majority" of scholars in the field.[4] To help

---

[1]N. T. Wright, *The Resurrection of the Son of God* (Minneapolis: Fortress Press, 2003); Michael Licona, *The Resurrection of Jesus: A New Historiographical Approach* (Downers Grove, IL: IVP Academic), 2010.

[2]I chose Montgomery partly because of the breadth of interests he has brought into the service of apologetics. I'm hoping his model of creative thinking will encourage others to think creatively as well.

[3]Gary R. Habermas, *The Historical Jesus* (Joplin, MO: College Press, 1996), pp. 158-67.

[4]Gary R. Habermas, "The Minimal Facts Approach to the Resurrection of Jesus: The Role of Method-

quantify the agreement among scholars, he has so far listed 3,400 sources[5] in English, French and German. He has made a special effort to include radical authors, even those without scholarly credentials who do not appear in scholarly publications. So if anything, his conclusions about what is accepted by the vast majority is skewed against a traditional understanding of the gospel.[6]

Classical apologist William Lane Craig commends Habermas's approach, pointing out that most nonspecialists do not realize that the central facts that "inductively imply the resurrection of Jesus are agreed upon by the majority of New Testament critics today. I know that this sounds unbelievable, but it is true." He expresses his classical apologetics view when he adds, "The problem lies not in the evidence, but in philosophical presuppositions."[7]

Habermas sees a weakness in the more traditional approach, which argues for the general trustworthiness of the Bible, then uses that to argue for various supernatural topics like its inspiration or the deity and resurrection of Christ. The problem with arguing for the reliability of an entire volume and not focusing on evidence for the particular passages in question (e.g., for the resurrection) is that we routinely accept works as generally reliable while discounting their specific unusual claims—such as those involving religion or the supernatural. He illustrates this using several highly respected ancient writers of history who include supernatural accounts that are universally discounted. Tacitus "made many allowances for Fate, the actions of the gods, and the divinity of some of the Caesars."[8] Suetonius included omens and other religious beliefs, including the divinity of five of the first dozen Caesars.[9] It would be difficult to argue from the general trustworthiness of the Bible in a way that makes its supernatural claims credible while showing that those of the other ancient authors are not. Their accounts are closer in time to many

---

ology as a Crucial Component in Establishing Historicity," *Southeastern Theological Review* 3, no. 1 (Summer 2012): 15–26, http://garyhabermas.com/articles/southeastern_theological_review /minimal-facts-methodology_08-02-2012.htm.

[5]He explains the number: "I am making no claim to having done an exhaustive study of all these resurrection sources. My figures reflect a difference between representative sources that have been catalogued in all their significant, exhausting details, to those that were surveyed more briefly, to those that are simply listed in my ongoing bibliography." Habermas, "The Minimal Facts Approach," p. 18 n. 8.

[6]Ibid., p. 18.

[7]William Lane Craig, "Closing Remarks," in Cowan, *Five Views on Apologetics*, pp. 325–26 n. 17.

[8]Gary R. Habermas, "An Evidentialist's Response" (responding to Feinberg), in Cowan, *Five Views on Apologetics*, p. 188. He cites Tacitus, *Annals* 1.11, 19, 28, 42, 55; 12.43.

[9]Habermas, "An Evidentialist's Response," p. 188. Gaius Suetonius Tranquillas, *The Twelve Caesars*, trans. Robert Graves (Baltimore, MD: Penguin, 1957): Tiberius, 74–75; Gaius Caligula, 57, 59; Titus, 10; Domitian, 23; Julius Caesar, 88; Augustus, 100; Claudius, 45–46; Nero, 56; Vespasian, 4, 25.

of the questionable events they chronicle than John's Gospel is to the life of Jesus. They used good sources, such as official records, and Suetonius even claims he used eyewitnesses.[10] Habermas says an easier way to show that the Bible's supernatural claims are credible while those of the ancient writers are not is by focusing specifically on the passages in question rather than trying to make the case from general reliability. Nevertheless, he believes that the "reliability" approach to the New Testament can be effective if it is done with exceptional care.[11]

Habermas in no way intends his approach as theology, nor as casting doubt on the reliability of the biblical record. It is strictly for apologetics.[12]

He emphasizes that, while the role of the Holy Spirit is indispensable and must draw people to faith, he uses believers in the process. Citing 1 Peter 3:15, he urges believers to be ready to answer what may be sincere questions on the part of the nonbeliever (though some who are sincerely interested might not require evidence). While the message of the gospel does not change, the method of presentation must be suited to the audience. In Acts Paul cites Scripture when talking to Jews, but when talking to Gentiles he cites secular writers and poets known to them (Acts 17:16-31). Responding to those who think it is wrong to try to support the gospel with evidence (i.e., fideists) and want only a believer's testimony, Habermas says that if it is wrong to support it with evidence it is wrong to support it with testimony. The apostles supported the gospel with evidence. Nevertheless, not everyone who resists the gospel does so for intellectual reasons, and for them, no amount of evidence will help, Habermas says.[13]

In a book he coauthored with Licona, he works with four minimal facts and adds the empty tomb as the fifth,[14] which "enjoys acceptance by an impressive

---

[10]Habermas, "An Evidentialist's Response" (responding to Feinberg), p. 189 n. 10. On Suetonius's use of eyewitnesses, Habermas cites Suetonius, *Twelve Caesars*, p. 7.

[11]Gary Habermas, personal email correspondence with the author, Nov. 1, 2013.

[12]Habermas, "The Minimal Facts Approach," p. 26.

[13]Gary R. Habermas and Michael R. Licona, *The Case for the Resurrection of Jesus* (Grand Rapids: Kregel, 2004), pp. 33-35.

[14]Habermas uses six in a more recent article: (1) "Jesus died due to the process of Roman crucifixion," (2) "once a persecutor of Christians, Paul became a believer because of an experience that he believed was an appearance of the resurrected Jesus," (3) "the disciples had already experienced what they also thought were actual appearances of the risen Jesus," (4) "the apostles' proclamation of the resurrection dates from an exceptionally early time after Jesus' death," (5) "James the brother of Jesus and a skeptic, was converted after experiencing what he also thought was an actual appearance of the risen Jesus," and (6) "the disciples were utterly transformed by their own conviction that they had seen the risen Jesus even being willing to die for this belief." Gary R. Habermas, "The Core Resurrection Data: The Minimal Facts Approach," in *Tough-Minded Christianity: Honoring the*

majority of scholars, although not by nearly all."[15] Its acceptance is not quite as high as the other four (though Craig includes it as part of his core evidence[16]). Incidentally, Habermas disagrees with Craig that we can argue from the "unnatural" qualities of the resurrection to a supernatural cause, since that allows the critic to argue that its very unnaturalness shows it is merely a freak of nature.[17] Of course, as an evidentialist, Habermas believes we can argue from evidences to the existence of God, just not from the "unnatural" nature of miracles like the resurrection.

Habermas and Licona begin with five commonsense principles that historians often use to assess the evidentiary value of testimony: (1) multiple, independent witnesses are usually better than one; (2) neutral or hostile testimony is better than friendly since there is less likelihood of favorable bias; (3) witnesses do not usually make up details that would weaken their story; (4) an eyewitness is better than a second- or thirdhand source; and (5) testimony close in time to the event is better than testimony years later.[18]

The first minimal fact is that Jesus died by crucifixion. It is attested not only by all four Gospels but also by a number of other sources. Josephus says that Pilate "had condemned him to be crucified."[19] Tacitus writes that "Christus" was crucified in the reign of Tiberius at the hands of Pilate.[20] The satirist Lucian of Samosata writes that the Christians worship a leader who was crucified.[21] Mara Bar-Serapion questions what advantage came to the Jews from the "murder of their Wise King."[22] The Talmud says that on the eve of Passover Yeshua (Jesus) "was hanged."[23] Even John Dominic Crossan, the critical scholar from the Jesus

Legacy of John Warwick Montgomery (Nashville: B & H, 2008), pp. 387–405.

[15]Habermas and Licona, *Case for the Resurrection*, p. 48.

[16]For other differences, some minor, see Gary R. Habermas, "The Resurrection of Jesus and Contemporary Scholarship: A Review Essay," *Bulletin of the Evangelical Philosophical Society* 14 no. 2 (1991): 44–51.

[17]Habermas, "An Evidentialist's Response" (to Craig), in Cowan, *Five Views on Apologetics*, p. 60. He cites William Lane Craig, *Historical Argument for the Resurrection* (Lewiston, NY: Edwin Mellen Press, 1985), p. 500.

[18]Habermas and Licona, *Case for the Resurrection*, p. 40.

[19]Josephus, *Antiquities* 18.64; quoted in Habermas and Licona, *Case for the Resurrection*, p. 49.

[20]Tacitus, *Annals* 15.44 (ca. A.D. 115); quoted in Habermas and Licona, *Case for the Resurrection*, p. 49.

[21]Lucian of Samosata, *The Death of Peregrine* 11–13 (ca. mid-second century); quoted in Habermas and Licona, *Case for the Resurrection*, p. 49.

[22]Habermas and Licona, *Case for the Resurrection*, p. 49. They note that the manuscript is currently at the London Museum, Syria mss. additional 14,658 (dated to ca. late first century to third century).

[23]The *Babylonian Talmud, Sanhedrin* 43a (probably second century); quoted in Habermas and Licona, *Case for the Resurrection*, p. 49.

Seminar, concludes, "That he was crucified is as sure as anything historical can ever be."[24]

The second fact is that Jesus' disciples believed that he rose and appeared to them. This is not the claim that he rose, only that the disciples believed it. About that there could be little doubt. They certainly claimed it, and were transformed into bold proclaimers of the gospel who were willing to suffer imprisonment, torture and death. Habermas stresses that accepting this fact does not depend on believing in the inspiration of the Bible, as important as that may be theologically. It assumes only that it is "an ancient volume of literature containing twenty-seven separate books and letters."[25] It is well accepted that all four Gospels were written in the first century, thus within seventy years of Jesus. Paul quotes a very early creed in 1 Corinthians 15:3-5, that Christ died for sins and was raised the third day, appearing to Cephas (Peter) and to the Twelve. This is backed up by the apostolic fathers, who succeeded the apostles. Irenaeus (ca. 185) says that Clement, bishop of Rome (ca. 30–100), knew the apostles. Tertullian (ca. 200) says that Polycarp knew the apostle John, and Irenaeus says Polycarp was taught by the apostles. Tertullian writes that Peter and Paul were martyred under Nero, a fact that could be found in the pubic records. In 110 Ignatius, bishop of Antioch in Syria, traveled to his martyrdom in Rome and on the way wrote letters to six churches and to his friend Polycarp, who was himself later martyred. Origen (ca. 185–254) and Eusebius (ca. 263–339) also left records, the latter's having the advantage of citing now-lost books. All of this shows, at the very least, that Christ's followers believed that Christ had risen.

This is very different from a myth, which often embellishes the facts over time. The resurrection account can be traced to the very earliest period, and it was believed so sincerely that Christians were willing to die for it. This also argues against the theory that the disciples stole the body.

The third fact is that Paul, who had been persecuting the church, was suddenly changed. He was clearly a powerful and dedicated foe yet became Christianity's great apostle. He wrote of his conversion in his letters to Corinth, Galatia and Philippi; and his testimony appears in Acts. There are also accounts from Clement of Rome, Polycarp, Tertullian, Dionysius of Corinth and Origen.[26] Paul's sudden and dramatic conversion offers powerful testimony, because he

---

[24]John Dominic Crossan, *Jesus: A Revolutionary Biography* (San Francisco: HarperSanFrancisco, 1991), p. 145; see also 154, 196, 201; quoted in Habermas and Licona, *Case for the Resurrection*, p. 49.
[25]Habermas and Licona, *Case for the Resurrection*, p. 51.
[26]Ibid., p. 279 n. 4.

claimed to have met the risen Christ, and suffered greatly for his new convictions. His conversion was not simply the outworking of inner changes already at work. He was convinced both that his sect of Judaism was true and of the need to suppress Christianity, but then he suddenly came to believe the opposite view. His suffering for it suggests he was sincere, and the radical nature suggests something beyond a natural explanation.

The fourth fact is that James the skeptical brother of Jesus suddenly changed. Like his siblings,[27] James did not believe the claims of Jesus,[28] though he seems to have been pious.

The early creedal material says that Jesus appeared to him (1 Cor 15:3-7), and by the meeting in Acts 1:14 he was among the believers. Later he appears as the leader of the Jerusalem church, at the center of Christianity (Acts 15:12-21; cf. Gal 1:19). He was so convinced of his beliefs that he died a martyr, as is attested by Josephus, Hegesippus and Clement of Alexandria.[29] As with Paul, clearly, something happened to James.

The fifth fact, the empty tomb, is not accepted quite as widely as the other four and so is treated separately. Nevertheless, at the time they he and Licona wrote the book, Habermas found that 75 percent of scholars believed that the tomb was empty.[30] After the crucifixion and burial in Jerusalem (we could add, *pace* Hume,[31] not an out-of-the-way place), the Christian movement could have been stopped immediately by its many Jewish and Roman enemies by simply pulling out the body of Jesus. But not one critic has ever suggested that happened. One recent suggestion is that, since the public proclamation of the gospel began at Pentecost, fifty days from the Passover crucifixion, the body had already decomposed beyond recognition. There would have been no point in bringing it out. But that ignores the fact that the dry local climate slows decomposition, and at the very least, the hair, stature and certainly the wounds would have been clear (a fact verified by the physician in charge at the medical examiner's office in Virginia,

---

[27]Habermas and Licona (ibid., p. 284 n. 16) remind us of Mt 12:46-50; Mk 3:31-35; Lk 8:19-21; Jn 2:12; 7:3, 5, 10; Acts 1:13-14; 1 Cor 9:5; Gal 1:19.

[28]Ibid., p. 68. Mk 3:21, 31; 6:3-4; Jn 7:5.

[29]Ibid., p. 68. On the genuineness of the Josephus passage, see p. 284 n. 17.

[30]Ibid., p. 70. Note that after the book he greatly expanded the number of sources he surveyed to 3,400. Habermas, "The Minimal Facts Approach," p. 18.

[31]Hume said in his *Enquiry* 10.2 that suspicious reports tend to spread in "country places and provincial towns," and "among ignorant and barbarous nations." Jerusalem hardly fits the profile. For an online copy of his work, see the website *Eighteenth-Century Studies*, http://18th.eserver .org/hume-enquiry.html#10.2.

even in their damp climate, which speeds decomposition).[32] Had a corpse in any condition been pulled out of the tomb, Christianity would have been very seriously damaged, and the incident would have been mentioned in hostile accounts. When critics charged that the disciples stole the body (Mt 28:12-13; Justin Martyr, *Dialogue with Trypho* 108; Tertullian, *De Spectaculis* 30), they were confirming that the tomb was empty. The fact that the first and primary witnesses to the empty tomb were women is highly significant. Jewish and Roman society uniformly held the testimony of women in very low regard. No one inventing a story, or even manipulating it, would have damaged its credibility by making women so prominent.

The established facts support each other against challenges to the resurrection. For example, the idea that the risen Christ was a mere grief hallucination cannot account for the empty tomb, nor the conversion of Paul, "nor more crucially, the group appearances recorded in very early sources."[33] The theory that the disciples stole the body does not fit with the evidence that they sincerely believed he appeared (and were willing to suffer for their belief). The resurrection was not a myth that developed over time because it can be shown to be very early.[34] Habermas and Licona argue further against alternate theories, such as that the resurrection was a legend, or outright fraud; that the disciples merely went to the wrong tomb, the death was only apparent, the accounts were biased, Jesus was an alien or that there is some psychological explanation (hallucination, delusion, vision).

CRITICISMS

As could be expected, the sharpest concerns about Montgomery's position come from presuppositionalists and those sympathetic with their Kuyperian tendency to deny that facts can point upward to their interpretations.[35]

Paul Feinberg defends Montgomery's position from Ronald Nash's criticisms, offering some helpful insights on the debate about the relationship between facts and their interpretation.[36] When Montgomery says that facts carry their interpretation, he does not mean that there is one and only one interpretation possible.

---

[32]Habermas and Licona, *Case for the Resurrection*, p. 287 n. 32.

[33]Gary Habermas, personal email correspondence with the author, Nov. 1, 2013.

[34]Habermas and Licona, *Case for the Resurrection*, p. 76.

[35]The summary is wrapped into this more extensive criticism section.

[36]Ronald Nash, "The Use and Abuse of History in Christian Apologetics," *Christian Scholar's Review* 1, no. 3 (Spring 1971): 217–26. Paul D. Feinberg, "History: Public or Private?," *Christian Scholar's Review* 1, no. 4 (Summer 1971): 325–31.

Rather, similar to the philosopher Ludwig Wittgenstein (1889–1951), he holds that the meaning of statements comes from their publicly known context, specifically our understandings of the words (and sometimes the nonverbal gestures) used to make those statements. Thus meanings are not private, but public.

However, as we have seen, Montgomery believes that historical facts, out of all their possible interpretations, do point to the correct ones. If it were not so, Feinberg argues, there would be no way to choose between wildly different interpretations. Rationality itself would be threatened. He offers what he believes to be an important correction.

Echoing Van Til, Nash says that there are no such things as "facts."[37] To Feinberg this implies that a "fact" is the combination of a brute event and mind-dependent interpretation. Yet a "fact" of history is roughly the same as an "event" of history. It happened, and it can be interpreted. It is objective. The crucial thing is that the significance of an event is not given by the mind; the mind only recognizes it. In that sense the fact cannot be connected with equal validity to just any interpretation. Facts point to their correct interpretation. This is the only way the nonbeliever is left without excuse, their rebellious will being the only problem.

The evidentialist is criticized by classical apologists for a similar reason. Norman Geisler commends evidentialism for acknowledging that truth is objective and public, and that "in a given context not just any interpretation can be given to any fact."[38] But he insists that a fact has meaning only in a context, and it can in no way point to that context, not to any degree. So the resurrection, for example, can be a miracle only if God exists. For the atheist, it is only an unusual event. Absent God in the worldview, the earthquake that swallowed Korah in the Old Testament (Num 16:31-32) would be explained only in geological terms. Again echoing Van Til, he says, "No bare fact possesses inherent meaning; every fact is an 'interprafact.'"[39] He says further that the very act of selecting certain events as having special significance requires a prior commitment to an interpretive framework. As the book by R. C. Sproul, John Gerstner and Arthur Lindsley puts it, "Miracles cannot prove God. God, as a matter of fact, alone can prove miracles. That is, only on the prior evidence that God exists is a miracle even possible."[40]

---

[37]Nash, "Use and Abuse," p. 222; cited in Feinberg, "History: Public or Private?," p. 328.

[38]Norman Geisler, *Christian Apologetics* (Grand Rapids: Baker, 1976), p. 98.

[39]Ibid., p. 96.

[40]R. C. Sproul, John Gerstner and Arthur Lindsley, *Classical Apologetics: A Rational Defense of the Christian Faith and a Critique of Presuppositional Apologetics* (Grand Rapids: Zondervan, 1984), p. 146.

Taking a slightly different approach, William Lane Craig points out that the existence of God makes the resurrection more plausible. If there is a God, then there is nothing implausible about the resurrection. Therein lies the value of arguments for theism: they can show that the inherent plausibility of theism is not low and thus that the inherent plausibility of the resurrection is not low. But he hastens to add that merely showing that God exists does not make the probability of the resurrection very high since we cannot know what God would do; he can do whatever he wants. But the mere fact that resurrections are extremely rare, which the Christian readily admits, is no argument against it happening in the case of Jesus, "since it may be precisely God's intent to reserve such a striking miracle solely for the vindication of his Son's radical claims and ministry."[41] So the existence of God makes the resurrection more plausible in that it would fit with our background beliefs (i.e., belief in God). The resurrection need not fit with previous events in the sense that it has happened before.

Craig says that if we attempt to argue from the resurrection to the existence of God, as the evidentialist does, we leave ourselves open to the charge that God is an ad hoc hypothesis. An ad hoc (Latin, "for this") hypothesis is one invented especially for a certain occasion, which we do not use to explain anything else, and does not appear anywhere else in our thinking. A defense attorney is creating an ad hoc hypothesis if he tries to argue that his client is innocent and a Martian lookalike committed the crime. The alien lookalike is unknown and figures in no other explanations. It seems created solely to make the client look innocent. Craig reasons that we are in a much stronger position if God is in our worldview by means of theistic proofs of various kinds so that it does not seem that we invented him only in connection with miracles. He adds, "If the arguments of natural theology alone suffice to warrant belief in theism, then the natural role for Christian evidences to play is not to reinforce the case for theism, but to narrow the focus to warranting a Christian form of theism."[42]

Though presuppositionalists and classical apologists agree against evidentialists that miracles, including the resurrection, cannot constitute evidence for God's existence, they differ as to how we arrive at the framework that interprets the facts. To review, classical apologists believe that we can arrive at the framework (of theism) as an inference, even though the framework is on the

[41]William Lane Craig, "A Classical Apologist's Response" (to Habermas), in Cowan, *Five Views on Apologetics*, p. 127.
[42]Ibid., p. 128.

level of a worldview, despite worldviews having a maximal impact on our ideas. Whether or not God exists has many implications for many of our ideas (e.g., it determines the nature of causality, purpose, morals and so on). Presupposition-alists say this will not work because in this case nothing is outside the framework, that framework being our entire worldview, which encompasses everything—including all facts we would use to try to prove the worldview. Besides, the highest authority is God's Word, and to evaluate it in order to conclude that it is true would require something higher and more authoritative, which does not exist. Furthermore, humanity's problem at root is not intellectual, but is mani-fested in the very desire to think independently of God, which is what we would be doing if we were to evaluate the Bible to see if it, rather than the writings of another religion or sect, is God's Word. So Van Til and Bahnsen claim that we can have indirect proof in that (Reformed) Christianity provides the only framework in which we can have knowledge of anything.

What some presuppositionalists and classical apologists are missing, according to the evidentialist, is that facts can point to the best interpretation without having to do so infallibly, unmistakably or deductively. It is not an all-or-nothing process in which facts indicate nothing about their interpretation and the perspective (e.g., theism or Christianity) determines knowledge. If someone says he will perform a phenomenally unlikely event and then it happens exactly as he predicted, the interpretation that it "just happened" versus the interpretation that the person or prophet has access to special knowledge and power are not on equal footing. Could it be explained as a freak event? Yes, but that would not be nearly as good an explanation as the alternative view. So to object that the freak-event view is as viable or rationally acceptable as any other misses the point of induction and reasoning to the best explanation. Suppose a person says he has divine power and then proceeds to heal people instantly, raise dead people, walk on water, multiply food, turn water into wine, calm deadly storms and successfully make detailed predictions. The view that he indeed has some special power is rationally pref-erable to the view that it is all a matter of coincidences.

Van Tillian presuppositionalist Greg Bahnsen critiques Montgomery's apolo-getic approach at some length in an article (space permits only a very brief overview).[43] As to Montgomery's criticisms of presuppositionalism, Bahnsen says

---

[43]Greg Bahnsen, "A Critique of the Evidentialist Apologetical Method of John Warwick Mont-gomery," *Covenant Media Foundation*, www.cmfnow.com/articles/pa016.htm. To indicate some-thing of the article's tone, it contains ninety-three exclamation marks.

he fails to distinguish between Van Til's presuppositionalism, which attempts to justify its presuppositions, and those of Dooyeweerd and the Toronto ICS school, which do not. Recall that Van Til claims that (Reformed) Christianity is deductively proved indirectly, in that if it is not assumed then there is no grounds for knowledge of any kind (as well as no grounds for other essentials, like predication and morals). On Montgomery's behalf, we can say that he believes the criteria set up by the presuppositionalist would seem like "stacking the deck" in the believer's favor: the presuppositionalist sets up the only acceptable qualifying criteria for a worldview and—no surprise—only the presuppositionalist's own worldview can meet it.

As we would expect, Montgomery's use of induction is a major point of criticism. For Bahnsen, as for Van Til, anything short of deduction—airtight and 100-percent certain—will allow the nonbeliever an excuse for his rebellion. So it is not enough that conclusions regarding the resurrection are shown to be highly probable. High probability does not coerce belief, according to the Van Til/Bahnsen type of presuppositionalism. This is a major divide between presuppositionalists and those on the right side of our chart at the beginning of this book (veridicalists, combinationalists, classical apologists and evidentialists); those on the right side believe induction is ultimately the best proof we have available, and adequate for the most serious decisions in life, including the question of religious truth. As such, high probabilities can indeed be decisive, and we routinely hold people to account based on probabilities.

Bahnsen insists that Montgomery prove his case for Christianity purely from the facts upward, without bringing in any assumptions. For example, Montgomery argues, "If Christ is God then He speaks the truth,"[44] but Bahnsen replies that on some religious views, God can indeed be dishonest (e.g., the Greek gods).[45] For Bahnsen this again demonstrates the impossibility of arguing from the facts upward, instead of working from the top down by appealing to presuppositions. Craig as a classical apologist would no doubt point to the importance of establishing a traditional theistic framework by means of the moral argument.[46] He might reply (similar to John Frame) that it is hard to see how all the attributes of the Christian God are transcendentally necessary for knowledge and predication. In other words, does God have to be perfectly loving, wise, just

---

[44]Part of Montgomery's six-point argument critiqued by Bahnsen in ibid. The argument appears in Montgomery, *Where Is History Going?*, p. 35; and Montgomery, *The Shape of the Past: A Christian Response to Secular Philosophies of History* (1975; repr., Eugene, OR: Wipf & Stock, 2008), pp. 138–39.

[45]Bahnsen, "Critique of the Evidentialist Apologetic Method."

[46]See, e.g., William Lane Craig, "Closing Remarks," in Cowan, *Five Views on Apologetics*, p. 321.

and so on for humans to have and communicate knowledge? While Bahnsen says Montgomery cannot go from the facts to something that looks like the Christian God, some would say that Van Til's transcendental argument cannot get there either. As we remember, Frame believes, in contrast to Van Til, that the transcendental proof is more like a goal that requires a number of arguments (including traditional ones) rather than a completely decisive, one-step proof.

Where Montgomery believes that, absent bias, the facts surrounding Christ will point to the resurrection, Bahnsen replies that to the nonbeliever, a resurrection is "scientifically ridiculous."[47] He implies that no amount of evidence can overturn that. When Montgomery accedes that his inferences could be unfounded, Bahnsen takes this to mean that his argument is "logically crippled."[48] Yet those who accept inductive arguments in apologetic contexts would see a very strong inductive argument as convincing, despite a small possibility that the premises could be true but the conclusion false. So an argument that could be considered at, say, .97 (where 1 is absolute certainty) would be convincing despite the .03 likelihood that the conclusion is false. The argument would in no way be considered "logically crippled." But again, to Bahnsen (and Van Til) anything less that absolute certainty is worthless because as they see it that leaves the nonbeliever with some excuse.

Montgomery argues that Jesus' claim to be God rested on his forthcoming resurrection, but Bahnsen doubts the disciples would have even remembered his claim. Montgomery points to Jesus' promise that they would have been divinely enabled to remember his words; however, Bahnsen objects that such a promise depends on him having that spiritual authority—making Montgomery's argument circular. However, remembering such a remarkable claim does not seem so difficult, given that it later happened (and they were in a semi-literate culture where presumably many things were entrusted to memory). Also, it was not as though they did not think about the promise and the resurrection until it was time to write the Gospels many years later. The event shaped their lives and that of the Christian community from their first realization of it, and likely the account was retold many times. Bahnsen goes on to show that someone's fulfilled prediction does not demonstrate their deity.[49] But it is hard to see how anyone could think that Montgomery is making the argument that it does, given that he is quite aware of many prophecies by individuals in the Old and

---

[47]Ibid.
[48]Ibid.
[49]Ibid.

New Testaments, and certainly no one claimed that the prophets were divine.

Habermas defends Montgomery by saying that the six-point argument he outlined was never developed in detail and does not appear intended as a developed case. Therefore, Bahnsen should not critique it as such. Habermas cites the principle of charity in logic, according to which we should give our opponent the benefit of the doubt by strengthening their argument in order to ensure that we are responding to its strongest form.[50]

Bahnsen charges that Montgomery believes that facts can be neutrally observed, that brute facts are inseparable from their meanings and that knowledge is objective.[51] Habermas replies that Montgomery agrees that facts must be interpreted, and makes no less than forty references to that effect in his classic article "The Theologian's Craft."[52] Montgomery further agrees that interpretations can be skewed, for example, by the individual's presuppositions, hopes and fears. In an apologetic context, various interpretations about Jesus must be tested against the historical data to see which fits. Nevertheless, Habermas admits Montgomery could have done a better job of showing how this works in apologetics.[53] Montgomery specifically critiques the view that Bahnsen claims he holds, saying that those who claim complete objectivity is possible in history (positivists) fail to realize that our "philosophies of life have always, and will always produce different interpretations of history." Besides, humans are "unique, free, and gloriously unpredictable."[54] Moreover, failing to realize that human nature is sinful will have grave consequences for the interpretation of history.[55] Habermas adds that virtually everyone today agrees that there are no completely neutral perspectives and that predispositions matter—but acknowledging this by no means makes a person a presuppositionalist.

To be clear, Bahnsen accepts inductive apologetic arguments, such as those from history, but only for the Christian, never the non-Christian. He says,

> The effectiveness of the evidence is felt by the believer because he is thinking within the context of revelational presuppositions, but the historical evidences

---

[50]Gary R. Habermas, "Evidential Apologetic Methodology: The Mongomery-Bahnsen Debate," in *Tough-Minded Christianity: Honoring the Legacy of John Warwick Montgomery* (Nashville: B&H Publishing, 2008), p. 433.

[51]Ibid., p. 427.

[52]John Warwick Montgomery, "The Theologian's Craft," in *Suicide of Christian Theology*, pp. 267–313.

[53]Habermas, "Evidential Apologetic Methodology," p. 429. He makes a similar point in "Evidential Apologetics," pp. 94–95 n. 10, and adds a list of critics and defenders.

[54]Montgomery, *Shape of the Past*, pp. 73–74.

[55]Ibid., p. 16.

are insufficient in themselves (even theoretically) to change the unbeliever's mind because his thinking is guided by apostate presuppositions. If the non-Christian's presuppositions are granted, then he has adequate reason to reject a simple historical apologetic built up from inductive evidences; this is why our apologetic to the unregenerate must be made up of stronger material.[56]

So the evidentialist believes that inductive arguments from facts such as those from history and miracles like the resurrection can change a person's upper-level beliefs, roughly, their presuppositions. Some classical apologists believe such a change is impossible (e.g., Geisler), which is why theistic proofs are needed to set the framework for interpreting the facts. Others (e.g., Craig) hold that it is possible but difficult, and theistic proofs definitely help strengthen the overall case. Presuppositionalists generally believe it is impossible, which is why presuppositions and the spiritual condition of the nonbeliever need to be the focus of an apologetic encounter.

For presuppositionalists, this is where belief in the self-attesting nature of Scripture plays an important part. Bahnsen writes,

> The fact that Christ and the apostles performed miracles does not imply that inductive, historical validation of the Scriptural miracles is our central apologetic thrust. Far from it. God expects us to accept the word and witness of the apostles on their own Christ-given authority. It is a grave thing not to submit to the authority of apostolic proclamation (which is the source of our information, after all, about the miracles and resurrection, etc.), for that proclamation is self-attestingly God's word.[57]

He believes God's confrontation of Adam provides insight into dealing with fallen beings. God does not try to convince Adam of the truth, nor does he submit evidences to him; rather, he confronts him on the issue of authority. The desire to offer humans "autonomous verification" of God's Word comes from the failure to grasp that humans are his special creation, and as such they naturally recognize his Word. They do not need evidence. He says, "Our apologetic must not assume that man's responsible knowledge of God has been lost (thus requiring autonomous corroboration of God's word to satisfy man's intellect)."[58] However, we must not think that the human intellect is undamaged from the

---

[56]Bahnsen, "Critique of the Evidentialist Apologetic Method."
[57]Ibid.
[58]Ibid.

fall. Bahnsen believes Montgomery makes both mistakes, offering evidences and overestimating the ability of the fallen human mind to process them.

All of this prompts Habermas to offer some criticisms of his own. The three most influential presuppositionalists (Van Til, Bahnsen and Frame) commend the use of evidences but have done little to produce their own, he says. Specifically, they say they value historical apologetics, and though they criticize how others do it, decades have gone by without an example of how they think it should be done. He quotes Frame, who admits, "Unfortunately, there has been very little actual analysis of evidence in the Van Tillian presuppositionalist school of apologetics."[59] Habermas welcomes them to show how it should be done—and does it not make sense for them to want to do that, since they "constantly scold, correct, and offer suggestions without ever attempting to perform the task themselves?"[60] Until such a work is produced, presuppositionalism is open to the charge that it is still an incomplete apologetic system.[61]

Habermas then takes a second look at scriptural passages that he believes Bahnsen has discounted too quickly. Bahnsen says he sees no Scripture that urges us to prove the resurrection by inductive research but rather that the apostles expect the resurrection to be accepted on its "own authoritative witness."[62] The person who gives us the example of resurrection faith, he says, is not doubting Thomas, but Abraham, who believes God "against all empirical probability or inductive reasoning."[63] However, Habermas points out that Abraham is given a remarkable amount of evidence. He hears directly from God (Gen 12:1-3; 13:14-17; 22:1-2), asks for and gets a sign that God will fulfill his promises (Gen 15:8-21), is visited by God and two angels (Gen 18:1-33), witnesses God's visible judgment on Sodom and Gomorrah (Gen 19:1-29), and hears from an angel twice (Gen 22:11-18). Yet he still has several crises of faith (Gen 12:11-20; 15:8; 17:15-17; 20:1-7). So it is far from true that Abraham's faith existed apart from, or even against, data from sense experience. As to Thomas, Christ tells him that it would be better had he believed without requiring his appearance (Jn 20:29), yet he nevertheless presents himself

---

[59]John Frame, *The Doctrine of the Knowledge of God* (Phillipsburg, NJ: P & R, 1987), p. 352; quoted in Habermas, "Evidential Apologetic Methodology," p. 434.

[60]Habermas, "Evidential Apologetic Methodology," p. 436.

[61]Ibid., p. 436. He adds (p. 448 n. 50) that this is one of his chief critiques of Van Tillian presuppositionalism, citing Habermas, "An Evidentialist's Response" (to Frame), in Cowan, *Five Views on Apologetics*, pp. 238-41; and Habermas, "Closing Remarks," pp. 343-44.

[62]Bahnsen, "Critique of the Evidentialist Apologetic Method." I added the material in the quote from Bahnsen to clarify his point.

[63]Bahnsen, "Critique of the Evidentialist Apologetic Method."

as evidence after the disciple has said that he will not believe without it. That leads directly to Thomas's faith. Jesus also presents himself to others in an empirically convincing way, allowing himself to be held (Mt 28:9; Jn 20:17), and showing his body and scars, as well as eating (Lk 24:36-43; Jn 20:19-20).

Paul reports that the resurrected Jesus showed himself several times to his followers, and over five hundred saw him, most of whom were then still alive. Habermas says that Montgomery, like most commentators, holds that Paul's point is that at the time the witnesses could still be consulted. Such resurrection appearances led directly to the conversions of Paul and James the brother of Jesus. Presenting the resurrection was Paul's customary way of presenting the gospel (Acts 17:2).

Bahnsen's point that most nonbelievers will fail to be convinced by Montgomery's apologetic approach is hardly relevant, Habermas contends. Few responded to Paul at the Areopagus (Acts 17:32-34), and people regularly walked away from Jesus in unbelief.[64] Not only do people come to belief from evidence, but God's people are told to examine those who claim to be prophets to see if their predictions come true (Deut 18:21-22). Elijah offers a test to see which God is real: the one who lights up his sacrifice is the real God; and Yahweh does (1 Kings 18:20-45). Jesus answers John the Baptist's doubts with miracles (Lk 7:18-23), and later says his resurrection will be the chief sign of his identity (Mt 12:38-40; 16:1-4). Peter (Acts 2:22-24; 1 Pet 1:3-4) and Paul (Acts 17:31) say the resurrection confirms Jesus' teachings. Habermas says that God apparently did not think that checking evidences "were out of line or that they somehow failed to take Him at His word. After all, it is God who even commanded the testing!"[65]

KEY TERMS

Minimal facts approach. The traditional approach first establishes the reliability of the Bible, then argues for supernatural topics, such as inspiration, deity and the resurrection. Habermas argues instead from facts that are agreed upon by a vast majority of scholars, including those who are hostile to belief in a literal resurrection.

THINKING IT OVER

1. What is the minimal facts approach? What does Habermas see as the difficulty with the traditional approach?

---

[64]Habermas, "Evidential Apologetic Methodology," p. 443.
[65]Ibid., p. 444.

2. How does Habermas respond to fideists?

3. What are the five commonsense principles that historians often use to evaluate the evidentiary value of testimony?

4. Summarize the four minimal facts, plus one.

5. How does Feinberg defend Montgomery's view against Nash, that there is no such thing as a "fact"?

6. How does Craig argue for proving theism before proving the resurrection? What does he say is the problem with not arguing first for theism?

7. What do evidentialists think that classical apologists and presuppositionalists are missing with regard to facts and interpretation?

8. What two approaches to justifying presuppositions does Bahnsen say Montgomery fails to distinguish?

9. How does Bahnsen argue against going from the facts upward? How would the critic argue that neither can Van Til go from presuppositions to the Christian God?

10. How does Habermas argue that Montgomery himself believes that facts cannot be neutrally observed, but must be interpreted?

11. What criticisms of presuppositionalism does Habermas offer?

GOING FURTHER

Baggett, David J., ed. *Did the Resurrection Happen? A Conversation with Gary Habermas and Antony Flew*. Downers Grove, IL: InterVarsity Press, 2009.

Habermas, Gary R. *Dealing with Doubt*. Chicago: Moody Press, 1990.

——. "Evidential Apologetics." In *Five Views on Apologetics*, edited by Steven B. Cowan, pp. 91–121. Grand Rapids: Zondervan, 2000.

——. *The Historical Jesus: Ancient Evidence for the Life of Christ*. Joplin, MO: College Press, 1996.

——. *The Risen Jesus and Future Hope*. Lanham, MD: Rowman & Littlefield, 2003.

Habermas, Gary R., and Michael R. Licona. *The Case for the Resurrection of Jesus*. Grand Rapids: Kregel, 2004.

CONCLUSION

Putting it all together

It is obvious that the question of apologetic methods is complex, and that brilliant, godly, dedicated people can disagree. With due respect for the intellects that have engaged this field, I offer some thoughts on four areas of disagreement that I believe are crucial and that to a significant extent shape the contrasting views: the relationship between faith and evidence, the possibility of using induction, the relationship between fact and theory (especially whether we can reason from fact to theory) and the rational capability of the fallen mind.

Faith and Evidence

As was clear from the introduction, I do not think fideism is a viable option biblically. Many people think it is partly true because faith is necessary and sometimes we, like Job, must believe without evidence. But according to fideism, faith can never be supported. So if you think there is ever any reason to believe, you are not a fideist.

The insight that we sometimes must believe things without support points to the varied nature of faith. A good deal of the time faith can have rational support. For example, Jesus pointed to evidence of prophecy about himself (Lk 24:25) and his miracles (Jn 10:37-38). Paul pointed to the resurrection (Rom 1:4; Acts 17:31). But sometimes faith has little or no support, which challenged Job (Job 23:8-9), and was expressed by the writer of Hebrews, "Faith is the assurance of things hoped for, the conviction of things not seen" (Heb 11:1).

We cannot expect to have 100-percent proof, in the normal sense of the term *proof*, for most of what we believe. As nonomniscient beings, we do not have absolute, airtight proof for real-world things. Proof is multifaceted, and varies according to what is proved. For example, we prove historical truths differently from those of physics or mathematics. Furthermore, we have different levels of certainty for different things. We have a higher level of certainty for the statement "circles are round" (a tautology) than we do for the statement "Booth shot Lincoln" (what if his legal name at the time was not "Booth" and the records were lost?). But that does not mean that we cannot have certitude, the inner assurance that something is true. We saw that Alvin Plantinga has argued that we can be considered rational for being sure of things we would have difficulty proving (e.g., the world wasn't created with apparent age a few minutes ago), so our level of certitude can exceed our level of proof. We can inwardly be just as sure of two things for which we have different levels of proof.

Some things are by nature rationally undeniable. As Norman Geisler and Mark Hanna point out, a person cannot, for example, deny their existence, since someone must be making the denial. A person cannot rationally deny that at least something exists (since that would be denying one's own existence), or deny the principle of noncontradiction. Such things would presumably be true in every worldview, and thus be common to every worldview. (Hanna regards those things as cognitive neutral ground.)

We also have immediate awareness of some things, such as our own existence. I don't know of anyone who wakes up in the morning and thinks through a rational argument in order to conclude they exist so they can start their day. There's no need. We simply know we exist. In fact, if anyone attempted to give us an argument to prove we do not exist, no matter how clever it was, it could not be more convincing than our simple awareness that we do in fact exist. Our response would be, "That argument seems correct but it is wrong," not, "I always thought I existed, but I guess I don't." In this sense a deductive argument with a conclusion that we know is wrong can give us grounds to reject the argument. In a sense the original argument gives us the form (called *modus ponens* in logic),

if *p* then *q*

p

therefore *q*.

But if we reject *q*, we can form a counterargument (called *modus tollens* in logic):

if *p* then *q*

not *q*

therefore not *p*.

It may help us to think of reasons behind our personal faith as having at least three aspects: There are the reasons that originally brought us to faith, which may for example have to do with a godly parent whom we found credible. Then there are the reasons why we currently believe. Then there are reasons we would offer someone who asks us, which might emphasize reasons that are more publicly accessible. It is possible that there are significant differences among all of these, as is the case with William Lane Craig having a strong intuition that Christianity is true, while offering others objective evidences.

So it seems that we do not need 100-percent proof in order to have 100-percent faith. Even if we feel we have 100-percent proof for ourselves, we may not be able to offer that same level of proof to others; in other words, we may not be able to offer absolute proof that is publicly demonstrable.

INDUCTION

This leads us to the pivotal question of acceptable ways of reasoning. Is induction appropriate for apologetics, or must we settle for nothing less than deduction? To review, deduction, on the one hand, is structured such that if the premises are true (and the form is valid), then the conclusion must be true. It works because the conclusion does not go beyond what was already granted in the premises. If I say that all the chairs in a room can hold five hundred pounds, and this is one of those chairs, I can conclude with certainty that this chair can also hold five hundred pounds. There is no way the conclusion could be false, because we have already granted that all the chairs hold five hundred pounds. So deduction is airtight because it goes no further than what we have already accepted as true. It merely draws out an implication of the premises.

The conclusion of an inductive argument, on the other hand, does go beyond what was granted in the premises; thus unlike deduction, the premises can be true but the conclusion false. I can say that all the chairs in the room except this one were tested and hold five hundred pounds, and this chair is just like all the rest, so I conclude that it will also hold five hundred pounds. It's a very good bet that the conclusion is true, but it is possible that we are wrong. If we can accept conclusions of strong inductive arguments as knowledge, then we can know a lot indeed. We can know that a medicine cures a disease even if we have not tested every case; we can know things about species of animals even if we cannot find every member of the species; and we can know that our brakes will work and that it's safe to drive our car. An omniscient being knows with absolute certainty whether the remaining chair can hold five hundred pounds, whether the medicine will cure the cases we could not test, whether every member of a species has a particular characteristic and whether our brakes will work. But we do not. We know only inductively. But most of what we know is by induction, and induction can be very powerful. Societies send people to prison and even death based on induction. We routinely stake our own lives on it, judging our level of safety while driving or even crossing the street, deciding how far we can go out in the water at the beach or how close we stand to the edge of a drop-off, or when to seek shelter in an electrical storm. Since you are reading this page, it's worked for you so far! We also use induction to decide values, weigh outcomes of actions and make important choices.

This means that we can claim to know things that could possibly be wrong in some highly unusual circumstances. Do we know that it was indeed our friend whom we talked to today, face to face? Yes, even though it is remotely possible that unknown to us, it was an identical twin we weren't aware they had. Do we know who the president is? Yes, even though it is remotely possible that he died in the past few minutes and news hasn't gotten out yet. Do we know who our parents are? Yes, even though it is remotely possible we were adopted and they decided not to tell us, and produced a fake birth certificate for the family files. Only if we can know things that it is remotely possible we could be wrong about—if it is possible to have "defeasible" knowledge—can we know our friends, the president, our parents and so on.

When it comes to religious belief, we can have faith that is supported by reasons, and where that is short of 100 percent certainty, we can have the kind of faith that believes when reasons are lacking. The latter is needed because as nonomniscient beings, our reasons for real-world beliefs (as opposed, for example, to tautologies and some mathematical proofs) will normally be less than absolute.

In practical terms deduction and induction are not as far apart as they look. For one, deductive cases propose that only *if* the premises are true is the conclusion certain. But in arguments about real-world things (events, the existence of God) with people who do not already accept our conclusion, the truth of one or more premises is likely to be challenged. How do we prove a premise? Well, we could set up another deductive argument, and that is fine, but at some point we will likely have to prove a premise using something that is less than 100-percent certain, such as history, science, common knowledge, expert opinion, authority and so on. So in practical terms, considering the entire argument that will have to be made, we may really have only inductive certainty once we go from the claim that if the premises are true then the conclusion follows to the claim that the premises actually are true and the conclusion does follow in the real world.

Induction is powerful and pervasive, and as nonomniscient beings we legitimately rely on it—and are accountable for our conclusions, legally, for example. God, too, clearly holds us accountable for moral behavior that depends on induction, which so much behavior does. We ought to know that a certain amount of force will injure someone, and we are accountable if we injure them. We ought to know that a vehicle with its windows rolled up on a very hot day can reach temperatures that are fatal to a child, and we are accountable for a death under those conditions. Christ also held people cognitively accountable for unbelief in the face of evidence, for example, in the face of his miracles (e.g., Mt 11:20-24), the knowledge of which entails at least some induction. (They had to realize, for example, that this is an unusual event, based on their memory of past events.)

There is a lot more that could be said, but I conclude that induction can be very useful in apologetics. If we can know something through a strong inductive argument, we know it clearly and God can indeed hold us responsible. Furthermore, the conclusion of a strong inductive case can amount to what we normally regard as knowledge. And we can have certitude, that inner sense that something is true,[1] for something we know inductively. I think these help address some of the issues that concerned Van Til, so I do not share his rejection of induction. (Neither does John Frame, though he would state it differently.)

If we accept induction, then it is a short step to accepting the use of inference to the best explanation, sometimes called "abduction." Unlike deduction, induction and abduction do not offer airtight proof since unlike deduction they go beyond what is given in the premises. Leaving aside discussions of whether one is a form of the other,[2] abduction can operate when people on both sides of an argument agree on *what* needs to be explained (e.g., there is order in the world), but they disagree on *how* it is to be explained (e.g., chance, or a creator). Legal arguments can be interpreted as abduction (that is, as arguments to the best explanation), where both sides strive to offer the better explanation for the evidence. A medical diagnosis can also be an explanation of the evidence, in this case,

---

[1]We could talk on the one hand in terms of the objective certainty of propositions, or on the other hand in terms of our subjective confidence that a proposition is true. The latter can be referred to as "certitude."

[2]See, e.g., John R. Josephson and Michael C. Tanner, "Conceptual Analysis of Abduction," in *Abductive Inference, Computation, Philosophy, Technology*, ed. John R. Josephson and Susan G. Josephson (Cambridge: Cambridge University Press, 1996), pp. 15-16.

symptoms. In apologetics, we consider the best explanation for the existence of the universe and what we find in it, and for the record of the empty tomb.

Bayes's theorem may also be useful, though fixing numbers is understandably controversial. It is a little less problematic if very broad estimates are used rather than exact numbers (e.g., .6 or .7 rather than .675). One of the things it shows is the relationships between elements of proof—that, for example, high explanatory power (ability to explain what cannot be explained any other way) can make up for low prior probability (where a theory does not fit well with everything else we know). Conversely, low explanatory power (where alternative explanations work nearly as well as the one we are trying to prove) can be made up for by high prior probability (where the theory fits well with everything we know). Explanatory relationships are not the only ones useful in apologetics, however.

FACT AND THEORY

The general relationship between theory and fact is crucial and is one of the main factors that divides proponents of the various apologetic methods. We see it on one level in the problem of how background knowledge shrinks as the scope of a theory expands up to the maximal level of a worldview. How can worldviews be evaluated when they affect the interpretation of everything? Richard Swinburne answers that simpler theories turn out to be true more often. Norman Geisler appeals to first principles that are undeniable, which informally stated are as follows: something exists; something is identical to itself; opposites cannot be true (the principle of noncontradiction); it takes something to cause anything; and like produces like.

As to what must be established first, Swinburne believes that because of the nature of the inductive case for Christianity, theism must be established first. Geisler agrees on grounds that explanations are effective only within worldviews. Van Til agrees that a worldview determines all interpretations and explanations and thus must be established first. And he does that with his claim that only the (Reformed) Christian view makes knowledge of any kind possible such that it is impossible to reason without it; thus even an argument against theism or Christianity covertly affirms it. Unlike fellow classical apologist Norman Geisler, William Lane Craig believes that it is better to argue first for theism, but not because it is impossible to do otherwise. If we argue from the resurrection to the existence of God, God can appear to be ad hoc (that is, something invented to save our theory but that has little or no relation to things we already believe).

John Warwick Montgomery believes that we can first establish theism, but it is by no means necessary, and fellow evidentialist Gary Habermas agrees. So theistic arguments are useful, he believes, but the proper way to resolve a conflict is to examine the facts and see which theory fits. This is opposite of the trend in recent decades to see theories as completely, or almost completely, determining facts, a trend in its earlier stages during Van Til's intellectually formative years. Montgomery agrees that "our existing worldview provides a structure within which we view particular issues. But, unless we are in effect paranoiacs, when the facts contradict some aspect of our worldview, we need to modify the latter to fit the facts."[3] He illustrates it using the Wittgenstein-Popper analogy of the shoe and the foot: "We need to adjust our theories (the shoe) to fit the facts of the world (the foot). I see no difference between this operation in science, in history, in law—or in religion. Our maturity level will be determined by our willingness to let factual reality be the ultimate determinant of our philosophy of life."[4]

John Frame sees the relationship between fact and theory holistically. Interpretations can be verified on the basis of facts, which amounts to comparing the contents of our beliefs with the external world—though neither is "a brute, incorrigible standard."[5] Either can be compared with the other such that they verify each other. Interpretations can be verified by comparing them with facts, and what you think are facts can be compared with your interpretations.[6]

Montgomery (without referring to Frame's views specifically) would see any back-and-forth comparison, an "equilibrium," as problematic because it suggests that "worldviews and facts are on an equal plane in some kind of interdependent, dynamic, paradoxical relationship." Having two such criteria gives us the same problem that he believes is inherent in the approaches of E. S. Brightman, followed by E. J. Carnell: What do we do when the elements of a multifaceted test for truth conflict?[7]

Montgomery's solution is to privilege facts, so that in a conflict between fact and theory (or worldview), facts always win. This does not mean we should give up "a worldview on the first appearance of problems, but it does mean a willingness to modify one's beliefs when the evidence against them becomes so powerful that one would accept that evidence in parallel, non-threatening situations."[8]

It seems that our theories influence what we consider to be facts and how we

---

[3]John Warwick Montgomery, email correspondence with the author, Oct. 12, 2013.
[4]Ibid.
[5]John Frame, email correspondence with the author, Aug. 24, 2013.
[6]Ibid.
[7]John Warwick Montgomery, email correspondence with the author, Oct. 12, 2013.
[8]Ibid.

interpret them. Does it make a difference if the theory is a worldview? (Van Til, Bahnsen, Geisler and Swinburne say yes; Montgomery, no; Craig, not crucially.) Can facts, such as those about the resurrection, point us to the proper worldview, such as theism? (Van Til, Bahnsen and Geisler say no; Swinburne and Craig, not effectively; Frame, yes, by interaction; Montgomery and Habermas, yes.)

Biblically, there is a clear path from fact to theory. In Exodus 4:1-9, when Moses seeks credentials from God to show his people that he has divine authority, God grants miraculous signs. A classic example of proof is Elijah offering a test to see who is the true God (1 Kings 18:23-24). The true prophet and the false ones agree on the common ground: the living God will burn up his own sacrifice. In terms of this issue, the theory that Yahweh is God is proved by the fact that he burns up his sacrifice. It is never suggested that the test will be ineffective because those committed to Baal will see the event only in the light of their theory that Baal is God. The appeal is to the fact of the burned sacrifice, which is taken to be decisive. Refusal to face the fact is then blind commitment to a disproven theory. Jesus presents himself as the fulfillment of prophecy, which could be checked against the facts of his life and deeds. Appealing to facts is, for example, how he resolves the doubts of John the Baptist (Lk 7:20-22), Thomas (Jn 20:27-28), the apostles (Lk 24:39-43) and the assembly to whom he gives "many convincing proofs" (Acts 1:3). He makes similar appeals to audiences that are more hostile, that is, who held to different theories about him.

On the other hand, Christ does not offer proof to those who are completely unwilling to consider it (high priest [Mk 14:61]; Pilate [Mk 15:4-5]). They are committed to their view of him and nothing will help. This is not a problem with the method of proof, but with the spiritual condition of the closed-minded. Such willful blindness—in effect the refusal to go from clear fact to theory—is biblically considered to be cognitive dysfunction, and renders those people culpable. Christ calls into account those who do not respond to his miracles (Mt 11:21; Lk 10:13, Chorizin, Bethsaida). Such censure is not unique to the ministry of Christ. The psalmist and the prophet Isaiah, for example, speak of the incongruity between belief in idols and the facts, that they are made of wood and cannot deliver (Ps 115:4-8; 135:15-18; Is 40:20; 44:9-20; 57:13). We could note too that in our common understanding, failure to allow our theories to be revised by adequately confirmed and persistent facts is considered bias, or prejudice.

Today, any appeal to miracles of course lacks the force it had for those who personally witnessed them, or for those who could talk to those who had witnessed them (1 Cor 15:6). Reports of miracles (and prophecy) are now mediated through the biblical record, as the apostle John anticipated (Jn 20:30). Since the veracity of Scripture has been challenged for over two centuries, a careful case must be developed for its reliability. But the point is that biblical reasoning sanctions using facts to prove theories.

Can the same process be used for a theory on the level of a worldview? That is a more difficult question. If we have atheists especially in mind, biblical figures and writers encountered few of them. However, appeals were made to those who rejected Yahweh in favor of one or more of the very different gods of the Near East. Also, Christ encountered Sadducees (who did not believe in an afterlife), and Paul encountered Epicureans and Stoics (Acts 17:18). The two witnesses in Revelation confront the people of their day and their religious beliefs (Rev 11:3-13; note miracles and miraculous events after their deaths). These widely different views—which in at least some cases could be considered worldviews—do not seem to be treated in an entirely different way, as if appeals from fact to theory no longer work for them. Paul, for example appeals to the resurrection when his audience includes mostly Epicureans and Stoics (Acts 17:18, 31-32). When talking to unphilosophical devotees of Greek paganism, he says that God "did not leave Himself without witness, in that He did good and gave you rains from heaven and fruitful seasons, satisfying your hearts with food and gladness" (Acts 14:17). What he says could be constructed as an appeal from the fact of providential order to the existence of God, which we would consider a teleological argument (cf. Ps 19:1-4).

There are, of course, other ways to argue. To show, for example, that theism provides the best ground (an inductive argument) for reasoning, ethics, logic and more is also open. The claim that it can be shown with deductive certainty that uniquely Christian theism alone accounts for all such things (Van Til's transcendental argument) is much more difficult to make, as Frame has pointed out. Frame also points out the difficulty of showing that attributes and characteristics of the uniquely Christian God (e.g., love, justice, patience, wisdom) are needed to ground knowledge.

In the face of conflict or doubt, there can be some tension between theory and fact. If we see at a distance someone we had heard was traveling to another city, we can wonder if it's merely someone who looks like them (fact), or if the report that they are away was wrong (the report being the basis for our belief, which in terms of this discussion would be the theory). If we cannot get closer to the person in question we might review each more carefully. We might think back over the report to determine if it was reliable, and also try to observe the person from a distance more carefully (reexamine the facts) to see if we can recognize their mannerisms, gait and so on. It is possible to decide either in favor of the report or of our observations of the person, depending on the details of the incident. But if we are able to walk closer and their appearance becomes clearer, we may decide that the report "must" be wrong. And if we talk to them and we find that they know us and have private knowledge that only our friend would have, we would be convinced that the report was wrong.

If, however, the report was that the person was not traveling but had died, we would go through a similar process, but would typically require more confirmation[9] in deciding that the report of death was not credible than we would in deciding that the report of travel plans was not credible. It is much more likely that the report of travel plans is inaccurate than that a report of death is inaccurate (although Mark Twain once had to clarify, somewhat wryly, that it was not he but his cousin that was ill, saying, "The report of my death was an exaggeration"[10]). How we would decide in a particular case depends on which we judge to be stronger, the report or our experience with the person. If we are very sure of the report but we are not that familiar with the person, we might decide that they merely look like the deceased, or that someone is playing a trick on us. We can accept the theory (report of death) over the fact (our encounter with the person) because in this case we are more sure of the theory. Normally, since what we are calling "facts" are closer to experience, being based on things like observation, we are more sure of them. Thus they normally take precedence in a conflict between theory and fact. But as in the case of being more sure of the report than what the person looks like, it is possible to give precedence to the theory. There are cases too where just what we "see" as far as facts is itself defined by the theory and is open to interpretation by competing theories. This may be the case, for example, in aspects of particle physics, where the visible evidence (to use an old example, streaks on a plate, or trails in a cloud chamber) has to be interpreted by the theory.

Philosopher of science Thomas Kuhn described potential tension between a theory and experimental data.[11] A theory can be held in spite of anomalies, in which case the theory takes precedence over the facts. But eventually the

---

[9]To borrow an illustration from Swinburne.

[10]His cousin was ill and a report had circulated in London that it was Twain. For corrections of a misquotation and details of his actual quote, see *Snopes.com*, www.snopes.com/quotes/twain.asp.

[11]Thomas Kuhn, *The Structure of Scientific Revolutions*, 3rd ed. (Chicago: University of Chicago Press, 1996).

anomalies can become too great and the theory is rejected, in which case the facts overwhelm the theory.

As far as science, we have to remember that there is a well-recognized path from fact to theory. A good example is the crucial observation during a total eclipse in 1919 of the sun bending light about as much as Einstein's theory of relativity had predicted. The observation was taken as confirmation of the theory of relativity—from the fact upward to the interpretive perspective of the theory. But to take the illustration a step further and show the complexity of the fact-theory relationship, there was some controversy over the observation. The bending of light was not quite as much as what Einstein's theory had predicted, and some also thought that contrary evidence from another telescope had been ignored. Some doubted too that the instruments at the time were accurate enough to measure such a fine difference,[12] showing how a different theory, about accuracy of instrumentation, affects interpretation of the same fact. So were they observing bent light, the "fact" that light bends around large masses—or not? Note that here at least, the question was resolved by further studies of the observation of the light during the eclipse, that is, the "fact."

In biblical terms, Nicodemus sees the facts of Jesus' deeds, and speaks for some who have changed their theory: "Rabbi, we know that You have come from God as a teacher; for no one can do these signs that You do unless God is with him" (Jn 3:2). Many others see the deeds and choose not to change their theories (Mt 11:21; Lk 10:13). Some demand ever more deeds in a way that brings criticism from Christ: "Unless you people see signs and wonders, you simply will not believe" (Jn 4:48). Some of the Pharisees who see his deeds become convinced that they are supernatural, but in order to hold on to their belief that he is not from God, they adjust their theory, saying that the deeds were done by the power of Satan (Mt 12:24). Christ disproves their adjusted theory by showing that it leads to the absurd conclusion that Satan would in effect be fighting himself, a reductio ad absurdum (Mt 12:26). He thus disproves it not by appealing to the facts (to show they are indeed miracles), but by pointing out a problem with their theory itself. Being a reductio ad absurdum it is a deductive argument, but its practical success as an argument depends on inductive knowledge from experiences, that like-minded beings do not fight themselves, and therefore that Satan would not

---

[12]Richard Ellis, Pedro G. Ferreira, Richard Massey and Gisa Weszkalnys, "90 Years On: The 1919 Eclipse Expedition at Príncipe," *A&G*, August 2009, www.astro.caltech.edu/~rjm/Principe/press /coverage/AAG0809_article.pdf, pp. 4.12–4.13.

fight himself. Christ rebukes them for their wrong conclusion (Mt 12:30-31). This is another example of the difficulty of doing without induction in any argument about the real world.

Job, however, is faced with the facts of his horrific health condition and the deaths in his family, but in this case it is right to hold on to his (theoretical) belief that God is just and cares for him. A closer examination of the facts about his health or the deaths would not have led him to the right theory about them, in other words, the right interpretation of them. In his extreme case it is a matter of resolutely holding to the theory (his faith) that God is good and just, and using it to interpret the facts of his suffering. This is different from Christ expecting the facts of his miracles to point upward to the proper theory about him.

When fact and theory conflict, the outcome is not predictable. For most things we are in a better position to be more sure of the facts than the theory. To decide whether someone we thought was traveling is actually on the street instead, we would go up to them and make sure of their identity.

One thinks of philosopher W. V. O. Quine's statement (though he was making a bit of a different point): "Any statement can hold come what may, if we make drastic enough adjustments elsewhere in the system. . . . Conversely, by the same token, no statement is immune to revision."[13] We would add that a person can make cognitive tradeoffs that are driven by the outcome they desire rather than by purely rational concerns. Some choices could be considered irrational, even culpable (as when a paranoid attacks an innocent person and claims self-defense).

Viewed from the standpoint of what is ultimately true (ontology), theories that are correct are also "facts" that are known by an omniscient being. But we are considering things from the standpoint of how we know things (epistemology), so we are separating what we normally call facts from theories, which are more interpretive.

Though I am oversimplifying a bit to do it, we are regarding some aspects of our beliefs (and those of the biblical figures noted above) as being interpretive and thus theory-like, and others as facts that are typically closer to experience. Simpler observations that are close to experience, such as that the lights are on, or the chair is at the table, tend to be those that people are more confident are correct, and are those that people from different worldviews can agree on—forming some degree of cognitive common ground. The atheist, Muslim, Buddhist and Christian can

---

[13]W. V. O. Quine, "Two Dogmas of Empiricism," in *From a Logical Point of View*, 2nd ed. (New York: Harper & Row, 1963), p. 43. He was questioning the analytic-synthetic distinction.

all agree that the lights are on, and many more things about what is in the room. They can even agree on the more theoretical issue of the definition of "room," and the nature of the light by which they see objects in it, and the visual process itself. Moving up the scale, slightly away from simpler observation, our diverse group might be able to agree on the existence of order within living things, which is dependent on some assumptions about what constitutes order.

More interpretive beliefs often depend on a variety of assumptions and conclusions. Verifying them is therefore more complex, and agreement among people more likely depends on other things they believe. So, for example, that people die physically would be agreed on by people of different worldviews, whereas the possibility and nature of life after death would likely be regarded differently by the various worldviews.

When considering how much cognitive common ground exists between worldviews, at least three things will tend to lessen it: (1) seeing facts as completely defined and determined by the theories that interpret them; (2) seeing what we know as highly interconnected such that facts are inextricably linked to the whole of what someone believes, entailing that those with different worldviews have little or nothing in common cognitively; and (3) making starting assumptions, and thus potential common ground, more about common beliefs rather than common methods of reaching the truth (such as the principle of noncontradiction and other tools of reasoning).

We need to recognize that not all assumptions (or starting points, or presuppositions) are equal. The more content we insist that another person adopt up front, the less the process is one of dialogue and the more it becomes a leap to our position (either provisionally for the sake of argument, or as the shift in convictions that accompanies a conversion), there being no way to get there in reasoned steps. Conversely, the less content we insist someone share up front, the more common ground there is between us. Traditional apologetics assumes less content needs to be shared between believer and nonbeliever in order to make progress. Additionally, the more that content has to do with the methods of reaching correct conclusions rather than actual beliefs, the more dialogue is open with a broad array of people. Of course the Christian holds unequivocally that his or her beliefs are true, ontologically speaking. But we are considering the matter of how we know they are true and how we show it to others, which is epistemology—the stuff of apologetics.

THE MIND'S CAPABILITIES

The question of how much the fallen human mind can process is another issue that divides apologetic methods. Most people agree that when dealing with things like medical inventions and space travel, the mind does very well. But spiritual and moral issues can complicate things. So does the mind's equipment stop working when considering spiritual or moral issues, or is the problem our fallen nature that operates the mind? To what extent can people process arguments for religious truth? Incidentally if (with the Holy Spirit's help or whatever way) they can be expected to process Van Til's transcendental argument, then they can be expected to process virtually anything—it being the most abstract and philosophical apologetic argument I know.

To answer that, we observe that biblical figures encounter nonbelievers of all sorts, and offer a wide variety of arguments, including those for Yahweh and Christ (e.g., Paul "reasoned" in the synagogues, Acts 17:2; 18:19). Also, as we've seen, Romans 1:20 says, "For *since* the creation of the world His invisible attributes, His eternal power and divine nature, *have been clearly seen*, being *understood through what has been made*, so that they are without excuse" (emphasis added; cf. Ps 19:1-4). If this means that we see creation and draw a conclusion about God's existence (rather than, or in addition to, creation causing us to have an intuition about God; see Alvin Plantinga), then the human mind is working just fine when it comes to religious reasoning.[14] So if Paul is indeed talking about a conclusion of some sort, it is the very fact that people can draw a proper conclusion that renders them "without excuse." If they could not, they would not be guilty. And that they are guilty is the point of the passage in the context of Paul's overall argument in this section of Romans. But if Paul is talking about an immediate awareness of God that is stimulated by the creation such that there is no inference (Plantinga, Hanna), then people are guilty for suppressing that awareness, and the passage does not necessarily tell us about the ability of the fallen mind to reason to conclusions in about religion.

If the mind functions but people in their fallen state suppress the conclusion that is reached, or could be reached (Rom 1:18), then offering arguments is entirely legitimate. Apologetically speaking, it is our job to offer reasons, and the Spirit cuts through our blindness, stubborn bias and the like (Jn 16:8).

In conclusion, what could be more important than how to decide life's most

---

[14]I am not claiming anything about Plantinga's view of how well the fallen mind works.

crucial question—what is ultimately true with respect to our worldview? The topic of apologetic methods is therefore of paramount importance, and there is much more work to be done. It is my hope and prayer that this book will motivate some to grasp the baton from those who are finishing their leg of the race, and run on.

NAME INDEX

SUBJECT INDEX

abduction. *See* reasoning: inference to the best explanation

agnosticism, 153, 256-57, 258, 264, 290

ancient documents rule, 312, 312n92, 330, 332

antirealism, 138

apologetics from below, 306-10, 330

atheism, 49n23, 86, 228, 252-53, 277, 279, 280, 281, 284, 291, 306

autonomy, 14, 85, 86, 89, 104, 177, 310

basic, properly, 14, 122, 124, 125, 126, 138, 139, 143, 222-23, 231, 232, 263

Bayes's theorem, 356
   Craig on, 227, 254
   Montgomery on, 304-5, 327, 331
   Swinburne on, 190, 193, 194-97, 210, 211, 212, 216, 304, 305, 327

borrowed capital, 14, 73, 86

brute fact, 63, 65, 86, 261, 292, 296, 346

classical apologetics, 15, 22, 23, 24, 25, 44, 105, 112, 142, 176, 180, 185-291, 304, 335
   common ground, 186-87
   evidences, Christian, 189, 201-2, 206-7, 208-10, 285-87
   theistic arguments, 198-204, 210, 211, 212,

233-35, 235-42, 243-51, 251-53, 254, 282-85, 288, 291

coherence theory of truth, 64, 88, 127, 143

combinationalism, 15, 21, 22, 24, 25, 142, 147-84, 269, 270, 271, 272, 290
   common ground, 160-62, 174-75, 183
   common values (Lewis), 168-69
   deduction, rejection of in theistic proofs, 154-55, 170, 174, 178
   empiricism, rejection of, 150-51, 169, 172, 173-74, 182
   induction, rejection of in theistic proofs, 155, 170, 178
   point of contact, 162-68
   spiritual living, apologetic value of (Schaeffer), 173
   systematic consistence, 150-60, 179, 182
   theistic proofs, rejection of, 150-51
   verificational (abductive) argument, 169-72, 174, 175, 176

common ground, 15, 21, 22, 51, 119, 142, 186-87, 215, 217, 227, 358, 362, 363
   Carnell on, 149, 152, 160-62, 166, 176, 180, 181, 183, 215
   Craig on, 227
   Frame on, 92

Geisler on, 262, 266
   Lewis on, 169, 174
   Montgomery on, 296-97, 299, 310
   Plantinga on, 119, 142
   Schaeffer on, 174
   Swinburne on, 215, 217
   Van Til on (common ground and common notions), 67, 75, 76, 77, 81, 87, 88, 180, 183, 215, 262, 270

correspondence theory of truth, 64, 88, 257

cosmological argument. *See under* theistic arguments

deism, 51, 52, 165, 272, 273

empiricism, 21, 101, 150, 151, 169, 172, 178, 182, 258, 328

empiricist, 46, 71, 151, 154

evidentialism, 11, 15, 18, 23, 24, 25, 52, 84n82, 120, 142, 186, 202, 253, 264, 287, 291, 292-350
   apologetics from below, 306-10, 330
   facts and interpretation, 292, 294-95, 307, 341-49
   historical and legal arguments, 306-7, 310-19, 330, 332
   Holy Spirit's role, 308-9, 336
   minimal facts, Habermas's argument from, 334-40, 349

SCRIPTURE INDEX

Finding the Textbook You Need

The IVP Academic Textbook Selector
is an online tool for instantly finding the IVP books
suitable for over 250 courses across 24 disciplines.

---

ivpacademic.com